THEORISING LABOUR LAW IN A CHANGING WORLD

This collection brings together perspectives from industrial relations, political economy, political theory, labour history, sociology, gender studies and regulatory theory to build a more inclusive theory of labour law. That is, a theory of labour law that is more inclusive of non-traditional workers (including those in atypical work, or from non-traditional backgrounds); more inclusive of collective approaches to work regulation that foster solidarity between workers; and more inclusive of interdisciplinary and complex explanations of labour law and its regulatory spaces. The individual chapters speak to this theme of inclusivity in different ways and offer different suggestions for how such inclusivity might be achieved. They break down the barriers between legal research and other fields, to promote fruitful and inclusive conversations across disciplines. In the spirit of inclusivity and intergenerational dialogue, the book blends contributions from early career and emerging scholars with those from leading scholars in the field, featuring critical commentary from senior labour law figures alongside theoretically and empirically informed work.

Theorising Labour Law in a Changing World

Towards Inclusive Labour Law

Edited by
Alysia Blackham
Miriam Kullmann
and
Ania Zbyszewska

•HART•
OXFORD • LONDON • NEW YORK • NEW DELHI • SYDNEY

HART PUBLISHING

Bloomsbury Publishing Plc

Kemp House, Chawley Park, Cumnor Hill, Oxford, OX2 9PH, UK

1385 Broadway, New York, NY 10018, USA

HART PUBLISHING, the Hart/Stag logo, BLOOMSBURY and the Diana logo are trademarks of Bloomsbury Publishing Plc

First published in Great Britain 2019

Reprinted 2020

A catalogue record for this book is available from the British Library.

Library of Congress Cataloging-in-Publication data

Names: Blackham, Alysia, editor. | Kullmann, Miriam, 1983- editor. | Zbyszewska, Ania, editor.

Title: Theorising labour law in a changing world : towards inclusive labour law / edited by Alysia Blackham, Miriam Kullmann, Ania Zbyszewska.

Other titles: Theorising labor law in a changing world | Theorizing labour law in a changing world | Theorizing labor law in a changing world

Description: Oxford [UK] ; Chicago, Illinois : Hart Publishing, 2019. | Includes bibliographical references and index.

Identifiers: LCCN 2019021083 (print) | LCCN 2019021902 (ebook) | ISBN 9781509921560 (EPub) | ISBN 9781509921553 (hardback)

Subjects: LCSH: Labor laws and legislation. | BISAC: LAW / Discrimination.

Classification: LCC K1705 (ebook) | LCC K1705 .T49 2019 (print) | DDC 344.01—dc23

LC record available at https://lccn.loc.gov/2019021083

ISBN: HB: 978-1-50992-155-3
ePDF: 978-1-50992-157-7
ePub: 978-1-50992-156-0

Typeset by Compuscript Ltd, Shannon
Printed and bound in Great Britain by TJ International Ltd, Padstow, Cornwall

To find out more about our authors and books visit www.hartpublishing.co.uk. Here you will find extracts, author information, details of forthcoming events and the option to sign up for our newsletters.

ACKNOWLEDGEMENTS

This book's individual contributions originated as papers presented at a two-day workshop held at Maastricht University in the Netherlands in December 2016. The workshop aimed to feature critical, innovative, and interdisciplinary perspectives on labour law and work regulation. It also sought to highlight the work of scholars at different career stages, featuring doctoral and emerging researchers alongside those who were already well established in their fields. In addition to the chapters collected here, several other contributions presented at the workshop have been published together in a special issue of the *International Journal of Comparative Labour Law and Industrial Relations*. This attests to the richness of our discussions during the workshop and since. We are grateful to everyone who participated in the workshop – we have relished the opportunity to work with such a diverse and talented group of colleagues and friends. The workshop was generously funded by the International Collaboration Fund at Melbourne Law School, the University of Melbourne; the Research Fund at the University of Maastricht Faculty of Law; Warwick Law School's Legal Research Institute; and Hart Publishing. We are exceedingly grateful for the generous financial and in-kind support of these sponsors, which allowed us to bring together a diverse range of academics, from all career stages, and drawn from five different continents. We also owe great thanks to Cate Read and the Melbourne Law School Academic Research Service, who spent many hours assisting with finalising this manuscript.

TABLE OF CONTENTS

PART C
ADVANCING THEORETICAL MODELS TO RESPOND TO THE NEW WORLD OF WORK

LIST OF CONTRIBUTORS

Alysia Blackham is an Associate Professor and Australian Research Council Discovery Early Career Research Fellow at Melbourne Law School, The University of Melbourne.

Nicole Busby is a Professor of Labour Law at the University of Strathclyde.

Manoj Dias-Abey is a Lecturer in Law at the University of Bristol School of Law.

Anja Eleveld is an Assistant Professor at the Faculty of Law VU University Amsterdam.

Cristina Inversi is a Lecturer and member of the Work and Equalities Institute at the Alliance Manchester Business School, The University of Manchester.

Andrea Iossa is a Postdoctoral Fellow at the Faculty of Law at Lund University funded by the Swedish Research Council for Health, Working Life and Welfare (FORTE).

Robert Knegt, sociologist of law, has been Director of, and is now Guest Researcher at, the Hugo Sinzheimer Institute, University of Amsterdam.

Miriam Kullmann is an Assistant Professor at the WU Vienna University of Economics and Business, Department of Private Law. She also is a guest researcher at Leiden University and at Radboud University Nijmegen.

Tonia Novitz is a Professor of Labour Law at the University of Bristol.

Vincenzo Pietrogiovanni is a Senior Lecturer at the Department of Business Law at Lund University.

Lisa Rodgers is a Lecturer in Law and Course Director of the LLM Employment Law course by distance learning at the University of Leicester.

Ralf Rogowski is a Professor of Law at the University of Warwick School of Law and Member of the Academic Board of the Marco Biagi Foundation, University of Modena and Reggio Emilia.

Supriya Routh is an Assistant Professor at the University of Victoria Faculty of Law, Canada.

Nicola Smit is a Professor of Law and Dean at Stellenbosch University Faculty of Law.

Fotis Vergis is a Lecturer in Law at the School of Law, The University of Manchester.

Rebecca Zahn is a Senior Lecturer in Law at the University of Strathclyde.

Ania Zbyszewska is an Assistant Professor in Law and Work at the Department of Law and Legal Studies, Carleton University.

1

Introduction

MIRIAM KULLMANN, ANIA ZBYSZEWSKA
AND ALYSIA BLACKHAM*

I. Introduction: The Paradox of Inclusion

In the twenty-first century, the world of work has undergone dramatic changes. How to respond to the increasingly obvious disjuncture between existing legal models and the realities of people's work lives, the global geographies of production and new modes of service delivery has stirred much critical reflection and debate in labour law scholarship. Over the last 20 years, the search for alternatives to traditional labour law models has involved various theoretical attempts to reconsider labour law's normative foundations, its purpose and scope, as well as its subjects, institutions, regulatory mechanisms and jurisdictions. These contributions have ranged from more restrained, sometimes defensive reassessments,[1] to bolder, more radical critiques and reconceptions,[2] or even calls to abandon

* Assistant Professor, WU Vienna University of Economics and Business, Department of Private Law; Assistant Professor, Carleton University, Department of Law and Legal Studies; and Associate Professor, Melbourne Law School, University of Melbourne.

[1] See, eg, G Davidov, 'The Reports of My Death are Greatly Exaggerated: "Employee" as a Viable (Though Over-used) Legal Concept' in G Davidov and B Langille (eds), *Boundaries and Frontiers of Labour Law* (Oxford, Hart Publishing, 2006) (arguing that the concept of employee, if properly used, can remain useful); A Goldin, 'Labour Subordination and the Subjective Weakening of Labour Law' in G Davidov and B Langille (eds), *Boundaries and Frontiers of Labour Law* (Oxford, Hart Publishing, 2006) (suggesting that we replace the concept of subordination with a broader notion of contractual inequality, also covering new forms of exercising power); M Freedland and N Kountouris, *The Legal Construction of Personal Work Relations* (Oxford, Oxford University Press, 2011) (revitalising the contract of employment through its reconceptualisation); ND Zatz, 'The Impossibility of Work Law' in G Davidov and B Langille (eds), *The Idea of Labour Law* (Oxford, Oxford University Press, 2012) (advocating for a 'work law' that treats different forms of work differently).

[2] See, eg, R Dukes, *The Labour Constitution: The Enduring Idea of Labour Law* (Oxford, Oxford University Press, 2014) (urging that labour law should be reorientated around the values of redistribution and economic democracy); J Fudge, 'A New Vocabulary and Imaginary for Labour Law: Taking Legal Constitution, Gender, and Social Reproduction Seriously' in D Brodie, N Busby and R Zahn (eds), *The Future Regulation of Work: New Concepts, New Paradigms* (Basingstoke, Palgrave MacMillan, 2016) (making a conceptual contribution to expanding the scope of labour law so as to include unpaid care work); J Howe, 'The Broad Idea of Labour Law: Industrial Policy, Labour Market Regulations,

labour law (as we know it) entirely.[3] Spanning this diversity, however, is a general recognition that labour law's continued relevance depends on its capacity to become more inclusive, representative and broadly solidaristic.

Thus, *inclusion*, and how to achieve it in theory and practice, is a key theme and point of contention in contemporary labour law scholarship. An enduring question, though, is how and whether legal norms and institutions built around historically specific[4] and deeply gendered (and racialised) ways of organising work (and society)[5] can ever be satisfactorily adapted to accommodate evolving labour markets; and, even if they could be so adapted, how representative they would be, given the growing casualisation of work and its widespread informality in the world's lower income and developing economies.[6]

Even more problematically, the idea of inclusion is itself contested, and able to be co-opted for multiple and disparate political ends. For example, labour law's internal critique has coincided with longstanding neoliberal policy-led efforts to dismantle or re-regulate existing employment protection regimes,[7] including on the basis of promoting 'inclusion'. Paradoxically, deregulation has often been advanced on the premise that employment protections for standard workers contribute to inefficiencies and rigidities in labour markets, not least because they reproduce labour market segmentation (that is, the insider/outsider divide) and,

and Decent Work' in G Davidov and B Langille (eds), *The Idea of Labour Law* (Oxford, Oxford University Press, 2012) (broadening the scope of labour law by including tariff protection or state aid regulations); LF Vosko, 'Out of the Shadows? The Non-Binding Multilateral Framework on Migration (2006) and Prospects for Using International Labour Regulation to Force Global Labour Market Membership' in G Davidov and B Langille (eds), *The Idea of Labour Law* (Oxford, Oxford University Press, 2012) (especially with a view to migrant labour, making a case for introducing a global labour market membership).

[3] H Arthurs, 'Labor Law as the Law of Economic Subordination and Resistance: A Thought Experiment' (2013) 34 *Comparative Labor Law & Policy Journal* 585 (imagining a law of economic subordination and resistance encompassing all economic relations characterised by comparable asymmetries of wealth and power).

[4] A Blackett, 'Emancipation in the Idea of Labour Law' in G Davidov and B Langille (eds), *The Idea of Labour Law* (Oxford, Oxford University Press, 2012).

[5] J Fudge and R Owens, *Precarious Work, Women, and the New Economy: The Challenge to Legal Norms* (Oxford, Hart Publishing, 2006); J Conaghan and K Rittich, *Labour Law, Work, and Family: Critical and Comparative Perspectives* (Oxford, Oxford University Press, 2005); J Fudge and E Grabham, 'Introduction: Gendering Labour Law' (2014) 4 *feminists@law*. While not a labour lawyer, LF Vosko, *Managing the Margins: Gender, Citizenship, and the International Regulation of Precarious Employment* (Oxford, Oxford University Press, 2009) proposed a particularly strong critique of legal norms based on the standard employment relationship, according to which the only way to address the exclusionary and gendered operation of those norms is to dissolve them.

[6] J Fudge, S McChrystal and K Sankaran (eds), *Challenging the Legal Boundaries of Work Regulation* (Oxford, Hart Publishing, 2012); D Ashiagbor (ed), *Re-Imagining Labour Law for Development: Informal Work in the Global North and South* (Oxford, Hart Publishing, 2019) (forthcoming); S Marshall and C Fenwick (eds), *Labour Regulation and Development: Socio-Legal Perspectives* (Cheltenham, Edward Elgar and ILO, 2016); S Routh and V Borghi (eds), *Workers and the Global Informal Economy: Interdisciplinary perspectives* (London, Routledge, 2016).

[7] S Lee and D McCann (eds), *Regulating for Decent Work: New Directions in Labour Market Regulation* (London, Palgrave MacMillan, 2011).

as such, impede the pursuit of more inclusive, diverse, and equal labour markets.[8] Advanced since the 1990s by the Organization for Economic Cooperation and Development (OECD) and the World Bank, and in Europe by the European Commission, this neoliberal version of inclusion has prioritised broader access to labour markets and paid work, without necessarily guaranteeing work quality or substantive equality to new labour market actors.[9] Critiques of this policy show that it is not only rooted in a market-first logic, and undergirded by truncated conceptions of redistribution and equality, but also that methodological problems put into question its evidence base, not least by probing the assumed correlation between employment protection and labour market segmentation.[10] Inclusion may also be used as a rationale and justification for coercive labour market reforms, designed to compel individuals to engage or re-engage with the labour market.[11] This is particularly apparent in social security reforms, where income support may be lowered or withheld entirely for a failure to engage with labour market processes,[12] ostensibly in a way that is in the individual recipient's 'best interests'.

Regardless of (or, perhaps, precisely due to) the paradoxical way in which the notion of inclusion has been constructed in, and co-opted by, mainstream discourse, significant diversification of work arrangements has made the issue of inclusivity an urgent one for labour law. In addressing issues of exclusion and inclusion, many scholars are committed to finding solutions to labour law's arbitrary distinctions between standard and non-standard employment, and tackling its diminishing ability to protect workers within existing models. These interventions have, for instance, sought to rethink how work relations and parties are classified or identified,[13] propose new legal categories,[14] reflect on how employment contracts can be extended to cover the self-employed, or how labour law's purposes can be reconceived to extend its protective ambit.[15]

[8] See, eg, J Rubery, *Re-regulating for Inclusive Labour Markets* (Conditions of Work and Employment Series No. 65, Geneva, International Labour Office, 2015); V De Stefano, 'A Tale of Oversimplification and Deregulation: The Mainstream Approach to Labour Market Segmentation and Recent Responses to the Crisis in European Countries' (2014) 43 *Industrial Law Journal* 253.

[9] Rubery, *Re-regulating for Inclusive Labour Markets* (n 8) 2, referring to the OECD's 1994 *Jobs Study*, the World Bank's *Doing Business Index* and the European Commission's 2011 *Annual Growth Survey* (COM(2011) 11 final).

[10] For comprehensive discussion and references to evaluations of these policies see Lee and McCann, 'Regulating for Decent Work' (n 7); Rubery, *Re-regulating for Inclusive Labour Markets* (n 8).

[11] H Collins, 'Discrimination, Equality and Social Inclusion' (2003) 66 *Modern Law Review* 16.

[12] J Peck, *Workfare States* (New York, The Guildford Press, 2001); A Daguerre and D Etherington, 'Workfare in 21st century Britain: The Erosion of Rights to Social Assistance' (2014) ESRC Working Paper http://workfare.org.uk/images/uploads/docs/Workfare_in_21st_century_Britain-Final.pdf accessed 20 December 2018; J Millar and F Bennett, 'Universal Credit: Assumptions, Contradictions and Virtual Reality' (2017) 16 *Social Policy & Society* 169.

[13] See, eg, J Prassl, *The Concept of the Employer* (Oxford, Oxford University Press, 2015).

[14] See, eg, SD Harris and AB Krueger, *A Proposal for Modernizing Labor Laws for Twenty-First-Century Work: The "Independent Worker"* (The Hamilton Project, Discussion Paper 10, 2015). In some European countries, in-between categories already exist, eg, Austria, Germany, and the UK.

[15] G Davidov, *A Purposive Approach to Labour Law* (Oxford, Oxford University Press, 2016).

Other scholars, however, have argued that only a major reconceptualisation of labour law's scope to encompass different forms of work,[16] such as unpaid care work[17] or informal work,[18] can make the law more inclusive and responsive to the realities of people's (work) lives. True inclusivity might require moving beyond employment to focus on social rights,[19] adopting different models of regulation,[20] or considering ways in which labour law intersects with other regulatory fields[21] to produce particular vulnerabilities and precariousness.[22] These more radical approaches may be key to tackling enduring inequalities in accessing employment protection, particularly given the growing diversification of work.

The idea of inclusivity is therefore both a touchstone and point of contention for labour law scholarship. It offers at once a potential guide for the future of labour law reform, and a telling critique of the limits of labour regulation. This is made more complex, of course, by the inherent paradox in the notion of inclusion, and how it is deployed in public policy making. The notion or paradox of inclusion seems to be representative of the bind in which labour law now finds itself, especially in its efforts to develop an encompassing theory or answer to these various challenges.

II. Towards Inclusive Labour Law

This book's individual contributions originated as papers presented at a two-day workshop held at Maastricht University in the Netherlands in December 2016. The workshop aimed to feature critical, innovative, and interdisciplinary perspectives on labour law and work regulation, and to highlight the work of scholars at different career stages, featuring doctoral and emerging researchers alongside those who are already well established in their fields. As such, the premise of

[16] Fudge, McChrystal and Sankaran, 'Challenging the Legal Boundaries of Work Regulation' (n 6).

[17] J Fudge, 'Labour as a "Fictive Commodity": Radically Reconceptualizing Labour Law' in G Davidov and B Langille (eds), *The Idea of Labour Law* (Oxford, Oxford University Press, 2011); Fudge, 'A New Vocabulary and Imaginary for Labour Law' (n 2).

[18] See, eg, S Routh, *Enhancing Capabilities through Labour Law: Informal Workers in India* (London, Routledge, 2014); Routh and Borghi, 'Workers and the Global Informal Economy' (n 6).

[19] S Fredman, 'Women at Work: The Broken Promise of Flexicurity' (2004) 33 *Industrial Law Journal* 299; A Supiot, *Beyond Employment: Changes in Work and the Future of Labour Law in Europe* (Oxford, Oxford University Press, 2005).

[20] See, eg, Zatz, 'The Impossibility of Work Law' (n 1); D Brodie, N Busby and R Zahn (eds), *The Future Regulation of Work: New Concepts, New Paradigms* (London, Palgrave MacMillan, 2016).

[21] A Bogg, C Costello, A Davies and J Prassl, 'Introduction: Exploring Autonomy' in A Bogg, C Costello, A Davies and J Prassl (eds), *The Autonomy of Labour Law* (Oxford, Hart Publishing, 2015) 18.

[22] C Costello, 'Migrants and Forced Labour: A Labour Law Response' in A Bogg, C Costello, A Davies and J Prassl (eds), *The Autonomy of Labour Law* (Oxford, Hart Publishing, 2015). The editors of *The Autonomy of Labour Law* agree that labour law should look at other legal disciplines, however, the key issue they highlight is the need to develop filtering criteria to assess whether a particular borrowing or influx from other legal domains is apt to fulfil or undermine labour law's aims and functions: Bogg, Costello, Davies and Prassl, 'Introduction' (n 21) 18.

inclusivity was both the organising idea for the workshop itself, and one of the key crosscutting themes that emerged over the course of our discussions.[23]

Building on this theme, this collection seeks to contribute to the ongoing debates in labour law scholarship by providing a diverse set of ideas and insights on what a more inclusive labour law theory might be. To be clear, the collection does not put forward a singular, coherent vision, nor do all contributions speak to the idea of inclusion directly. Instead, as emerges in the coming pages, inclusive labour law, as we see it, is a multifaceted umbrella concept, and an approach to scholarship, that is characterised by a number of shared commitments. An inclusive labour law theory is diverse and multiple, reflecting the complexity of the globalised world we live in. As a regulatory field, inclusive labour law eschews exclusions by remaining open to a multiplicity of regulatory approaches, which are capable of addressing different problems, rather than seeking one-size-fits-all solutions. While it pays homage to some of labour law's traditional values and goals, and is informed by established scholarship and legal history, inclusive labour law is self-reflective and not laden by nostalgia in thinking about contemporary conditions or future possibilities.[24] As a scholarly discipline, it embraces diverse conceptual framings, methodological approaches, and scholarly voices. It seeks to engage in a dialogue with other disciplines and across generations of scholars. Finally, as a political project, it is emancipatory and democratic, and seeks to bolster sociality and solidarity between differently situated workers. Inclusive labour law rejects co-optation by economic rationalities and political agendas that seek to weaken protections and fragment solidarity under the guise of inclusivity.

III. Themes and Structure

The individual contributions in this collection are arranged across three parts. Part A considers work regulation in the context of a shifting socio-economic order; Part B reviews the role of collective institutions; and Part C seeks to develop and extend theories already present in labour law scholarship. These thematic sections broadly align with what we identify above as features of inclusive labour law; namely, rejection of economism, commitment to sociality and solidarity, and openness to a multiplicity of regulatory and conceptual tools. These themes are focal points for the book's organisation, and also traverse the collection, being

[23] While the contributions in this volume are largely European-centred and engage with developed countries, other papers at the workshop had a more global scope, also pertaining to Australia, South Korea and South Africa. These contributions have been published together as a special issue of the *International Journal of Comparative Labour Law and Industrial Relations*, entitled 'Scrutinizing the Standardized Worker: International and Comparative Perspectives' (2018) 34, 345–96.

[24] In this sense, we accept Bob Hepple's urging to reject nostalgia in a search for alternatives, and instead let the 'close analysis of the present and an understanding of the past' guide these efforts: B Hepple, 'The Future of Labour Law' (1995) 24 *Industrial Law Journal* 303, 305.

echoed in many of its contributions. We examine these shared themes in more detail before turning to a description of the book's three parts and the individual chapters that comprise them.

First, the critique of a regulatory approach or strategy where economic logics are privileged over social, usually non-quantifiable, values, is most clearly articulated by the contributions in Part A.[25] That said, the need to prioritise qualitative and normative principles such as democracy, social justice and dignity in our efforts to address the challenges facing labour law is evident in many of the book's other contributions. Taking a long-term historical perspective, the present moment may be exceptional in the extent to which neoliberal market rationality has usurped the justificatory authority of all other competing normative values (Knegt). Echoing the neoliberal capture of the notion of inclusion we noted earlier, regulatory approaches such as reflexive law have also been appropriated by neoliberal governance agendas, and now need to be re-evaluated (Blackham). When considering ways to counteract the resulting 'normative erosion' of labour law, we should not underestimate the role of the courts in challenging so-called 'emergency measures' induced under the guise of economic and financial crises (Rodgers) or refining legal doctrines to transform labour law from within (Pietrogiovanni). At the same time, challenging neoliberal and deregulatory ideas and strategies might require the introduction of new conceptual and justificatory tools (Eleveld) or the facilitation of horizontal means for organising production, to address the imbalance of power embedded in the employment relationship (Iossa). While trade unions seem to have adapted to the 'economic rationales of efficiency and productivity', they must become credible again in their representation function if they are to regain their role in shaping social consensus and relations (Vergis). Economism can also be rejected from the point of view of those who are excluded from the scope of labour law, as in the case of unpaid care workers, whose work – though societally indispensable – is often not seen as 'market' work and as such remains grossly undervalued (Zbyszewska and Routh).

Secondly, this commitment is supplemented by a shared understanding that developing a more inclusive approach to labour law requires us (and labour market actors) to recast and reimagine solidarity, so as to ensure its relevance to the changing world of work. Solidarity is better seen as a bond that extends beyond occupational or class-based allegiances to encompass relations with and between differently situated workers,[26] and perhaps even those excluded from the

[25] See also, eg, Dukes, *The Labour Constitution* (n 2); K Rittich, 'Making Natural Markets: Flexibility as Labour Market Truth' (2014) 65 *Northern Ireland Legal Quarterly* 323. In a European context see, eg, C Crouch, 'Entrenching neo-liberalism: the current agenda of European social policy' in N Countouris and M Freedland (eds), *Resocialising Europe in a Time of Crisis* (Cambridge, Cambridge University Press, 2013); D Ashiagbor, *The European Employment Strategy: Labour Market Regulation and New Governance* (Oxford, Oxford University Press, 2005). Offering a gendered critique: Fudge and Owens, *Precarious Work, Women, and the New Economy* (n 5).

[26] Supiot, *Beyond Employment* (n 19).

scope of work regulation. As the contributions in Part B make apparent, this has implications for collective forms of organisation and resistance, with a more inclusive approach potentially also being a source of renewal for traditional labour law institutions and collective actors (Zahn). That said, some situations might require the establishment of new types of collective actors and activism, especially where existing ones, even if transformed, might not be suitable (Dias-Abey). Other contributions also address solidarity that extends to relations between workers and those who are, by contemporary labour law, seen as non-workers (Zbyszewska and Routh). By stressing the need to elevate non-market logics or principles, including those operating in the civic sphere (Knegt), re-embed the economy in society through solidaristic structures and collective voice (Vergis), make work organisation more horizontal (Iossa), and rebalance power relations at work (Inversi), the chapters reiterate the importance and potential of collective action in transforming new work arrangements and structures.

Thirdly, and as the book's contributions make apparent, adopting a one-size-fits-all approach is inadequate, be it in relation to collective representation, regulatory tools, or theoretical perspectives. Instead, different strategies, values and principles are needed to steer a shift away from the current overreliance on neoliberal ideologies. Multiplicity is therefore a third theme that runs through all chapters; that is, the idea that diverse work and national circumstances require multiple tools and types of regulation, actors, disciplinary approaches and methods, as well as a grounding in normative values and goals, to design a decent and socially just labour market in which diverse groups of workers can participate. Multiplicity acknowledges and seeks to accommodate diversity in: the different forms of work and workers captured by the scope of labour law (Zbyszewska and Routh); the economic organisation of work (Iossa); regulatory instruments (Inversi, Blackham); legal institutions (Rodgers, Pietrogiovanni); and ways of representing the diverse workforce (Vergis, Zahn, Dias-Abey). With this diversity in mind as a guiding principle, we can, in the long-term, envision and create a more inclusive labour law.

These three themes are further developed across the three parts of the volume, as we detail below.

A. Part A: Work Regulation and the Socio-Economic Order

The notion of crisis has provided a critical entry point into theoretical debates on labour law over the last two decades. In this first set of contributions, the crisis – both that which afflicts labour law itself (as a regulatory model and academic discipline), and that pertaining to transformation in the socio-economic conditions within which this law is embedded – serves as the basis for reflections on labour law's constitutive operations and its possible futures. In keeping with the book's theme of conceptual and methodological multiplicity, the contributions in this Part shed light on this subject using distinctive lenses, ranging from historical and economic sociology to doctrinal approaches. Underpinning all three contributions, however, is a critique of economic and market rationality or, rather, its disproportionate privileging over social concerns, which has permeated broader policy discourse, unsettling (and increasingly influencing) labour law's justificatory and technical apparatus.

To start, Robert Knegt's chapter positions labour law's current adaptation problems and search for new normative and institutional paradigms against a historical account of centuries-long (crises and) transformations in European labour relations. His aim is to expose the dynamics of normative ordering in labour relations, so as to inform future institutional design and dispel a number of common assumptions that constrain labour law's imagination. While adopting a historical methodology, conceptually Knegt draws on economic sociology,[27] which posits an interdependent or co-constitutive relation between societal spheres (including the 'already embedded market'), that is nonetheless dynamic, negotiated, and subject to change. Normative orders of labour relations, as an aspect of broader social relations and life, undergo similar processes of negotiation, institutionalisation, and change. Knegt illustrates this with examples dating back to Europe's medieval period, to show how successive models of industrial relations emerged, crystalised, and eventually gave way to others; in each case, their precise institutional design an outcome of negotiated settlement between co-existing and often competing 'orders of worth', or justifications for action, associated with particular societal spheres or domains. What is exceptional about the present moment, Knegt urges, is that neoliberal market rationality has usurped the justificatory authority over orders pertaining to 'civic' or 'domestic' spheres, with the effect of shaping social life, including labour relations, around the values of the market and the individual, entrepreneurial self. Breaking the grip of this logic in designing future models of labour relations will require more inspiration than simply clutching onto the industrial and Fordist-era past, the conditions and societal compromises of which no longer hold. While Europe's institutional history provides a rich repertoire of ideas, the labour relations and legal regimes of the future must reflect new societal compromises.

Picking up the theme of labour law in the clutches of neoliberal market rationality, Lisa Rodgers's contribution addresses labour law's more recent transformations, brought about by the post-2008 economic crisis reforms adopted across the European Union (EU). Rodgers adopts a 'state of exception' conceptual lens, drawing on Giorgio Agamben, to examine the mechanics and logics of crisis governance and, within them, the double-edged operation of law and the role of legal actors. Applying this lens to labour law, Rodgers shows how

[27] For other examples of how an economic sociology approach has been developed and used in socio-legal scholarship, including in relation to work and labour, see two special issues by Diamond Ashiagbor, Prabha Kotiswaran and Amanda Perry-Kessaris: *Towards an Economic Sociology of Law* in the *Journal of Law and Society* (2013) and *Continuing Towards an Economic Sociology of Law* in the *Northern Ireland Legal Quarterly* (2014).

invocation of a 'state of emergency' associated with the crisis enabled adoption at the EU-level of a series of rapid and wide reaching macroeconomic and fiscal governance reforms, often through technocratic means, extension of the executive power, and with involvement of democratically unaccountable institutions, such as the European Central Bank. Contra their exceptional (ie, of temporary need) justifications, Rodgers argues these reforms have had permanent and transformative consequences for labour law; they have also been consistent with existing policy preferences seeking to align labour law with economic and employer-focused requirements of flexibility and efficiency. At the same time, as she illustrates by reference to several national court rulings concerning the implementation of reform measures, the resulting normative erosion of labour rights has not been uncontested. These rulings, in Rodgers's view, demonstrate that when bolstered by civil society and the mobilisation of social movements, law and legal actors (including the judiciary) can still play an important role in challenging re-regulatory measures that aim to downgrade employment rights.

Conviction in law and legal actors' transformative possibilities also informs Vincenzo Pietrogiovanni's contribution. As he shows, the crisis of labour law partly derives from its inability to respond to contemporary conditions of work, especially the growth in insecurity and precarity associated with technology-enabled forms of work organisation, and the blurring of the boundaries of the workplace. In particular, Pietrogiovanni notes, the realities of crowd-work or platform-assisted work are not captured by mainstream concepts of autonomy and subordination, as invoked in judicial decisions about employment status (as opposed to self-employment) (see also Iossa, Part C). The solution, he suggests, is to reconceptualise subordination, and he proposes to do so by drawing on the concept of subordination as 'double alienness', as developed in Italian jurisprudence. As Pietrogiovanni explains, the Italian Constitutional Court has used the concept of double alienness to capture a situation wherein one party provides a service, but another party effectively owns both the service product itself and the means by which the service delivery is organised. With reference to fractal work, specifically car ride services provided through the Uber platform, he shows that this concept could be useful in extending protection to workers who are deemed autonomous, but in fact operate in the '"grey zone" … where traditional indices of subordination coexist with typical elements of autonomy'. Ultimately, then, although he highlights labour law's limitations and exclusionary operation, Pietrogiovanni is interested in the possibilities offered by existing legal doctrine to transform labour law from within. In a similar vein to Rodgers, he demonstrates the important role of the courts in interpreting and developing labour law protections for new forms of work.

Notwithstanding their differences of emphasis and approach, as Nicole Busby notes in her commentary, the key point of convergence between the three contributions in Part A, and with Busby's own comment, is the pointed critique of the prioritisation of economic concerns as labour law's primary antecedents and justification for its existence. While labour law's role in the constitution of socio-economic orders is certainly not new (Knegt and Rodgers), its privileging of economic logics and objectives reflects and reproduces the broader hegemony of market rationality as a key organising principle of contemporary social life. To harness law's constitutive power for socially progressive ends, labour lawyers must elevate other concerns and rationalities that have historically animated labour law, not least those of democracy and social justice. As Busby urges, labour law's emancipation from the market must involve the broadening of its scope, so that its reinvention also produces instruments or regulatory approaches that promote inclusion and justice. While this should be guided by our past, Busby maintains, in agreement with Knegt, that we have to be mindful of contemporary conditions to develop rules that ultimately respond to and reflect day-to-day human practices. Being open to a multiplicity and plurality of approaches, supporting collective mobilisation of workers and civil society, and embedding labour law in wider socio-economic strategies, rather than making the law subservient to the latter, are some proposals Busby invokes as steps forward.

B. Part B: Revitalising the Role of Collective Representation

The contributions in this Part take up the theme of collective mobilisation and solidarity. As they exemplify, the challenges that collectivism and collective representation face relate, in part, to the shrinking base for these forms of workplace regulation. As all three contributions and the two commentaries make clear, traditional collective institutions have often neglected to address and include in their policies and strategies marginalised workers, particularly women and racialised workers. As such, trade or labour unions have missed out on opportunities to engage with groups of workers that could stimulate their renewal. The question these contributions pose is whether there is any role left for traditional and conventional trade unions (Zahn); and, if so, what that role ought to be (Vergis); or, if not, whether new institutions can provide a solution (Dias-Abey).

Fotis Vergis considers the contemporary role of collective institutions by going back to the conceptual roots of the idea of labour protection, including the mechanisms developed to ensure labour's safeguarding from coercion and abuse of power. Drawing on both Marxist and liberal theory, and examining the political history that gave rise to collective labour institutions, Vergis explores their role as a catalyst for market democratisation, something he sees as a prerequisite for a functional liberal democracy. Like Knegt (Part A), Vergis also puts forward a social constructivist conception of the market (and economy) as embedded in particular social structures, institutions and norms, with the choice of the latter being ultimately a negotiated and political one. As Vergis notes, historically, collective labour institutions have played a key role in embedding the economy or the market through their regulatory and solidaristic functions. Labour unions' current representational crisis, he claims, stems partly from their acquiescence to a purely economic role, and the concessions and accommodations unions have made around economic rationales of efficiency and productivity. Despite this critique,

Vergis maintains that collective labour institutions are still uniquely positioned to re-embed the market in its new social context. To do so, however, they have to act beyond their current market regulation shackles, and re-embrace their solidaristic and regulatory functions, alongside the pursuit of individual dignity and freedom for their members. Unions also have to re-engage in identity building, albeit on terms that correspond with contemporary realities and diversity among workers, so that they can again partake meaningfully in shaping the (new) socio-political consensus.

Picking up on the need to rebuild collective identities in a manner that is more inclusive and representative, Rebecca Zahn's contribution engages with the historical experiences of trade unions in organising and protecting atypical workers. Her starting point is that while expanding their representational reach among non-standard workers (ie, women workers in the gig economy) could be an important source of trade union renewal, in practice, unions are still perceived as representing the quintessential white, working-class blue-collar man, who was the model for the once prevalent standard employment relationship.[28] In reflecting on why traditional trade unions have had only limited success in shifting this presumption, Zahn considers how they tend to prioritise their functions, which, as classified by Keith Ewing, include functions of service, representation, regulation, government and public administration. She observes that unions will have to rethink not only which functions they prioritise, but also what these functions entail, if they are to be more successful in reaching women workers, those in the gig economy, and other non-standard workers. The historic prioritisation of regulation[29] over service functions, she notes, reflects organised labour's gendered understanding of the labour market. Moreover, while the service function has typically focused on legal advice at work or discounts for holiday insurance, these matters are less relevant for female workers who struggle to manage work and care or who do not know how many hours they will work week to week, making their income highly precarious. Thus, if traditional trade unions are to respond effectively to the rise in non-standard work, Zahn argues they ought to actively show their willingness to adapt to the realities of this work and the needs of people who perform it.

Continuing and developing the theme of adaptation, Manoj Dias-Abey explores the emergence of alternative collective representation in the United States (US) by so-called worker centres. Despite not being protected by labour regulations, these organisations have grown in prominence and impact, including due to their focus on serving and organising those workers left out from the New Deal, namely African-Americans and other racialised workers. As Dias-Abey demonstrates through his study of the Coalition of Immokalee Workers (CIW), alternative forms of collective organisation can be more effective than traditional

[28] See, eg, J Conaghan, 'Labour Law and Feminist Method' (2017) 33 *International Journal of Comparative Labour Law & Industrial Relations* 93; Vosko, *Managing the Margins* (n 5).

[29] That is, bargaining on behalf of workers to regulate work through collective bargaining.

models, not least because they may be open to a broader and more creative range of strategies. In the case of the CIW, activists went beyond the labour law paradigm which long marginalised migrant farm workers, instead deploying strategies pertaining to different regulatory and discursive 'fields' and devising a private regulatory system, the Fair Food Program. As Dias-Abey shows, by enlisting large fast food chains and supermarkets that purchase Floridian tomatoes to sign up to the Fair Food Program, the CIW managed to put pressure on growers in fast food/supermarket supply chains to comply with a series of labour standards the Program stipulates, ultimately improving the conditions of work on farms. Even if it primarily pertains to a private regulatory mechanism – a code of conduct – rather than formal legal reform, the CIW case affirms that law (albeit broadly construed) remains an important and effective instrument, thereby echoing other contributions' views of law as having enduring strategic utility. At the same time, Dias-Abey remains cautious, pointing out law's frequent limitations and, drawing on the example of immigration law, its problematic operations. Notwithstanding these reservations, his study invites us to think about law and legal strategies pertaining to work more broadly, and to more seriously consider how, when combined with political engagement, law can be used to benefit those traditionally left out of regulatory protection.

Ultimately, what all the chapters in this Part show is that a necessary requirement for strengthening collective institutions is reimagining the role or functions such institutions could or should play. They also show that a multiplicity of different approaches can be adopted to that end, though the kind of institutional set-up and regulatory and strategic tools needed will depend on the political and socio-economic context. The comments by Tonia Novitz and Nicola Smit also pick up on this theme of multiplicity and need for context specific adaptation. Novitz acknowledges the concerns raised by Zahn, but emphasises that, at least to some extent, we should aim to preserve the more traditional functions of trade unions, while simultaneously 'developing a multiplicity of tools to achieve further objectives that address the intricacies and dynamics of our twenty-first-century labour markets'. Among others, she notes that international and cross-border regulation (ie, international labour standards in combination with rules on trade) should provide additional methods of strengthening the role of collective institutions. Smit is more cautious about the role and scope of international labour and social labour protection. The latter, she notes, tends to focus on the formal sector, ignoring the complexity of informality, which is the reality in many low income and developing countries. She particularly questions whether the tripartite structure promoted by the International Labour Organization (ILO) is of use in countries where informal markets dominate and trade unions are marginalised. When considering the potential future role for collective actors in the non-standard work context, Smit suggests that a mix 'between social, enterprise and network bargaining and persuasive influence has become relevant'. She adds that it might be necessary to establish 'new hybrid models of collectivism' – issues to which Zahn and Dias-Abey speak – which are able to involve more non-traditional players and could also cover 'subjects other than traditional terms and conditions of employment and social benefits'. As many workers do not enjoy decent work, existing regulatory and collective models are in need of review.

C. Part C: Advancing Theoretical Models to Respond to the Contemporary World of Work

While canvassing a wide array of theoretical approaches, from reflexive law (Blackham), to regulatory space (Inversi), to anarchist theory (Iossa), to the republican theory of non-domination (Eleveld), to feminist theory (Zbyszewska and Routh), the chapters in this Part are united in recognising both the limits and potential of different theories for reconceiving labour law and labour regulation for the contemporary world of work.

The chapters by Cristina Inversi and Alysia Blackham engage with the regulatory function(s) of labour law. Inversi uses the concept of 'regulatory space' to capture the multiplicity of regulatory levels, dimensions, instruments and actors that already coexist and interact in the context of labour relations. This perspective decentres mandated legal norms, which it treats as only one among various dimensions of regulation, with the others being generated through negotiation (between employers and workers) and unilateralism (imposition of rules through managerial prerogative). At the same time, law's capacity to produce hierarchies renders it crucial for facilitating both self-regulation and particular interactions between other regulatory dimensions. As Inversi points out, it is not only what law does, but also what it does not do that matters. Law's limits and inconsistencies shape spaces for other regulatory dimensions and differently situated actors. As Inversi shows, drawing on the case of working time in the United Kingdom (UK), the benefit of this pluralist approach is that it better captures the dynamism and complexity of regulatory change.

While the approach that Inversi adopts highlights reflexivity and self-regulation as integral elements of the regulatory space, Blackham more specifically addresses the theory of reflexive law, highlighting that, at least for equality law in the UK, this theory does not work in practice as would be predicted. In contrast to Inversi's contribution, Blackham's chapter highlights reflexive (labour) law's 'exclusivity'. While reflexive law – in theory – is fundamentally inclusive, drawing on regulation at multiple levels and encouraging self-regulation by local actors, this is not borne out in practice. As Blackham's chapter shows, it 'appears difficult to translate systems theory and reflexive law into practical regulatory interventions', especially where mechanisms are lacking to 'moderate the power of organisations and public bodies'. What this chapter shows, then, is that ideas and theories are fundamentally beholden to their implementation, and are therefore also dependent on political will and political values. Reflexive law in particular has the potential to be captured by neoliberal actors to (further) deregulate existing labour protections. Blackham concludes by canvassing some emerging developments in critical systems theory, which may offer a path to develop reflexive law as a useful tool that escapes its current limitations.

Anja Eleveld's contribution builds on these ideas to consider how labour law and work regulation might be defended from the incursions of neoliberal policy. Eleveld suggests that the answer might lie in the application of the republican theory of non-domination as an interpretative tool to contest deregulatory ideas and strategies. In doing so, she reflects on and joins recent labour law engagements with republicanism.[30] Unlike most, however, Eleveld is not interested in republican theory as a source of new philosophical or normative foundations for labour law. Rather, she endorses a 'post-foundationalist' approach, with the objective of ascertaining whether republican theory is helpful from a justificatory perspective. Eleveld considers whether conceptions of domination, the power on which it rests, and its particular theory of justice and equality provide a more convincing language with which to defend labour law than other alternatives that labour lawyers have considered, such as the capabilities approach and theories of vulnerability and subordination. Eleveld finds republican theory more suited to the task, as the theory is inherently relational rather than individualistic (a fault she finds in the capabilities approach, for example). Moreover, Eleveld shows, drawing on Philip Pettit's work, that the objections that republican theory makes to the exercise of 'arbitrary power' – especially in so far as it has consequences for personal freedom, including the ability to enjoy free choice and make future plans – are more likely to effectively contest neoliberal rationales (which, after all, profess to maximise individual freedoms). Thus, defending against the erosion of labour law on the basis that its insufficiency might lead to domination and the exercise of arbitrary power by employers is an argumentative strategy that neoliberal policy might find harder to counter.

Countering neoliberal ideology by taking advantage of the conditions and opportunities it has brought about is a thread taken up by Andrea Iossa's contribution. Iossa argues that traditional labour law has, alongside its protective function, also institutionalised and perpetrated subordination (that is, a form of labour exploitation). At the same time, neoliberal ideology, notwithstanding all its harms, has also effectively diminished the importance of both the employer and the state as traditional expressions of authority. This context, Iossa suggests, invites us to consider how anti-authoritarian, anarchist theories might be usefully applied to

[30] A Bogg, 'Republican Non-Domination and Labour Law: New Normativity or Trojan Horse?' (2017) 33 *International Journal of Comparative Labour Law and Industrial Relations* 391; K Breen, 'Non-Domination, Workplace Republicanism, and the Justification of Worker Voice and Control' (2017) 33 *International Journal of Comparative Labour Law & Industrial Relations* 419; D Cabrelli and R Zahn, 'Theories of Domination and Labour Law: An Alternative Conception for Intervention?' (2017) 33 *International Journal of Comparative Labour Law & Industrial Relations* 339; G Davidov, 'Subordination vs Domination: Exploring the Differences' (2017) 33 *International Journal of Comparative Labour Law & Industrial Relations* 365.

rethink labour regulation. Specifically, Iossa proposes a horizontal organisation of production, as an alternative to subordinate and hierarchical relations inherent in the bilateral employment relationship. A horizontal organisation of work would enable the redistribution of earnings among workers, challenging the idea that workers must work for the employer's benefit and profit. Referring to successful examples of workers' cooperatives, Iossa therefore shows that there is an alternative to capitalist undertakings as a form of economic organisation. What he makes clear is that the current labour law model, which favours capitalist economic ordering of work (relations), is not fit for the contemporary socio-economic reality, as it only serves a few and excludes workers from most of the benefits of production. A horizontal economic production or work organisation would allow us to focus on workers' dignity, and therefore would give the reinvented labour law a human touch. In this way, Iossa's contribution speaks to the inclusion of workers in a more dignified work organisation, focusing on the quality rather than the quantity of work and production.

As discussed above, 'inclusion' in the labour market can become coercive. This risks undermining individual autonomy and the value placed on other social goods. The conversation between Ania Zbyszewska and Supriya Routh illustrates this idea in their critique of the implicit (or unintentional) productivism underlying labour law as a discipline and regulatory field. Engaging with feminist scholarship, Zbyszewska and Routh probe the extent to which critical contributions to labour law debates have managed to challenge productivism, and question the extent to which a 'productivism' lens should be used to expand labour law's scope. Zbyszewska emphasises labour law's exclusionary scope, derived from its focus on productive work, which has particular implications for the family/work divide and the exclusion of unpaid household and care labour from labour law's remit. To counteract that productivist lens, feminist political economists have stressed the need to consider the role and place of social reproduction, which is needed to uphold the productive workforce. Reconceiving labour law's subjects and domains thus requires addressing the interdependence of production and social reproduction. However, Routh questions whether feminist labour law scholars have not reproduced a productive bias in justifying the contributions made by homework and care work (as non-market activities). Rather than seeking recognition of home and care work by the market, Routh uses the notion of 'public good' to argue that a justification must be found outside the market for care work. Yet, as Zbyszewska argues, promoting such a justification poses a danger in – again – not recognising home and care work as something of value and, more importantly, possibly opens the door to coercive obligations to provide such work because it is in the public interest. Zbyszewska and Routh's contribution therefore neatly illustrates the tensions inherent in labour market inclusion and exclusion, and the potential interplay between the market and other social goods, such as care.

The final contribution in this Part comes from Ralf Rogowski, who recalls Ton Wilthagen's two-decade old proposal for advancing labour law theory, and uses it as a framing device for his comment. As Rogowski reminds us, the elements of this proposal to make labour law fit for contemporary conditions included: multidisciplinarity; attentiveness to the relations between labour law, employment relations, labour markets and the state; deconstruction of neoliberal economism and its normative assumptions; inclusion of the policy dimension; and development of a theoretical frame for labour law based on the notion of reflexivity. While Rogowski's comment is refracted through his own interest in reflexive law – a theoretical approach to which he has greatly contributed – the fact that each chapter in this last section tackles at least one of the elements Wilthagen identified attests to the need for a multiplicity of tools and approaches for inclusive labour law theory. Moreover, Rogowski's comment picks up on the broader concern that traverses this volume, namely challenging the link between work regulation and neoliberal policy, be it through revitalisation of collective action (Part B), or the search for alternative logics to those that prioritise markets and emphasise production as a key aspect of social life (Parts A, B and C). Rogowski's comment also helpfully identifies ways in which this agenda can be advanced, via areas for future research and scholarship. He particularly emphasises the global nature of labour law, and reiterates the need to consider global conditions in research and scholarship.

IV. Conclusion

This volume advances the conversation about how we might develop a more inclusive labour law theory. Rather than proposing a singular vision, and while acknowledging the contestable nature of 'inclusiveness', we propose the notion of inclusivity as an overarching umbrella concept and an approach to scholarship.

To that end, this book showcases the diverse ways in which labour lawyers and our colleagues in adjacent disciplines theorise possibilities for labour law's future development. Within this diversity, the contributions are united by a number of joint commitments. The three overarching features of inclusivity that we have highlighted here are: a rejection of economism that seeks to weaken protections and fragment solidarity under the guise of inclusivity; a commitment to sociality and solidarity between differently situated workers; and openness to a multiplicity of regulatory, methodological and conceptual tools and approaches, as well as to scholarly voices across generations and jurisdictional boundaries.

As the contributions highlight, these commitments are not necessarily novel. Rather than being beholden to history, however, the vision of inclusive labour law that emerges here is conceptually and normatively informed by and grounded in the past, but also unafraid of change, so long as this change advances the values of democratic participation, social justice, and protection of a broader range of work activities and the people who perform them. This collection, then, offers a roadmap and a rallying call for a future of inclusive labour law scholarship.

PART A

Work Regulation and the Socio-Economic Order

2

Recovering the Impact of Normative Regimes on Labour Relations Practices: A Socio-Historical View of Institutional Requirements

ROBERT KNEGT*

I. Introduction

When Hugo Sinzheimer coined the term 'labour law' (*Arbeitsrecht*) in 1911, the term represented two developments partly realised by him: first, that academic lawyers had become aware that state law could be relevant to labour relations; secondly, that part of the labour movement was giving up its suspicion of state law as repressive law, and discovering its potency to contribute to freedom, equality, and security for workers.[1] Sinzheimer gave a strong impetus to a wide institutional re-embedding of labour relations that was only halted when the hegemony of neoliberal economic perspectives afflicted government policies in the 1980s. The consecutive institutional downshift generated strife among labour law scholars for restoring or reinventing the goals of labour law.[2] Strategies diverge: some authors tend to submit to the hegemony of economics and try to convince economists that labour law rules do not disturb, but actually contribute to the efficiency of labour markets.[3] Others stress the autonomy of labour law's goals and criteria: it is rather markets that ought to bow to the superior political principle of democracy or the legal principles of justice and equality.[4]

* Guest Researcher, Hugo Sinzheimer Institute, University of Amsterdam.

[1] H Sinzheimer, *Grundzüge des Arbeitsrechts* (Jena, Fischer, 1927).

[2] See, for instance, the different contributions in G Davidov and B Langille (eds), *The Idea of Labour Law* (Oxford, Oxford University Press, 2011).

[3] S Deakin and F Wilkinson, *The Law of the Labour Market: Industrialization, Employment, and Legal Evolution* (Oxford, Oxford University Press, 2005).

[4] M Weiss, 'Re-Inventing Labour Law?' in G Davidov and B Langille (eds), *The Idea of Labour Law* (Oxford, Oxford University Press, 2011).

Since the 1980s, the political embrace of neoliberal doctrine has tended to obscure sight of the importance of institutional conditions for well-functioning labour relations. I argue that a broader historical perspective on developments in the regulation of labour relations can assist us in recovering a clearer view of these conditions, and may assist us in considering the possible futures of labour law.

This argument requires, first, a lessening of the strict limits to which 'labour law' has been subjected. Its history is then, secondly, reconstructed as one of successive transformations of normative models, which are not just ideological refractions of, but are actively co-constituting labour relations. A succinct outline of labour relations regimes in Western Europe, over a period of roughly eight centuries, substantiates the importance of institutionally embedding the strange market on which the commodity of 'labour' is said to be traded, and suggests the need to find (new) ways of doing so if we are to prevent its future collapse.

II. Seven Common but Deplorable Limits of Labour Law

With a view to a broader historical perspective, I need to dissociate myself from what I will list – for the sake of brevity – as seven common, but deplorable limits that are regularly placed on the scope of labour law. Whatever the reasons have been for setting up fences, they tend to obstruct our view of the actual continuity of the norm-imbued domain.

First, labour law is often depicted as if it originated with the Industrial Revolution.[5] Wage labour and its regulation, however, have existed in considerable volume for much longer. In Europe, wage labour has been reported as far back as the seventh century. It existed on a large scale in monasteries at the start of the last millennium. In the fourteenth century, more than half of all labour was, at least in Britain and the Netherlands, wage labour.[6]

Second, labour law is widely identified with *state* law, or rules formally based upon the latter at supranational level. This is in keeping with conceptions of law that have gained dominance since the nineteenth century. However, if we do not impose such a narrow definition of 'law' upon reality, we rediscover a not inconsiderable amount of law regarding labour relations at 'lower' levels, in different forms; for instance, local conventions, or rules of associations, or enterprises that were explicitly perceived as 'law' by those associated with them. In a prolonged struggle during the nineteenth century, nation states gradually succeeded in usurping most of it. Labour law may acknowledge their claim to victory, yet without submitting to the conqueror's narrow perspective.

[5] eg, B Hepple (ed), *The Making of Labour Law in Europe: A Comparative Study of Nine Countries Up to 1945* (London, Mansell, 1986) 12.

[6] C Dyer, *An Age of Transition?: Economy and Society in England in the Later Middle Ages* (Oxford, Clarendon Press, 2005) 211–13.

Third, labour law is argued as concerning the *protection* of *workers*.[7] But, for instance, it also authorises employers to direct the activities of 'their' employees and protects employers from some of their whims. Labour law is about normatively structuring labour relations by generally attributing powers, rights, and responsibilities in a certain way. The protection of workers is only part of it. In substantially different labour market conditions, even the protection of employers might become urgent – as has occurred in specific situations in the past.[8]

Fourth, this protection is argued as applying in principle to *employees* only, because of their specific subordinate position. This argument corresponds with the currently dominant, strict division between employment and entrepreneurship. However, the strictness of this division is just a recent aberration. In the past, governments have devised regulations protecting self-employed workers; for instance, formally independent textile workers who were economically dependent on merchants running a 'putting-out' system.[9]

Fifth, the types of protection are deemed to be characteristic of labour relations under *industrialised* relations. However, terms of dismissal, continued payment of wages in case of illness, and several other conditions have been documented elements of labour relations at least from the fourteenth century.[10] Terms of dismissal have also been conferred upon legally independent textile craftsmen working under the conditions of a 'putting out' system.[11]

Sixth, labour relations are thought to have always been based on *contract*. Whilst incumbent duties will generally be based upon a certain type of formal confirmation of entering a relationship, this need not be the current conception of contract as a 'concordance of wills' – an eighteenth-century innovation. Previously, commitment was typically entered by a *unilateral* act, the self-description of which was 'hiring oneself out'.

Seventh, labour law tends to be conceived as a normative framework *imposed* 'from the outside' upon a 'naturally' functioning market. However, conceived less narrowly, law is an integral element of practical interactions. And, until the eighteenth century, the 'market' did not have the naturalised character that orthodox economics assigns it nowadays. The market was conceived as a public place of justice;[12] as a device that would, by its technical design, realise justice

[7] Hepple, *The Making of Labour Law* (n 5) 11.

[8] K Schulz, *Handwerksgesellen und Lohnarbeiter: Untersuchungen zur oberrheinischen und oberdeutschen Stadtgeschichte des 14. Bis 17. Jahrhundert* (Sigmaringen, Thorbecke, 1985) 74–76.

[9] K Schermer, 'Handwerker und Verleger: Das Verlagssystem der frühen Neuzeit als rechtshistorisches Problem' in K Schermer and D Willoweit (eds), *Vom Gewerbe zum Unternehmen: Studien zum Recht der gewerblichen Wirtschaft im 18. und 19. Jahrhundert* (Darmstadt, Wissenschaftliche Buchgesellschaft, 1982).

[10] W Ebel, *Gewerbliches Arbeitsvertragsrecht im Deutschen Mittelalter* (Weimar, H Böhlhaus, 1934); W Klatt, *Treuepflichten im Arbeitsverhältnis* (Pfaffenweiler, Centaurus Verlag, 1990) 36–39.

[11] J Brand, *Untersuchungen zur Entstehung der Arbeitsgerichtsbarkeit in Deutschland* (Pfaffenweiler, Centaurus Verlag, 1990) 240–41; Schermer, 'Handwerker und Verleger' (n 9) 53.

[12] M Foucault, *The Birth of Biopolitics: Lectures at the Collège de France 1978–1979* (M Senellart ed, G Burchell tr, New York, Palgrave Macmillan, 2008).

between trading parties. Only liberalism has turned it into a quasi-natural mechanism, and thereby isolated it from a discourse of justice.

III. Repertoires of Evaluation and Legal Models of Labour Relations

By steering these critical notes in a positive direction, towards an approach that recognises (labour) law as a constitutive element of day-to-day human practices, I build upon the work of Luc Boltanski and Laurent Thévenot.[13] They have urged social science to take the imperative to justify human action seriously. In the face of uncertainty, people ordinarily 'seek to carry out their actions in such a way that these can withstand the test of justification … to establish associations among things that count, to identify beings independently of circumstances, and to reach agreement on forms of generality'.[14] Coordination of human beings at work requires *investments of form* that endow human beings, and objects, with capabilities and thus ensure an adjustment of diverse resources. Boltanski and Thévenot identify six different orders of worth, with each based upon mutually incommensurable ways of establishing equivalences amongst beings, in order to coordinate human action: *Inspired* (passion, creativity); *Domestic* (trust, authority); *Civic* (equality, solidarity, rights); *Opinion* (recognition, repute); *Market* (exchange, desire); and *industrial* (functionality, productivity, expertise). Below, I use the first letter in parentheses to refer to each mode, with the exception that (U) stands for 'industrial'.

Organisations partake of different orders at the same time, and can be analysed as composite arrangements of compromise between them – the business firm, for instance, as 'a compromising device between several modes of coordination, which engage different repertoires of evaluation'.[15] In this view, labour law is the equipment of a central compromise between civic and industrial orders around the constitutive concept of the 'worker'.[16]

Boltanski and Thévenot stress the incessant *dynamics* of coordination, thus disentangling their composite 'repertoires of evaluation'. Whilst their research orientation leads them to treat compromising devices as derivative phenomena, such phenomena may be valued for their capacity to construct a relative *stability* that allows them to be mobilised in the coordination of (labour) relations as *composite modes of evaluation*. The stability of these compositions is being pursued by material arrangements that support the regularity of practices

[13] L Boltanski and L Thévenot, *On Justification: Economies of Worth* (C Porter tr, Princeton, Princeton University Press, 2006).

[14] ibid 32, 37.

[15] L Thévenot, 'Organized Complexity: Conventions of Coordination and the Composition of Economic Arrangements' (2001) 4 *European Journal of Social Theory* 405.

[16] Boltanski and Thévenot, *On Justification* (n 13) 325.

(rituals, written rules), and by investments of form that culminate in the design of *normative models of labour relations*. My analysis focuses on the role that these normative models have played, and are playing, in the structuring of labour relations.

As to which normative models are being used, this depends primarily upon three conditions. First, on the prior *availability* of *normative models* of relations: what is already in the 'toolkit', and how may it be used to normatively shape practices? Secondly, on the availability of certain *technical devices* and arrangements that facilitate the implementation of models (oath, meeting places, writing). Thirdly, on the capacity of an available model to be adjusted to *fit* current requirements. This fit has to be judged both in terms of the model's internal consistency and legitimacy (do participants in the unit sufficiently recognise it as a valid framework for what they are doing collectively?), and of its performative power within the configuration of interdependent actors of which the unit is a part.

Distinguishing between types of configurations of actors, types of technical arrangements, and types of normative structuring allows me to argue for the role of normative models in different historical *regimes of labour relations*.

IV. Regimes of Labour Relations: An Outline

The outline below is selective in several respects. It aims, not of course at completely rewriting the history of labour relations, but at highlighting the role of differential normative models in their development. It comprises 'regimes' that have been relatively stable and widespread in Western Europe, and that might still somehow be relevant to our thinking about the future of labour law. My sources, though, are to a large extent on developments in Germany, as these have been documented and analysed more thoroughly than elsewhere. The point is to highlight a number of relevant types of regimes as combinations of configurations of actors, types of technical arrangements and relevant knowledge, and types of normative structuring.

A. Craft Guild Regime

Economic developments during the High Middle Ages allowed cities to be revived or newly founded, and to develop into craft centres. Craftsmen, working in workplaces connected to their homes (D)[17] which were often spatially collected in a quarter of the town, were basically equal competitors in one trade. Their configuration in the political space of the city, yet to be defined, urged them to organise

[17] The letters between parentheses refer to Boltanski and Thévenot's (n 13) six orders of worth, introduced in the text above.

themselves collectively (C). In their search for a normative mould, the religious model of a *sworn brotherhood* offered itself; the mutual oath (*coniuratio*) being the basis to claim and organise the rule-making capacity and jurisdiction of the guild.[18] In the Middle Ages, the oath was one of the few devices permitting the constitution of binding relations of parity between non-kin people of equal status.[19] Guild members used to bind themselves by oath to comply with the rules – even those not yet issued – and to accept, in advance, sanctions in case of infringement. The brotherhood model has clear legal implications of equality and of common decision-making. Competition (M) allows for different earnings, but brotherhood (C) forbids excessively large differences in potentials (rules on the maximum number of journeymen employed). In accordance with a conception of markets as places where *justice* would be realised, guild rules aimed at guaranteeing a just division of the amount of work, and a reasonable level of subsistence to all members.

The expertise of the trade (U), transferred from masters to apprentices, constituted a secret kept from outsiders (D); the 'mystery' of the trade – a term that might be related to the contemporary legal conception of the corporation as a *persona mystica*.[20] The meetings at which guild masters took collective decisions (C) were characterised by secrecy as well, maintained through ritual, and strictly oral in character. What members called the 'law' of the guild was not something 'external', but was actually being *lived* by them, performed by participating in ritual meetings, meals, drinks, greetings, funerals of members, and in the festive processions in the town.[21] To be effective, guild rules required force also towards outsiders and, in this respect, guilds were dependent upon city governments for official proclamation. It allowed the city to monitor general interests; for instance, the city's valued reputation as an exporter of quality products (O).

Could the craftsmen have made another choice of legal model? Their positions as urban citizens and independent economic competitors made the craftsmen prefer 'horizontal' over more hierarchical models available. In order to forge a strong compromise between civic and domestic orders, they transformed models of association already developed in the religious world. Since the thirteenth century, this fraternity structure and its legal rules have been constantly copied and partly adjusted by other guilds all over Europe – metaphorically they might be regarded as a kind of 'Operating System' that could everywhere base the 'application programs' of locally different craft practices.[22]

[18] G Dilcher, 'Die genossenschaftliche Struktur von Gilden und Zünften' in B Schwineköper (ed), *Gilden und Zünfte* (Sigmaringen, Jan Thorbecke, 1985) 71–11 (79).

[19] W Reininghaus, *Die Entstehung der Gesellengilden im Spätmittelalter*, vol Beiheft 71 (Viertelsjahrschrift für Sozial-end Wirtschaftsgeschichte, Wiesbaden, Franz Steiner Verlag, 1981) 79.

[20] Schermer, 'Handwerker und Verleger' (n 9) 23.

[21] Brand, *Untersuchungen* (n 11) 77–85.

[22] HJ Berman, *Law and Revolution: The Formation of the Western Legal Tradition* (Cambridge, Mass., Harvard University Press, 1983) 391–92.

The basis of the craft guild regime could be undermined by deficiencies or changes in power configurations. If the city was an insufficiently closed space, outsiders had an opportunity to ignore the guild's borders of control (D), and take away part of the internal demand. Individual members could be seduced to cheat on the rules (C); for instance, by employing more journeymen than allowed. In particular, with textiles, merchants could acquire a dominant position at the demand side (M), and thereby force guild masters into a dependent position (more on this below in IV(C)). Finally, the domestic relationship between masters and journeymen could be contested by a civic solidarity of journeymen.

B. Journeymen's Associations and the Tripartite Structure of Relations in Cities

At an early stage, journeymen figured as 'adolescent' members of guilds, subordinate to their masters (D), and lacking a voice at guild meetings. Over the course of the fourteenth century, German journeymen started to distance themselves from their domestic subordination and to organise separately (C), allegedly to defend their 'honour' (O) against intrusions by masters. In search for a normative mould, some of the journeymen's collectives selected a domestic alternative and appointed a 'king' to guide and represent them. Others claimed legitimacy on the basis of a reduced guild model, organising themselves around 'boxes', and creating collective funds (C) to provide for the costs of member funerals or festivities – or, as masters tended to suspect, subversive actions. The journeymen created their own space in town: they met in their inns (*Stuben*) and claimed their own jurisdiction. Their wandering practices, which involved regularly moving between cities in order to learn more of the trade, contributed to their organising at regional and even at empire level. It enabled them to enforce measures at a regional level which gave them temporary weight over (primarily locally organised) masters. The collective action of journeymen incited masters to take counteractions; for instance, to make regional collective agreements on maximum wages, and incited city governments to mediate between conflicting parties.[23] During 'the golden age of wage labour' – a term used to describe a short period in the mid-fourteenth century – masters complained to city governments that journeymen were trying 'to become lords over their masters' which, to some extent, mirrored actual relations.[24]

The divide between masters and journeymen, and the role of city governments in their relationship, established a now familiar triangular structure comprised of employers, employees, and government. It can be regarded as a device that effects compromise between domestic, civic, market, and industrial orders.

[23] Schulz, *Handwerksgesellen und Lohnarbeiter* (n 8) 72–75.
[24] Reininghaus, *Die Entstehung der Gesellengilden* (n 19) 38.

Under normal conditions, all parties strive to realise their legitimate interests and, at the same time, desire to keep relations peaceful. As a compromise between incommensurable orders of worth, it institutes a balance that cannot be celebrated as a safe accomplishment, as it remains subject to changes in the (power) configuration underlying it.

C. Putting Out System and Corporate Structure

For a lengthy period until the end of the nineteenth century, the production of textiles dominated craft activities in the cities. Traditionally, it was organised as a *serial* processing of textile materials, in which each process was conducted by a separate trade, represented by a guild with its own jurisdiction and 'honour' within the social order of the city. As early as the fifteenth century, there are reports of a shift in the power configuration caused by the increasing concentration of capital in the hands of merchants. Textiles are predominantly products exported to foreign markets, therefore traders are interested both in increasing the efficiency of processes, and in gaining control of all of the consecutive stages of production. That way, they can attune the production process to increasingly rapid changes in preferences for textile styles and shifts in fashion. Merchants claiming expertise in marketing (M) started to impose the changing demands of international markets upon primarily traditionally (D) producing craftsmen. Merchants provided masters with raw materials and required well-defined products to be delivered to them – often, exclusively to them. The domestic-civic parataxis of the trades, each of which took relatively independent care of its 'own' part of the textile production process, tended to break down with the industrial logics of merchants orientated to market requirements. At the same time, merchants undermined guild regimes by exploiting the labour potential of farmers in the countryside, providing them with spinning wheels, looms, and raw materials, and requiring them to spin and weave at their homes (ie, a 'putting out' system).

The new commercial regime, however, conceiving of the production process as a chain of contractual deliveries, typically lacked some of the controls and commitments that made up the strength of guild regimes. Merchants were facing at least five problems.[25] First, they lacked direct supervision, so how were they to make sure that the work was done correctly? Secondly, they usually competed between themselves for workers, so how were they to ensure that the workers engaged by them were not poached by another? Thirdly, if the merchant had provided a worker with materials or given him an advance payment, how would they be retrieved if the worker disappeared? Fourthly, how to keep the worker committed and prevent him from using his machinery to produce textiles for others as well? Finally, the lack of control increased the risk of conflict at the moment of delivery.[26]

[25] Brand, *Untersuchungen* (n 11) 172.
[26] ibid 399.

Are, for instance, product failures due to bad work or to bad materials provided by the merchant? How to deal with these conflicts? Brand highlights the massive embezzlement of raw materials that occurred in spite of penal sanctions, on which a whole black market could flourish, and interpreted this as a protest by independent workers against the constrictions to which they were subject. It was behaviour aimed at damaging the 'putting out' merchant, inspired by a fundamentally different normative model of labour relations that made the merchant appear to them as an 'uncompaniable alien'.[27]

The problems mentioned above urged the merchants to try, not just to rule out the guild regime, but to exploit its excellent disciplinary potential, and therefore look for compromises between their commercial and the 'old' guild regime. This was primarily achieved in one of two ways. Either the commercial regime was incorporated into officially proclaimed guild regulations, whose character was largely preserved. Or guilds (or collectives of its members) figured as parties to civil law contracts, and committed themselves to collective deliveries to merchants.[28] The guild masters could retain the formal independence that was so important to their perceptions of 'honour' (O), and of their rightful place in city communities (C), whilst their economic position shifted towards an actual dependency (M) on a small number of merchants.

In this conflict of regimes, city governments have been ambivalent, and have changed their position over time. For a considerable period, their 'economic policy' (C-U) has been characterised by two basic tenets. First, international trade depended upon a city's reputation (O), which required supervision over the quality of its export products. Apart from institutional facilities (weigh-house, cloth hall), the city had to check the internal quality control mechanisms of the guilds involved. Secondly, the city had a duty of care to the common wealth of the city, in particular, to monitor whether its population had insufficient means of subsistence or if there were unused possibilities for economic growth. An important means to further economic activities was to attract skilled craftsmen from elsewhere by offering them easy entrance to citizenship, protection of their religion, or fiscal privileges.

Since the eighteenth century, there has been a persistent discussion regarding whether, or to what extent, guilds should be seen as conservative, monopolising forces resisting modernisation – as they have been depicted by revolutionaries in France, most protagonists of strong national states, and many orthodox economists; or whether their organisational structure has contributed significantly to the economic development of cities – a position nowadays supported by socio-economic historians.[29] Government policies towards guilds gradually developed

[27] ibid 199–207.

[28] Schermer, 'Handwerker und Verleger (n 9) 38–45.

[29] J Lucassen, 'Labour and Early Modern Economic Development' in K Davids and J Lucassen (eds), *A Miracle Mirrored: The Dutch Republic in European Perspective* (Cambridge, Cambridge University Press, 1995).

from legal recognition of their relative autonomy, to efforts to supervise and control them and make them subservient to national economic policies (under absolutism) and, finally, to the withdrawal of support and efforts to eradicate them in favour of the commercial regime pursued by merchants.

D. Commercial/Contract Law Regime

The commercial regime, normatively based upon contract law, was initially pushed by commerce, then embraced by states that were gradually increasing their power at the cost of cities. Configurations changed in favour of states, firstly of newly developing absolutist states, in the nineteenth century of nation states. They rose by countering city-level structures such as the guilds, by supporting the commercial development of the countryside, and by pushing a universal civil law regime of *contract* upon labour relations. Initially, the purport of this regime was predominantly *negative*: to deny legitimacy to *Ancien Régime* structures, particularly the *domestic* elements of these structures in the cities.

The regime shift was prepared both in legal theory and in economics. 'Labour', as an abstract indication of productive activities, had been unknown until economics developed it in the eighteenth century as a measure of the value of things.[30] The idea that 'hiring oneself out' could be legally constructed as a transfer of *property*, had been developed by Samuel von Pufendorf and Hugo Grotius,[31] who treated labour as a 'particle of freedom' that is owned, and thus may be alienated by a subject without thereby detracting from his freedom.[32] A key concern in Enlightenment philosophy was how to reconcile the formal autonomy and equality accorded to free citizens, with the functional relations of inequality. The usual answer was 'by contract', and the smart 'solution' in relation to labour relations was to combine the notion of *property* of labour power with the legal freedom to transfer it by contract (C) to another, provided that this was for a *limited* period (no 'slavery'!). The possibility of transfer, however, introduced labour into the market order. To treat labour as a 'commodity', as we have come to characterise it, remains a tortuous exercise (I have elsewhere outlined eleven reasons why it is still problematic to treat 'labour' as something that could be traded on a market).[33] A recent comparative,

[30] NJ Theocarakis, 'Metamorphoses: The Concept of Labour in the History of Political Economy' (2010) 20(2) *Economic and Labour Relations Review* 7, 13.

[31] S Pufendorf, *The Whole Duty of Man According to the Law of Nature* (A Tooke tr, Indianapolis, Liberty Fund, 2003); H Grotius, *De iure belli et pacis* (Amsterdam, G Blaeuw, 1631).

[32] K-P Nanz, *Die Entstehung des allgemeinen Vertragsbegriffs in 16. Bis 18. Jahrhundert* (München, J Schweitzer Verlag, 1985) 141.

[33] R Knegt, 'A Farewell to "Protection": Rethinking the Labour Law-Market Nexus' (2nd Labour Law Research Network Conference, Amsterdam, 25 June 2015) 15–16 www.researchgate.net/publication/277308450 accessed 20 December 2018.

historical study of societies in which labour had been commodified, found that commodification contributed to a short period of economic growth, but was then followed by increasing social inequalities that have in all cases internally generated the downfall of market economies.[34]

The contractual model was deployed as a crowbar to break up the local arrangements and normative models that characterised labour relations under the *Ancien Régime*. The way in which this model was subsequently received in practice has significantly differed across local cultures. In France, the model was initially applied quite radically, to the detriment of employers who suddenly lacked the traditional means of disciplining workers, whilst workers used their newly acquired freedoms to 'vote with their feet' and walked away in the event of disagreement. A solution, in part, was found with the introduction of the *Conseils de Prud'hommes*, a low-threshold dispute-resolution body that had not been saddled with substantial rules, and quickly began to refer back to 'old' conventional rules, thus succeeding in playing a reconciling role.[35] In Germany, in spite of regulation to the contrary, the guilds succeeded in upholding their local regimes, to a large extent, until the third quarter of the nineteenth century. Guild journeymen could not keep non-guild workers from being hired by a factory owner, but they could – and sometimes with a claim to their 'honour', they successfully did – resist working with non-guild workers in the same building.[36]

Generally, the positive impact of the contractual regime has, at first, been minimal. No wonder *Civil Codes* only devoted three articles to labour contracts: it may retrospectively be regarded as the legislator's adequate recognition of the sparse role that national law could play in this field – one that, primarily, was normatively structured by non-state law. In factories, workers were the 'subjects' of a patron-manufacturer. The domestic logic of this arrangement was incompatible with the civic logic of the new contractual regime. Workers were reluctant to address their patrons in terms of their 'rights', and patrons were furiously disappointed when they started to do so – it was only late in the nineteenth century when gradual industrialisation led to a change of configuration that elicited the normative figure of the 'employment contract' proper.

E. From the 'Labour' to the 'Employment Contract'

During the last quarter of the nineteenth century, configurations of relevant actors were again changing significantly. The number of factory workers increased.

[34] B van Bavel, *The Invisible Hand? How Market Economies have Emerged and Declined since AD 500* (Oxford, Oxford University Press, 2016).

[35] A Cottereau, 'Droit et bon droit: Un droit des ouvriers instauré, puis évincé par le droit du travail (France, XIXe siècle)' (2002) 57 *Annales HSS* 1521.

[36] Brand, *Untersuchungen* (n 11) 118.

National states acquired an ever-firmer position, and the extension of the franchise required broader support for political decisions. Meanwhile, the negative consequences of capitalism and liberal economic politics were becoming more visible and frightening.

Industrialisation elicited pressures to change the normative structuring of relations between factory owners and workers. In the 1870s, industrial logic induced British, French, and German employers to claim that 'subordination' of the worker had always been, or would have to be, part of the labour contract. Assigning a right of direction (D) to the employer is, however, not easily reconcilable with the formal equality of contractual parties (C).[37] In Britain, an 'employment contract' only applied to a few categories of professional workers, with 'master and servant' rules applicable to most workers. These rules were significantly tightened in the last quarter of the century. Absent workers were threatened with criminal sanctions that were enforced on a large scale. In German writing on labour relations, legitimation of the subordinate position of workers was sought in the putative 'German' tradition of allegiance ('*Gefolgschaft*') as a domestic basis for mutual relations of obedience, trust, and protection in factories. In France, suggestions from employers that subordination had always been part of the contract were obviously incompatible with French jurisprudence, and elicited heavy resistance from workers' organisations, but were nevertheless legally adopted.[38]

In Germany, around 1900, one million German workers had contracts covered by collective labour agreements, at a moment that German law did not cover them in any way. Legal theory had shown no interest in labour relations which, from a conceptual Roman law standpoint, belonged to the legal wastelands of local conventions. Around 1900, Philip Lottmar started to reclaim the terrain and, in the 1910s, Sinzheimer developed the legal concept of *collective agreement*, which forged a compromise between the industrial logic of enterprises, the contractual autonomy of employers and workers, and civic requirements of democratic decision-making. After which, an alliance of legal professionals and politicians developed and lasted until the post-World War II heyday of the welfare state.

Around the turn of the twentieth century, the rise of protective legislation, in particular against risks of industrial injury, established a conception of *employment* as a contract of 'subordinated, and therefore vulnerable' workers. Rapid growth in the further protection of workers, and the codification of rules, led to the constitution of employment as an historical compromise between industrial, domestic, civic, and market orders. Control of production was left to employers, provided that employees were sufficiently protected against risks associated with their subordination to employers, as well as their dependency on the 'labour market'.

[37] Sinzheimer, *Grundzüge des Arbeitsrechts* (n 1).
[38] Cottereau, 'Droit et bon droit' (n 35).

F. Paternalist Welfare Capitalism

Stanzani has suggested that, at the start of the twentieth century, capitalism underwent significant change, transforming from a capitalism that for centuries had been based upon labour-intensive growth, and therefore sought to intensify its grip on the labour force, to a capitalism where innovation in the organisation of the work process, training, and qualifications became much more important.[39] This change may have inspired enterprises to develop, in the 'golden years of capitalism' between 1870 and 1920, a normative model that revived a paternalistic (D), next to a contractual (C) relation. In particular, family-run enterprises started to provide their employees with all kinds of facilities, such as housing, sport facilities, training, and education, for example.[40] This resulted in the creation of 'factory villages'by enterprises, which gained widespread support in the United States (US), France, the United Kingdom (UK), and Germany. They were intended to attract workers who would develop a stronger commitment to the enterprise, but the paternalistic attitude of capitalistic entrepreneurs also served to legitimate their position both to themselves and to others. It has been argued that a change in power configurations, in particular towards shareholder capitalism, has put an end to this development. One wonders whether future supply shortages on the labour market might urge employers to again explore comparable composite models.

G. The 'Legal Order' of Labour as a Post-War Social Compromise

During the first half of the twentieth century, the protective regulation of workers gradually intensified, by way of both state legislation and collective agreements. After World War II, labour-orientated parties enjoyed a stronger political position which, along with the cultural climate of restructuring the commonality of social life, resulted in many European countries becoming welfare states and establishing a 'legal order' for labour relations; namely, a well-defined legal framework that bestowed rights upon employees, in order to compensate them for risks that were deemed to follow from their dependent position. In Germany, the 'labour constitution', developed by Sinzheimer for the Weimar Republic, could now partly be realised.[41] The employment model gained pre-eminence; and the distinction between employees and small businessmen or the self-employed, who had

[39] A Stanziani (ed), *Labour, Coercion, and Economic Growth in Eurasia, 17th–20th Centuries* (Leiden, Brill, 2013).

[40] E de Gier, *Capitalist Workingman's Paradises Revisited: Corporate Welfare Work in Great Britain, the USA, Germany and France in the Golden Age of Capitalism, 1880–1930* (Amsterdam, Amsterdam University Press, 2016).

[41] R Dukes, *The Labour Constitution: The Enduring Idea of Labour Law* (Oxford, Oxford University Press, 2014).

to bear most of the risks themselves, was intensified.[42] The triangular structure was restructured at a state level: employer and employee organisations were, as 'social partners', invited to participate in the socio-economic decision-making of governments. Economic developments, processes of industrial organisation, and the cultural climate favoured long-term labour relations and, in many countries, dismissal regulation endowed employment with a new social significance as a contract of indefinite duration.

This social compromise allowed labour law as a scholarly discipline to influence political decision-making, and to play an important role in shaping regulations. Prevailing concepts of citizenship came to regard citizens as *social* beings, differing in their economic dependency, and in their capacity to deal with its consequences; the state was considered to have a role in correcting for inequalities generated by these differential dependencies. The post-war employment model has thus strengthened, within the space of its compromise, the *civic* elements of equality and rights at the cost of market elements, which were integral to the contractual model.

H. Neo-Liberal Turn Towards 'Entrepreneurial' Citizenship

Now that I am reaching, in my concise overview, the more familiar ground of the labour relations of the last three decades, I can be more brief. The economic developments that elicited the turn to neo-liberal socio-economic policies occurred in the 1980s, although it should be remembered that their theoretical foundations were formulated in the period directly after World War II – in Europe, by the German 'ordo-liberal school'; in the US, by Chicago School economists.[43] The primacy which they accord to markets over other types of coordination, and the definite but restricted role that they require of governments in guaranteeing competition, were foundational to the construction of the European Union's forerunner (EEC) in 1957. The EEC's deliberately one-sided approach in promoting economic competition, whilst leaving 'social' matters to member states, was not just a matter of respecting the peculiarities of national social policies, but was also compatible with ordo-liberal priorities. Since financial markets became dominant in the 1990s, and took the lead in economic relations, a quasi-natural development called 'globalisation' has been promoted to nation states as an argument for deconstructing legal frameworks of labour relations, in a manner that is reminiscent of what nation states did to cities at the start of the nineteenth century.

Next to, and often instead of (labour) law, it is now economics that is being embraced by politics as a framework of universalisation, and as a guide to shaping socio-economic policies. As a consequence, non-market (in particular: civic)

[42] Deakin and Wilkinson, *Law of the Labour Market* (n 3).
[43] Dukes, *Labour Constitution* (n 41) 123; Foucault, *Birth of Biopolitics* (n 12).

types of coordinating activities have increasingly been placed under suspicion, from the perspective of both market ('too costly') and industrial orders ('bureaucratic', 'inefficient'). Instead of being compensated for their differential capabilities to participate in economic life, the citizen is now constructed 'as *autonomous activity* geared at the actualization of his productive and vital necessities'. Michel Foucault conceptualised this decollectivising shift, this increased attribution of individual responsibility, as a change in 'governmentality'. Neoliberal governmentality primarily operates towards fostering the maximum participation of the populace in labour markets. In the composite normative model of 'employment', the civic logic of equality and rights, dominant in the post-war era, is gradually being abandoned in favour of market logic. In the neoliberal normative model of labour relations, the worker appears as an entrepreneur, individually responsible for turning their capacities into money.[44]

V. Conclusions and Outlook

In light of renewed discussions on the goals and methods of labour law, I argue for the importance of types of normative structuring for practices of labour relations, and for the need to take some distance from their current legal forms. I use Boltanski and Thévenot's six orders of worth to re-examine part of the history of labour relations in Europe, from the perspective of the impact of choices that had to be made from a repertoire of available legal models, and of the changes that were made to make these models fit requirements related to changes in power configurations.

From a long-term perspective, the idea that work can be the object of a contract of transfer of property (of labour power) is of relatively recent origin. The concept remains burdened with the consequences of its problematic presuppositions. It may be important to remember that the 'employment contract' as we know it, and tend to use it – as an almost timeless standard by which to judge the precariousness of recent types of contracts – has existed for no more than two generations.

This re-examination has brought to light how normative models of labour relations have been a constituent part of actual practices, and can fruitfully be analysed as compromises between mutually incompatible modes of evaluation. In the city economies of medieval and pre-modern times, civic and domestic logics were constitutive of normative models of labour relations. Guilds were a dominant framework of production for markets, the logic of which was tamed by civic notions of equality and fairness. Gradually, the universalising impact of the merchants' market-industrial logic, in combination with a political move towards

[44] Foucault, *Birth of Biopolitics* (n 12); A Rossi, *The Labour of Subjectivity: Foucault on Biopolitics, Economy, Critique* (London, Rowman & Littlefield, 2016) 161.

the formation of nation states, undermined the domestic base of the guild regime. Contract was pushed forward, in a negative sense, as an individualising crowbar to break up collective structures that were resisting the universalising powers. Their resistance was tenacious, and it was only late in the nineteenth century that contract, as a normative model of labour relations, had a real impact on labour relations.[45] It developed into 'employment' – a post-war compromise in which the logic of market, industrial, and domestic orders were tamed by civic notions of equality, fairness, and workers' rights. Neoliberal governmentality has shifted the balances embodied in the compromise of employment in favour of a normative model of individual entrepreneurship.

So what about normative models of the future? The strong point of 'contract' and 'price' (at market), in light of historically changing power configurations, is their universalising power. A century ago, Max Weber argued for the selective force of such formal mechanisms.[46] For comparable reasons, politicians prefer the appearance of value-free calculability offered by economics,[47] over and above evaluations supplied by (labour) law. At first sight, this might make the labour contract an unlikely candidate for replacement. However, the possibility of *other* formal mechanisms arising in the future – for instance, by way of new ICT facilities – should not be discarded prematurely. The outline above also suggests that the institutional 'embedding' of such formal mechanisms may strengthen their potential, and possibly prevent societies from succumbing to the inequalities that flow from use of these mechanisms by new elites seeking to monopolise power.[48]

Medieval towns experienced a level of institutional variety that evened out different interests within the town, in a way that recognised conflicting positions, but did not let them undermine the communal base of city life. It has been argued that this strong (domestic and civil) base of communal institutions – which spread over Europe, from the Italian cities, through France and Germany, up to Britain – was the most important factor in the economic rise of parts of Europe, rather than the factor markets that established themselves afterwards.[49] Without some of the unique legal inventions (eg, the notion of a 'corporation') that were part of this communal movement, scientific progress and the Industrial Revolution would probably not have occurred.[50] Europe, one is tempted to argue, ought to be proud of its rich institutional past rather than dismantle it, because of the false hopes held out by orthodox economists of a millennium of 'free markets'.[51]

[45] A Stanzani, *Bondage: Labor and Rights in Eurasia from the Sixteenth to the Early Twentieth Centuries* (New York, Berghahn, 2016) 204–7.

[46] M Weber, *Wirtschaft und Gesellschaft* (Tübingen, Mohr, 1976).

[47] B Latour, *An Inquiry into Modes of Existence: An Anthropology of the Moderns*, 5th edn (C Porter tr, Cambridge, Harvard University Press, 2013) 446–49.

[48] van Bavel, *The Invisible Hand?* (n 34) 268.

[49] ibid 251–55.

[50] TE Huff, *Intellectual Curiosity and the Scientific Revolution: A Global Perspective* (Cambridge, Cambridge University Press, 2011).

[51] van Bavel, *The Invisible Hand?* (n 34) 255.

The task of labour law, therefore, is to lay theoretical foundations for a revised or new institutional design that breaks the dominance of market logic, and reinstates the relevance of domestic and civic orders of worth in labour relations. But this is not the only task: according to Sinzheimer, labour law also has to 'find the forces that may realize the emerging ideas'. The current power of economic elites and financial markets, and the hegemony of economic theories that ignore the institutional foundation of markets, make these forces hard to find.[52] In the meantime, labour law should not be blindfolded by the legal forms that preoccupy it now and, instead, should profit from broadening the perspective on its past manifestations, be aware of the character of compromise between different orders of worth, and search for possibilities to help design normative models that may be constitutive of labour relations in the future.

[52] J Beckert, 'The Social Order of Markets' (2009) 38 *Theory and Society* 245, 246.

3

Theorising Labour Law in the State of Exception: Political and Judicial Responses to Crisis

LISA RODGERS*

I. Introduction

In the realm of constitutional law, there is a wealth of literature on the actions of states in situations of 'emergency'.[1] The traditional understanding is that in times of crisis or emergency, the normal constitutional order and balance of powers between the executive, legislature, and judiciary can be varied in order to enable a swift and efficient response to a perceived threat or crisis. Under this 'emergency paradigm',[2] the executive is authorised to take measures which would not ordinarily be permitted under the legal constitutional order, including measures that fall foul of the demands of the rule of law or human rights norms. Such authorisation is premised on the basis that the suspension of normal constitutional and legal norms only takes place for a short time and as far as necessary to re-establish the status quo. Once the crisis has passed, the legal constitutional order resumes. The operation of emergency powers has most often been studied in the context of the action of executives in response to threats to national security – although, more recently, there has been the suggestion that economic crises might also be considered 'emergencies' requiring a particular state response. For example,

* Lisa Rodgers is Lecturer in Law and Course Director of the LLM Employment Law course by distance learning at the University of Leicester, Leicester UK. ORCID 0000-0001-6712-2342.

[1] See D Dyzenhaus, *The Constitution of Law: Legality in a Time of Emergency* (Cambridge, Cambridge University Press, 2006); K Roach, 'Ordinary Laws for Emergencies and Democratic Derogations from Rights' in V Ramraj (ed), *Emergencies and the Limits of Legality* (Cambridge, Cambridge University Press, 2008) 229; LC Feldman, 'Lockean Prerogative: Productive Tensions' in C Fatovic and BA Kleinerman (eds), *Extra-Legal Power and Legitimacy: Perspectives on Prerogative* (New York, Oxford University Press, 2013) 75.

[2] K Loevy, *Emergencies and Public Law: The Legal Politics of Containment* (Cambridge, Cambridge University Press, 2016) 48.

in the European Union (EU), the financial crisis of 2008 has been set alongside the 'refugee crisis' and the 'jobs crisis' as setting the agenda for action.[3]

The idea that economic crises can enable states to enact a 'state of emergency' is deeply troubling.[4] For a start, emergency responses to economic crises are unlikely to fit the model of the 'economic paradigm'. The assumption that the executive is in the best position to carry out the response to economic crisis needs to be brought into question given the wide availability of economic data, and the possibility for those outside the executive to predict the spread of pernicious economic effects. It also appears that measures undertaken in response to economic crises are rarely 'temporary' either in operation or effect. Rather such measures tend to effect permanent change and establish a 'new' status quo rather than reverting to the previous state of affairs. That economic crisis can lead to a state of emergency is also extremely troubling from the point of view of labour law. During a state of emergency, labour law norms would tend to be eroded or ignored in the same way as other human rights norms. Furthermore, labour law goals and economic goals are often presented as in conflict: labour law acts as a drag on economic functioning and the free flow of market transactions. Hence, the prioritisation of resolving economic issues arising from economic crisis is likely to lead to the deregulation of labour law over time.

The assumption that economic crisis can form the basis of an 'emergency response' bolsters the argument that we are no longer living in a liberal constitutional order under which emergency powers are enacted on a specific, temporary basis. Rather, we have entered a 'state of exception' in which the exigencies of emergency have come to define action in all state functions. This state of exception involves several features. First, the action of the executive proceeds without proper Parliamentary or judicial scrutiny leading to the 'technocratisation' of decision-making. In the context of economic crisis, this is justified on the basis of the need to respond swiftly to an ever changing global financial scene. Secondly, executive, legislative, and judicial action is increasingly directed towards the management and confinement of emergency and, in the economic context, the avoidance of future economic crisis. All bodies are implicated in establishing and maintaining legitimacy in the face of rising politico-economic pressure. Thirdly, there is an overall trend in the downgrading of social norms. Social norms tend to be viewed as part of the problem in the context of economic crisis. As a result, some social laws might be actively repealed. Others are downgraded to 'soft law' measures in order to ensure maximum flexibility for those actors with the most economic power (ie, employers).

The aim of this chapter is to investigate the claims that the state of exception exists in relation to labour law, and to argue that it represents a useful and interesting

[3] President Jean-Claude Juncker, 'Opening Remarks' (EP Plenary session, Conclusions of the European Council Meeting of 17 and 18 December 2015, Brussels, 19 January 2016).

[4] A Greene, 'Questioning Executive Supremacy in an Economic State of Emergency' (2015) 35 *Legal Studies* 594, 594.

lens through which to view current labour law developments. Section II looks at the claims that we have entered a state of exception, and considers the implications of the state of exception for labour law. Section III looks at the possible response to this state of exception from the point of view of labour law theory: namely, to challenge politico-economic domination by collective action and democratisation of the economic sphere. Section IV analyses the possible judicial responses to this state of exception in the form of rejecting the use of 'crisis' as a valid means to downgrade (constitutional) social norms. The final section seeks to address and counteract the negative view of the usefulness and power of law in the state of exception literature and to suggest that, in combination with collective action, it can be a useful tool for supporting workers.

II. The State of Exception and Labour Law

The state of exception thesis proposes that the 'emergency paradigm' under which there is a distinct separation between the actions of government in times of crisis, and the actions of government during normal conditions, no longer represents reality. The argument is that the sense of emergency has become so engrained in the language of policy making that it represents a continual technique of government. Although a state of emergency is not declared in a technical sense, the voluntary creation of a permanent state of emergency has been 'one of the essential practices of contemporary states'.[5] According to this thesis, the existence of the permanent state of emergency transports emergency politics from a technique to deal with a temporary threat in order to re-establish the status quo, to something transformative.

It is argued on this thesis, that the nature of the transformation is deep and wide-ranging. First, the existence of the state of exception profoundly affects the operation of the balance of powers between the legislative, executive, and judiciary, as the power of the executive is strengthened. The state of exception allows the extension of executive power into the legislative sphere through the issuance of decrees and measures which do not require legislative scrutiny.[6] The role of the legislature is reduced to ratifying measures in a technical sense, rather than debating the value and effect of the proposed legislation. Secondly, there is the progressive extension of governmental action into fields previously excluded from the realm of 'law'.[7] This is particularly important in terms of the examination of the actions of government in response to economic crisis. However, the government exhorts the need to remove the burden of regulation from the financial sphere, whilst at the same time producing 'rules' to govern it. These 'rules'

[5] G Agamben, *State of Exception* (K Attell tr, Chicago, University of Chicago Press, 2005) 3.
[6] Greene, 'Questioning Executive Supremacy' (n 4) 595.
[7] Agamben, *State of Exception* (n 5) 39.

are technocratic in nature, and can take the form of 'soft law' under which rules do not have to be recognised to be effective, and are capable of 'self-regulation'.[8]

Finally, the state of exception involves the (semi-)permanent suspension of the civil liberties of the liberal democratic state. It is argued that the normative content of civil law is eroded as a result of the change in the balance of power and the transformation of the nature, and application, of law under the state of exception. According to the analysis of Giorgio Agamben, the use of emergency powers over the course of the twentieth century has undermined the rule of law to a dramatic extent. Agamben argues that the use of emergency powers is an example of the 'paradox of sovereignty' under which the sovereign acts at the same time inside and outside the juridical order.[9] The state relies on the existence of some form of legal order in order to legitimate its use of emergency powers, but at the same time suspends that law in order to apply the exception. As the use of emergency powers is now a technique of government rather than a response to a one-off event, the exceptional has become the rule. The implication is that, in the state of exception, rules and orders are issued which have the force of law (they legitimate the actions of governments), but their normative content is eroded to the extent that they can no longer be applied in any meaningful way.[10] This presents a challenge to the operation of liberal structures of law which rely on an immoveable normative hierarchy in order to be effective. It also, paradoxically, threatens the legitimacy of the liberal state: it brings into question the operation of democracy and the freedom of those within the state to mount a challenge to state action.

The aim of this section is to investigate these propositions with reference to labour law. It is argued that labour law suffers in a cumulative and compounded way under the scheme of the state of exception. On the one hand, labour law is becoming increasingly contaminated by financial regulation. In a number of ways, it is conflated with economic law, and is required to meet the needs of economic markets. This is achieved through technocratic legislation and the extension of the power of the executive to operate outside the strict rule of law. On the other hand, labour law is suffering a normative erosion. Again this is achieved through direct action of the executive, but also the more nuanced action of the legislature in allowing the downgrading of constitutional rights.

A. The Financial Crisis and Emergency Action

There is evidence of the rise in executive action to disable labour law in a number of different geographic and substantive contexts. At the level of the EU, the action

[8] A Supiot, *Homo Juridicus: On the Anthropological Function of the Law* (S Brown tr, London, Verso, 2007).

[9] G Agamben, *Homo Sacer: Sovereign Power and Bare Life* (Stanford, Stanford University Press, 1998) 15.

[10] L Brännström, 'How I Learned to Stop Worrying and Use the Legal Argument – A Critique of Giorgio Agamben's Notion of Law' (2008) 5 *No Foundations* 22, 40.

of governments in the wake of the 2008 financial crisis provides a stark indication of the use of the techniques and language of emergency to effect permanent and dramatic changes to labour law.[11] However, this must be seen against the background of the increasing extension of macroeconomic policy to the labour law field prior to the financial crisis,[12] which had already transformed labour law into a secondary consideration of economic policy rather than normatively important in its own right. Indeed, in the United Kingdom (UK), the government had proceeded to downgrade employment rights on the basis of the need for improved macro-economic performance without specific reference to the financial crisis. For example, the Employment Law Review, which was launched in 2010, set out a package of reforms designed to reduce the burden on business of compliance with employment law. It was posited that such reforms would allow businesses more flexibility, and hence make them more competitive in the long run.[13]

In terms of the EU response to the financial crisis, a number of 'exceptional' measures were introduced. These were executive measures which, despite having legal effects, were introduced without the usual inter- and intra- institutional deliberations expected in the formation of EU law. The argument was that these (temporary) measures were required to restore fiscal stability to the EU area, and that it was necessary to bypass the normal legislative mechanisms in order to ensure that these measures were introduced within a timescale which would ensure their effectiveness. Concerns have been raised in relation to these measures. There is a concern about the relationship between these measures and the provisions of the European Union Treaties (the Treaties); there has even been the suggestion that certain of these measures violate the agreed competency compromises.[14] There is also the concern that such measures allow unjustified political interference into the formation and management of the law. This disrupts the functioning of the rule of law, and reduces the legitimacy of legal judgments.[15]

[11] C Kilpatrick, 'On the Rule of Law and Economic Emergency: The Degradation of Basic Legal Values in Europe's Bailouts' (2015) 35 *Oxford Journal of Legal Studies* 325; C Kilpatrick, 'Are the Bailouts Immune to EU Social Challenge because they are Not EU Law?' (2014) 10 *European Constitutional Law Review* 393, 393; S Deakin, 'Social Policy, Economic Governance and EMU: Alternatives to Austerity' in N Bruun, K Lörcher and I Schömann (eds), *The Economic and Financial Crisis and Collective Labour Law in Europe* (Oxford, Hart Publishing, 2014) 83.

[12] M Schmitt, 'Evaluation of EU Responses to the Crisis with Reference to Primary Legislation (European Union Treaties and Charter of Fundamental Rights)' in N Bruun, K Lörcher and I Schömann (eds), *The Economic and Financial Crisis and Collective Labour Law in Europe* (Oxford, Hart Publishing, 2014) 195; S Garben, 'The Constitutional (Im)balance between "the Market" and "the Social" in the European Union' (2017) 13 *European Constitutional Law Review* 23.

[13] Department for Business Innovation & Skills (BIS), *Employment Law Review: Annual Update 2012* (March 2012) https://assets.publishing.service.gov.uk/government/uploads/system/uploads/attachment_data/file/49015/12-p136-employment-law-review-2012.pdf accessed 21 May 2018.

[14] M Ruffert, 'The European Debt Crisis and European Union Law' (2011) 48 *Common Market Law Review* 1777, 1801.

[15] G Beck, 'The Court of Justice, Legal Reasoning, and the *Pringle* Case – Law as the Continuation of Politics by Other Means' (2014) 39 *European Law Review* 234.

There are numerous examples of these 'crisis' law measures which could be cited. For example, the 'Euro Plus Pact' is one such measure, agreed in March 2011.[16] This is an intergovernmental agreement made by the European Council for increased coordination of policies on competitiveness, employment, public finances, financial stability, and tax policy in the wake of the crisis. Concerns have been raised that this measure stretched the competency compromise agreed in the Treaties, with increased monitoring of national wage agreements, and the 'highest attention' paid to 'the sustainability of pensions, healthcare and social benefits' at a national level.[17] However, the commitment in the Euro Plus Pact to soft law measures and enforcement by 'peer-review' has meant that its impact on national systems (and the principle of subsidiarity) has been less than might have been expected.[18] By contrast, other 'executive' measures have been more far-reaching. The Six-Pack on macroeconomic and fiscal surveillance[19] created a set of hard law measures (one Directive and five regulations) which set public debt and deficit targets for Member States in the Eurozone, and provided for escalating financial sanctions to be applied to those states in breach of those debt and deficit targets. In addition, the Treaty on Stability Coordination and Governance, agreed in January 2013, supplemented and reinforced the Six-Pack regime.[20] This intergovernmental agreement set out a balanced budget rule under which a Member State's deficit cannot normally exceed 0.5 per cent of GDP and a debt-break rule, which determined that a Member State must take steps to reduce public debt if it goes above the 60 per cent threshold.[21]

Furthermore, the involvement of the European Central Bank (ECB) in the market for sovereign debt has been criticised.[22] According to Article 123 of the Treaty on the Functioning of the European Union (TFEU), and the no-bail-out clause in Article 125, the ECB is prohibited from lending to public authorities

[16] Conclusion of the European Council (24–25 March 2011) EUCO 10/1/11, 18.

[17] ibid.

[18] C Barnard, 'The Financial Crisis and the Euro-Plus Pact: A Labour Lawyer's Perspective' (2012) 41 *Industrial Law Journal* 98, 109.

[19] Regulation (EU) 1175/2011 of the European Parliament and of the Council of 16 November 2011 amending Council Regulation (EC) 1466/97 on the strengthening of the surveillance of budgetary positions and the surveillance and coordination of economic policies [2011] OJ L306/12; Council Regulation (EU) 1177/2011 of 8 November 2011 amending Regulation (EC) 1467/97 on speeding up and clarifying the implementation of the excessive deficit procedure [2011] OJ L306/33; Council Directive 2011/85/EU of 8 November 2011 on requirements for budgetary frameworks of the Member States [2011] OJ L306/41; Regulation (EU) 1173/2011 of the European Parliament and of the Council of 16 November 2011 on the effective enforcement of budgetary surveillance in the euro area [2011] OJ L306/1; Regulation (EU) 1176/2011 of the European Parliament and of the Council of 16 November 2011 on the prevention and correction of macroeconomic imbalances [2011] OJ L306/25; Regulation (EU) 1174/2011 of the European Parliament and of the Council of 16 November 2011 on enforcement measures to correct excessive macroeconomic imbalances in the euro area [2011] OJ L306/8.

[20] Treaty on Stability, Coordination and Governance in the Economic and Monetary Union 2012 (TSCG).

[21] Deakin, 'Social Policy, Economic Governance and EMU' (n 11).

[22] M Everson, 'An Exercise in Legal Honesty: Rewriting the Court of Justice and the *Bundesverfassungsgericht*' (2015) 21 *European Law Journal* 474, 482.

of the Union or Member States. These measures were grounded in the ethos that one Member State should not get involved in effectively underwriting the debts of other national governments, and were thought a necessary incentive to ensure that Member States endeavoured to avoid spiralling national deficits. However, despite these legal barriers set out in the Treaties, the ECB did get involved in the sovereign debt market following the crisis. A number of initiatives were instigated, including the Outright Market Transactions Programme (OMT). Under the OMT, the ECB made a commitment to buy unlimited amounts of sovereign bonds from secondary sources (commercial banks) to support the solvency of a Member State if it agreed to the conditions for financial assistance under a Memorandum of Understanding, or via the European Stability Mechanism. Ostensibly then, the ECB was getting involved in fiscal transfers which were forbidden by the Treaties.

The legality of these mechanisms was subject to challenge in the *Pringle* case.[23] In *Pringle*, a challenge was brought against the Treaty amendment made in 2011 which empowered the EU to establish a programme of financial assistance to Member States (Article 136(3) TFEU). Relatedly, the validity of the European Stability Mechanism Treaty (ESMT) (which established the European Stability Mechanism (ESM)) was also brought into question. However, the Court of Justice of the EU held that Article 136(3) was validly adopted, and that the ESMT was also lawful. It held that the EMST was compatible with both Article 123 TFEU and Article 125 TFEU. The strict conditionality of the financial assistance provided under the ESM furthered the objectives of the Treaty clauses; namely, to ensure budgetary discipline amongst Member States. The stance of the Court of Justice of the European Union (CJEU) on this matter has been robustly criticised, and the argument made that the judgment fails the rule of law. For example, according to Gunnar Beck, the reasoning adopted by the Court was driven not by the systematic application of legal rules, but by political expediency. This blurring of the line between politics and law disrupted the essential role of the Court (and law) in constraining political action. This in turn disrupted the legitimacy of legal (as opposed to political) action and left the techniques of legal argumentation meaningless.[24]

The legality of these executive measures is of direct importance to labour law. The Euro Plus Pact and the Six Pack regulations had labour law within their remit, and encouraged deregulatory measures in the Member States to ensure continued competitiveness and economic growth. Furthermore, the conditions attached to Memoranda of Understanding produced by the Troika have resulted in dramatic (deregulatory) changes to national labour law systems.[25] For example, Portugal committed to a number of deregulatory measures as part of its bail-out package. In its Memorandum of Understanding, it agreed to implement reform to severance

[23] Case C-370/12 *Pringle v Government of Ireland* (ECJ, 27 November 2012) (*Pringle*).

[24] Beck, 'The Court of Justice, Legal Reasoning, and the *Pringle* Case' (n 15) 238.

[25] S Deakin and A Koukiadaki, 'The Sovereign Debt Crisis and the Evolution of Labour Law in Europe' in N Countouris and M Freedland (eds), *Resocialising Europe in a Time of Crisis* (Cambridge, Cambridge University Press, 2013) 163, 176.

payments. These reforms included aligning severance payments for open-ended contracts with those of fixed-term contracts, and also reducing the total severance payments for new open-ended contracts. The Portuguese government also committed to reform the law on individual dismissals, and subsequently new laws were introduced to reduce both the notification period for individual dismissals and dismissal compensation payments.[26] Similar reforms were introduced in Spain and Greece as part of their bail-out conditions. Further deregulatory changes have also been introduced in these countries, in particular with regard to increasing the possibility of recourse to atypical contracts, and amendments to the regulation of working time. In Portugal, for example, the duration of fixed term-contracts was extended, and additional overtime reduced by 50 per cent, along with the elimination of compulsory time off.[27] In Spain, Act 3/2012 introduced a number of measures to promote working time flexibility, including increasing the scope for flexible allocation of working hours over a year, and the abolition of the need to obtain public authority permission for flexibilisation measures. In all three countries, the scope of recourse to collective bargaining was also systematically reduced.

The question arises as to whether this action was justified on the basis of the severity of the crisis event. If the 'emergency paradigm' methodology is adopted, it could be argued that these exceptional measures were necessary in order to stabilise national economies and prevent further economic threat. These measures were temporary actions in order to re-establish well-functioning national economies and labour law systems. However, the state of exception literature can be used to argue that, in fact, these measures were part of a more general trend towards the use of exceptionalism to pursue (economic) goals.[28] Furthermore, the argument that this action was necessary according to the 'emergency paradigm' could only be sustained where the effects on labour law and the national systems were temporary, and where labour law changes went only as far as necessary to re-establish the status quo. In fact, as we shall see in the next section, the changes enacted as result of the financial crisis have had long term effects on the national system of labour law in the EU Member States.

B. The State of Exception and Labour Law Development

It can be argued that 'crisis law' measures following the financial crisis are merely an intensification and cumulation of processes already at work in the labour law sphere. At EU level, labour law has long existed at the intersection between the

[26] Act 53/2011; Act 23/2012.

[27] Act 23/2012.

[28] The argument that such 'exceptionalism' predates the financial crisis is also supported by analysis in the following text: A Zbyszewska, *Gendering European Working Time Regimes: The Working Time Directive and the Case of Poland* (Cambridge, Cambridge University Press, 2016) 53 ff.

'hard law' and standard setting of Directives and Regulations, and the 'soft law' of economic policy.[29] Indeed, to a large extent, the hard law of Directives and the soft law of economic policy have been seen as complementary elements of the same system with, for example, the Employment Guidelines on economic policy directly influencing the development of a series of employment law Directives.[30] These Guidelines and their integration into the labour law system at EU level is a strong example of the incorporation of economic considerations into the development of labour law. The policy rules under the Employment Guidelines are technocratic in nature and are enforced through a system of monitoring, and benchmarking, originally referred to as the Open Method of Coordination. The aim of these Guidelines has been the achievement of certain macro-economic goals, including high employment and the promotion of 'flexible working arrangements' to ensure that employers are best able to respond to changes in global economic conditions. The incorporation of these elements into EU labour law has been transformative, and has guided the alignment of many of the Directives on labour law in line with securing flexibility for employers, with weaker provisions for worker protection alongside. For example, in the preamble to the Part-time Work Directive (PTWD),[31] the need to balance employer flexibility with employee security is recognised.[32] However, the actual provisions concerning worker security are limited,[33] and there is the possibility for derogation from the non-discrimination provisions on 'objective' grounds.[34]

Indeed, there is evidence of the intensification of these processes, with negative consequences for labour.[35] The Employment Guidelines have been combined with the Economic Guidelines, meaning that there is now not even notional separation of employment from economic considerations. Monitoring and surveillance of national (wage) policy has increased, with a consistent downward pressure exerted on labour provisions in the name of 'competitiveness' and 'job creation'.[36] Furthermore, the social partners have been progressively excluded from input into employment policy (and hence employment law) through a series of technocratic adjustments. Theoretically, the institutionalisation of the Tripartite Social Summit for growth and employment through the Lisbon Treaty implies the formal

[29] L Rodgers, 'Labour Law and Employment Policy in the EU: Conflict or Consensus?' (2011) 27 *International Journal of Comparative Labour Law and Industrial Relations* 387.

[30] ibid 394.

[31] Council Directive 97/81/EC of 15 December 1997 concerning the Framework Agreement on part-time work concluded by UNICE, CEEP, and the ETUC [1999] OJ L14/9 (PTWD).

[32] PTWD, Preamble, para 3.

[33] Under clause 5(2) PTWD, it is stated that: 'A worker's refusal to transfer from full-time to part-time work or vice-versa should not in itself constitute a valid reason for termination of employment, without prejudice to termination in accordance with national law, collective agreements and practice, for other reasons such as may arise from the operational requirements of the establishment concerned'.

[34] PTWD, cl 4(1).

[35] E Menegatti, 'Challenging the EU Downward Pressure on National Wage Policy' (2017) 33 *International Journal of Comparative Labour Law and Industrial Relations* 195, 200.

[36] ibid 205.

recognition of the social partners in the development of economic policy. The role of the social partners in the development of economic and budgetary policy is also specifically recognised in the Preamble to one of the Six-Pack Regulations, and in the same Regulation, specific reference is made to Article 152 TFEU. However, it appears that the European Semester, which determines Member States' compliance with the economic and employment guidelines of Europe 2020 post-crisis, acts independently of the Tripartite Social Summit, so that the social partners have no input into these guidelines. This is evidenced most starkly by the fact that, in 2012, the spring Tripartite Social Summit was held on 1 March, the same day as the European Council's announcement of the guidelines for economic and employment policies in the Member States.[37]

Furthermore, the normative erosion of labour law enacted at national level in response to the demands of the bail-out packages is neither new, nor temporary, either in scope or effect. There is significant evidence that they are having a permanent transformative effect on national labour law systems. Member States are required to follow a 'flexibility-orientated' approach, and this has infiltrated deep into decision-making on the content of labour law. For example, in Italy, the government was quick to implement deregulatory changes in labour law following the crisis. Italy responded promptly to the demands of the ECB as part of the bail-out package, allowing companies to derogate from employment provisions laid down in high-level collective agreements and the law, and promoting decentralised collective bargaining. This was done in the name of promoting employment growth and in allowing flexibility for companies to maximise growth. Since the advent of these changes, there have been progressive waves of reforms which have continued the deregulatory trend in the name of flexibility and employment growth. The Fornero reform,[38] implemented in 2012, exempted companies from complying with technical requirements in the use of temporary employment contracts and increased the possibility of recourse to contracts of a fixed term nature. Flexibility was cited as one of the primary motivations of this action. In 2014, the Jobs Act introduced a new open-ended contract with significantly reduced unfair dismissal protection, and reduced the compliance requirements for fixed-term and apprenticeship contracts in the name of job creation and stimulation of the economy.[39] This pattern has been repeated in a number of other countries.[40]

The normative erosion of labour law can also be seen in the 'better' and 'smarter' regulatory agendas of the Commission, as well as Member States not

[37] Schmitt, 'Evaluation of EU Responses to the Crisis' (n 12) 239.

[38] Law No 92/2012.

[39] A Pizzoferrato, 'The Economic Crisis and Labour Law Reform in Italy' (2015) 31 *International Journal of Comparative Labour Law and Industrial Relations* 187, 196.

[40] eg, see C Kilpatrick and B de Witte (eds), 'Social Rights in Times of Crisis in the Eurozone: The Role of Fundamental Rights Challenges' (EUI Working Paper Law 2014/05) http://cadmus.eui.eu/handle/1814/31247 accessed 18 December 2017.

affected by the crisis measures. For example, at EU level, the Commission has given its commitment to the Better Regulation Agenda,[41] which seeks to reduce the burden of social regulation on Member States and to simplify legislative documents. In the UK, the Government's commitment to the Red Tape Challenge[42] has downgraded employment protection over a number of years, and led to a preference for 'voluntary' regulatory measures in the employment field over measures which require detailed legislative scrutiny. For example, when the Equality Act was introduced in 2010 to consolidate previous equality legislation, it was hoped that this would form the basis for the extension of equality rights. However, the most ambitious elements of the Act have not come into force[43] and it has since been supplemented by only very weak provisions.[44] The effect on legislation pertaining to trade unions has been particularly pernicious, with the Trade Union Act 2016 introducing changes which severely restrict the ability of trade unions to take strike action.[45]

It appears then that economic 'crisis' is increasingly reshaping the normative content of labour law. The 'state of exception' literature is useful in this regard as it shows how states are able to manipulate law and policy in the name of crisis to pursue certain (economic) goals. These changes are transformative rather than exceptional, and tend to reproduce already existing policy preferences. However, if the literature on the state of exception helps to identify these trends, it does not suggest ways in which these trends can be countered. Fundamentally, the state of exception is a story of disempowerment under which law and democratic politics are captured by oppressive state power. Under this scheme, the state gradually annexes all law for itself, but does so in a way which is normatively damaging. It brings groups within the law by bringing them within a particular state scheme, but excludes them from the possibility of using that law for their own ends, or challenging the operation or content of those rules. Within this scheme, groups must go beyond or overcome the law; the law cannot itself be used for emancipatory purposes.[46]

It is argued here that a challenge to the dominance of the state of exception must adopt a different premise. It must adopt a premise that either law or politics have emancipatory potential. It must take on the claims of traditional labour law

[41] Communication from the Commission to the European Parliament, the Council, the European Economic and Social Committee and the Committee of the Regions, *Better Regulation for Better Results – An EU Agenda* (COM/2015/0215 final, 19 May 2015).

[42] Cabinet Office, 'Press Release: Red Tape Challenge' (7 April 2011) www.gov.uk/government/news/red-tape-challenge accessed 22 May 2018.

[43] eg, s 1 of the Equality Act 2010, which would have created a public sector duty in relation to socio-economic inequality.

[44] eg, 'mandatory' gender pay reporting under the Equality Act 2010 (Specific Duties and Public Authorities) Regulations 2017, SI 2017/353, to which there are no sanctions attached for non-compliance.

[45] See the commentary in KD Ewing and J Hendy, 'The Trade Union Act 2016 and the Failure of Human Rights' (2016) 45 *Industrial Law Journal* 391.

[46] Brännström, 'How I Learned to Stop Worrying' (n 10) 41.

theory that the capture of dominant political and legal ideology by the state can only be counteracted forcefully by the work of sub-state actors in taking back political and economic power for themselves. These claims will be discussed in Section III. Alternatively, the challenge must come on the basis that law does have emancipatory potential and that the judiciary can 'push back' against excessive state power to uphold important rights. This second challenge involves disproving, and challenging, some of the claims of the state of exception literature, and will be discussed in Section IV.

III. Means of Resistance: Recognising and Employing Crisis for Labour

It is possible to see recognition of the role of economic 'crisis' in the administration of labour law in the work of certain classical labour law scholars. For example, Otto Kahn-Freund, the founding father of British labour law, was influenced by the work of Karl Marx, and the understanding of employment relationships as intimately bound up with the capitalist system.[47] On this analysis, the starting point is that capitalist relations of production are constitutive of the employment relationship and determine the power differential between the two groups. For example, the capitalist system determines that there is an imbalance of bargaining power between the employer and the worker. Employers own the means of production and control the surplus value created by the labour of workers. The accumulation of surplus value allows the proper functioning of the capitalist system, but means that workers are maintained in a permanent position of subordination, as they have no real alternative but to engage with the system to meet their subsistence needs. It follows that in times of economic crisis or recession, the accumulation of surplus value fails and this in turn disrupts the social relations upon which the economy depends. Labour laws which were created on the basis of raising the price of labour cannot be sustained in the absence of demand, and collective bargaining struggles in the face of mass unemployment. Economic crisis could be seen as a direct threat to labour law as, in times of crisis, workers are not in a position to take advantage of that law and employers are reluctant to divert limited funds to honour social commitments.[48]

However, the impact of crisis can be more far reaching if it is adopted as state ideology. According to Marx, the employer class (bourgeoisie) can translate

[47] O Kahn-Freund described the differential priorities of management as opposed to labour in the capitalist system. He recognised therefore that the labour/capital relationship was not only unequal but inherently conflictual. See P Davies and M Freedland, *Kahn-Freund's Labour and the Law*, 3rd edn (London, Stevens, 1983) 66.

[48] R Dukes, 'Conflict and the Crisis in Labour Law: From Weimar to Austerity' in PF Kjaer and N Olsen (eds), *Critical Theories of Crisis in Europe: From Weimar to the Euro* (London, Rowman & Littlefield International, 2016) 107.

economic into political dominance and has a direct influence on state action.[49] This political dominance allows the bourgeoisie to pursue its own interests more widely, and to disseminate and enforce ideologies which function to legitimate its own practices.[50] This does not mean that the crises and contradictions of capitalism presented above disappear, only that the bourgeoisie is able to present those crises/contradictions in a way which suits their own ends. One pertinent example is the very notion of 'crisis' as emergency. Under the economic/bourgeois conception of crisis or emergency, a crisis is a 'dysfunctional moment that ruptures an otherwise harmonious functioning of the "system"; a moment that will pass when equilibrium is established'.[51] This narrow conception of crisis excludes the contradictions and class struggles which are part of capitalism. Furthermore, the conception of crisis as emergency serves to mask the very real and necessary function that economic crises have in the reproduction of capitalism itself. In this way, crisis can be externalised and blamed on a set of factors external to the economic system; in particular, the restrictive functions of labour law.

It is for this reason that traditionally labour law scholars have favoured political over legal solutions to the problems faced by labour and the downgrading of labour law protection.[52] Law and legal ideology is dominated by employers as represented by the state. In order to challenge the structure of that law, workers need to capture a level of social power for themselves. For Kahn-Freund, this involved individuals joining together in trade unions which would engender the 'creation of a social power on the workers' side to balance that of management.[53] For Hugo Sinzheimer, the answer lay in the creation of an economic constitution under which democracy was extended from the political to the economic sphere. Under this economic constitution, trade unions would act together with management to produce policies which corresponded to the public interest. This action would be backed by the state, which would recognise the importance of labour law to the functioning of the economy.[54]

In a similar way, authors proclaiming the state of exception are very sceptical of the power of legal rights to improve the position of social groups.[55] For Agamben, what lies at the heart of rights declarations is essentially a cooption of 'bare life' and

[49] K Marx, 'The Communist Manifesto' in D McLellan (ed), *Karl Marx: Selected Writings*, 2nd edn (Oxford, Oxford University Press, 2000) 245, 247.

[50] A Giddens, *Capitalism and Modern Social Theory: An Analysis of the Writings of Marx, Durkheim and Max Weber* (Cambridge, Cambridge University Press, 1971) 41.

[51] 'Interview with Nicos Poulantzas' in J Martin (ed), *The Poulantzas Reader: Marxism, Law and the State* (London, Verso, 2008) 387.

[52] A Bogg, 'Labour, Love and Futility: Philosophical Perspectives on Labour Law' (2017) 33 *International Journal of Comparative Labour Law and Industrial Relations* 7, 8.

[53] Davies and Freedland, *Kahn-Freund's Labour* (n 47) 19.

[54] H Sinzheimer, 'Zur Frage der Reform des Schlichtungwesens (1929)' in H Sinzheimer, *Arbeitsrecht und Rechtssoziologie: Gesammelte Aufsätze und Reden* (Frankfurt, Europäische Verlagsanstalt, 1976) 226.

[55] O Gross and F Ní Aoláin, *Law in Times of Crisis: Emergency Powers in Theory and Practice* (Cambridge, Cambridge University Press, 2006) 110.

a spread of disempowerment. The allocation of rights implies a political loss. This political loss is intensified in the current environment, because we have entered an extreme phase of the separation of the rights of man from the rights of the citizen.[56] Essentially 'the social' cannot be included in the rights scheme in any satisfactory way because that scheme is apolitical, and life is intensely political (or should be allowed to be so). The question is, of course, how the social can be recaptured in this bleak scenario. In the state of exception, this cannot be achieved by an increase in legal rights in the current economic and social climate. There must be a move 'beyond' law to a political society: '[W]hat Marx called class conflict … is nothing other than the civil war that divides every people and that will come to an end only when, in the classless society or the messianic kingdom, People and people will coincide, and there will no longer be, strictly speaking, any people.'[57] This is a departure from the work of traditional labour law theorists who view a role for both civil society and rights in improving workers' lives. For Kahn-Freund and Sinzheimer, it is through this combination that industrial peace can be achieved.[58]

IV. Means of Resistance: Recourse to Law

At this juncture, it is worth exploring in more detail the attitude to law in the state of exception. According to this literature, the law is useless as a tool to improve the situation in which we now find ourselves. The very nature of the exception relies on an exploitation of law to the extent that its content and norms become useless.[59] The state of exception opens up a gaping hole within which law exists, but cannot be applied in any way which is useful to challenge the exclusion it creates.[60] This is a very negative view of the operation of law, and one which does not stand up to analysis. It appears that even in the most lawless of places (one of the most catastrophic examples being Guantanamo Bay), law exists and is followed. There may be problems in the way in which that law is defined and applied, but those problems are not founded on complete exclusion – rather, 'more or less pleasant ways of being included'.[61] Likewise, it is the argument in this chapter that law can

[56] Agamben, *Homo Sacer* (n 9) 128.

[57] ibid 178.

[58] O Kahn-Freund, *Labour Law: Old Traditions and New Developments* (Toronto, Clarke, Irwin, 1968) 10.

[59] Hence the action of the executive in times of crisis is 'extra-legal': O Gross, 'Chaos and Rules: Should Responses to Violent Crises Always Be Constitutional?' (2003) 112 *Yale Law Journal* 1011, 1096.

[60] This assertion can be said to draw upon Carl Schmitt's claim that a state of emergency exposes the limits of the law. See C Schmitt, *Political Theology: Four Chapters on the Concept of Sovereignty* (George Schwab tr, Cambridge, Mass., MIT Press, 1988) 1. However, Schmitt is a controversial figure and some authors actively distance themselves from his work: C Fatovic, 'Constitutionalism and Contingency: Locke's Theory of the Prerogative' (2004) 25 *History of Political Thought* 276, 296.

[61] Brännström, 'How I Learned to Stop Worrying' (n 10) 46.

be an effective mechanism through which to challenge the operation of the state of exception. A number of authors have suggested that the judiciary is best placed to mount the challenge, given the closeness of the workings of the legislature and executive under the state of exception.[62] The judiciary also exists to uphold the normative content of the law, particularly those norms of greatest constitutional value.

There are a number of examples of this 'push back' effect, where national courts have found that the downgrading of social rights in the wake of the financial crisis runs counter to national constitutional law. For example, the Portuguese Constitutional Court has ruled on the constitutionality of a number of the provisions adopted as part of the Government's response to the demands of its Memorandum of Understanding with the EU, IMF and the ECB. In April 2013, the Portuguese Constitutional Court found that the provision in the Budget Law 2013 setting out a reduction and suspension of salary for public sector workers was in breach of the principle of equality and proportionality, and therefore void.[63] Similarly, the Constitutional Court ruled on the constitutionality of changes to dismissal laws brought into force in the wake of the crisis. It ruled that the downgrading of dismissal laws, and particularly the removal of the employer's duty to offer the employee alternative suitable employment was unconstitutional. As a result of this decision, the Government was forced to reinstate this duty in the Portuguese labour code.

A particularly interesting feature of these judgments is the Court's willingness to challenge the Government's justification for the removal of employment protection on the basis of 'emergency'. In the judgment of April 2013, the Constitutional Court of Portugal questioned the length of time that the 'emergency' measures were in place, stating that workers should not be asked to 'bear an additional effort' indefinitely.[64] The Court's judgment suggested that, although the identification of 'crisis' was a political matter, it could be subject to challenge where such 'crisis' conditions could not be adequately demonstrated, or where there was insufficient connection between the (economic/social) crisis and the reduction of worker rights effected. Similarly, the Constitutional Court of Italy found that certain labour law measures introduced in the wake of the crisis were unconstitutional, particularly given their length of application and effect.[65] As an example, measures which extended the freezing of bargaining procedures were deemed to have 'structural effect', leading to the conclusion that 'the regime itself violates the principle of freedom of association' enshrined in the Constitution.[66] The impact

[62] F de Londras and FF Davis, 'Controlling the Executive in Times of Terrorism: Competing Perspectives on Effective Oversight Mechanisms' (2010) 30 *Oxford Journal of Legal Studies* 19.

[63] Case No 187/2013 (Judgment) Portuguese Constitutional Court (5 April 2013).

[64] ibid para 40. See also the commentary in F Fabbrini, 'The Euro-Crisis and the Courts: Judicial Review and the Political Process in Comparative Perspective' (2014) 32 *Berkeley Journal of International Law* 64.

[65] Case No 178/2015 (Judgment) Constitutional Court of Italy (24 June 2015).

[66] ibid para 15.2.

on constitutional values of government action was not 'occasional', but (semi-) permanent, and therefore unconstitutional. The Italian government could not hide behind the notion of 'crisis' to effect a permanent reduction in worker rights.

These trends can also be seen at the international level. In the case of GSEE, the Committee of Experts was asked to consider complaints that a number of trade union and collective rights had been breached in the wake of the financial crisis of 2008.[67] In its judgment, the Committee listed the arguments made by the trade unions involved, which asserted that the actions of the government were neither temporary, necessary, nor proportionate. They could also have long-term damaging effects on workers' rights, and so could not be considered as maintaining workers' living standards for the duration of the crisis. In its conclusions, the Committee stated:

> While noting the reasons advanced for the exceptional circumstances in this case … the Committee observes that … repeated recourse to statutory restrictions on collective bargaining could, in the long term, only prove harmful and destabilize labour relations, as [they] deprived workers of a fundamental right and means of furthering and defending their economic and social interests.[68]

A similar position was adopted in the case, FSC-CCOO.[69] The conclusions in GSEE were stated even more starkly. Here the Committee observed that, in the context of economic stabilisation, priority should be given to collective bargaining as a means of determining the employment conditions of public servants, rather than adopting legislation to restrain wages in the public sector.[70] Collective bargaining could actually provide a way out of crisis conditions, and so should not automatically be restricted in times of economic uncertainty (even if temporary, necessary, etc).

These judgments demonstrate that the judiciary can play an important role in challenging 'emergency' measures which downgrade employment and other social rights. To this extent, the state of exception literature underestimates the enduring nature of constitutional rights and the ability of the judiciary to challenge the dominant discourse of emergency. This does not imply an end to scepticism about the role of legal rights, by themselves, in promoting lasting change for workers. Nor does it imply that judicial decisions will always protect the interests of workers. Indeed, at EU level, the track record of the CJEU in this regard has been extremely mixed.[71] Rather, it is to suggest that there are situations in which law

[67] Case No 2820, *Greek General Confederation of Labour (GSEE), Civil Servants' Confederation (ADEDY), General Federation of Employees of the National Electric Power Corporation (GENOP-DEI-KIE) and Greek Federation of Private Employees (OIYE) supported by the International Confederation of Trade Unions (ITUC)*, Report No 365 (November 2012) (784–1003).

[68] ibid para 995.

[69] Case No 2918, *Citizens' Service Federation of the Trade Union Confederation of Workers' Commissions (FSC-CCOO)*, Report No 368 (June 2013) 323–64.

[70] ibid para 362.

[71] Garben, 'The Constitutional (Im)balance' (n 12) 23.

and legal rights can be captured in order to promote the interests of workers. Of course, this process of capture relies on a strong civil society mechanism to support claims and challenge conservative interpretations of the extent of constitutional rights. However, it is possible for the 'social' and 'legal' power to work together to challenge the state of exception in which we now find ourselves.

V. Conclusions

The state of exception literature is very interesting from a labour law perspective, as it demonstrates how far the discourse of crisis and the use of 'emergency' measures by states has come to dominate our experience of the law. Indeed the extension of use, of the discourse of emergency, to determine action in response to economic 'crisis' is particularly worrying from the point of view of labour law. Labour law tends to be portrayed negatively in relation to economic development, so that reference to economic 'crisis' can be used to justify dramatic restrictions in protection. Moreover, it appears that reference to 'crisis' in this context means that the normal legislative production cycles can be abandoned in favour of (inter)governmental decision-making, and the independence of labour law from economic governance policies can be eroded to the extent that it becomes unrecognisable. This is damaging from the point of view of individuals, but also from the point of view of democracy, given the importance of work-related institutions in embedding democratic values in society as a whole.

The problem with the state of exception literature is that it does not suggest ways in which such trends can be countered. This literature suggests that state power has come to override and dominate the law to the extent that the law has become meaningless to ordinary citizens. In turn, those citizens are unable to use the law to any emancipatory effect. This position must be challenged. On the one hand, it can be challenged on the basis that the state of exception literature is simply a restatement of the problematic recognised by Marx and taken up by labour law scholars: the state as representative of employers will always try to dominate economic and social discourse to keep employees in a position of subordination. The language of crisis is simply one way in which to achieve this and must be countered by politico-social challenge to this domination. On the other hand, it can be challenged on the basis that the state of exception literature underestimates the role of the judiciary and civil society in protecting and supporting employee rights.

V. Conclusions

[illegible]

4

Redefining the Boundaries of Labour Law: Is 'Double Alienness' a Useful Concept for Classifying Employees in Times of Fractal Work?

VINCENZO PIETROGIOVANNI*

I. Back to the Future: Fractal Work and Fundamentals of Labour Law

The future of work is a key issue for debate, even outside of labour law scholarship.[1] With the emergence of a 'new capitalist vanguard', and the proliferation of companies such as Foodora and Deliveroo, the struggles of today's workers have much in common with those of the late nineteenth century; namely, agitation against worker exploitation, and demands for fairer salaries and better protections. Labour law today, as 100 years ago, is challenged by the following questions: 'Which work does deserve protection? Which protection does work deserve?'[2]

Labour law has constantly been declared 'in emergency' since the 1973 oil crisis.[3] If every crisis entails a change of paradigm,[4] or a break with the *épistémè*,[5]

* Senior Lecturer, Department of Business Law, Lund University.

[1] Executive Office of the President, *Artificial Intelligence, Automation, and the Economy* (December 2016) https://obamawhitehouse.archives.gov/sites/whitehouse.gov/files/documents/Artificial-Intelligence-Automation-Economy.PDF accessed 8 January 2019. The ILO has formed the Global Commission on the Future of Work, whose publications are available at 'The Future of Work' *(International Labour Organization)* www.ilo.org/global/topics/future-of-work/lang--en/index.htm accessed 8 January 2019.

[2] R Voza, 'Il lavoro e le piattaforme digitali: The Same Old Story?' (WP CSDLE, 'Massimo D'Antona', IT–336/2017, 29 August 2017) http://csdle.lex.unict.it/docs/workingpapers/Il-lavoro-e-le-piattaforme-digitali-the-same-old-story/5649.aspx accessed 8 January 2019.

[3] M D'Antona, 'Diritto del lavoro di fine secolo: una crisi di identità' (1998) 48 *Rivista Giuridica del lavoro e della Previdenza Sociale* 311.

[4] TS Kuhn, *The Structure of Scientific Revolutions* (Chicago, University of Chicago Press, 2012).

[5] You can find these concepts developed and applied in works such as: M Foucault, *Folie et déraison: Histoire de la folie à l'âge classique*, vol 169 (Paris, Plon, 1961); M Foucault, *Les mots et les choses: une archéologie des sciences humaines* (Paris, Gallimard, 1966).

then crises are a developmental process in which the values and principles that will shape the new paradigm are the result of a complex articulation of factors; in this process, scholars and interpreters in general definitely play a role. In times of digitalisation, labour law has been declared 'in crisis' once again and, in many opinions, its fundamental categories appear unfit to solve current regulatory problems. The challenges arising from the use of new technologies – including an unprecedented increase in managerial power over the control and direction of labour – have questioned the nature of twentieth century labour law and its main purpose: protecting the dignity, freedom, privacy, and health and safety of working people against exploitation and discrimination, together with improving democracy and transparency in labour market regulation, through 'collective labour freedoms'.[6]

The recent wave of far-reaching reforms of labour market regulation in many European Union (EU) Member States,[7] often inspired by neoliberalism but justified to increase employability,[8] has deconstructed the traditional features of labour law as it developed during the twentieth century, especially with the Fordist business model. This deconstruction could be symbolised by the break of famous Aristotle's three unities of classical drama as applied to work:

- fixed-term and temporary agency contract or independent contractors broke the unity of action;
- posting of workers and other forms of outsourcing labour broke the unity of place;
- part-time jobs or on-call jobs broke the unity of time.

But if labour law has been in crisis for more than 40 years, what is different now? It looks like the just-in-time production of Toyotism (making only what is needed, only when it is needed, and only in the amount that is needed) has been transferred also to the management of labour demand. Indeed, through a technological cluster comprised of computers, algorithms, and digital devices, all connected through the internet, employers can now resort on-demand to forms of work that are repeated in their main tasks in the same way on different scales, potentially throughout the whole globe. We can define the result of these forms of acquiring and managing workforce labour as 'fractal work'; work that has an

[6] See V Bavaro and V Pietrogiovanni, 'A Hypothesis on the Economic Nature of Labour Law: The Collective Labour Freedoms' (2018) 9 *European Labour Law Journal* 263.

[7] For a comprehensive perspective, see A Koukiadaki, I Távora and M Martínez Lucio (eds), *Joint Regulation and Labour Market Policy in Europe during the Crisis* (Brussels, European Trade Union Institute, 2016).

[8] The literature on this topic is wide, but for a more grounded reading, see T Wilthagen and F Tros, 'The Concept of "Flexicurity": A New Approach to Regulating Employment and Labour Markets' (2004) 10 *Transfer* 166. See also V Pietrogiovanni, 'Reality Still Bites: A First Look on Labour Law and Jobless Youth in Nordic and Southern European Countries' [2014] (3) *European Journal of Social Law* 141.

extremely irregular surface formed of an indefinite number of similarly irregular parts. The term, 'fractal' – introduced by the French-Polish mathematician, Benoît Mandelbrot, in 1975 – comes from the Latin word, *fractus*, the past participle of *frangere*, which means 'to break'. If the work is divided up and spread across an indefinite number of people (the 'crowd'), and thus outsourced, then all Aristotle's traditional unities seen above are broken.

Capitalism in its current version of platforms and 'gigs' shows a great capacity, induced by new technologies, to overcome the traditional division between working time (directed by the factory) and life time (directed by the Welfare State). In times of total consumerism, when the citizen is identified as a purchaser and valued by their purchasing power,[9] the current iteration of capitalism has overcome the time of 'production', and the time of 'reproduction', by expanding its ability to create profit not only out of labour, but also out of social interactions – thus, out of 'society'.[10] This expansion, however, is reinforcing the inherent power of capitalism to control and inform people's lives (the discipline)[11] outside traditional workplaces, by reproducing more and more similar patterns – or fractals – of social actions, and making them all uniform while disguising them as 'customised' or tailored on individuals' needs and wills.

Indeed, this fractal work is often characterised by intrinsic informality and casualisation:[12] in order to further lower the employers' responsibility for social transactions, the contractual relationships are usually translated into autonomous collaborations – which supports the idea of an escape from subordination,[13] with all the relating consequences in terms of employment protection and social security.

At this point, however, we need to acknowledge that the concept of a 'gig economy' is vague. This makes it even harder to define under a specific category the *crowdwork* to which the gig economy is linked and which, in its socio-economic reality, constitutes very different situations[14] that are not necessarily connected to the 'proliferation of intermediate categories'.[15]

Whatever these terms might denote at an economic or organisational level, for labour law, they are relevant to the blurring of boundaries surrounding the concept

[9] L Cohen, *A Consumer's Republic: The Politics of Mass Consumption in Postwar America* (New York, Knopf, 2003).

[10] M Fana and S Fana, 'Postfazione' in F Chicchi and E Leonardi (eds), *Manifesto per il reddito di base* (Bari, Laterza, 2018) 42–43.

[11] S Pollard, 'Factory Discipline in the Industrial Revolution' (1963) 16 *Economic History Review* 254.

[12] V de Stefano, 'Casual Work Beyond Casual Work in the EU: The Underground Casualisation of the European Workforce – And What to Do About It' (2016) 7 *European Labour Law Journal* 421.

[13] W Däubler and T Klebe, 'Crowdwork: Die neue Form der Arbeit – Arbeitgeber auf der Flucht?' (2015) Heft 15 *NZA* 1032.

[14] L Ratti, 'Precarious Digital Work and the Role of Online Platforms: The Inefficacy of Traditional Tests and the Need for an Indirect Approach' (ReMarkLab Final Conference, Stockholm, 19–20 May 2016) www.jurinst.su.se/polopoly_fs/1.281328.1462279693!/menu/standard/file/Ratti%20-%20Precarious%20digital%20work.pdf accessed 20 December 2018.

[15] G Davidov, *A Purposive Approach to Labour Law* (Oxford, Oxford University Press, 2016) 135.

of 'workplace' which, therefore, indicates the need to redefine the boundaries of labour law *per se*. Accordingly, this pressure on the fundamental structures of labour law re-opens one of the most traditional topics in labour law scholarship; that is, the classification of employment status based on the classical dichotomy between subordination and autonomy. For labour law as a system, that is, a working machinery of social regulation, many European countries rely on the concept of subordination as the key to access the protective statute addressed to employees; thus, it is necessary to update the hermeneutical operation through which subordination is interpreted in order to meet the challenges as briefly presented above.

In order to revitalise the debate on the concept of subordination,[16] innovative approaches are required. This chapter introduces an alternative definitory technique for use at an international level, which originates from Italian case law: the concept of subordination as *double alienness*. Applied for the first time by the Italian Constitutional Court in 1996, and then recalled by the Supreme Court and lower courts in other cases, this concept defines subordination as the alienness (ie, the exclusive destination to other persons or entities than the worker) of the results attained by the work performance, and of the productive organisation in which the worker's activities are performed. This chapter contextualises the definition and applies it to the example of 'crowdworkers', in order to test its utility in solving questions of misclassification.

II. A Few Necessary Premises

While reviewing the recent debate on the classification of crowdworkers, some premises – mainly in the form of acknowledgements – would seem appropriate to clear the discourse of theoretical misunderstandings or normative confusions.

The first acknowledgement concerns the simple fact that employment and self-employment are not ontological concepts but legal notions: all forms of human activity that have an economically appreciable value, and are defined as work, can usually be conducted through a contract of employment or a contract of self-employment. There is no intrinsic or ontological activity that must necessarily be conducted in one way or another. The fundamental freedom of contract gives parties the chance to choose (even though it is clear that, in the labour market, employers have major bargaining power in this process) how to define the regulation of their interests raising from professional collaboration. Therefore, the classification of work as subordinate or autonomous is a normative process that starts from each actual relationship as it occurs in socio-economic reality and then connects it to the norms of the legal system. In some countries, like civil law systems, this process goes beyond the *numen juris* of the contract and takes into consideration how the

[16] L Nogler, *The Concept of 'Subordination' in European and Comparative Law* (Trento, University of Trento, 2009).

parties *de facto* have arranged their interests during the negotiation, at the conclusion of the contract, and during its subsequent execution.[17]

Crowdwork, however, is not a legal concept: it refers to a variety of different activities whose status has not yet been subject to any form of legal definition. The evidently sociological and economic nature of the concept of crowdwork does not prevent it, nevertheless, from being too vague for use in categorising a multitude of works, and 'gigs', which are often very different to each other. Attempts to create a taxonomy of crowdwork[18] – from the cyclists who deliver food wearing a Foodora or Deliveroo jacket, to the driver who is allocated work via the Uber app, to the lonely (intellectual) manufacturer who accomplishes small tasks from home on the Amazon Mechanical Turk, to the graphic designer or tax accountant who finds clients on Upwork – are challenged by the diversity of such cases (these being particularly well known ones) with few common elements that might link them, and thus enable identification of a genus/species relationship.

In the socio-economic dimension of crowdworkers, nonetheless, two aspects are quite evident. The first is that the demand for work is managed through virtual platforms – this is why many authors refer to them as 'platform-workers' (in line with the expression, 'platform capitalism', which in turn is more convincing than 'gig economy'). The second aspect is that, as for the performance of their tasks to customers, these platforms strongly rely on a spread condition of availability of workforce, which in Marxist terms is defined as 'reserve army' – now, instead, is defined with a more neutral term 'crowd'. Indeed, these platforms are operational as long as there is a 'crowd of people' willing to accept work in accordance with the platforms' terms and conditions, and therefore fulfil the need for the provision of services or goods to customers on demand. Given the immanent evanescence of the concept of crowdwork, any hermeneutical effort that aspires to find a key or a universal interpretative method to classify all platforms' workers in terms of subordination or autonomy, may result in a vain operation, or in fallacious results.[19] Hence, the last premise of this contribution is that the proposed method must be applied on a case by case basis.

III. A Matter of Classification from an Italian Perspective

Three main positions, in particular, are evident concerning the regulatory gaps created by the increasing practice of crowdwork. First, many labour law scholars see the problem as a matter of classification. Secondly, others call for legislators,

[17] This is the principle of primacy of facts, also supported by the International Labour Organization, in *The Employment Relationship* (International Labour Conference, 95th Session, Report V(1), 2006) 24.

[18] Ratti, 'Precarious Digital Work' (n 14).

[19] Voza, 'The Same Old Story?' (n 2) 10.

at the regional (EU) and domestic levels, to introduce a *tertium genus*, or an intermediate category for platform workers. A third approach goes beyond an investigation into the subordinate or autonomous nature of the relationship, and calls for a sort of Charter of fundamental rights for all workers.

Briefly, the second position[20] is *de iure condendo*, although in many civil law systems like Italy, there is a principle of 'unavailability of the contractual type' (in Italian: *indisponibilità del tipo contrattuale*),[21] according to which neither the legislator nor the parties can 'deny the legal qualification of employment relationships subject to relationships that objectively have such a nature, where this results in the inapplicability of the mandatory provisions of the law to implement the principles, guarantees and rights established by the Constitution to protect subordinate employment'.[22] So, at least for labour law scholars in civil law systems, the regulatory gaps created by the diversity of crowdwork cannot easily be solved without first addressing the contract classification.[23] The last approach is dangerous: labour law, already deeply deregulated and fragmented, does not need an intervention that appears technically weak at combatting abuses.

Consequently, the main problem is still the classification of the contract; in this part of the debate, two contributions have remarkably renovated the hermeneutical tools at disposal of labour law – even though there is not enough room, unfortunately, to analyse them in-depth in this chapter: the first one passes through a redefinition of the 'employer' and her functions,[24] while the second one is based on the expansion of agency work.[25] While these are worthy attempts at accommodating the notion of crowdworkers within the traditional foundations of labour law, the first approach conflicts with the laws of evidence applicable to court proceedings, and the second one is not convincing with its exclusion of the necessity for additional legislation.

As Lord Wedderburn said, the contract of employment is like an elephant: '[A]n animal too difficult to define, but easy to recognise when you see it';[26] it would be useful to draw the elephant with a different pencil. Deep reflections on

[20] See, inter alia, JR Mercader Uguina, *El futuro del trabajo en la era del digitalización y la robotica* (Valencia, Tirant lo Blanche, 2017), as well as the proposals reported in A Aloisi, 'Il lavoro "a chiamata" e le piattaforme online della "Collaborative Economy": nozioni e tipi legali in cerca di tutele' (Bocconi Legal Studies Research Paper No 1, 10 December 2016) 38 https://ssrn.com/abstract=2883530 accessed 10 January 2019.

[21] M Novella, *L'inderogabilità nel diritto del lavoro: norme imperative e autonomia individuale* (Milano, Giuffrè, 2009); E Ghera, 'Subordinazione, statuto protettivo e qualificazione del rapporto di lavoro' (2006) 109 *Giornale di Diritto del Lavoro e di Relazioni Industriali*, 17.

[22] Case No 121/1993 (Judgment) Constitutional Court of Italy (25 March 1993).

[23] M Biasi, 'Dai pony express ai riders di Foodora. L'attualità del binomio subordinazione-autonomia (e del relativo metodo di indagine) quale alternativa all'affannosa ricerca di inedite categorie' [2017] (11) *Bollettino Adapt*.

[24] J Prassl and M Risak, 'Uber, TaskRabbit, and Co.: Platforms as Employers? Rethinking the Legal Analysis of Crowdwork' (2016) 37 *Comparative Labor Law & Policy Journal* 619.

[25] L Ratti, 'Online Platforms and Crowdwork in Europe: A Two-Step Approach to Expanding Agency Work Provisions' (2017) 38 *Comparative Labor Law & Policy Journal* 477.

[26] L Wedderburn, *The Worker and the Law* (3rd edn, Harmondsworth, Penguin, 1986) 116.

classification have generated different methods since the early stages of labour law. Now mainly Italian labour law is considered, where the emphasis on the employment contract lies in the concept of subordination. On this point, Luigi Mengoni observes that:

> the insertion of subordination in the content, and therefore in the cause, of the contract satisfies the need to re-personalize the relationship respecting the civil law principle of formal equality, which excludes that the contracts can differentiate due to the differences of the parties' economic positions and logically implies the need to consider (pretend) the consent of the worker as free as any other contractor.[27]

In Italian scholarship, classification of an employment contract has usually been addressed by identifying the will of the parties, and their choice of contractual type, whether of employment or self-employment.[28] The classification 'calls for a reflection on the identity of the employment contract and, in particular, on the very idea of subordination and its relation to the worker's protective status'.[29] Italian case law has produced a range of different notions of subordination, examples of which include hetero-direction, socio-economic dependency, collaboration, and availability or coordination.

According to Article 2094 of the Italian Civil Code, the subordinate worker is someone 'who binds [themselves], in exchange [for] remuneration to collaborate in the enterprise, performing [their] own intellectual or manual work, depending and under the direction of the entrepreneur'. Therefore, the subordination is 'legal-technical', because it is strictly connected to the element of dependency, according to which the contract of employment is an open contract whose content must be constantly filled by the orders of the creditor (the employer) towards the debtor (the employee).[30] In this sense, subordination is also meant as hetero-direction. The Civil Code, while referring to the entrepreneur, underlines the almost unique position that the head (and the owner) of the enterprise enjoys before her employees: she is, indeed, entitled to the three managerial (private) powers on them, that is, the power of giving directives and orders, the power to control and monitor and the power to punish against any breach of the contract.[31] Some scholars have defined this concept of subordination as 'technical-functional', underlying the functionality of such a contract within the enterprise as an organisation of production (of goods or services).[32]

[27] L Mengoni, 'Il contratto di lavoro nel secolo XX' (Intervention at AIDLASS Congress, 2002) www.aidlass.it/wp-content/uploads/2015/11/mengoni.rtf accessed 20 December 2018.

[28] Ghera, 'Subordinazione' (n 21) 1.

[29] ibid 1.

[30] ibid 1; L Mengoni, 'Il contratto individuale di lavoro' [2000] (86) *Giornale di Diritto del Lavoro e di Relazioni Industriali*, 181.

[31] C Zoli, 'Subordinazione e poteri dell'imprenditore tra organizzazione, contratto e contropotere' [1997] (2) *Lavoro e diritto* 241.

[32] M Napoli, 'Dallo Statuto dei lavoratori allo Statuto dei lavori' [1998] (3) *Diritto delle Relazioni Industriali* 297; P Ichino, *Subordinazione e autonomia nel diritto del lavoro* (Milano, Giuffrè, 1989).

Probably the most common method used by Italian courts to identify subordination – irrespective of its concept – is the 'subsumption' method (*sussunzione* in Italian, or *subsumtion* in German), which is the technique through which a given concrete relationship, in practice, is reconnected to a general and abstract rule. The method of subsumption starts from the reality of the relationship as it has occurred between the contractual parties, and then connects it to the abstract provision of the law, in order to classify it as an employment relationship or not.[33] The concept of subordination *ex* Article 2094 of the Italian Civil Code – based on subordination, collaboration, onerousness and synallagma – has been complemented by courts through empirical 'subsidiary' indices derived from experience such as: observance of a working schedule; fixed and constant remuneration; the absence of the risk of the result and therefore of the productivity of the work; the insertion of the worker in the organisation of the enterprise; continuity or duration of work performance.[34] The classification functions through the identification, in the concrete relationship, of a certain number of indices that are symptomatic of subordination.

The dominant concept of subordination is the hetero-direction, at least in the case of traditional blue-collar workers in Fordist industries. In many examples of workers in atypical positions characterised by high intellectual content and/or creative tasks – managers or high-skilled employees – as well as in cases of extremely elementary performance, which are repetitive and predetermined in their implementing rules, the criterion of the hetero-direction may not be significant for qualification of the employment relationship. In all these examples, the Supreme Court stated that it is legitimate to resort to subsidiary criteria of differentiation, such as the presence of a small entrepreneurial organisation of the worker, the incidence of economic risk, the observance of working time, the form of remuneration, or the continuity of performance.[35]

However, the concept of hetero-direction has some limitations as a result of significant changes in production processes over recent decades. As stated in the introduction, many employees currently enjoy increasing levels of autonomy (or smaller dependency) in carrying out their tasks, while many atypical workers – often freelance and self-employed – face the condition of being dependent from their (unique) client – such as a web designer working for one webpage but not in an employment relationship. In these situations, the method of double alienness may become more and more valuable and, above all, useful in detecting subordination where it would otherwise appear to be absent.

[33] G Ghezzi and U Romagnoli, *Il rapporto di lavoro* (Bologna, Zanichelli, 1995); L Mengoni and M Napoli, *Il contratto di lavoro* (Milano, Vita e Pensiero Università, 2004).

[34] Ghera, 'Subordinazione' (n 21) 10–11.

[35] L Pagani, 'Dipendente, Lavoratore' (*Dizionario di Economia e Finanza* on *Treccani*, 2012) www.treccani.it/enciclopedia/lavoratore-dipendente_%28Dizionario-di-Economia-e-Finanza%29/ accessed 12 January 2019.

IV. The Concept of Subordination as Double Alienness

Before explaining the concept of 'double alienness', a linguistic clarification is required. The term chosen to translate the Italian word, 'alienità', into English, is *alienness*, and not *alienation*; the latter is undeniably a more common expression, which translates into Italian as 'alienazione'. The reason behind this choice is that 'alienation', in legal terms, refers to the transfer of ownership of property rights to another person; whilst in Marxist theory, it describes the condition of psychological estrangement (*Entfremdung* in German) of workers in the capitalist mode of production, resulting from a lack of identity with the products of their activities, and the feeling of being controlled and exploited by their employers.[36] The Italian expression, 'alienità', does not refer to the condition of workers, but adjectivises the status of their labour in relationship to the organisation in which they collaborate, so as to express the exclusive destination of their labour to the employer. The concept of double alienness first appeared in the Italian legal system in a judgment issued by the Constitutional Court, whose main task is to guarantee, inter alia, that ordinary legislation is in compliance with the Constitution.

In Case No 30/1996, the Constitutional Court was asked to evaluate the constitutionality of a provision regarding severance pay and pensions,[37] within a dispute between members of a workers' cooperative and the INPS (the National Social Insurance Agency). Indeed, the Tribunal of Catania, which referred the case to the Constitutional Court, believed that the failure to apply the same pension rules to members of the workers' cooperative was a violation of the principle of equality enshrined in Article 3 of the Constitution. Although the employment arrangement for members of a cooperative was different to an employment contract, they were nonetheless characterised as having a weak economic position in relation to the cooperative, which is similar to the position of subordination experienced by employees as against their employer. According to the referring judge, this comparison was confirmed by several laws that extended protections enjoyed by employees – for example, of working time and weekly rest – to members of the workers' cooperatives.[38]

It is important to highlight that the Constitutional Court rejected the case for reasons that will soon be explained; nevertheless, what matters here lies in the argumentation that led to the decision. To implement specific labour protections, particularly those concerning remuneration, the relevant aspect is not the fact of carrying out a work activity characterised by elements of subordination, but the type of interests to which the activity is functionalised, and the corresponding arrangement of legal situations in which the activity is inserted. In this respect, 'subordination in the strict sense, peculiar to the employment relationship … is a

[36] See I Mészáros, *Marx's Theory of Alienation*, 5th edn (Delhi, Aakar Books, 2006).

[37] Law No 297/1982, Art 2.

[38] Case No 30/1996 (Judgment) Constitutional Court of Italy (12 February 1996) 1–2 [1].

more pregnant and together qualitatively different concept from the subordination of other contracts involving the working capacity of one of the parties'.[39] The difference is determined by the coincidence of two conditions which, in other cases, are never combined: 'the alienness (meaning the exclusive destination to others) of the result whose attainment the work is finalised to, and the alienness of the productive organisation in which the activity is inserted'.[40] When integrated with these two conditions:

> subordination is not simply a way of being the performance set in the contract, but it is a classification of the performance resulting from the type of regulation of the interests chosen by the parties by concluding a contract of employment, involving the incorporation of someone's work in a productive organisation on which the worker has no power of control, being formed for a purpose in respect of which [they] ha[ve] no (individual) interest legally protected.[41]

The Court argued that, beside the employee defined by Article 2094 of the Italian Civil Code, the members of a workers' cooperative are not legally indifferent to the purpose of the business because they have the powers and the rights to contribute to the formation of their company's will and have control over its social management; moreover, they have also the right to a share of the profits. These rights and powers, and the correlative assumption by the individual member of a business risk level, justify the provision in question, which excludes cooperatives' employees from the protection of the Guarantee Fund for severance indemnities that is addressed to standard employees.

This innovative concept of subordination has been applied in a small number of judgments from the Supreme Court of Cassation,[42] and other lower courts.[43] However, 'double alienness' is the only concept of subordination that groups together the unskilled worker (whose tasks are set on a routine basis), the driver of a CEO, the high-skilled engineer, and the manager of a department, because they all enjoy different levels of hetero-direction, but do not own the outcome of their activities, nor do they own the organisation in which their collaboration is inserted. Double alienness perfectly represents the rationale behind the legal institution of the employment contract as an object of legal protection. This 'constitutionally driven' interpretation of the notion of employment provides a single criterion for distinguishing between autonomy and subordination, rather than traditional multiple criteria.[44] For all these characteristics, 'double alienness' seems to be a

[39] Case No 30/1996 (Judgment) Constitutional Court of Italy (12 February 1996) 1–2.

[40] ibid.

[41] ibid.

[42] Namely, Case No 21646/2006 (Judgment) Constitutional Court of Italy (9 December 2006), Case No 820/2007 (Judgment) Constitutional Court of Italy (16 January 2007), and Case No 18692/2007 (Judgment) Constitutional Court of Italy (6 September 2007).

[43] Case (Judgment) of Court of Appeal, Genoa (30 September 2013).

[44] M Roccella, 'Lavoro subordinato e lavoro autonomo, oggi' (WP CSDLE 'Massimo D'Antona', IT–65/2008, 14 January 2008) 37 http://csdle.lex.unict.it/docs/workingpapers/Lavoro-subordinato-e-lavoro-autonomo-oggi/1806.aspx accessed 20 December 2018.

very useful tool in the so-called 'grey zone' of the labour market, where traditional indices of subordination coexist with typical elements of autonomy.

V. Applying Double Alienness to the Fractal Work of Platforms

The platform economy is essentially based on two forms of work: 'crowdwork' and 'work on-demand via apps'.[45] Workers are usually contracted as self-employed, freelance, or independent contractors. However, many contracts are not truly autonomous; an indication of which is the increasing number of court proceedings on the issue of misclassification. Courts dealing with fractal work of platforms have adopted the usual method of subsumption, but have reached different conclusions in similar cases. Yet, what would happen if the concept of double alienness were adopted? In this section, the concept of double alienness will be 'tested' on the well-known example of Uber drivers.

The classification of Uber drivers has achieved prominence due to the large number of disputes brought before courts, at all levels, around the world. Many courts have recognised the employment status of drivers, but many have not; therefore, the pattern of judicial consideration on this issue is fragmented. Sometimes courts have explicitly requested that legislators provide for a new category of worker to cater for this type of employment.[46]

In this chapter, it is not possible to describe, in full, details of how Uber acquires its workforce; nevertheless, what we need to consider is that an Uber driver is a self-employed worker who, in driving their own car, is connected to a platform that sends through information on where to pick up clients who have reserved a 'ride' via the Uber app, and where to take them via a precise route. Uber always declared itself as a tech company that connects independent drivers and people in need of a ride: this interpretation of its 'mission', however, has been rejected by several courts – above all, the Court of Justice of the EU in *Asociación Profesional Élite Taxi v Uber Systems Spain, SL* (*Uber Systems*).[47] The case against Uber is that it is a transport service, where all transactions between drivers and clients are managed by Uber, which extracts a fee for having mediated and processed the transaction.

As seen above, the double alienness consists of the 'exclusive destination' of the results of labour, and of the organisation of production by the contractual party other than the worker – a further iteration of the counterparty owning, directly and originally, the product or the service made by the worker, as well as organising and managing, directly and originally, the means of production in which the worker is placed.

[45] V de Stefano, 'The Rise of the "Just-In-Time Workforce": On-Demand Work, Crowdwork, and Labor Protection in the "Gig-Economy"' (2016) 37 *Comparative Labor Law & Policy Journal* 471.
[46] ibid 18.
[47] Case C-434/15 *Asociación Profesional Elite Taxi v Uber Systems Spain, SL* (ECJ, 20 December 2017).

In *Uber Systems*, the results of the activity performed by the drivers are, without doubt, directly and originally owned by Uber. In order to clearly understand this aspect, we need to consider the following factors. First, Uber customers can only use the Uber app to book their 'rides', therefore their main interface is with Uber. The fact that 'taking an Uber' is now common parlance amongst Uber customers for booking a 'ride' using the app is an illustration of the degree to which this legal fact has infiltrated social reality. Moreover, for the service of transportation, clients usually pay Uber directly through the app. Whilst it is possible to pay cash, this option must be selected before the 'ride', after customers have entered their destination, but not yet 'requested' the 'ride'. Drivers will only get their remuneration after Uber has deducted its fees. So, the result of the activities of the drivers is that its exclusive destination is Uber, not the drivers producing those activities.

More problematic for Uber drivers appears the issue of the alienness of the organisation of the production, nonetheless it takes a minor effort to overcome the superficial appearance. If we consider (superficially) the production of the service of transportation, we might conclude that the activity of Uber drivers mainly consists of taking customers from one place to another, with the primary means of doing so being the driver's own car. So, as a consequence, it would be difficult to argue that the second factor of alienness exists, as the process of production is entirely on the drivers. But if we consider the Uber service as part of a broader picture – that is, as an economic phenomenon – then we will realise that the drivers' car is only part of the business organisation, and probably not even the most significant. Uber's activity is essentially based on the platform and application that connects drivers and passengers. The 'ride' is only one part of such an activity, whose prologue and epilogue comprise several important steps: creating an account; reserving the ride; rating the driver; checking information relating to drivers (eg, their driving licence or the condition of their cars) – all of which is completely owned and directly managed by Uber, without any participation or direct access to the process by drivers. Moreover, the algorithm that creates the match between the driver and the customer is probably the biggest part of the entire production process. Indeed, it is through the app that the drivers get their information about each 'ride'. Once the journey has commenced, the app provides the driver with turn-by-turn directions – which are not obligatory on paper, but if drivers fail to follow them, they may encounter negative results. As the Employment Tribunal in London has acknowledged, 'at the end of any trip, the fare is calculated by the Uber servers, based on GPS data from the driver's smartphone. The calculation takes account of time spent and distance covered. In "surge" areas, where supply and demand are not in harmony, a multiplier is applied to fares resulting in a charge above the standard level'.[48]

[48] Case Nos 2202550/2015 & Others (Judgment) Employment Tribunal of London (28 October 2016) 4 [18] It is worth noting that the appeal in this case was recently heard in the Court of Appeal (Civil Division): *Uber BV v Aslam* [2018] EWCA Civ 2748 (19 December 2018).

Yet again, it is Uber, and not the drivers, which directly and exclusively owns and manages this tool. And if we consider the EU Court of Justice's ruling that Uber should be considered a transportation service, then we can argue that this is the way in which Uber organises its service of transport, whereby the drivers are merely the last cog in a much more structured and complex machine. The alienness of the organisation of production in Uber is capable of further appreciation when another aspect is considered. Specifically, that Uber sets recommendations to standardise its quality of service, as acknowledged by the courts, and that driver non-compliance with these recommendations potentially constitutes a breach of the partner term/license conditions – this set of recommendations is accompanied by a rating system that is also completely inaccessible to drivers.[49]

The current high levels of irregularity in the patterns of courts' argumentation is probably due to the use of traditional methods of classification. For instance, in a recent French case, the Paris Conseil de Prud'Hommes ruled that Uber drivers cannot be classified as employees because they 'are at liberty to accept or to refuse a trip and that they are at liberty to disconnect if they so wish'; moreover, the plaintiff 'was also at liberty to work according to the hours and days that suited him, since it cannot be contested that these matters were not imposed on him'.[50] The concept of subordination, in terms of hetero-direction, needs to find support in the total lack of 'autonomy' of workers to set their working schedule, because the employment contract entails the continuity of the obligation to perform.[51]

In this regard, double alienness clearly defines the arrangement of the interests raising from the relationship between Uber and its drivers in terms of employment without taking into consideration the traditional indices of subordination.

Application of the double alienness standard by courts would likely increase the number of findings that Uber drivers are in fact employees, as on each occasion that a driver activates the Uber app and performs activities for Uber, the arrangement of both parties' interests is set according to the employment contract. Now, if an element of continuity in the relationship is fundamental, judges (or legislators) should bear responsibility for making it socially acceptable that a driver might conclude hundreds (if not thousands) of fixed-term contracts each year with the same employer, Uber, but certainly not deny the existence of dependent work; otherwise the more reasonable solution would be to recognise that there has been one single employment contract.

VI. Conclusion

The concept of subordination used by the Italian Constitutional Court – in terms of double alienness or hetero-organisation – has great potential to be applied

[49] G Pacella, 'Gig Economy, Rating, Labour Relationship' (2017) 3(1) *Labour & Law Issues* R1.

[50] General Role No F 16/11460 (Judgment) Conseil de Prud'Hommes de Paris (29 January 2018).

[51] L Spagnuolo Vigorita, *Subordinazione e diritto del lavoro: problemi storico-critici* (Napoli, Morano, 1968).

to a broader number of cases concerning possible misclassification, compared to what is possible with subordination as hetero-direction. This re-definition of the grounding idea of employment may conceive the employment relationship as dilated on both subjective and objective levels, and as structurally more 'open to incorporate different ways of working, and structured around a conception of subordination that is less technical-functional and with more marked socio-economic, as well legally relevant, characteristics'.[52] This hermeneutical operation does not aim at overcoming previously established concepts, but rather it suggests an additional tool (for judges as well) for accurate classification of a given relationship. As Massimo Roccella comments:

> [I]n view of the indications of the Constitutional Court, one cannot keep from verifying that the real 'strangeness' of the recent debate on the topic of subordination is certainly apparent in the attitude of the doctrine: in its negligence, in its omissions, in its silences, perhaps understandable (at least for those who are aware of the anything but neutral character of legal interpretation), but really difficult to justify.[53]

Indeed, Roccella suggests that, notwithstanding occasional exceptions, the case law of the Constitutional Court relating to subordination (especially the above-mentioned Case No 30/1996) lacks doctrinal analysis and seems to lack due consideration. He writes: 'Amnesia? Removals? […] all the more so when the different point of view comes from a not exactly irrelevant pulpit, such as the Constitutional Court.'[54]

The possible reasons for such an attitude may lie in the fact that criticism against double alienness confuses it with socio-economic dependency, but it is obvious that these are two completely different concepts. Hetero-organisation, indeed, considers only the legal status of the results of work, and of the production organisation, which both depend exclusively on the contractual arrangement of the parties. There could be, perhaps, two other reasons behind the scepticism towards double alienness. First, judges and scholars may feel that hetero-direction is still the best way to classify those relationships in which elements of subordination are intertwined with factors of autonomy; but the risk of dishomogenous patterns of decisions is evident. Secondly, double alienness might be underestimated because it is considered as an 'ideological' approach, with assonances to the Marxist theory of alienation, rather than as a positivistic one. All concerns regarding a lack of positivism in the double alienness approach should be easily overcome; indices are not more 'positivistic' than double alienness. There was, however, an attempt to regulate crowdworkers from the current Italian Government through a Law

[52] G Ferraro, 'Flessibilità in entrata: nuovi e vecchi modelli di lavoro flessibile' (2012) 4 *Rivista Italiana di Diritto del Lavoro* 567 (translated into English by author).

[53] Roccella, 'Lavoro subordinato' (n 41) 35.

[54] ibid.

Decree – now abandoned – in which the concept of subordination, in terms of double alienness, was clearly adopted.[55]

It is evident that all attempts to avoid classification problems by calling for a sort of Charter of fundamental labour rights to all workers can be fascinating, nonetheless it is also evident from recent history that the goal of improving labour conditions cannot be attained by downsizing the purpose and the scope (ie, the identity) of labour law. Challenging practices of acquiring a workforce through platforms or any other digital tool need a redefinition of the boundaries of labour law in the sense of expanding its protective force that brings about social justice.

The efforts, indeed, to ensure the application of labour law also to the 'new capitalist vanguard' of platforms, moreover, brings about also a fairer economy. As the Californian Supreme Court has acknowledged, the misclassification of workers creates 'the unfair competitive advantage the business may obtain over competitors that properly classify similar workers as employees and that thereby assume the fiscal and other responsibilities and burdens that an employer owes to its employees'.[56] Moreover, Ewan McGaughey has recently raised the question of whether 'contriving' to 'misrepresent' something enables fraud claims, either by staff who seek employment rights, or by public authorities for tax receipts or social security contributions.[57]

As for the big questions posed in the introduction to this chapter, regarding which work deserves protection, and which protections work deserves, double alienness pushes the interpreter to focus on the pillar aspect of labour law. That is, a law that regulates socio-economic powers within capitalist production, in order to understand which economic and legal powers can be exercised by a worker and the entrepreneur within the production process, through the arrangement of interests as set by both parties. It is these aspects in relation to which double alienness proves most valuable and effective; and it is the familiar challenge concerning the balance/imbalance of power between employers and employees in which labour law has been exercising its democratising force throughout its existence. And, frankly, there is no evidence that this will be any different in the era of platform capitalism.

[55] V Conte, 'Di Maio e il "decreto dignità" per cambiare il Jobs Act' (*La Repubblica*, 15 June 2018) https://ricerca.repubblica.it/repubblica/archivio/repubblica/2018/06/15/di-maio-e-il--decreto-dignita-per-cambiare-il-jobs-act10.html accessed 12 January 2019 (regarding the draft, so-called 'Dignity Decree').

[56] *Dynamex Operations West, Inc v Superior Court*, No 5222732 (Cal S Ct, 30 April 2018) 2.

[57] E McGaughey, 'Uber, the Taylor Review, Mutuality, and the Duty Not to Misrepresent Employment Status' (2018) *Industrial Law Journal*, doi:10.1093/indlaw/dwy014.

5

Comment

Reconsidering Historical Perspectives Anew – Old Ideas Adapted to New Forms of Work

NICOLE BUSBY*

In this commentary, I address what I see as a key theme underpinning the three thought-provoking chapters in this section; that is, the need to broaden labour law's scope to incorporate wider policy concerns which are of great significance to the exchange of labour for wages. My comments, thus, focus on the importance of expanding labour law's reach, in its configuration as both a scholarly endeavour and a practice, in its ambition, as well as in its practical effect. As historical perspective shows us, this does not require a redesign, but rather a restatement of the origins of labour law and their contextualisation within contemporary arrangements. The notion that labour lawyers should adapt old or pre-existing ideas to fit new forms of work is clearly supported by the three chapters in this section, which I will refer to in order to illustrate my own thoughts on theorising labour law in a changing world.

Although the three chapters deal quite specifically with rather different propositions, they are quite rightly, in my view, linked through their shared wariness of the current predominance of economic concerns as a precursor to law. Robert Knegt emphasises the importance of understanding the past in considerations of contemporary social and economic ordering and the requisite place of labour law. In a sophisticated and layered analysis, Knegt argues that the Foucauldian conception of the market as a public place of justice has been lost in the (neo)liberal turn, which has reformulated our understanding of the market as 'a quasi-natural mechanism', and isolated it from a discourse of justice. Lisa Rodgers provides an analysis of labour law's place within the specificities of the contemporary

* Professor, Law School, University of Strathclyde.

political economy, in particular the notion that the 2008 global economic crisis has led to a rationalisation of the existence of a state of exception. Rodgers warns that, if left unchecked, this movement could pose a significant threat to labour law's democratic function due to the negative juxtaposition of what is perceived as costly regulation with the positive spin of economic development. In his contribution, Vincenzo Pietrogiovanni offers a potential solution to the very real problem posed by contemporary arrangements for labour-wage exchange through what has become known as the 'gig economy'. Pietrogiovanni posits how the definitional dilemma surrounding the 'crowd workers', who populate online platforms, might be resolved with reference to the Italian concept of 'double alienness' as a means of determining their degree of subordination, and thus enabling their inclusion in labour law's reach. What all three contributions tell us is that, in order to fully appreciate labour law's pivotal role in the development of the social and economic order, labour law, perhaps more than any other area of legal study and practice, demands the application of a longitudinal and broad perspective. This is also the best route to achieving any meaningful articulation of its most useful future direction.

In reconsidering the historical perspectives of labour law anew, it is helpful to return to what are widely acknowledged to be its foundational goals, which are intrinsically linked through their operationalisation. In its simplest formulation, the value of labour law as a distinct field of practice and scholarship can be seen as two-fold: first, it is through the application of rules and principles, which together form the body of labour law, that disputes are resolved and justice instilled in relations between the two sides of what has become a contractual relationship. Its second, and equally important, value can be found in its contribution to wider understandings of the economic and social conditions with which workers and employing organisations are confronted, as one of the means by which social and economic goals can be implemented.[1] The transformation of such potentially wide aims into meaningful action cannot be achieved effectively through traditional legal means alone, although hard law does have a role to play, be it through legislation or common law that strategically converts objectives into action. I will return to complementary and/or alternative forms of regulation below, but staying with legal intervention for now, this does not happen by chance and takes place in clear view through targeted political activity. Such activity should acknowledge that the contractual relationship between employer and worker, although 'private' in the legal sense, serves a public function and requires the application of wider public law principles. This places an obligation on decision-makers, including those charged with the implementation of law and policy, to act fairly and rationally, in good faith, and by using the powers that they have for their proper purposes. Using Keith Ewing's classification, the two functions of labour law can be identified as

[1] KD Ewing, 'Democratic Socialism and Labour Law' (1995) 24 *Industrial Law Journal* 103, 110.

the wider or social justice purpose, and the traditional or democratic purpose.[2] Both go straight to the heart of traditional conceptions of labour law as evidenced in the work of its foundational scholars.

Labour law's democratic function brings to mind Hugo Sinzheimer's idea of the 'labour constitution' through its use as a means of limiting the power of capital and freeing labour.[3] Sinzheimer's work on industrial democracy, as both a scholar and a politician, gave rise to broader views of regulatory development encompassing workers' representation and regulation through industrial councils. In the context of the Weimarian collective labour law to which Sinzheimer's conception of the constitution refers, this is explicit in Article 165 of the Weimar Republic's Constitution which provided that: 'Workers and employees are called upon to cooperate, on an equal footing, with employers in the regulation of wages and of the conditions of labor, as well as in the general development of the productive forces.'

In his classic conception of labour law, Otto Kahn-Freund, Sinzheimer's one-time student, recognises its duality through its regulation of the employment contract, and its goal of correcting imbalance in the bargaining power – as a 'countervailing force' – between employer and employee.[4] The world in which Kahn-Freund wrote about labour relations no longer exists, yet his observations are still capable of capturing the problems arising from the increased marketisation of labour, although insufficiently positioned to respond effectively in the contemporary context. We seek new solutions and, as Knegt reminds us in reference to Sinzheimer, changed political and economic conditions may mean that received wisdom, however fundamentally important to our understanding, may require reconsideration.

The dominance of pervasive economic concerns as a means of structuring labour law is raised as problematic in all three chapters. As the contributors show, both labour law's social justice purpose and its democratic purpose have been crowded out in recent years by the dominance of narrowly conceived economic concerns, so that labour law – or more precisely, its pursuit of justice through democratic means – has become subordinated to the market. Rodgers' analysis attributes this to the use of exceptional action (or non-action), rationalised by the need to respond to the economic crisis, which has had a deregulatory effect on labour markets as protective measures are incinerated in a 'bonfire of the regulations'.[5] Rodgers uses the 'exceptional state' thesis to argue that temporal concerns with economic performance should not provide the basis for long-term

[2] ibid 111.

[3] H Sinzheimer, *Arbeitsrecht und Rechtssoziologie: Gesammelte Aufsätze und Reden* (first published 1928, Frankfurt, Europäische Verlagsanstalt, 1976); R Dukes, *The Labour Constitution: The Enduring Idea of Labour Law* (Oxford, Oxford University Press, 2014).

[4] O Kahn-Freund, *Labour and the Law*, 2nd edn (London, Stevens, 1977) 6.

[5] S Coulter and B Hancké, 'A Bonfire of the Regulations, or Business as Usual? The UK Labour Market and the Political Economy of Brexit' (2016) 87 *Political Quarterly* 148; see also N Bruun, K Lörcher and I Schömann (eds), *The Economic and Financial Crisis and Collective Labour Law in Europe* (Oxford, Hart Publishing, 2014); S Walby, *Crisis* (Cambridge, Polity Press, 2015).

strategy which reconstitutes labour law in ways that reorientate it away from its original purpose of protecting workers from the exploitative excesses of the market order. Knegt argues against the predominance of the 'modern economy', as the starting point for understandings of how and why labour law should operate. He posits that economics has toppled (labour) law as the primary political 'framework of universalisation' upon which socio-economic policies are based. Pietrogiovanni shows the effects of labour law's own narrow concern with a particular economic model so that wage labour, which takes place outside of the familiar employing entity embodied by the traditional firm, escapes its protective reach. In seeking an alternative interpretative tool, which would enable inclusion of those workers previously excluded, Pietrogiovanni seeks to prevent their surrender to self-identification as entrepreneurs of themselves.[6]

So, in becoming subsumed by the market order, labour law has lost its democratic grounding, thus placing its goal of social justice in peril. The timeline of Knegt's recall of the past, Rodgers' warning regarding the present, and Pietrogiovanni's quest for the future bring to mind Antonio Gramsci's assessment, recorded in his *Prison Notebooks*, that '[t]he crisis consists precisely in the fact that the old is dying and the new cannot be born; in this interregnum a great variety of morbid symptoms appear'.[7] Labour law's way out of the interregnum, through its emancipation from the market, must surely rest on the broadening out of its scope.[8] This will require both micro- and macro-level industrial relations actors to reclaim what has been conceptualised as the 'regulatory space',[9] defined as 'the range of regulatory issues subject to public decision. Proponents claim that its dimensions and occupants can be understood by examining regulation in any particular national setting, and by analyzing that setting in terms of its specific political, legal and cultural attributes'.[10]

This is not a new endeavour – history shows us nothing is – and in the context of scholarship, at least, there is much to be learned from previous considerations. In her engagement with, and advocacy for Sinzheimer's work, Ruth Dukes warns against a closer realignment of the study of labour law with the labour market

[6] M Foucault, *The Birth of Biopolitics: Lectures at the Collège de France 1978–1979* (M Senellart ed, G Burchell tr, New York, Palgrave Macmillan, 2008) 240; K Rittich, 'Making Natural Markets: Flexibility as Labour Market Truth' (2014) 65 *Northern Ireland Legal Quarterly* 323.

[7] A Gramsci, *Selections from the Prison Notebooks of Antonio Gramsci* (Q Hoare and G Nowell-Smith eds, Q Hoare and G Nowell-Smith trs, London, Lawrence & Wishart, 1971) 276.

[8] C Arup and others (eds), *Labour Law and Labour Market Regulation: Essays on the Construction, Constitution and Regulation of Labour Markets and Work Relationships* (Annandale, Federation Press, 2006).

[9] C Crouch, 'Sharing Public Space: States and Organised Interests in Western Europe' in JA Hall (ed), *States in History* (Oxford, Basil Blackwell, 1986); L Hancher and M Moran, 'Organizing Regulatory Space' in L Hancher and M Moran (eds), *Capitalism, Culture, and Economic Regulation* (Oxford, Clarendon Press, 2000); C Scott, 'Analysing Regulatory Space: Fragmented Resources and Institutional Design' [2001] (Summer) *Public Law* 329.

[10] SV Berg, F Gasmi and JI Tavari, *Glossary for the Body of Knowledge on the Regulation of Utility Infrastructure and Services* (World Bank, 2005) 73.

as the primary object of study. The danger is that such reorientation 'can tend towards an acceptance of market logic as the organising principle of the field', so that in transnational and international considerations, the motivations and policy decisions of national governments are viewed and predicted through the lens of a market-based model. Dukes asserts that this model is unhelpful, because the assumption of national governments' primary goals of wealth maximisation (in the economic sense), and global competitiveness, allows scholars 'little scope for arguing in favour of the protection of social rights and labour rights as goods in themselves'.[11] This restates labour law's social justice and democratic functions as primary to any other purposes that it might serve.

A return to labour law's traditional conception of its purpose and function is required, but with modification so as to ensure that it is fit for the specific contemporary challenges presented by the regulatory space that has opened up in the absence of collective bargaining. In keeping with labour law's wider purposes, particularly its democratic function which is most affected by the demise of trade unions, it must avoid the managerial unilateralism and institutional risk avoidance that has filled the void through the elevated status of the human resource function.[12] In our quest for appropriate modifications, we must be mindful of what Knegt calls 'seven common but deplorable limits' on labour law's scope, amongst them the assumption of state involvement, the focus on the protection of workers, and the preoccupation with employment. In drawing attention to these (and other) self-imposed limitations, he argues that labour law needs to free itself from constraint in order to reinvigorate the regulatory space that it inhabits. The lesson to be learned from a longitudinal analysis is that better use should be made of the potentially broad scope pertaining to the various forms of regulation (in the widest possible sense) of what is after all human behaviour. The system of rules that we end up with should derive from that behaviour and not simply be imposed upon it. Although the application of free market principles to the labour for wage exchange gives the illusion of a *laissez faire* approach by the state, labour market policy is in fact a highly regulated area, and the approaches adopted by states epitomise just how seamlessly mainstream economics has become subsumed by ideology, narrowing regulatory choice, and stunting institutional imagination. The mythical alchemy of political constructs such as austerity,[13] apparently justifies the surrendering of control to invisible and mysterious forces, and obscures that it is in fact through the careful targeting of imposed rules and regulations that labour law's scope has been narrowed.[14] The reconstitution of pluralism through the opening up of regulation to participative processes involving workers and

[11] R Dukes, 'A Global Labour Constitution' (2014) 65 *Northern Ireland Legal Quarterly* 283, 284.

[12] L Barmes, *Bullying and Behavioural Conflict at Work: The Duality of Individual Rights* (Oxford, Oxford University Press, 2015).

[13] L Clarke and J Newman, 'The Alchemy of Austerity' (2012) 32 *Critical Social Policy* 299.

[14] A Bogg, 'Beyond Neo-Liberalism: The Trade Union Act 2016 and the Authoritarian State' (2016) 45 *Industrial Law Journal* 299.

their representatives, as well as wider civil society actors, is the only way in which the democratic function of labour law can be reinstated; in Knegt's estimation, through '... an approach that recognises (labour) law as a constitutive element of day-to-day human practices'.

Rather than being subordinated to wider economic strategy, including employment policy, law should be embedded in it. The broadening of regulatory space should be aimed at recasting employment relations and reversing the movement towards individualised regulation, and the shift from union to non-union voice. Without such a radical overhaul, the same regulatory challenges persist in groundhog-day fashion, albeit in new guises, so that according to Pietrogiovanni (quoting Roberto Voza), labour law is likely to ask itself, once again, 'as one hundred years ago ... "Which work does deserve protection? Which protection does work deserve?"'

How widely should labour law redraw its own boundaries? What is included in 'labour market policy'? Does it stretch to social security? To immigration policy? To public procurement and the development of infrastructure? In the contemporary transnational capitalist economy, all of these fields seem relevant as capital's capacity to seek out labour markets, both nationally and transnationally, with lower standards and costs presents the greatest challenge to labour law's social justice function. The globalisation of capital has led to changes in the ability and willingness of national governments to maintain social protection so that, as Rodgers reminds us, the regulatory space has been filled with new neoliberal theories of labour markets and their impact on economic goals. This underlines labour law's subordination to the dominant preoccupation with the smooth running of the market. If its underlying purpose is indeed the protection of workers, then the relationship between this aim and wider labour market policy must be acknowledged. If the new subject of labour law is indeed 'the worker', actual or potential (see Pietrogiovanni), a holistic approach is necessary in order to encompass the related concerns beyond employment protection of such an individual, in a volatile and ever changing environment.

Thus, labour law which is capable of encompassing employment protection as well as collective bargaining, *and* actively responding to labour market policy, has a far greater capacity for effectiveness in its operation than a system which passively accepts state-imposed regulation and/or deregulation, and which demobilises its social justice and democratic functions. Heeding Rodgers' warning regarding the potential erosion of 'the normative content of civil law ... as a result of the change in the balance of power', we must be mindful in broadening the scope of labour law that its objectives return to their protective origins, rather than the current concern with profitability of the employing organisation, and macro- and micro-economic efficiency. The reaction of States to the global financial crisis provides a perfect illustration of this shift, with the creation and retention of jobs seen as the primary regulatory goal in place of the protective measures necessary to improve the quality of jobs. As Pietrogiovanni's chapter shows, the transfer of risk to the worker facilitated by the growth in assistive technologies has resulted in the proliferation of crowdworking whose diversity prevents its inclusion within the narrowly drawn boundaries of employment. To counter this, a broadened focus is necessary; one that seeks to modernise and supplement Kahn-Freund's normative conception of labour law by ensuring that it not only protects workers, but also concerns itself with the quality of jobs.

Recalling labour law's historical legacy is again informative in this context, as it shows us that the orthodoxy and received wisdom of the discipline are limited in time and place. As Knegt demonstrates, the stable employment model on which the traditional subject matter of labour law is based was relatively short lived in the history of labour market regulation, as is its legal formulation as one of contract. Furthermore, the story told of labour law's conceptualisation and development has been dominated by European and North American scholarship, and is thus reflective of the economic conditions and industrial practices in those jurisdictions. Even in this narrow purview, changes in labour market practices within and beyond employing organisations, including in the composition of the paid workforce and the corresponding rise in 'non-standard' working arrangements, have rendered traditional labour law prone to avoidance. Pietrogiovanni and Rodgers remind us of the importance of courts in preserving and reshaping its application, so that its underlying purpose is retained in the face of contemporary challenges, but this is not enough. Labour law needs to adapt to changes in both time and space.

The adoption of a pluralist conception of regulation, not confined to legislation and the common law, but concerned with a wider variety of regulatory approaches including soft law and self-regulation, and using the tools of participative democracy, is required to (re)instil labour law's public function in new approaches. This should encompass a wider subject matter incorporating social security law, supply side employment policy (including immigration law), and access to justice concerns so as to ensure labour law's effectiveness. The ILO's original constitution included broader policies beyond the improvement of working conditions to preserve universal peace by addressing 'the regulation of the supply of labour' and the 'prevention of unemployment'.[15] In this reimagining, should labour law be viewed as part of the political economy? Such an approach is more likely to capture current issues in labour regulation which impact on social and economic inequality. In the contemporary setting, the achievement of social justice goals such as equality requires more than addressing the imbalance of bargaining power between employers and employees. Furthermore, to focus on the traditional subjects of labour law using the narrowly drawn, and historically short-lived, contractual nexus (see Knegt) risks ignoring others dependent on their labour for a living (see Pietrogiovanni).

As the chapters in this section demonstrate, a broader perspective for labour law reinforces that markets are not autonomous and self-generating (Knegt), and

[15] Constitution of the International Labour Organization (ILO Constitution) Preamble, available at www.ilo.org/global/about-the-ilo/history/lang--en/index.htm accessed 7 January 2019.

shows the importance of national or transnational policy in constituting, structuring, and mobilising those markets (Rodgers). Carefully targeted regulation provides a means of doing all three. Labour demand is driven by broader economic policy and that has an important impact on how labour markets are constituted, and what labour standards can be achieved. In seeking to protect, expand, and enhance those standards, the democratic and social justice functions of labour law should remain its primary drivers, so that our understandings of where the discipline has come from can shape its current conceptualisation and effect – in the words of Michel Foucault, 'to let knowledge of the past work on the experience of the present'.[16]

[16] Foucault, *Birth of Biopolitics* (n 6) 30.

PART B

Revitalising the Role of Collective Representation

6

Back to the Future: Rediscovering the Non-Economic Role, Value and Scope of Labour Law and Collective Labour Institutions in a Changing World

FOTIS VERGIS*

I. Introduction

'All this has happened before; and all this will happen again.' It is rare for a historian, a biblical[1] or Marxist[2] scholar, or simply a fan of modern fairy-tales[3] or good contemporary sci-fi to converge on a statement they all can agree on. However, the value of drawing lessons from our socio-political past to understand and address the seemingly novel challenges of the present should not escape our attention. As we observe, often bewildered, the rapidness with which contemporary social, economic, political and technological developments unfold, we barely have time to grasp the full details of the changes they bring about. The frantic pace makes it appear as if our traditional analytical and theoretic constants – our fundamental assumptions – are inadequate to grasp the new reality and in dire need of revision. In a world economy that is, in developed economies, post-Fordist and increasingly deregulated for the sake of flexibility and which, in developing countries, almost mirrors the appalling conditions of early Fordist industrialised production, traditional conceptions of labour law and its mechanisms are increasingly perceived as ill-equipped to provide a coherent framework for labour protection. Regulatory concepts and institutional structures, embedded in post-World War II western social regulation, reflect not only bygone production models but also the balance of political and market forces' power as it existed at a fixed point in time that now seems ancient.

* Lecturer in Law, School of Law, The University of Manchester.

[1] Ecclesiastes 1:9.

[2] K Marx, *The Eighteenth Brumaire of Louis Bonaparte* (New York, International Pub Co, 1852).

[3] The phrase is the opening line of the 1953 animated film 'Peter Pan'.

However, reinventing the wheel might not be necessary. Perhaps all we have to do is take a breath, go back and remember the lessons of the past on how and to what end labour law and its collective labour institutions first came about. This chapter proposes going back to the historical and conceptual roots of collective labour organisation, to recall the value of the concept of labour itself, and the objectives of the mechanisms that emerged to ensure its protection from coercion and abuse of power.

It is certainly possible to rethink the role and function of collective mechanisms within a market economy, and suggest that balance is possible, by placing our discussion in the dominant narrative, which focuses on the economic aspect and effect of labour institutions, and adopting a similarly retrospective rationale. In that case, our dive into the past would entail reconnecting with institutional and neoclassical economic theory to reveal the fallacies of contemporary dominant economic theses, influenced by neoliberal musings, that display an aversion to labour rights and collective labour institutions, as they consider them 'externalities', rather than inherent features of the market and the economic system as a whole. However, such a discussion would exceed the scope and space this chapter can afford.

Similar conclusions to such an economic analysis can be reached by moving away from the economic rationale that has dominated discourse to date. This chapter seeks to reconnect the concept of 'labour', the fundamental core of the protective nexus of labour law, to its normative content, as an element of identity and social recognition. By examining the political history and the theoretical basis of the emergence of collective labour institutions, the chapter discusses the role of collective labour organisation and action as an inherent catalyst for market democratisation and, therefore, as a prerequisite for a functional liberal democracy. By looking into the historical roots of labour law, collective autonomy and self-determination – as opposed to top-down regulation – will be shown to be the foundations of fundamental labour law concepts and ensuing rights. Furthermore, building upon ideas expressed by Karl Polanyi and Hugo Sinzheimer, among others, solidaristic structures of collective expression of voice are demonstrated to be integral in embedding the economy in its socio-political context, inducing structural systemic democratisation, and promoting an ethos of participation.

II. Collective Labour Law and the Challenges of the Modern Global Economy

The non-economic value of labour law and collective labour processes has almost receded into obscurity in the judicial and political understanding and approach of recent years. In fact, reference to the 'social' nature of labour rights is often used to highlight the suggested discrepancy between social and economic rights, and perpetuate the perception that collective labour institutions are almost by definition directly at odds with economic rights, as interpreted by reference to established economic rationales. In that respect, collective labour institutions are merely tolerated insofar as the primacy of economic freedoms and interests is not found to be at risk.

This understanding of collective labour law, however, is hardly definitive. Rather, it merely reflects a very particular strand of thought rooted in neoclassical economic theory.[4] Such a narrow economocentric approach, based on a very specific understanding of economic theory, essentially allows analyses to ignore the constitutive role of collective institutions and the inherent symbiotic relationship of institutional mechanisms and their societal and socio-political context.[5]

Further, this predominantly economic approach conveniently obscures the dynamic essence of collective labour institutions. It presents them as a more or less fixed, albeit not entirely desirable, fixture of an economic system that is in itself largely a given constant judged against the aspired golden standard of the rational, competitive free market economy. What is conveniently downplayed, if not entirely forgotten, is that labour law and its institutions might be a fixture of the modern capitalist system, but they are not a *conditio sine qua non* of the aspired free market standard of neoclassical theory, nor were they ever a given. On the contrary, they were forged in the conflicts[6] that followed the early industrialisation of labour[7] and the emerging need to rebalance the worker/employer relationship within a system of organised mass production.

Labour law systems and relevant legal conceptions across Western Europe, now seen as the 'traditional' rigid systemic fixtures that ought to be reconsidered as antithetical to market flexibility, emerged as a response to challenges brought about by the full adoption of the Fordist model of mass production, its ensuing narrow specialisation of labour[8] and the reorganisation of businesses into the

[4] See, inter alia, GR Boyer and RS Smith, 'The Development of the Neoclassical Tradition in Labor Economics' (2001) 54 *Industrial & Labour Relations Review* 199; see also W Lord Wedderburn, *Employment Rights in Britain and Europe* (London, Lawrence and Wishart, 1991) 204 discussing a Thatcherite interpretation of Hayek anti-union sentiments.

[5] See N MacCormick, *Institutions of Law: An Essay in Legal Theory* (Oxford, Oxford University Press, 2007) 171–240.

[6] T Van den Bergh, *The Trade Unions: What Are They?* (Oxford, Pergamon Press, 1970) 3–4. Van den Bergh provides a series of accounts of the history of industrial conflicts in the UK labour market, which evolved alongside the industrialised capitalist economy.

[7] See S Deakin and F Wilkinson, *The Law of the Labour Market: Industrialization, Employment, and Legal Evolution* (Oxford, Oxford University Press, 2005) 11–18, 34–35, 108 (also, see 4–18, 00–05); BE Kaufman, 'Labor Law and Employment Regulation: Neoclassical and Institutional Perspectives' in DS Kenneth, S Harris and O Lobel (eds), *Labor and Employment Law and Economics* (Cheltenham, Edward Elgar, 2009) 3.

[8] A Supiot, *Beyond Employment: Changes in Work and the Future of Labour Law in Europe* (Oxford, Oxford University Press, 2005) 1.

model of the hierarchical workplace, usually as a centralised, largely self-contained unit.[9] The resulting traditional institutional paradigm took the form of a labour market regulatory structure constructed upon the twin pillars of autonomous regulation through collective bargaining and of the welfare state.[10] The economic rationale for sacrificing some freedom from regulatory intervention in the market and slightly retreating from the individualistic ideal of the worker as a rational economic actor in favour of more collective processes was to ensure a standard of living for workers that would induce consumption, completing and perpetuating a stable mass production-mass consumption cycle.[11]

However, the ground upon which the institutional apparatus of labour law was built has since shifted, as the world moved towards today's meta post-Fordist[12] globalised economy. This new mass-consumption-driven paradigm is founded upon transnational, integrally connected markets which have free movement of capital, production and services and are focused on unrestrained competition.[13]

This shift has been followed by the incorporation into theory and policy of a combination of neoclassical, post-Fordist and post-modern[14] market characteristics, such as an individualistic ethos and an aversion to trade unionism and labour market self-regulation through collective labour law mechanisms.[15] Increasing emphasis on the globalised free market ideal, devoid of any regulatory

[9] ibid.

[10] A Lipietz, 'Post-Fordism and Democracy' in A Amin (ed), *Post-Fordism Reader* (Oxford, Blackwell, 1994) 342. See also G Esping-Andersen, *The Three Worlds of Welfare Capitalism* (Cambridge, Polity Press, 1990).

[11] Lipietz, 'Post-Fordism and Democracy' (n 10).

[12] The term 'post-Fordism' is ambiguous and has been used in an attempt to describe many a characteristic of market and production modernisation (technologic advance, 'flexible specialisation', post-industrialism and shift to services, to name a few). Post-Fordism has thus been criticised as a vague and inaccurate concept of convenience. See A Amin, 'Post-Fordism: Models, Fantasies and Phantoms of Transition' in A Amin (ed), *Post-Fordism: A Reader* (Oxford, Blackwell, 1994) 1–39; R Munck, 'Labour Dilemmas and Labour Futures' in R Munck and P Waterman (eds), *Labour Worldwide in the Era of Globalization* (Oxford, Palgrave MacMillan, 1999) 10. *cf* K Kumar, *From Post-Industrial to Post-Modern Society: New Theories of the Contemporary World*, 2nd edn (Oxford, Blackwell, 2005) 61ff (87–88). It is for this reason that Munck has warned against identifying a clear divide between 'Fordism' and Post-'Fordism' as two supposedly coherent distinct stages of the evolution of capitalist market economy: Munck, 'Labour Dilemmas and Labour Futures' 5; *cf* K Williams, T Cutler, J Williams and C Haslam, 'The End of Mass Production?' (1987) 16 *Economy and Society* 405, 438.

[13] Munck, 'Labour Dilemmas and Labour Futures' (n 12) 10; R Smith, 'The Convergence/Divergence Debate in Comparative Industrial Relations' in M Rigby, R Smith and T Lawlor (eds), *European Trade Unions: Change and Response* (London, Routledge, 1999) 11.

[14] The term alludes to aesthetic, ethical, moral and cultural characteristics, shaped in part by the evolution of economic structures. See, inter alia, D Harvey, *The Condition of Postmodernity: An Inquiry into the Origins of Cultural Change* (Oxford, Blackwell, 1989). *cf* P Anderson, *The Origins of Postmodernity* (London, Verso, 1998); F Jameson, *The Cultural Turn: Selected Writings on the Postmodern, 1983–1998* (London, Verso, 1998); A Callinicos, *Against Postmodernism: A Marxist Critique* (Cambridge, Polity, 1989). For a fiercer critique see A Sokal and J Bricmont, *Fashionable Nonsense: Postmodern Intellectuals' Abuse of Science* (New York, Picador, 1998).

[15] M Rustin, 'The Politics of Post-Fordism: Or, the Trouble with "New Times"' (1989) May–June *New Left Review* 54, 61–62.

intervention (including on the basis of collective autonomy) that would impede competitiveness and set upon further promoting 'flexibility' of labour forms and relations, ultimately reflects a neoclassical, and increasingly neoliberal,[16] evolution[17] of capitalist market economies on a global scale. The rapid pace at which this change has unfolded in recent decades has brought with it a radical departure[18] from familiar norms, structures and their certainties,[19] leading Scott Lash and John Urry to describe the result as 'disorganised capitalism'.[20]

This paradigm change, therefore, demanded established collective labour institutions to reconnect with their dynamic element, which had always grounded them in socioeconomic and political reality, and had been the power that defined their character since their emergence. It was this element that had allowed such institutions the flexibility to adapt to the changing demands of the evolving market and production system, on the one hand, and the readiness to act as a countervailing force against violent changes that would threaten the interests of workers on the other. Instead of this essential reboot, however, decentralisation and the emphasis on establishment-level labour relations,[21] in conjunction with the advent of flexible and atypical work relations, had a significant impact on the strength and role of trade unions, even in relation to their narrower function as market actors and co-regulators.[22] Perhaps more importantly, trade unions, displaying the instinctive rigidity that established institutions develop in lieu of the more dynamic character of their early days, instead of resisting or reinventing themselves[23] to better connect with their changing base and its needs, apparently chose to embrace the new ethos and attempt to adapt to contemporary economic rationales of efficiency and productivity as their primary focus,[24] essentially accepting the argument that achieving these aims for the business would trigger the 'trickling down' of benefits for workers. In other words, trade unions essentially conceded to a purely economic understanding of their role.

[16] According to Rustin, 'Thatcherism may be understood as a strategy of post-Fordism initiated from the perspective of the right': ibid 75. See also D Harvey, *A Brief History of Neoliberalism* (Oxford, Oxford University Press, 2007) 13–19; C Crouch, *The Strange Non-Death of Neoliberalism* (Cambridge, Polity Press, 2011).

[17] RJ Antonio and A Bonanno, 'A New Global Capitalism? From "Americanism and Fordism" to "Americanization-Globalization"' (2000) 41 *American Studies* 33.

[18] See Supiot, *Beyond Employment* (n 8) 283, 50.

[19] S Lash and J Urry, *The End of Organised Capitalism* (Cambridge, Polity, 1987) 312–13. *cf* F Traxler, 'Collective Bargaining and Industrial Change: A Case of Disorganization? A Comparative Analysis of Eighteen OECD Countries' (1996) 12 *European Sociological Review* 271, who is critical of the disorganisation thesis as a synonym of a linear, unavoidable (or 'deterministic', at 272) and unitary (at 275) process of convergent deconstruction. However, he does concede to evidence of shifts in perceptions, structures and paradigms, albeit resulting in diversity and multiplicity rather than convergence (at 279–83).

[20] Lash and Urry, *The End of Organised Capitalism* (n 19).

[21] R Hyman, 'European Unions: Towards 2000' (1991) 5 *Work, Employment and Society* 621, 626–27.

[22] Smith, 'The Convergence/Divergence Debate in Comparative Industrial Relations' (n 13) 11.

[23] Supiot, *Beyond Employment* (n 8) 50–51.

[24] W Streeck, *Social Institutions and Economic Performance: Studies of Industrial Relations in Advanced Capitalist Economies* (Londen, Sage, 1992).

This retreat to economic pragmatism, however, also inherently includes the adoption of a more conciliatory ethos, that impliedly accepts a commonality of interests between labour and management. This is a stark departure from the conscious understanding of the inherent conflict of interests in the unbalanced power relationship between workers and their employer that had been the foundation of the identity of trade unions as vehicles of collective expression of workers' interests and instruments designed to rebalance the relationship not only through negotiation and conciliation but also coercion. This change in stance has arguably contributed to trade unions losing their 'representational credibility'[25] in the eyes of individual workers and their position in the collective imagination as actors of not only an economic, but also a social and political, role.

It could be maintained, then, that a narrow economic understanding of collective labour law as a mainly cooperative institution within the context of advancing the interests of the business, as a supposed all-encompassing unitary whole, has contributed to the 'disaggregation of the working class'[26] into isolated business-related pockets of workers with no sense of commonality, and hence no broader solidarity and interconnection.[27]

However, the ideological dominance of a particular economic theory should not result in us adopting its assumptions as religious dogma, setting aside all other analyses or, indeed, disregarding the reality that led to the emergence of certain institutions. The non-economic objectives and functions of labour law, in general, and collective labour institutions, in particular, are critical and remain topical, regardless of the evolution of market structures.

III. Collective Labour Law as an Instrument in the Service of Social, Democratic, and Political Values and Objectives

The 'social' element of labour law has largely provided the core of traditional analyses as well as the popular understanding of the function and utility of labour regulation. Regardless of the form of political or economic mantle under which a human community operates, people are inherently dependent on each other[28] and on the subsequent social and legal structures that govern human labour

[25] R Hyman, 'Trade Unions and the Disaggregation of the Working Class' in M Regini (ed), *The Future of Labour Movements*, 2nd edn (London, Sage, 1994) 150.

[26] ibid 150ff.

[27] ibid 151.

[28] See GWF Hegel, *Elements of the Philosophy of Right* (AW Wood ed, H Nisbet tr, Cambridge, Cambridge University Press, 1991) §183, 221, 189, 227. See also T Kohler, 'Civic Virtue at Work: Unions as Seedbeds of the Civic Virtues' (1995) 36 *Boston College Law Review* 279, 295.

and its organisation.[29] This interdependence manifests as the interconnection of the outcomes of each individual's labour to produce the necessary means of subsistence[30] for all, but it also describes the cooperative element inherent in work and in any labour market as a whole.[31] In that sense, labour, its function and the organisation of its provision and division, have a dual, individual and collective, character, relevant to the basic individual needs of labourers, on the one hand, but also to the fundamental political and social structures of any given society on the other.[32] Therefore, any economic system cannot by itself define, regulate or explain its structures. There will always arise a social impetus to reconnect economic arrangements and conceptions back to considerations that relate to the individual, as well as the collective, element of the society and polity she lives in. Within that context, after all, individuals are identified and defined in their three, inherently coalescent, capacities: as persons, as bourgeois citizens (members of a particular societal configuration and the classes therein), and members of a particular political community, a particular polity.[33]

Workers retain these three capacities, even as labour actors, in their activity within the workplace. The multiple functions of collective labour law structures correspond to considerations that are relevant to each of those, be it individualistic (eg, economic freedom and interests) or collective (eg, solidaristic or class-related) in nature. In that respect, trade unions act as hubs of socialisation and democratisation within a market structure, allowing these three properties of individual activity to emerge in the workplace, and their broader social and political effects to be mirrored in that context. Trade unions are as much economic institutions as they are elements of civic society. As such, they reflect and promote communal values, such as cooperation, solidarity and the sense of human interdependence and commonality of interests, as opposed to the individualistic, selfish ethos,[34] the 'atomism ascendant',[35] of neoclassical economic perceptions.[36]

[29] NH Smith and JP Deranty, *New Philosophies of Labour: Work and the Social Bond* (Leiden, Brill, 2012) 6.

[30] Hegel, *Elements of the Philosophy of Right* (n 28) §182–83, 220–21; Smith and Deranty, *New Philosophies of Labour* (n 29).

[31] Smith and Deranty, *New Philosophies of Labour* (n 29).

[32] See, eg, JA McCartin, *Labor's Great War: The Struggle for Industrial Democracy and the Origins of Modern American Labor Relations, 1912-1921* (Chapel Hill, University of North Carolina Press, 1997) 95, where 3 primary workers' demands are highlighted: those for a rule of law in the workplace, for workers' voice in the determination of working condition, and for claiming workers' rights as citizens through their labour.

[33] HC Schmidt am Busch, 'The Legacy of Hegelian Philosophy and the Future of Critical Theory' in NH Smith and JP Deranty (eds), *New Philosophies of Labour: Work and the Social Bond* (Leiden, Brill, 2012) 63, 71.

[34] Kohler, 'Civic Virtue at Work' (n 28) 294–96.

[35] ibid 295.

[36] P Levine, 'The Legitimacy of Labor Unions' (2001) 18 *Hofstra Labor & Employment Law Journal* 529, 559–60.

A. Collective Labour Institutions as a Catalyst of Social Re-Embedding of the 'Market Economy'

It follows that, in Polanyian terms, collective labour institutions can provide an anchor for re-embedding the market in its specific social context, coupling economic considerations with their inherent social base.

For Polanyi, the neoclassical idea of a self-calibrating market, that is neutral and can exist outside and beyond social and legal frameworks, is a fallacy.[37] The market, as socially constructed, is always inherently connected with specific social structures, institutions, and norms, and with specific political choices.[38] It is impossible to commodify everything, turning the entirety of human behaviour and activity into something that can be objectively explained by the rules of trade or economic rationales.

Human labour, in particular, is for Polanyi a 'fictitious commodity'. It was never intended as something to be 'produced' and 'traded' in a market like any other commodity, thereby following the market's 'natural' laws.[39] It is a human activity that cannot be detached from its multiple functions,[40] including as a catalyst of personal self-awareness and development, as an expression of the worker's very physical, 'moral, psychological and moral' entity[41] and identity, and as a vehicle of social participation.[42] Therefore, labour cannot be entirely stripped down to its economic value, to be construed as merely a market commodity, despite the need for its economic function to be regulated to fit particular economic structures, the latest of which is the modern capitalist market.[43] There cannot be a market that exists outside and beyond specific social, political and legal institutions, which support the human web that constitutes the very fabric of the economy.[44]

Any effort to 'disembed' the economy from society will inevitably lead to strains that will, in turn, result in resistance. That is the essence of Polanyi's double movement thesis:[45] dislocating the economy from its social context will undoubtedly result in a social reaction[46] to bring the economy and society back together.

Resistance, however, can take either of two forms: it can manifest as disorderly reaction via revolts and social unrest or, alternatively, it can be funnelled through

[37] K Polanyi, *The Great Transformation: The Political and Economic Origins of Our Time*, 2nd edn (Boston, Beacon Press, 2001) 1–2.
[38] ibid 2.
[39] ibid 75.
[40] ibid.
[41] ibid 76.
[42] ibid.
[43] ibid 72–79.
[44] K Veitch, 'Law, Social Policy, and the Constitution of Markets and Profit Making' (2013) 40 *Journal of Law and Society* 137.
[45] See Polanyi, *The Great Transformation* (n 37) 136–40.
[46] ibid 156–57.

pre-existing democratic institutions. Collective organisation is one such democratic hub that, by definition, exists to couple economic and social considerations and infuse democratic ethos in the labour market. In that respect, Polanyi meets Sinzheimer. The Polanyian objective of balance and re-connection of the economy to society through democratisation is served by the democratisation of the economy itself. That, according to Sinzheimer, is the ultimate goal of collective labour law and its institutions.[47]

It is the inherent interconnectivity of any economic system that regulates labour to social considerations and to the autonomy of the individual that informs the Hegelian idea of the necessity of an 'ethical basis'[48] of the economy, which operates as a moral anchor.[49] In other words, any economic system must take into account and cater for social considerations and relevant objectives, functioning as part of a coherent whole which encompasses the political, the social and the economic. In turn, by doing so, a socially embedded economic system can be accepted by its actors and thus be perceived as morally,[50] and therefore socially and politically, legitimate. This holistic picture of any socioeconomic system resonates with the thesis of the fundamental socioeconomic duality of the function of collective labour law.

The social element of that duel character operates at both the individual and the collective level. Collective labour rights can be understood as a factor safeguarding individual autonomy, ensuring a dignified life and personal development. However, collective institutions are also critical in the formation of social identity and culture.

In that respect, the working class, as the broad social cell through which a worker perceives her social identity and status, is not to be entirely economically construed, in the traditional Marxian fashion. It may start with the position one has within the market, but it might be better understood as a broader concept that encapsulates all aspects of social identity and experience, and involves a communion of not only overarching interests, but also of experiences, fundamental relation patterns, needs and consumption habits, community and political life.[51] In turn, in a world where globalisation of capitalism has not yet led to complete homogeneity, this working class experience, if not the perception of class itself, is influenced by specific social and state structures, as well as by perceptions of different racial,

[47] R Dukes, 'Constitutionalizing Employment Relations: Sinzheimer, Kahn-Freund, and the Role of Labour Law' (2008) 35 *Journal of Law and Society* 341, 346; R Dukes, *The Labour Constitution: The Enduring Idea of Labour Law* (Oxford, Oxford University Press, 2014) 18–19.

[48] Smith and Deranty, *New Philosophies of Labour* (n 29) 17–18.

[49] A Honneth, 'Work and Recognition: A Redefinition' in HC Schmidt am Busch and C Zurn (eds), *The Philosophy of Recognition: Historical and Contemporary Perspectives* (Plymouth, Lexington Books, 2010) 229–30.

[50] ibid 230; Smith and Deranty, *New Philosophies of Labour* (n 29) 17.

[51] E Arnesen, J Greene and B Laurie, *Labor Histories: Class, Politics and the Working Class Experience* (Chicago, University of Illinois Press, 1998) 4.

ethnical, regional or even gender paradigms.[52] The result is often that the working class is initially constructed on the basis of a fragmented consciousness formed by already existing prejudices and dividing lines.

This formational process through, and despite, pre-existing fragmentations was evident in the United States (US) in the early days of the labour movement. In a land of extreme diversity, with cultural, ethnic or even religious lines clearly dividing the minds of workers, unions initially formed around those traditional societal divisions.[53] As a consequence, prejudice and antagonisms ensued.[54] However, over time what prevailed was the commonality of needs, experiences and industrial struggle, and the gradual emergence of a shared consciousness; a sense of belonging to a community, a class, on the basis of worker status, and not because of traditional divisions, but through them.[55] An illustrative example was the revolt of garment worker representatives in 1914, forged in the fire of unyielding strikes that preceded it,[56] against the old establishment of union elites that had tried to maintain racial divides as a means of controlling the Union of Garment Workers (UGW) and the American Federation of Labor (AFL).[57] The worker base demanded and eventually succeeded in bringing about change in the structure and ethos of the union itself, to reflect the sentiment it had voiced in the 1914 AFL convention: 'Let us unite in order to fight our common enemy, capitalism, instead of picking suicidal quarrels among ourselves.'[58] The socialising force that allowed for the transcendence of old lines of segregation and suspicion was the presence and operation of collective labour law institutions and the interaction and discourse they fostered.

However, commonality of interests and collective mobilisation can also transcend the traditional institutional structures of collective autonomy. It is useful

[52] ibid.

[53] M Dubofsky and F R Dulles, *Labor in America: A History*, 8th edn (Wheeling, Harlan Davidson 2010) 72. See, eg, references in the creation of unions along national/ethnic lines (of Greeks, Italians and Mexicans) in GW Peck, 'Mobilizing Community: Migrant Workers and the Politics of Labor Mobility in the North American West, 1900–1920' in E Arnesen, J Greene and B Laurie (eds), *Labor Histories: Class, Politics and the Working Class Experience* (Chicago, University of Illinois Press, 1998) 175–200; or racial lines (African American/white unions) in E Arnesen, 'Charting an Independent Course: African American Railroad Workers in the World War I Era' in E Arnesen, J Greene and B Laurie (eds), *Labor Histories: Class, Politics and the Working Class Experience* (Chicago, University of Illinois Press, 1998) 284–308.

[54] See Arnesen, 'Charting an Independent Course' (n 53) 296–302.

[55] An excellent example is revolt of the multinational force of Colorado Miners in 1913–1914, comprising workers of 21 nationality groups, led by Louis Tikas and resulting in the infamous Ludlow Massacre of 1914. See S Martelle, *Blood Passion: The Ludlow Massacre and Class War in the American West* (London, Rutgers, 2007); Z Papanikolas, *Buried Unsung: Louis Tikas and the Ludlow Massacre* (Salt Lake City, University of Utah Press, 1982); W Fink, *The Ludlow Massacre* (New York 1971, 1st edn 1914, Denver, Williamson-Haffner, 1914).

[56] P Foner, *History of the Labor Movement in the United States Volume V: The AFL in the Progressive Era, 1910–1915* (New York, International Publishers, 1980) 226–56.

[57] ibid 260–64.

[58] CE Zaretz, *The Amalgamated Clothing Workers of America: A Study in Progressive Trade-Unionism* (New York, Ancon Publishing Company, 1934) 96.

to note that while these specific structures and mechanisms were put in place to organise collective mobilisation, they also had the effect of reigning in its force within specific preordained boundaries, including the scope of participation and coverage. Transcendence of those formal boundaries in practice, due to the substantive commonality of interests and of broader groups of de facto (but not necessarily *de lege* in any given legal order) workers signals the need of change as regards the institutional nexus of collective labour relations itself. An early institutionalist like John Commons, writing in 1913, while discussing obstacles to the emergence of class consciousness among unionised workers in early twentieth century US, pointed to immigration and, therefore, racial, ethnic and religious tensions and ensuing antipathy, as a factor that would 'undermine'[59] and, eventually, 'shatter'[60] class solidarity. Commons was of course referring to the oldest trick in the book: the use of immigrant workers as the scapegoat for the plight of the 'domestic' working class. By employing low-paid and non-unionised immigrant workers to circumvent established trade unions and their coercive mobilisation, employers also succeeded in aggravating racial and religious antipathies, effectively diverging workers' focus away from the commonalities of their status and experience that could incite class consciousness. The solution, according to Commons, was the prohibition or radical limitation of immigration,[61] rather than the integration of immigrant workers into existing communities and their collective labour institutions or, indeed, the transformation of those communal and institutional structures themselves under the effect and influence of their new members. Commons was desperate to see that trade union structures, those newly formed institutions which had finally endowed disorganised labour with a structural framework, be allowed to breathe and function, without any external factor distorting the delicate balance upon which they had been built.

Institutions, however, are shaped, and can be transformed by the communal bonds that emerge out of necessity, as a result of common experience. These bonds are revealed through the raw social function of collective organisation, irrespective of whether this process is dominated by already established internal groups and union elites (as in the case of UGW and AFL) or whether it can even be made to fit pre-existing institutional frameworks.

Commons had already been proven wrong a few years before his assumptions about the obstacles to achieving class consciousness. The summer of 1909, in McKees Rock, Pennsylvania, saw the eruption of the steel workers strike against Press Steel Car Co and the might of US Steel.[62] The company, one of

[59] J Commons, *Labor and Administration* (New York, MacMillan, 1913) 78.

[60] ibid 79.

[61] ibid. *cf* Dubofsky and Dulles, *Labor in America* (n 53) 88, who point out that, of course, immigration was not really the determinant obstacle to the attainment of labour's goals.

[62] JN Ingham, 'A Strike in the Progressive Era: McKees Rocks, 1909' (1966) 90 *The Pennsylvania Magazine of History and Biography* 353; A Snyder, 'A Window of Solidarity in Steel: McKees Rocks,

the largest railroad cars manufacturers in the US, had embraced the tactic of employing immigrant labour (mostly of Slavic, East-European origin), subjected to appalling living conditions and inhumane abuse[63] and, of course, devoid of institutional representation through established structures. The straw that broke the proverbial camel's back was a pay-related grievance.[64] An ethnically diverse and unorganised workforce of 3,500 immigrant steel workers[65] of 16 different nationalities rose quickly to challenge not just the employer but also, and perhaps more importantly, the representatives of 'native' workers and their unions, who attempted to control the strike and steer the relevant negotiations. Though the unorganised immigrants initially achieved the rejection of agreements negotiated supposedly on their behalf that would amount to capitulation, ultimately they were overwhelmed by the 'native' representatives who dismissed 'the violence of the uneducated Slavs' and proceeded to reach a settlement with management, enforce the return to work, impose their established institutions and, patronisingly, create a night-school programme to 'educate' immigrant workers on American institutions.[66]

It was clear that those who embraced established collective labour institutions at the time were sceptical and underprepared for,[67] if not completely averse to,[68] 'foreigners' who did not necessarily share their own societal and political perceptions, including as regards the role, function and objectives of collective mechanisms and their means of reaction. Nevertheless, McKees Rock proved that not only were 'unorganisable' immigrants perfectly capable of organising, but also that, through the shared experience with local workers, they were capable of inviting and inciting the support of their base, slowly building a community and common identity that would ultimately, and relatively quickly, come to inform and affect the institutional establishment over the following years and decades. In fact, by World War I new unions had emerged (such as the Amalgamated Clothing Workers of America (ACWA) in the garment and clothing sector) by achieving the successful organisation of 'unorganisable' immigrants, but also by attracting women and ensuring that they would have equal status and role to their male colleagues,[69] irrevocably changing the formerly dominant trade union paradigm.

1909' (2000) *Honors Theses Paper* 5, https://knowledge.library.iup.edu/honors_theses/5/ accessed 20 December 2018.

[63] Ingham, 'A Strike in the Progressive Era' (n 62) 354–55; Snyder, 'A Window of Solidarity in Steel' (n 62) 6–8.

[64] Snyder, 'A Window of Solidarity in Steel' (n 62) 359.

[65] ibid 371.

[66] ibid 372.

[67] B Ramirez, *When Workers Fight: the Politics of Industrial Relations in the Progressive Era, 1898–1916* (Connecticut, Greenwod Press, 1978) 136–37.

[68] Ingham, 'A Strike in the Progressive Era' (n 62) 376–77.

[69] Dubofsky and Dulles, *Labor in America* (n 53) 188.

This important community and collective identity building function of collective labour institutions is often overlooked in mainstream discussion. As Gordon Clark argued, this function and the inter-community solidarity it fostered have been 'overwhelmed'[70] by economic imperatives and financial objectives that transcend the traditional localised community and have ascended to become the absolute priority. Throughout his work looking into the history of organised labour in the Cold War period (1950s–1989),[71] Clark demonstrated and emphasised the absolute interconnectivity between specific communities and their local conditions, unions, and collective labour institutions. What Clark uncovered was that the rise, life, and decline of unionism cannot be disassociated from its spatial context, that is, from the particular characteristics and divides that define the community in which union structures emerge and which unionism serves.

As a result, even the often cited problems of representativeness and membership decline that have plagued trade unions in recent decades in the US, but, also, arguably, throughout the Western world, should not merely be attributed to the supposed adverse effect union structures have on economic efficiency and, thus, on the economy as a whole, which leads to reduced profits and, thereby, reduced returns for workers and employers alike. On the contrary, a more thoughtful and holistic approach could reveal the effect geographical divides[72] and local interests can have on any attempt to form a single collective voice capable of expressing the interests of unionised, yet geographically fragmented, workers. However, as Lash and Urry's 'disorganised' capitalism is also 'dislocated': globalised and inherently fluid and mobile. Corporate strategies transcend local and national boundaries, as does the capability of transnational capital to weather, if not completely nullify, the presumed adverse effects (not merely the purely economic cost)[73] that collective worker mobilisation can have, by simply relocating[74] its operations. This inherent capacity of capital and production mobility can disjoint unionisation from its spatial and social context, making it harder for community bonds to emerge and give rise to credible union structures as their institutional vehicle and voice. This mobility, then, could present one plausible explanation for the decline in union density and membership in recent years.

Overall, failing to understand the complex social communal character of collective labour institutions leads to a monolithic, one-dimensional approach towards them that misses the complexity of their functions and objectives.[75] In turn, this approach leads to the marginalisation of another process that builds on

[70] G Clark, *Unions and Communities under Siege: American Communities and the Crisis of Organized Labor* (Cambridge, Cambridge University Press, 1989) ix.

[71] ibid.

[72] ibid 40.

[73] ibid 53–56.

[74] ibid 45–66.

[75] ibid 40.

social bonds and re-organises them into forms and institutions that facilitate the constitution of a community into a particular political system which prioritises this sense of commonality: democracy.

B. Collective Labour Rights as the Vehicle of Market Democratisation

What labour law analyses often forget is that the mere existence of labour law institutions, especially those related to collective autonomy, is the product of an intense political struggle that was not conceived as narrowly as the contractual context that usually constitutes the basis of legal interpretation. Collective labour law was born out of the sweat and blood of massive movements demanding not only bargaining equality, but also dignity, control of the tyrannical paradigm of the employer as absolute sovereign and, ultimately, a share in the power to determine the norms and orders imposed on them.[76] In other words, the labour movement that pushed the state and the courts to create the set of principles and statutory norms that would effectively create a new field of law (today taken for granted), was analogous in its fundamental aspirations and development to the popular and political movements that dragged the western world out of the systemic middle ages of monarchy, feudalism and aristocracy, into the modern era of liberal western democracy.

It is important to recall that both these movements were not so much, if at all, concerned with the economic characteristics of the market or the effects of regulation on its structure and perceived qualities. The focus was on countering autocratic control of the lives of workers and citizens respectively by demanding the exercise of authority through democratic processes and respect of fundamental rights. Workers did not see themselves as merely elements of an economic framework (and a relevant normative structure that was to be taken for granted and in isolation from its context), but as societal and political actors as well. And although early movements could not necessarily articulate exactly what their demand for 'democracy in the industry' entailed, they had a gut feeling that such a demand was not only natural, but indeed patriotic,[77] the logical extension of their civic duties and entitlements and the normal corollary of a democratic polity.

Indeed, as Nelson Lichtenstein and Howell John Harris remark, the term 'industrial democracy'[78] in the US, at its initial conception and emergence,

[76] Indicatively, for an overview of the US example, and the political characteristics and variety of demands and objectives relating to worker struggles therein, see Ramirez, *When Workers Fight* (n 67).

[77] McCartin, *Labor's Great War* (n 32) 1, 7.

[78] See also D Milton, *The American Idea of Industrial Democracy, 1865–1965* (Chicago, University of Illinois Press, 1970).

was practically understood to mean something broader than mere collective bargaining. It was construed to signal the penetration of democratic principles and values into production processes and industry, and to indicate that 'industry', or the labour market, should conform to the democratic character of the political culture and systemic and constitutional framework that constitute its context.[79]

Consequently, the demand for the creation of labour standards and institutions was ultimately a demand for democratisation and systemic fairness. Its realisation unfolded through conflict and concessions at the social and political level, that went beyond industry or the labour market and engulfed national politics,[80] before the outcomes became mantled in legal theories and arguments and transposed into legal norms.

i. Workplace Democratisation

Some early collectivist constructions of the phrase 'industrial democracy' in the US, adopted by activists[81] and certain workers' factions, effectively implied collective ownership of the means of production and collectivisation of industry.[82] Conditions of employment and the division of profits ought to be determined by workers themselves; work supervisors ought to be chosen by workers to serve them, and work and production itself should be organised so as to benefit the collective, ensuring equality for all participant labourers.[83]

More conservative American trade unionists of the time, however, espousing a form of 'working-class republicanism'[84] that did not wish for radical departures from the established systemic status quo,[85] adopted a more modest definition. For them, democratising industry simply was the natural extension of citizenship,[86]

[79] N Lichtenstein and HJ Harris, *Industrial Democracy in America: The Ambiguous Promise* (Cambridge, Cambridge University Press, 1993) 2.

[80] McCartin, *Labor's Great War* (n 32) 4–5. McCartin's book is a wonderful account of precisely the interplay between worker movements and industrial demands, on the one hand, and national politics (including multiple complex considerations, from foreign policy and conducting war to dealing with immigration and combating social divisions).

[81] HD Lloyd, *Men, The Workers* (New York, Doubleday, 1909) 91.

[82] Lichtenstein and Harris, *Industrial Democracy in America* (n 79) 4.

[83] Lloyd, *Men, The Workers* (n 81).

[84] Lichtenstein and Harris, *Industrial Democracy in America* (n 79) 3–4.

[85] D Montgomery, 'Industrial Democracy or Democracy in Industry?: The Theory and Practice of the Labor Movement 1870–1925' in N Lichtenstein and HJ Harris (eds), *Industrial Democracy in America: The Ambiguous Promise* (Cambridge, Cambridge University Press, 1993) 41–42. *cf* HJ Harris, 'Industrial Democracy and Liberal Capitalism' in N Lichtenstein and HJ Harris (eds), *Industrial Democracy in America: The Ambiguous Promise* (Cambridge, Cambridge University Press, 1993) 46, noting that the fallacy of the working-class republicanism position is that it disregards the orthodox liberal position that separates the public and private sphere. As the employment relationship is based on economic freedom, encompassing freedom of contract, it sits firmly within the private sphere, and, therefore, transposition of public sphere arguments, principles and mechanisms is inappropriate.

[86] Montgomery, 'Industrial Democracy or Democracy in Industry?' (n 85) 25.

and the fundamental principles and (civil and political) rights it entails, so as to manifest in the context of the market.[87] The relevant unit of potential conflict (establishment; company; sector; industry) ought to be organised in accordance with the principles that govern the relationship between the state and individuals, including the guarantee of fundamental rights and mechanisms that would prevent abuse of power by the dominant authority (in this case, the employer, as analogous to the state). This form of 'industrial citizenship' would be funnelled through specific institutions and mechanisms, with trade unions at their core. That is precisely why, as Clark notes, not just formal electoral processes but, more importantly, electoral *politics*, were transplanted into collective labour institutions in the US straight from the political sphere.[88]

Analysing conditions and developments in the United Kingdom (UK) at the time, Sidney and Beatrice Webb seemed to share the broad tenets of 'working class republicanism' as opposed to ideas of collectivisation of production. The observations, arguments and theories they developed in 1898 under the moniker 'Industrial Democracy'[89] also considered the paradigm of the liberal democratic state as the basis for their examination of the internal workings of trade unions and their counterbalancing role vis-a-vis the dominant authority of the employer. They remarked: 'trade unions are democracies: that is to say, their internal constitutions are all based on the principle of "government of the people by the people for the people"'.[90]

Ultimately, that same paradigm is what Otto Kahn-Freund adopted as the basis for his analysis. For Kahn-Freund, the workplace micro-polity is not to be necessarily organised on the basis of direct democracy, as a commune or a collective. To use his own words, workplace democracy simply means 'that those who have to obey the rules have an active share in making them, and this is true of political as well as of "industrial" democracy'.[91] Therefore, democratisation of the workplace, and hence the market, does not inherently refute the dominant decision-making position of the employer, nor does it entail the nullification of employers' economic freedom. It simply denotes participation in the making of workplace rules through representative agents,[92] and not necessarily absolute codetermination or collective self-administration.

Thus, the more modest model that early US 'working class republicans', UK Institutionalists and traditional scholars such as Kahn-Freund had in mind does not contradict traditional liberal theory and its inherent respect for individual autonomy and economic freedom. In fact, it is entirely compatible with

[87] Lichtenstein and Harris, *Industrial Democracy in America* (n 79) 4.
[88] Clark, *Unions and Communities under Siege* (n 70) 37. See also 91–109.
[89] S Webb and B Webb, *Industrial Democracy*, 2nd edn (London, Longmans, Green and Co, 1902).
[90] ibid v–vi.
[91] P Davies and M Freedland, *Kahn-Freund's Labour and the Law*, 3rd edn (London, Stevens, 1983) 23.
[92] ibid.

that tradition,[93] and therefore with capitalism and the modern version of the labour market. That said, if we are to accept this balanced liberal interpretation, all the features and virtues of the liberal representative polity paradigm are to be transplanted to the workplace:[94] from respect for individual rights, to the democratic processes by which the collective voice of all 'industrial citizens', majority and minority included, is to be expressed by their elected representatives, so as to influence the construction of the norms that affect them. Therefore, not only can collective worker processes and institutions be judged using democracy and democratic theory as a standard, but they constitute a concrete manifestation of democracy and the political method it entails.[95] In fact, the inherent interconnectivity of the social and democratic function of (particularly local) collective labour institutions suggests that they are best suited to act as a primary hub of democracy and democratic expression, due to the immediateness of their processes to their spatial and social context, and to the relationships, particular characteristics and issues that characterise it.[96] Democratic standards and theory applies to both internal trade union democratic procedures and the 'external' process of collective bargaining.

The mechanism of workplace democracy culminates in setting, through collective agreements, norms that ultimately constitute the 'negotiated law'[97] which governs the workplace micro-polity. Collective agreements often go beyond just configuring working conditions. They also establish mechanisms and processes for the resolution of conflict and for providing a fair hearing before the imposition of penalties. Disciplinary and grievance procedures constitute the internal 'judicial' processes of the workplace that ensure accountability and transparency, but also respect for individual rights. This illustrates that collective labour law is the means that guarantees that the workplace mini-polity,[98] as a system of 'industrial self-government',[99] does not merely produce 'negotiated law', but is actually 'governed by an agreed upon rule of law'.[100]

Furthermore, the idea that those who are affected by employment related decisions, norms and conditions are entitled to participate in the regulation of labour, connects with deeper, substantive (rather than merely procedural) democratic

[93] See H Collins, 'Theories of Rights as Justifications for Labour Law' in G Davidov and B Langille (eds), *Boundaries and Frontiers of Labour Law* (Oxford, Hart Publishing, 2006) 144–46.

[94] H Arthurs, 'Landscape and Memory: Labour Law, Legal Pluralism and Globalisation' in T Wilthagen (ed), *Advancing Theory in Labour Law and Industrial Relations in a Global Context* (Amsterdam, North-Holland, 1998) 27–28.

[95] J Barbash, *Labor's Grass Roots: A Study of the Local Union* (Westport, Greenwood Press Publishers, 1974) 215–16.

[96] ibid 240.

[97] A Supiot, *Homo Juridicus: On the Anthropological Function of the Law* (S Brown tr, London, Verso, 2007) 162.

[98] See Webb and Webb, *Industrial Democracy* (n 89) 808.

[99] Steelworkers v. American Mfg. Co., No 363, 363 U.S. 564 (1960), 570.

[100] Kohler, 'Civic Virtue at Work' (n 28) 298.

themes. Freedom from coercion, the need to scrutinise the exercise of power, and the avoidance or peaceful resolution of conflict,[101] are all linked to the idea of participation, and, therefore, the expression of collective voice.[102] These objectives are relevant to the workplace context but also more broadly, crucial for any political community. They constitute rights and expressions of individual freedom[103] for the person in her capacities as both a worker and a citizen. In essence, collective labour institutions are the conduits through which the rule of law is established in the workplace,[104] to curtail the absolute sovereignty of the employer.

Collective labour institutions, therefore, are not merely precursors of conflict and clashes of interest between labour and management. As with any democratic system of governance, their main objective is to promote reconciliation and consensus through mutual concessions and respect of individualism, and to achieve an agreeable balance and peaceful coexistence to the benefit of the whole. Consequently, their existence and effective operation is not antithetical to the unfettered functioning of a free market economy; it is imperative for its balance and stability. Further still, democratising the workplace can ultimately result in the democratisation of the market itself.

Economic analyses of the function of collective labour law, no matter how 'labour-friendly', unavoidably accept the centrality of economic arguments, regardless of the particular school of economic thought they might be derived from. Inherently, therefore, they construe the modern systemic structure of capitalism as a given, seeking only to restrain its effects. By adopting this premise and the theoretical tools it restricts them to, economic approaches inadvertently adopt the fundamental reasoning of the system they seek to restrain, albeit attempting to use it to the benefit of workers. What is ultimately adopted is the basic tenet of the self-regulated market; what is sought is simply an alternate path to self-regulation.

Instead, the real need is to do away with the neoclassical fallacy of the autonomous operation of markets and place them within the social, constitutional and legal environment in which they operate, subduing market forces to the collective choices made by the people the economic system is meant to serve.[105] The democratisation of the market is but a facet of systemic democratisation.

ii. Systemic Democratisation

The democratisation of the market is systemically connected with the democratisation of the society within which the market operates.[106] Substantive market

[101] Davies and Freedland, *Kahn-Freund's Labour and the Law* (n 91) 27.

[102] R Freeman and J Medoff, *What Do Unions Do?* (New York, Basic Books, 1984) 7–11.

[103] Dukes, *The Labour Constitution* (n 47) 30–31.

[104] Kohler, 'Civic Virtue at Work' (n 34); McCartin, *Labor's Great War* (n 32) 95.

[105] *cf* McCartin, *Labor's Great War* (n 32) 206–07.

[106] See Webb and Webb, *Industrial Democracy* (n 89) 842. See also Lichtenstein and Harris, *Industrial Democracy in America* (n 79) for an account of this parallel process in the US context.

democratisation contributes to the overall perception of the legal superstructure as being democratically legitimate, emerging from popular participation and resulting in collective benefit.[107] Any discussion of a democratically regulated polity cannot be insulated from an examination of the degree to which its economic system complies in practice with that polity's fundamental standards of democratic functioning. Equally, any economic system and its inherent processes and institutions cannot be examined without reference to their systemic democratic legal and political context. This highlights the importance of considering, in any analysis, the function and role of labour law[108] and of collective labour mechanisms as its 'democratisation tools'.

Undoubtedly, the economic and social effects that collective organisation produces for individuals can positively impact upon structural systemic democratisation and the promotion of an ethos of participation. Furthermore, substantively, participation in collective labour law structures can benefit the quality of democracy,[109] building upon and going beyond the economic emancipation of workers.

At a basic level, and corollary to the economic function and objective of collective labour law, collective organisation in pursuit of the protection of the narrow economic interests of workers within the workplace can result in their personal and political emancipation. A worker given the chance to participate in the regulation and organisation of her own working conditions and the provision of her labour, and thus to have her own economic freedom fully respected, develops into a citizen that demands and enjoys greater freedom from coercion. Stability and relative economic security allow for greater liberty of choice. Moreover, as we have seen, that sense of commonality facilitates the transcendence of racial, gender or ethnic prejudices, and the forging of an inclusive social consciousness and identity. An individual forged in collective organisation and a sense of commonality, on a primary level deployed as a means to escape abuse and subordination from her direct economic superior, the employer, can employ these learned tools to safeguard her community against abuse from any overbearing group or institution.

Therefore, beyond the narrow confines of workplace democratisation, collective organisation can operate as a vehicle for the exertion of political pressure towards central political actors on issues relevant to worker interests, including those pertaining to the regulation of the labour market, and the consequent interventions of state institutions.[110]

[107] See Smith and Deranty, *New Philosophies of Labour* (n 29) 21; Honneth, 'Work and Recognition: A Redefinition' (n 49) 223.

[108] See Smith and Deranty, *New Philosophies of Labour* (n 29) 22–23.

[109] *cf* the relevant point, though more based on a predominantly economic understanding of modern democracy, in J Atleson, *Values and Assumptions of American Labor Law* (Amherst, MA, University of Massachusetts Press, 1983) 35–43.

[110] G Lester, 'Beyond Collective Bargaining: Modern Unions as Agents of Social Solidarity' in G Davidov and B Langille (eds), *Boundaries and Frontiers of Labour Law* (Oxford, Hart Publishing, 2006) 331. *cf* Levine, 'The Legitimacy of Labor Unions' (n 36) 562–67.

The political value of collective organisation and action cannot be overstated. The labour movement, as a precursor to legal and normative change, cannot be separated from the realm of politics; nor can its historical examination[111] or theoretical framing. On the contrary, this movement has always been interwoven with the political process, itself an expression of civic rights and a manifestation of the social forces that drive political developments, which, ultimately, legitimise and transpose to the legal realm social, political and economic change.[112] And if we consider trade unions, or any such collective institution, as a primary hub of politicisation and a Petri dish of micro-democracy, then to understand the effect of the worker movement on politics and, consequently, the broader reality and true nature of a particular polity, we also need to examine their inner workings and culture.[113] As much as the accounts of worker mobilisation and the labour movement as a whole help us to reconnect with the roots of the normative concepts that form labour law's analytical tools, so too does examining the 'internal' history of trade unionism, so as to understand the effects that participation in collective processes can have on workers as individuals.

At the same time, through their participation in the collective institutions that allow for the promotion of their economic interests, workers develop their bourgeois identity. They develop their sense of belonging to a commonality of interests, while concurrently realising that those interests can be better promoted through dialogue and mutual concessions with those of opposing objectives. In other words, besides the ethos of participation, workers develop the deeper, substantive, democratic reflexes and 'skills',[114] as well as the relevant experience, that allows for quality debate, deliberation and balancing of opposing views.[115]

Thus, workers are schooled[116] in the prerequisites of effective, respectful engagement in the public sphere and democratic processes. This is not merely an abstract process. It can entail, and has taken the form of, a practical pedagogical aspect.[117] Trade unions in the past have actively engaged in educating workers, not only in the technical skills and processes related to collective bargaining and lobbying (such as communication, negotiation, dealing with financial information and engaging with state institutions), but also in the social, democratic, political,

[111] A Fox, *History and Heritage: Social Origins of the British Industrial Relations* (London, Allen & Unwin, 1985) xii.

[112] J McIlroy, A Campbell and N Fishman, 'Approaching Post-War Trade Unionism' in J McIlroy, A Campbell and N Fishman (eds), *British Trade Unions and Industrial Politics: The Post War Compromise, 1945–1964* (Aldershot, Ashgate Publishing, 1999) 10.

[113] D Marsh, *The New Politics of British Trade Unionism: Union Power and the Thatcher Legacy* (Ithaca, ILR Press, 1992).

[114] Levine, 'The Legitimacy of Labor Unions' (n 36) 561–62.

[115] ibid 567–69; Kohler, 'Civic Virtue at Work' (n 28) 300.

[116] Kohler, 'Civic Virtue at Work' (n 28) 299.

[117] J McIlroy, 'Making Trade Unionists: The Politics of Pedagogy, 1945–79' in J McIlroy, A Campbell and N Fishman (eds), *British Trade Unions and Industrial Politics: The Post War Compromise, 1945–1964* (Aldershot, Ashgate Publishing, 1999) 37–65.

and, ultimately, systemic context of collective labour processes. Using trade unions as actual 'schools' – mechanisms to ensure the education of the working class – had been suggested in post-World War II UK, not only as a means of enhancing trade unionism as such, but also as a tool that could help improve industrial efficiency and the quality of systemic participatory democratic processes, essentially creating a better educated, more informed and, thereby, more mature populace.[118]

John McIlroy charts unions' gradual transition from attempts to ensure such broad emancipatory education, to eventually providing much narrower and more superficial 'industrial relations training'.[119] He argues that reducing the scope of education to just the technical skills required to deal with the specific established contemporary framework of industrial relations essentially implied capitulation on the part of labour, embracing not only that particular institutional framework,[120] but also its ideological and conceptual premises. Workers might still recognise the disparity of interests between management and labour, but they essentially agreed to and affirmed an idea of what balance between those interests might entail.[121] More importantly, however, McIlroy's analysis and arguments suggest that, to an extent, we can trace the seeds of resignation to the inevitability of contemporary free market structures and neoliberal tenets to the dilution of workers' education. Unconsciously embracing the established framework, workers and unions often struggle to perceive broader political and economic implications or possibilities,[122] and to engage in transformative practices akin to those that produced by what we understand today as 'labour law'.

In summary then, and regardless of the demise of actual education schemes, even the mere act of participation in collective organisation helps individual workers realise the commonality of interests among them and the value of solidaristic structures and cooperation. Moreover, it opens them to the experience of collective, and consequently political, processes, and it helps them forge a solid understanding of the broader socioeconomic and political context, and the interplay between the various state and non-state actors engaged in it. In other words, trade unions and collective labour law mechanisms become incubators of civic virtues.[123] They forge workers in their micro-democracies, so as to evolve, in turn, into conscious, engaged citizens within the greater polity.

This was certainly the effect of early labour movements in the nineteenth and twentieth century, which cannot be disconnected from their political character. The result of that interplay was also tangible in the political awakening and

[118] ibid 38.
[119] ibid 42–59.
[120] ibid 56–57.
[121] ibid 47.
[122] ibid 59.
[123] Kohler, 'Civic Virtue at Work' (n 28) 279–304.

subsequent active engagement of workers,[124] ultimately leading to the adoption of progressive policies and the strengthening of protective social regulation, but also to the enhancement of social inclusion and social equality in all forms.[125] It is certainly not coincidental that unionisation is related to the civil and political right of association under Article 11 ECHR, with its caveats, or why it is argued that it should be fully recognised and protected, including the corollary right to strike, as a civil right in the sense of the American legal and political tradition of those rights as expressed in the US Civil Rights Act.[126]

C. Systemic Democratisation: Overcoming Contemporary Boundaries

The analogies to be drawn from the US experience of the early twentieth century illustrate the integrative effect of worker participation in the struggle to democratise the market as a preamble to systemic democratisation. More importantly, however, they indicate the potential for social and political emancipation, and the emergence of a common consciousness that defies boundaries, either those based on the traditional narrow scope of worker interests as confined to workers alone, or those that restrain their expression within certain geographic or national bounds.

Conscious of the social interconnectivity of interests, modern trade unions often break the boundaries that delimit their traditional function to be within the workplace or the confines of the labour market, to connect with their broader communities[127] in pursuit of wider social objectives.[128] More recent examples of trade unions engaging in community wide local initiatives to push for social policy reforms,[129] or leading social movements, such as that against water privatisation in Greece during the Eurozone crisis, illustrate the capacity of collective structures to open up to the greater society, and function as hubs of social and

[124] Inter alia see C Bucki, 'The Worker's State: Municipal Policy, Class and Taxes in the Early Depression' in E Arnesen, J Greene and B Laurie (eds), *Labor Histories: Class, Politics and the Working Class Experience* (Chicago, University of Illinois Press, 1998) 124–49. *cf* McCartin, *Labor's Great War* (n 32).

[125] See, eg, the link Kahlenberg and Marvit identify between collective worker organising and the objectives of human dignity and equality, particularly as regards people of colour, of the Civil Rights Act in the US in R Kahlenberg and M Marvit, *Why Labor Organizing Should Be A Civil Right* (New York, The Century Foundation Press, 2012) 89–101.

[126] ibid.

[127] KVW Stone and S Cummings, 'Labour Activism in Local Politics: From CBAs to "CBAs"' in G Davidov and B Langille (eds), *Boundaries and Frontiers of Labour Law* (Oxford, Hart Publishing, 2006) 273–92.

[128] Munck, 'Labour Dilemmas and Labour Futures' (n 12) 15; Supiot, *Beyond Employment* (n 8) 132.

[129] Stone and Cummings, 'Labour Activism in Local Politics' (n 127).

political mobilisation.[130] Therefore, reality appears to disprove Rawlsean interpretations by which trade unions are judged to be inherently undemocratic, because their core objective is to induce wealth redistribution for the promotion solely of the interests of the closed caste of their members.[131]

On a greater scale, forums of transnational cooperation between national trade unions have increasingly been challenging market globalisation by approaching common problems (not solely related to labour, but also to democratic, social and ecological considerations[132]) from an international perspective.[133] These transnational collective cooperation webs provide an invaluable means for ensuring that the voice of workers can be heard in an environment which has developed into a space virtually free of the democratic intervention, accountability and control traditionally exercised through state structures.

As the Brexit vote and 2016 presidential elections in the US perhaps indicate, we may have reached the point where the first cracks are appearing to the inevitability of the free market dogma in its neoliberal form, with its aversion to the perceived 'obstacles' that democratic processes erect to market flexibility. As public trust in the institutions and functions of both the market and the state wanes in the post-Thatcherite neoliberal globalised world, recalling the galvanising and catalytic effects of market democratisation in the previous major crisis of capitalism might be useful.

IV. Conclusions: Rediscovering the Multiple Constitutive Value of Collective Labour law in a Contemporary Context

The origins and inherently complex functions of collective labour institutions and processes reveal their multidimensional value. Precisely due to their complex economic and socio-political nature and role, collective labour institutions can play a constitutive role, helping shape new identities, social structures and political ideas from the bottom up, leading to renewed systemic consensus.

Ruth Dukes's compelling work[134] brought into light Sinzheimer's conviction that collective labour law is a catalyst to bring about the constitutionalisation and democratisation of the economy. For Sinzheimer, collective labour processes and state institutions are symbiotic, feeding from each other and affecting

[130] *cf* P Waterman, 'The New Social Unionism: A New Union Model for a New World Order' in R Munck and P Waterman (eds), *Labour Dilemmas and Labour Futures* (Oxford, Palgrave MacMillan, 1999) 260–61.

[131] See Levine, 'The Legitimacy of Labor Unions' (n 36) 536.

[132] *cf* Waterman, 'The New Social Unionism' (n 130) 256–57.

[133] Munck, 'Labour Dilemmas and Labour Futures' (n 12) 15.

[134] Dukes, *The Labour Constitution* (n 47).

one another.[135] Collective autonomy, according to his model, uses state created institutional structures, including the legal framework, to affect the economic sphere. However, through its multiple functions, it helps shape and promote broader systemic normative objectives, including the pursuit and protection of individual autonomy and freedom, hence improving the quality of systemic democracy.

In that respect, labour law, and collective labour institutions, should not be regarded purely through a traditional lens which considers them 'private law'[136] stemming out of contractual freedom and the self-regulating capacity of the market. On the contrary, they better resemble elements of public law; they are, in essence, applied constitutional law, subjugating the economic realm to the normative will of the democratic, political constitution.[137] In that respect, state intervention to facilitate the constitutionally prescribed balance is welcome.[138] Consequently, collective labour institutions emerge as an instrument of Razian 'common ideology'. They are part of a coherent, pluralistic whole, which includes economic structures and interests as elements of the overall polity,[139] as means to the ends of the common constitutional good, including social coherence, democracy and social justice.[140]

Moreover, collective labour processes can go deeper than merely facilitating superfluous democratic participation, reach the heart of qualitative democracy and social cohesion: the rediscovery of a broader sense of belonging and solidarity.[141] The first step towards that is the realisation of worker individual, class and bourgeois identity. Unquestionably the socialising, democratising and emancipating effects of collective labour law processes shape workers' self-awareness and identity as individuals and bourgeois citizens. Through these processes workers are reconnected with a sense of belonging to a particular class, but also to a particular community.

Alain Supiot has argued that, as an aspect of the shake-up of market structures, labour mobility and the 'flexibility' of employment forms have disrupted and reshaped the largely homogenous[142] (at least in terms of nationality, gender and cultural background) labour force.[143] This is suggested to have led to disarray in familiar patterns of self-identification with an easily defined working class.[144]

[135] ibid 69–91; Dukes, 'Constitutionalizing Employment Relations' (n 47) 344, 356–60.

[136] Dukes, *The Labour Constitution* (n 47) 31; *cf* Dukes, 'Constitutionalizing Employment Relations' (n 47) 360–61 on Kahn-Freund.

[137] Dukes, *The Labour Constitution* (n 47); Dukes, 'Constitutionalizing Employment Relations' (n 47).

[138] *cf* Kahn-Freud's disagreement illustrated in Dukes, 'Constitutionalizing Employment Relations' (n 47) 343–44.

[139] Dukes, *The Labour Constitution* (n 47) 31.

[140] *cf* ibid 66–67.

[141] G Monbiot, *Out of the Wreckage: A New Politics for an Age of Crisis* (London, Verso, 2018) 71–92.

[142] Supiot, *Beyond Employment* (n 8) 25.

[143] ibid 94.

[144] Lash and Urry, *The End of Organised Capitalism* (n 19) 283–84.

Realisation of that common identity is necessary for the emergence of the sense of commonality that underlines solidarity and its institutional manifestations, in the form of participation in collective labour structures and systemic democratic processes. Re-constructing this thread of a realised common fate, which is ultimately what connects the members of any constitutive demos as citizens of a shared polity, is imperative. The urgency of this becomes clearer once we consider the emerging dangers of extremist populism, which comes with disillusionment and disenfranchisement in the absence or loss of that connecting thread of commonality and the tools to express it.

It is therefore no coincidence that, in the US context, suggestions have been made to reframe the freedom to associate in collective labour law institutions as a civil right.[145] Richard Kahlenberg and Moshe Marvit, for example, look beyond the confines of the market role of trade unions, and even their function as schools of the democratic process, incubators of political ideas or emancipatory mechanisms. To Kahlenberg and Marvit, the right to organise and participate in collective action is a means of ensuring a dignified existence. Therefore, it shares the fundamental objective of the civil rights movement: that all people should be treated with decency.[146]

Collective labour law institutions ought to be perceived beyond their 'market regulation' shackles of economic thinking, in order for their multiple functions to bear fruit. Freedom of association and collective action, in any form and in relation to any aspect of socio-political and socioeconomic life, are fundamental prerequisites of a functioning democratic society. They are designed to infuse the market with democratic principles, but also to ensure the diffusion of checks and balances that ensure protection from abuse, exploitation and inequality and a dignified life, beyond the state governmental context, to extend to every institution that operates within a certain polity.

The tools to accommodate this shift in our perception of collective labour law are there; we do not need to reinvent them. We merely need to recover them from the dusty corners of history, where we left them.

All this has happened before.

[145] Kahlenberg and Marvit, *Why Labor Organizing Should Be A Civil Right* (n 125).
[146] ibid 12.

7

Trade Unions, the Gig Economy, and the Feminisation of Work: Lessons from the Past?

REBECCA ZAHN*

I. Introduction

The world of work is changing rapidly, and concerns abound that 'non-standard' forms of work are challenging the social and collective dimension of work. In particular, the rapid growth of the 'gig economy' has brought these concerns to the forefront of the debate. For trade unions, the growth in non-standard work has long been considered problematic. However, the high degree of individualisation and lack of human contact characterising the gig economy raise profound questions about how trade unions should both organise, and represent, workers in this 'sector' at a time when trade union membership is in decline and there is a continuing lack of legislative support for collective bargaining. Much of the debate in the existing literature takes as its point of departure, the 'standard' (male) worker, and sees the rise in 'non-standard' work and work in the gig economy as a threat to this model. This is despite the fact that trade unions have been challenged by 'non-standard' work since their inception: the non-standard arrangements, which have now entered the mainstream, have long been the norm for many women workers.[1] Yet historically, within the labour law and industrial relations literature, women and gender have rarely been the subject of discussion, although this has

* Senior Lecturer in Law, University of Strathclyde. I am grateful to the editors of this collection, Erika Kovàcs, Lydia Hayes, Jeremias Prassl, a number of anonymous reviewers, and the participants and discussants at the workshop, *Theorising Labour in a Changing World: New Perspectives and Approaches*, held at the University of Maastricht in December 2016 for providing invaluable comments on earlier drafts. The usual disclaimers apply.

[1] See K Rittich, 'Feminization and Contingency: Regulating the Stakes of Work for Women' in J Conaghan, RM Fischl and K Klare (eds), *Labour Law in an Era of Globalization: Transformative Practices and Possibilities* (Oxford, Oxford University Press, 2004) 117.

changed since the 1980s.[2] In addition, much of the British literature examining the novelty of the gig economy has focused on the scope and ability of labour law to respond to these work arrangements, and there has been less engagement with trade union responses to these 'new' forms of work, even though the growth in such work also creates pressure for changes in the institutions that regulate labour markets.

Against this background, and in light of this book's overarching theme, this chapter calls for a new research agenda that considers the challenges of non-standard work, and of work in the gig economy, for trade unions within the context of the 'feminisation of work'. The geographical focus of this chapter, in this regard, is the United Kingdom (UK). The chapter argues that trade unions are struggling to shake off their image as the representatives of white, working-class, and blue-collar men. As a result, many of the successful efforts at organising non-standard workers, including workers in the gig economy, have been undertaken by 'non-traditional' trade unions (and other forms of grassroots organisations). This raises the question as to whether 'traditional' trade unions are able to effectively respond to the rise of non-standard forms of work, and to the gig economy in particular. It is suggested that part of the difficulty for these trade unions lies in the way in which they prioritise the functions that they adopt within the labour market, and the labour law system; functions which are based on a gendered understanding of the labour market,[3] and which in turn hamper trade union efforts to reach out to an increasingly feminised labour force. The chapter therefore suggests that a conscious conceptual shift should take place, when thinking about the purpose of trade unions, if these organisations are to respond effectively to the feminisation of work.

II. The Rise of Non-Standard Work and the Gig Economy in a Changing Legal Landscape

There is a considerable and diverse body of literature which examines the changing nature and composition of labour – which uses various terms such as precarious,

[2] Feminist scholarship mainly emerged in the 1980s and there is now a rich and diverse body of literature. For an excellent overview, see the footnotes in J Conaghan, 'Labour Law and Feminist Method' (2017) 33 *International Journal of Comparative Labour Law and Industrial Relations* 93; J Fudge, 'From Women and Labour Law to Putting Gender and Law to Work' in M Davies and VE Munro (eds), *The Ashgate Research Companion to Feminist Legal Theory* (Farnham, Ashgate, 2013) 321. There are still relatively few works that examine trade unions and women. For an overview of the debates, see S Fredman, *Women and the Law* (Oxford, Clarendon Press, 1997). Other works are cited as appropriate throughout this chapter.

[3] J Fudge and R Owens, 'Precarious Work, Women, and the New Economy: The Challenge to Legal Norms' in J Fudge and R Owens (eds), *Precarious Work, Women and the New Economy: The Challenge to Legal Norms* (Oxford, Hart Publishing, 2006) 3.

non-standard, contingent, atypical, insecure, and flexible to describe it.[4] Global economic factors and the changing contours of work, and workplace relations, have led to a reorientation of the social, economic, political, and cultural environment within which labour law has developed, as well as precipitating a changing role for labour law itself.[5] While collective bargaining in conjunction with legal intervention to protect workers who fell outside its sphere used to be the primary source of protection for workers in the UK, in the post-war era,[6] individual rights were increasingly extended during the 1960s and 1970s to workers both within and outside the collective bargaining arena. Instead of targeting workers considered particularly vulnerable, the legislation introducing individual rights was based on two general principles: first, that the floor of rights should not be available to those who were entrepreneurs in their own right; and secondly, that some rights at least must be 'earned' by a period of service with the employer.

From 1979, labour law was increasingly used as a tool to 'reduce the burdens on business', and thereby to facilitate a low-cost flexible workforce. Labour law policies were driven by the view that a low cost and highly flexible workforce was essential for increased competitiveness and lower unemployment.[7] This entailed the adoption of a series of measures, including the removal of minimum wage protection, the weakening of trade unions, and diminishing the coverage of employment protection legislation, as well as facilitating a ready-supply of low cost labour both within and from outside the UK.[8] Marginal workers were seen as attracting not more, but less, protection from the law than standard workers; a policy decision which had a 'disproportionately serious impact on women'[9] who were over-represented in non-standard work. Although the (then) European Community took a different approach, any attempts at establishing a floor of social rights and European-wide collective bargaining structures have also faltered in recent years.[10] At the same time, the reform of welfare and tax regimes encouraged a fundamental shift away from the male breadwinner employment norm to a new multi-earner family model, whereby women were actively encouraged to

[4] For comprehensive references to the debate, see ibid, 10; N Kountouris, 'The Legal Determinants of Precariousness in Personal Work Relations: A European Perspective' (2012) 34 *Comparative Labor Law & Policy Journal* 21.

[5] See further Fudge and Owens, 'Precarious Work' (n 3) 5.

[6] Subsequent paragraphs summarise Fredman's argument in: S Fredman, 'Labour Law in Flux: The Changing Composition of the Workforce' (1997) 26 *Industrial Law Journal* 337. See also Lord Wedderburn, 'Labour Law 2008: 40 Years On' (2007) 36 *Industrial Law Journal* 397.

[7] See S Deakin and F Wilkinson, *Labour Standards: Essential to Economic and Social Progress* (London, Institute of Employment Rights, 1996).

[8] See further D Harvey, *The Condition of Postmodernity: An Enquiry into the Origins of Cultural Change* (Oxford, Blackwell, 1989).

[9] S Fredman, 'Precarious Norms for Precarious Workers' in J Fudge and R Owens (eds), *Precarious Work, Women and the New Economy: The Challenge to Legal Norms* (Oxford, Hart Publishing, 2006) 174, 184.

[10] See, eg, A Bogg and KD Ewing, 'The Continuing Evolution of European Labour Law and the Changing Context for Trade Union Organizing' (2017) 38 *Comparative Labor Law & Policy* 211.

work outside the household.[11] This had a profound impact on women's labour, and labour market participation, at a time when there has been an 'intensification and erosion of gender in the labour market'.[12] Following the 1997 election, a 'Third Way' developed under the New Labour government which rejected both the earlier neoliberal view, and the post-war consensus, that employment standards are a 'burden on business' and, instead, considered employment rights as facilitating productive and committed non-standard workers.[13]

In addition to these policy decisions, which reshaped the legal framework regulating the work relationship and had a knock-on effect on the constitution of the labour market, factors such as the decline in manufacturing and the rise of a new economy based on modern information-based systems, and technologies, have all contributed to a 'rapid disintegration of the old industrial model of employment'.[14] In legal terms, there has been a proliferation of non-standard contractual arrangements which govern the work relationship, including: part-time work; fixed-term work; temporary agency work; dependent self-employment; and work on the basis of zero hour contracts.[15] The level of protection afforded to such workers by law varies. Particular concerns arise, however, in relation to dependent self-employment[16] and work on the basis of zero hours contracts;[17] both of which are growing phenomena in the UK, and are often associated with insecurity, precarity, and limited, if any, employment rights. In 2016, it was estimated that close to one million workers were working under a zero-hours contract, and that self-employment had grown to 4.6 million.[18]

In recent years, work in the so-called gig economy has also undergone exponential growth.[19] The gig economy is generally understood to include two

[11] Fudge and Owens, 'Precarious Work' (n 3) 14–15.

[12] J Fudge and B Cossman, 'Privatization, Law, and the Challenge to Feminism' in B Cossman and J Fudge (eds), *Privatization, Law, and the Challenge to Feminism* (Toronto, Toronto University Press, 2002) 3.

[13] S Fredman, 'Women at Work: The Broken Promise of Flexicurity' (2004) 33 *Industrial Law Journal* 299; S Fredman, 'The Ideology of New Labour Law' in C Barnard, S Deakin and GS Morris (eds), *The Future of Labour Law: Liber Amicorum Bob Hepple QC* (Oxford, Hart Publishing, 2004) 9.

[14] Fudge and Owens, 'Precarious Work' (n 3) 3.

[15] These are not mutually exclusive categories and additional variations also exist.

[16] The rise in self-employment was the subject of a Government Review published in 2016. See J Deane, *Self-Employment Review: An Independent Report* (February 2016) www.gov.uk/government/publications/self-employment-review accessed 3 November 2018. For a discussion, see M Freedland, 'The Deane Review of Self-Employment' (*The Institute of Employment Rights*, 3 March 2016) www.ier.org.uk/blog/deane-review-self-employment accessed 3 November 2018.

[17] See further Z Adams and S Deakin, *Re-Regulating Zero Hours Contracts* (Liverpool, Institute of Employment Rights, 2014).

[18] In 2016, the UK government ordered a review (the 'Taylor Review') of such employment practices. For a discussion of the Review's findings, see E McGaughey, 'Uber, the Taylor Review, Mutuality and the Duty Not to Misrepresent Employment Status' (2018) *Industrial Law Journal* doi:10.1093/indlaw/dwy014 accessed 3 November 2018.

[19] Accurate figures are hard to come by, but some data is provided by R Smith and S Leberstein, *Rights on Demand: Ensuring Workplace Standards and Worker Security in the On-Demand Economy* (National Employment Law Project, September 2015).

main forms of work: 'crowdwork' and 'work on-demand via app'.[20] The former refers to a work situation where a series of tasks are completed through online platforms. The online platforms establish contact between individuals and organisations (eg, Uber). The latter describes a form of work where the execution of traditional working activities such as transport, clerical work, or cleaning is channelled through apps that are managed by firms who require minimum quality standards of service, and intervene in the selection and management of the workforce.[21] A thorough review of work practices in the gig economy is provided elsewhere;[22] however, to summarise, work within the gig economy is enabled by IT, and the internet is used to match supply and demand. Workers are required to be extremely flexible (which is often cited as a positive aspect of the work, but which leads to increased competition between workers, often on a global scale; to very long hours worked; and extremely low earnings); are afforded few, if any, labour protections; and are only remunerated for actual time worked and work completed.

How then can one classify work in the gig economy? Is it really a new form of 'standard' or 'non-standard' work? Within the context of the gig economy, one rarely comes across the term 'work', 'worker', or 'labour', thereby suggesting that this form of work is a separate and 'new' form of engagement. In practice, many platforms or firms classify their 'workers' as independent contractors. However, in most cases, the evidence suggests that workers are rarely operating independently[23] and that, for many workers, money earned in the gig economy is an essential source of income.[24] Against this background, Janine Berg and Valerio De Stefano present a convincing argument that suggests 'gig economy work is simply twenty-first century casual work rebranded'.[25] Thus, contractual models such as zero-hours contracts, bogus self-employment, or agency work can also occur within the gig economy. Worker profiles in the gig economy vary from highly skilled IT and creative professionals to unskilled workers.[26] However, Miriam A. Cherry argues that in its extreme form, and particularly in the area of unskilled or low-skilled work, work in the gig economy – while not necessarily different

[20] This is explored in great detail by V de Stefano, 'The Rise of the "Just-in-Time Workforce": On-Demand Work, Crowdwork, and Labor Protection in the "Gig-Economy"' (2016) 37 *Comparative Labor Law & Policy Journal* 471; see also, the references in fns 1–2 of de Stefano.

[21] See further V De Stefano, *The Rise of the 'Just-in-Time Workforce': On-Demand Work, Crowdwork and Labour Protection in the 'Gig-Economy'* (International Labour Office, Conditions of Work and Employment Series No 71, 2016).

[22] De Stefano, 'Rise of the "Just-in-Time Workforce"' (n 20).

[23] This was confirmed by the employment tribunal in *Aslam v Uber BV* [2017] IRLR 4.

[24] De Stefano, *Rise of the 'Just-in-Time Workforce'* (n 21).

[25] J Berg and V De Stefano, 'It's Time to Regulate the Gig Economy' (*Speri*, 18 April 2017) http://speri.dept.shef.ac.uk/2017/04/17/its-time-to-regulate-the-gig-economy/ accessed 16 November 2018.

[26] See further G Valenduc and P Vendramin, 'Work in the Digital Economy: Sorting the Old from the New' (European Trade Union Institute, Working Paper 2016.03) 33 www.etui.org/Publications2/Working-Papers/Work-in-the-digital-economy-sorting-the-old-from-the-new accessed 16 November 2018.

from other nonstandard forms of work in terms of contractual arrangement – is a 'return to industrial (or even pre-industrial in terms of its pay by the piece and work at home) systems … featur[ing] highly rigid control systems and deskilled work'.[27] Work in the gig economy must therefore be seen as a continuation of the rise in non-standard forms of work identified above, and will be considered under the broader umbrella of non-standard work for the remainder of this chapter.[28]

III. Non-Standard Work, the Gig Economy, and Gender

The language of atypical, precarious, crowdwork, work on demand, or non-standard work suggests that these 'new' forms of work differ from 'standard' work; that is, 'a full-time and year-round employment relationship for an indefinite duration with a single employer'.[29] However, this normative understanding of the standard employment relationship relied upon particular parameters – the growth of heavy manufacturing industries after World War II; and a clear work-life arrangement whereby men were primary breadwinners, while women stayed at home and had primary care responsibilities.[30] As Simon Deakin points out, the standard employment relationship was based upon 'an anachronistic notion of the division of labour in the household'.[31] The increase in precarious or non-standard work undermines labour law, and labour institutions, which have been created around the concept of standard employment relationships. Yet the dichotomy in language ignores the nature of women's work – during this and earlier periods – which was often concentrated in precarious or 'non-standard' work (which, for them, was 'standard') that sought to supplement the declining male wage, but did not

[27] MA Cherry, 'Beyond Misclassification: The Digital Transformation of Work' (2016) 37 *Comparative Labor Law & Policy Journal* 577, 601–2.

[28] There is an entire debate in the literature on whether there is a difference between this form of work and others. Space precludes discussion of the debate here. See further B Rogers, 'Employment Rights in the Platform Economy: Getting Back to Basics' (2016) 10 *Harvard Law & Policy Review* 479; J Prassl, 'Reconsidering the Notion of "Employer" in the Era of the Fissured Workplace in the UK: Should Labour Law Responsibilities Exceed the Boundary of the Legal Entity?' in R Blanpain and others (eds), *The Notion of Employer in the Era of the Fissured Workplace: Should Labour Law Responsibilities Exceed the Boundary of the Legal Entity?* (Alphen aan den Rijn, Wolters Kluwer, 2017) 81; the contributions in G Davidov and B Langille (eds), *The Idea of Labour Law* (Oxford, Oxford University Press, 2011).

[29] Fudge and Owens, 'Precarious Work' (n 3) 3.

[30] See further J Conaghan, 'The Invisibility of Women in Labour Law: Gender-Neutrality in Model-Building' (1986) 14 *International Journal of the Sociology of Law* 377; Fredman, 'Labour Law in Flux' (n 6); L Dickens, 'Problems of Fit: Changing Employment and Labour Regulation' (2004) 42 *British Journal of Industrial Relations* 595.

[31] S Deakin, 'The Many Futures of the Contract of Employment' in J Conaghan, RM Fischl and K Klare (eds), *Labour Law in an Era of Globalization: Transformative Practices and Possibilities* (Oxford, Oxford University Press, 2004) 177.

provide sufficient income for independence.[32] As more men are working in precarious forms of work – previously identified with women – the language of the 'standard' employment relationship loses credibility, and we see a shift away from the male breadwinner model towards a 'feminisation of work'.[33]

'Feminisation' in this case has a double meaning, referring both to 'the increased labour market participation of women and the proliferation of forms of employment historically associated with women, that is, jobs that are part time, temporary, poorly paid, and lacking benefits and collective forms of representation'.[34] This is not to say that there has been complete convergence between men and women's work, as occupational gender segregation and equal pay differentials persist.[35] The feminisation of work in this dual sense also permeates work in the gig economy. It is becoming increasingly widespread in sectors traditionally occupied by women, and female participation in the gig economy is also high. The idea that work can be done outside a 'standard' workplace, and fit around workers' other responsibilities (such as care responsibilities), harks back to an earlier time when women's work often took place in their own or someone else's home.[36] The gender pay gap prevalent in other sectors of work also exists in the gig economy, where women experience discrimination at the hands of algorithms or ratings which are used to allocate work.[37] In a recent survey completed in the United States (US), a third of female gig workers adopted a gender neutral username in order to maintain anonymity.[38] As Gérard Valenduc and Patricia Vendramin point out, the flexible nature of work in the gig economy entrenches gender segregation in the private sphere and reproduces gender power.[39]

IV. Challenges to Trade Unions

The 'non-standard' worker is thus increasingly becoming the 'standard' worker. Yet, from an institutional perspective, there have been limited attempts at

[32] J Fudge and L Vosko 'Gender Paradoxes and the Rise of Contingent Work: Towards a Transformative Feminist Political Economy of the Labour Market' in W Clement and LF Vosko (eds), *Changing Canada: Political Economy as Transformation* (Montreal, McGill-Queen's University Press, 2003) 183; R Owens, 'Decent Work for the Contingent Workforce in the New Economy' (2002) 15 *Australian Journal of Labour Law* 209.

[33] Fudge and Owens, 'Precarious Work' (n 3).

[34] ibid 12.

[35] ibid.

[36] See N Schoenbaum, 'Gender and the Sharing Economy' (2016) 43 *Fordham Urban Law Journal* 1023; DE Roberts, 'Spiritual and Menial Housework' (1997) 9 *Yale Journal of Law and Feminism* 51.

[37] See M Kullmann, 'Platform Work, Algorithmic Decision-Making, and EU Gender Equality Law' (2018) 34 *International Journal of Comparative Labour Law and Industrial Relations* 1.

[38] C MacFarlane, 'The Future of Gig Work is Female' (*Hyperwallet*, 30 August 2017) www.hyperwallet.com/resources/ecommerce-marketplaces/the-future-of-gig-work-is-female/ accessed 16 November 2018.

[39] Valenduc and Vendramin, 'Work in the Digital Economy' (n 26) 37.

comprehensive reform of the 'classical' labour law model, which 'may be seen as a triangle whose three sides are companies, trade unions, and the state'.[40] Trade unions, in particular, have struggled to move away from the basic post-war model of which they were an integral part, and upon which collective bargaining systems were premised. Although the growth in non-standard work has long been considered problematic – and has been the subject of much debate in the academic literature[41] – much of this debate takes as its point of departure the 'standard' (male) worker and considers the challenges posed by the recent growth in non-standard work. This is despite the fact that, since their inception, trade unions have been challenged by 'non-standard' work, which is described by Sidney and Beatrice Webb as work carried out by 'casual workers with no skills who are *chiefly the daughters, wives and widows of these men who turn to labor of this kind*'.[42] According to the Webbs, it is

> for ever hopeless to attempt, by Mutual Insurance or Collective Bargaining, to raise appreciably the wages of the common run of women workers. Where, as is usually the case, female labor is employed for practically unskilled work, needing only the briefest experience; or where the work, though skilled, is of a kind into which every woman is initiated as part of her general education, no combination will ever be able to enforce, by its own power, any Standard Rate, any Normal Day, or any definite conditions of Sanitation and Safety.[43]

If this is the premise, then it is perhaps not surprising that trade unions have historically been largely ineffective in organising women. Indeed, Wally Secombe, writing in the 1970s, demonstrates how women, and housewives in particular, challenge the organised labour movement by remaining as a 'massive labouring population […] completely outside the organizations and struggles of the proletariat'.[44] Rather than seeking to represent such 'workers', trade unions often played a significant part in maintaining women's disadvantage in the labour market.[45]

Between 1888 and 1918, overall trade union membership in the UK grew from 750,000 to six and a half million. The number of women members also increased

[40] A Supiot, *Beyond Employment: Changes in Work and the Future of Labour Law in Europe* (Oxford, Oxford University Press, 2001).

[41] For an overview, see H Arthurs, 'Labour Law After Labour' in G Davidov and B Langille (eds), *The Idea of Labour Law* (Oxford, Oxford University Press, 2011) 13; R Gumbrell-McCormick and R Hyman, *Trade Unions in Western Europe: Hard Times, Hard Choices* (Oxford, Oxford University Press, 2013).

[42] S Webb and B Webb, *Industrial Democracy* (London, Longmans, Green & Co, 1902) 757, quoting from C Booth (ed), *Life and Labour of the People*, vol 9 (London, Macmillan, 1897) 193.

[43] ibid 757–58.

[44] W Secombe, 'The Housewife and Her Labour under Capitalism' (1974) 83 *New Left Review* 3.

[45] Although there have been some exceptions. See further, the growing literature on trade unions and the feminisation of the labour market. See, eg, Fredman, *Women and the Law* (n 2); L Briskin and P McDermott (eds), *Women Challenging Unions: Feminism, Democracy, and Militancy* (Toronto, University of Toronto Press, 1993); S Boston, *Women Workers and the Trade Unions* (London, Lawrence & Wishart, 1987).

during that period. However, by 1910, women made up almost one third of the workforce but only 10 per cent of members; over 90 per cent of women workers remained unorganised. Although women were incorporated in mixed unions, in sectors such as the cotton and textile industries where they often outnumbered male operatives (a high proportion of women were also members of teaching, clerical, and shop workers' unions), for the most part, women organised themselves. Trade union opposition to women workers – notably their concerns regarding equal pay and treatment – continued well into the twentieth century, even though female participation in the labour market, especially in traditionally male-dominated industries, increased during both world wars.[46] Following World War II, in particular, women became a far more visible part of the paid workforce than in earlier periods. However, Sandra Fredman notes that 'the trade union movement was surprisingly slow to reflect the increased participation of women in the paid work-force' and it was not until the 1960s, with the growth of white collar trade unionism, that trade unions began to systematically recruit women workers. Today, also as a result of the decline in heavy industry, women trade union members outnumber men and the average British trade unionist is a young, degree-educated, white, professional woman (although it may be of little comfort to find that women's influence is expanding in a labour movement that is declining). Nonetheless, trade unions have often failed to adapt their structures to the changing make-up of the labour force and to changing employment relationships. As Dorothy Sue Cobble states, the feminisation of unions does not necessarily reflect a change in attitude to women workers by trade unions, but is 'a result of the decline of private sector unionism, which tends to be male-dominated, and the rise of public sector unionism, a sector in which large numbers of women work.'[47] In addition, a large proportion of women members are not always reflected in the demographics of branch officers, workplace representatives, and national officers. As a result, trade unions are struggling to shake off their image as the representatives of white, working-class, blue-collar men.[48]

The rise in the gig economy has added an extra layer of complexity to the challenges facing trade unions, as well as injecting a sense of urgency into the debate on how trade unions should respond to the rise in non-standard work. According to Ursula Huws, 'one way of looking at the recent exponential growth of online platforms in service delivery is to see it as a formalisation of the informal economy, with the transparency of an open market replacing the old word-of-mouth methods of finding work.'[49] The lack of human contact and the wide dispersal of people

[46] See Fredman, *Women and the Law* (n 2).

[47] DS Cobble, *Gender Equality and Labor Movements: Toward a Global Perspective* (Solidarity Center, 2013) 12 www.eldis.org/document/A101076 accessed 16 November 2018.

[48] This is due, in part, to the under-representation of women within trade unions; but even where this was not the case, women's domestic responsibilities made it difficult for them to participate actively in a trade union. See Fredman, *Women and the Law* (n 2) 137.

[49] U Huws, 'Logged In' *Jacobin* (6 January 2016) www.jacobinmag.com/2016/01/huws-sharing-economy-crowdsource-precarity-uber-workers/ accessed 16 November 2018.

across large geographical areas poses a particular challenge for trade unions; one that does not exist in the same way for other non-standard forms of work. This (again) raises the question of how to organise, represent, and regulate non-standard work at a time of union decline[50] and limited legislative support. The move to individual rights, rather than a labour law system which includes collective bargaining (outlined above), underlines this dilemma for unions[51] and 'weakens trade union capacity to regulate work and employment within the national boundaries in which they are embedded'.[52] Moreover, 'changes in social values and expectations of workers towards unions'[53] have forced unions to reassess their traditional role as worker associations.

In light of the nature of work in the gig economy – precarious and often low-skilled – it is therefore, perhaps, not surprising that we find certain parallels with women worker attempts at organising in the nineteenth century. In the gig economy, much of the organisation of workers has occurred outside established union structures, and there is limited evidence that traditional trade unions have been able to successfully organise non-standard workers.[54] Most responses have focused on litigation.[55] Thus, in the UK, there have been recent victories by unions over the taxi app, Uber; the food delivery empire, Deliveroo; and the delivery firm, CitySprint.[56] At the EU level, in *FNV Kunsten Informatie en Media v Netherlands*,[57] the European Court of Justice (ECJ) ruled that competition law does not apply to collective agreements amongst freelance substitute orchestra musicians, which aim to improve their working conditions, if they can be classed as 'workers' (to be determined by national law) rather than 'undertakings'. In light of recent decisions in the UK, which have held that non-standard workers are to be classified as 'workers' even if their contract says otherwise, the ECJ's ruling opens the door for trade unions to include 'false self-employed' non-standard workers, who have a position that to all intents and purposes is similar to that of a standard worker in collective agreements.

[50] See further, 'Special Issue: Union Decline: Causes, Consequences and Cures' (2011) 17(2) *European Journal of Industrial Relations* 95–203.

[51] Equally, much of the literature that has considered alternative conceptions of 'worker' – in order to encompass workers in the gig economy – does not seem to move away from the individualised approach.

[52] Gumbrell-McCormick and Hyman, *Trade Unions in Western Europe* (n 41) 29.

[53] B Ebbinghaus and J Visser, 'When Institutions Matter: Union Growth and Decline in Western Europe, 1950–1995' (1999) 15 *European Sociological Review* 135, 143.

[54] For an overview of recent campaigns in the UK, see Trade Union Congress, Written Evidence (WOW0062) to Business, Energy and Industrial Strategy Committee, *The Future World of Work and Rights of Workers Inquiry*, 19 December 2016 (published 10 January 2017) http://data.parliament.uk/writtenevidence/committeeevidence.svc/evidencedocument/business-energy-and-industrial-strategy-committee/future-world-of-work/written/44647.html accessed 17 November 2018.

[55] See further, Cherry, 'Beyond Misclassification' (n 27), for litigation that has taken place in the UK.

[56] Not all of these cases involved 'traditional' trade unions. The Uber case involved the GMB, whilst the Deliveroo and CitySprint cases were supported by the Independent Workers' Union of Great Britain.

[57] [2015] 4 CMLR 1 (ECJ, First Chamber).

The fact that trade unions are focusing strongly on litigation as a response to the rise of the gig economy is indicative of the way in which trade union strategies have changed over the years. The same observation can be made in relation to calls for legislative action by trade unions which have become widespread.[58] As Alan Bogg and Keith Ewing point out, using litigation as a political strategy, or calling for greater government involvement, highlights

> the extent to which British trade unions have reconceived their methods of engagement. Historically, of course, it was one of the defining features of collective laissez-faire that British trade unions operated on the basis of a distrust of courts. As the political and constitutional landscape has shifted, the forms of trade union action have undergone a transformation as well.[59]

In light of falling trade union membership, a decline in trade union density, and limited legislative support for trade unions, Lord Wedderburn suggested in 2007 that the 'union movement could no longer sustain the weight of a "collective *laissez faire*" model'.[60]

Looking at trade union responses to workers in the gig economy seems to confirm Wedderburn's scepticism. Despite some success in the courts for 'traditional' trade unions, much of the litigation has been taken by the Independent Workers Union of Great Britain (IWGB). The IWGB was founded in 2012 and is a small, independent trade union – not affiliated with the TUC – whose members are predominantly low paid migrant workers in London. In its work, the IWGB focuses on high-profile campaigns and member representation, and also provides very limited services (mainly English language classes). It does not seek regulation of the labour market more generally. Thus far, it has acted as a dynamic and cooperative model with very limited or no hierarchies (in contrast to the democratic centralism which characterises 'traditional' trade unions),[61] and with noticeable success in organising and campaigning within specific sectors dominated by non-standard (male and female) workers, including for couriers working in the gig economy.

[58] See, eg, the statements made by Hannah Reed (Senior Employment Rights Officer, TUC) to the House of Commons' Business, Energy and Industrial Strategy Committee's Inquiry into the Future World of Work: Hannah Reed, Trade Union Congress, Oral Evidence (HC 929) to Business, Energy and Industrial Strategy Committee, *The Future World of Work and Rights of Workers Inquiry*, 7 March 2017 http://data.parliament.uk/writtenevidence/committeeevidence.svc/evidencedocument/business-energy-and-industrial-strategy-committee/future-world-of-work/oral/48743.html accessed 17 November 2018.

[59] Bogg and Ewing, 'Continuing Evolution of European Labour Law' (n 10) 226. Bogg and Ewing are referring here to the *Unison* litigation over the introduction of tribunal fees; however, similar lessons can be drawn from the litigation surrounding the gig economy cases. On collective laissez faire, see AD Flanders, 'The Tradition of Voluntarism' (1974) 12 *British Journal of Industrial Relations* 352.

[60] Wedderburn, 'Labour Law 2008' (n 6) 405.

[61] See U Mückenberger, E Schmidt and R Zoll (eds), *Die Modernisierung der Gewerkschaften in Europa* (Westfälisches Dampfboot, 1996) 12.

The success of the IWGB in organising non-standard workers raises the question as to whether 'traditional' trade unions are able to effectively respond to the rise of non-standard forms of work, and to the gig economy, in particular. It is suggested that part of the difficulty for these trade unions lies in the way in which they prioritise the functions adopted by them within the labour market and the labour law system; functions which are based on a gendered understanding of 'norms of employment, assumptions about who workers are and what they need, and ideas about how regulation works'[62] which, in turn, hamper trade union efforts to reach out to a feminised – in both senses of the word – labour force. The next section therefore considers the extent to which the functions adopted by trade unions in the UK display gendered understandings of the labour market and the labour law system.

V. Trade Union Functions

Ewing identifies five principal functions of unions: a service function; a representation function; a regulatory function; a government function; and a public administration function.[63] The different functions sit along a scale, with the service function at one end as the 'activity of a fledgling and immature organisation', and the public administration function at the other representing 'the apotheosis of trade union ambition in a social democratic society'.[64] The ambit of each function is largely self-evident. According to Ewing, 'a service function means a function which involves the provision of services and benefits to members'.[65] The meaning of the representation function is, again, obvious. All trade unions represent the interests of the worker at their place of work. This occurs through individual representation – that is, an extension of the union's service function – or collective representation, where overlaps occur with the regulatory function. Rule-making through collective bargaining, which is limited to individual members of the trade union, will thus fall under the umbrella of the representation function whereas the regulatory function 'acknowledges that trade unions are involved in a process of rule-making that extends beyond their members or the immediate colleagues of their members'.[66] Finally, the governmental and public administration functions of trade unions have two dimensions: first, trade unions represent 'the organised political representation of working people, both as a means of restraining the power of the State and a means of harnessing the power of the State';[67] secondly, trade unions engage 'in the process of government

[62] Fudge and Owens, 'Precarious Work' (n 3) 3.
[63] KD Ewing, 'The Function of Trade Unions' (2005) 34 *Industrial Law Journal* 1.
[64] ibid 3.
[65] ibid.
[66] ibid 4.
[67] ibid 5.

in the sense of being involved in the development, implementation and delivery of government policy'.[68] Ewing's analysis of trade union functions took place against the background of New Labour's 'Third Way', where trade unions were encouraged to provide both a universal service function to all and any workers wishing to become members, and to 'cooperate' with employers in representing members.[69] Trade unions thus expanded their service function in relation to work (by providing *inter alia* legal representation), but also outside of work (by offering commercial or social services),[70] and changed their way of working to support 'partnership industrial relations'.[71] The latter policy was most visible in relation to industries that required a 'flexible, skilled and motivated workforce',[72] and where trade unions are established. However, the policy has had limited impact on women workers: trade unions still lack a presence in sectors dominated by non-standard work, where 'flexibility' usually equates to numerical (which results in precarity) rather than functional flexibility.[73]

At the same time, the regulatory role of collective bargaining receded due to lack of public policy support and the abolition of an appropriate legal structure to accommodate, and support, such a function. Regulation of work has become a State rather than a trade union responsibility[74] with unions' 'regulatory ambitions to be secured by political campaigning and by legislation rather than by collective bargaining'.[75] While New Labour sought to encourage more women to participate fully in the labour market through the introduction of family-friendly norms (in contrast to earlier State preferences),[76] gender inequalities were not directly addressed; and although women and non-standard workers were beneficiaries of many of New Labour's initiatives, the primary drive behind many of the labour law measures was efficiency rather than fairness considerations. This has only increased in recent years.[77] As a result, there has been a dilution of norms which seek to benefit non-standard workers but which, because of their underlying policy rationale, are not as effective as they could be. The recommendations which have been made as a result of the current Government's review into 'modern

[68] ibid 5.

[69] ibid, 3.

[70] ibid 7.

[71] On partnership and unions, see T Novitz, 'A Revised Role for Trade Unions as Designed by New Labour: The Representation Pyramid and "Partnership"' (2002) 29 *Journal of Law and Society* 487.

[72] Department of Trade and Industry, *Fairness at Work* (Cm 3968, 1998) para 4.7.

[73] On the distinction between the two, see J Atkinson, *Flexibility, Uncertainty and Manpower Management* (The Institute for Employment Studies, Report 89, 1985) www.employment-studies.co.uk/resource/flexibility-uncertainty-and-manpower-management accessed 17 November 2018.

[74] See P Davies and M Freedland, *Labour Legislation and Public Policy: A Contemporary History* (Oxford, Clarendon Press, 1993) ch 1.

[75] Ewing, 'Function of Trade Unions' (n 63) 15.

[76] See Fredman, 'Precarious Norms' (n 9).

[77] Examples of this are evident in the recent welfare reforms, as well as any attempts to regulate non-standard work, including the recommendations of the Taylor Review.

working practices' are a case in point.[78] It is therefore not surprising that the working patterns of women – predominantly in low-paid, precarious work – have not changed substantially.

Ewing's analysis of trade union functions is based on his observations of organisations that are characterised by democratic centralism and a hierarchical power structure.[79] Their functions reflect their historical legacy as well as their members' priorities. These unions have long struggled to reach out to workers who do not fit within the mould of the 'standard' worker. During the nineteenth and the first half of the twentieth century, there was no desire or perceived need to engage with non-standard or women workers. Although trade union attitudes to women workers have since fundamentally changed, where they have been successful in organising women, this has largely been restricted to white collar professionals who slot more easily into the 'standard' worker paradigm. However, unions continue to struggle to respond effectively to the majority of women workers who are employed in non-standard work. By extension, it is not surprising that they are also challenged by the rise in non-standard work amongst male workers and the growth of the gig economy.

VI. Rethinking of Priorities?

In order to effectively respond to non-standard workers, including workers in the gig economy, this chapter concludes by calling for a new research agenda which requires trade unions to confront problems that women workers have struggled with for decades, and develop innovative strategies which take account of women's work and women's experience; insights from the gender domain could facilitate an effective response to the rise in non-standard work.[80] A successful reaching out to non-standard workers will also enhance the effectiveness of industrial relations law, and practice, by broadening unions' representational base and strengthening their claims to act as worker representatives and work regulators. Since non-standard work is fast becoming the norm, and shows no signs of abating, unions

[78] See IER (The Institute of Employment Rights) summaries of the different recommendations: 'The IER Guide to the Taylor Review' (*The Institute of Employment Rights*, 13 July 2017) www.ier.org.uk/news/ier-guide-taylor-review accessed 17 November 2018.

[79] Crain convincingly argues that power structures, which reflect patriarchal visions of power, sacrifice the solidarity that once served as the source of workers' empowerment. See M Crain, 'Feminism, Labor, and Power' (1992) 65 *Southern California Law Review* 1819.

[80] ibid; A Forrest, 'A View from Outside the Whale: The Treatment of Women and Unions in Industrial Relations' in L Briskin and P McDermott (eds), *Women Challenging Unions: Feminism, Democracy, and Militancy* (Toronto, University of Toronto Press, 1993) 325. Fudge therefore calls for 'the development of new forms of broader-based bargaining and inclusive unionism which do not replicate and reinforce the deeply fragmented, gendered, and hierarchical labour market which currently exists': J Fudge, 'The Gendered Dimension of Labour Law: Why Women Need Inclusive Unionism and Broader-Based Bargaining' in L Briskin and P McDermott (eds), *Women Challenging Unions: Feminism, Democracy, and Militancy* (Toronto, University of Toronto Press, 1993) 231, 244.

have to shift their focus to a new 'standard' worker – one long neglected by unions. It is argued that this shift in focus must begin with a shift in priorities relating to different functions, and to issues within those functions.

Ewing singles out the regulatory function as 'the most important function of trade unions, this being the most visible manifestation of the trade union role in promoting fairness and social justice not only at work but within the economy as a whole'.[81] The service function, on the other hand, can be found at the bottom end of the scale as 'the activity of a fledgling and immature organisation'.[82] The focus on regulation as the ultimate goal of trade union action persists, even though the most successful trade union responses to non-standard workers to date – particularly workers in the gig economy – have centred on the service function (the successful actions of the IWGB are a case in point). The devaluation of the service function hinders trade unions in terms of identifying and placing matters of concern to these workers centre-stage. This is not to say that trade unions should abandon their goal of seeking to regulate work through collective bargaining. There are examples of trade unions in other countries that manage to successfully bargain on behalf of non-standard workers.[83] However, collective bargaining, as traditionally conceived, proceeds on the presumption that trade unions represent a majority of workers in individual work-sites and negotiate collective agreements for individual groups of workers (or sectors); neither of these presumptions hold for non-standard workers. In addition, bargaining and work regulation in this regard often concerns industrial or economic matters, which are of secondary concern to workers who have limited or no job security, or access to employment rights. Issues of relevance to non-standard workers such as job segregation, (numerical) worker flexibility, and a systematic undervaluing of their work are considered social or equality issues.[84] Those examples where trade unions have been successful at organising, and bargaining, on behalf of non-standard workers have occurred where unions have broadened their bargaining agenda to prioritise, for example, equal pay, the elimination of discrimination, the provision of childcare at work, and the opening up of employment and training opportunities to non-standard (women) workers.[85]

The service function as traditionally conceived by trade unions – legal advice at work, discounts for insurance or holidays, and so on – fails to take into account the precarious and flexible nature of non-standard work. Such services will be of little appeal to workers who, for example, struggle to combine childcare and work, or who do not know how many hours they will work in any given week. Instead,

[81] Ewing, 'Function of Trade Unions' (n 63) 13.

[82] ibid 3.

[83] See Cobble, *Gender Equality and Labor Movements* (n 47).

[84] See A Blackett and C Sheppard, 'Collective Bargaining and Equality: Making Connections' (2003) 142 *International Labour Review* 419, 432.

[85] For examples, see Cobble, *Gender Equality and Labor Movements* (n 47).

trade unions need to think much more deeply about the types of services that could empower non-standard workers to better represent themselves, vis-à-vis a range of different actors such as employers, government officials, or consumers. In rethinking the service function, they could, for example, act as a form of employee mutual. Cautious parallels can be drawn with the labour market of the nineteenth century, where it was often not possible for trade unions to bargain with employers concerning regulation of the employment relationship; both because of the craft nature of many jobs (which entailed unilateral regulation), and because of the extreme precariousness and instability of many employment relationships, such as the casual (female) labourers identified by the Webbs above, and where the weakness of public social protections required the direct assumption of solidaristic tasks by trade unions.[86] British trade unions therefore controlled the labour supply, and supplied – and (where possible) bargained for – 'friendly benefits' and allowances for workers. As Gian Primo Cella highlights, this was the typical action of trade union representation before the spread of the 'new unionism';[87] namely, to bargain minimum standards with employers and provide fairness criteria around which to organise unilateral regulation. The distribution of benefits (in case of accident, illness, or unemployment) served the same purpose: to ensure that a temporary or permanent decline in the market power of individuals did not prompt breach of the wage levels, and employment conditions, established by custom or tradition.[88] In the labour market of the twenty-first century, many of these benefits are provided by the State. However, due to the nature of the work relationship, non-standard workers often either do not qualify for such benefits, or they are so meagre that they do not prevent workers from taking on jobs that undermine established wage levels or employment conditions – thereby leading to a dehumanisation of the workers, and increasing precarity across the labour market.

It must, of course, be borne in mind that these nineteenth-century trade union policies are associated with 'craft unions', where workers organised along the lines of a particular craft, occupation, or trade within local and controllable labour markets (thereby discriminating against 'outsiders' to the craft); and that, of course, women were often excluded from craft unions. However, research in recent decades, especially in North America, has shown that elements of these policies can be used in today's context with regard to unskilled jobs in services, and to the high-tech jobs of semi-self-employment in the gig economy.[89]

[86] The parallels between the end of the nineteenth and twentieth centuries was also remarked upon by Dahrendorf: R Dahrendorf, *Economic Opportunity, Civil Society and Political Liberty* (Geneva, United Nations Research Institute for Social Development, 1995).

[87] See further EJ Hobsbawm, *Worlds of Labour: Further Studies in the History of Labour* (London, Weidenfeld & Nicholson, 1984) ch 9.

[88] See HA Clegg, A Fox and AF Thompson, *A History of British Trade Unions since 1889*, vol 1 (Oxford, Clarendon Press, 1964) 6–7.

[89] See further GP Cella, 'The Representation of Non-Standard Workers: Theory and Culture of Collective Bargaining' (2012) 18 *Transfer* 171, 176.

In this context, it must be questioned whether it is possible to change trade union behaviour, or whether non-standard workers would be better served by the establishment of new trade unions. This chapter does not seek to advocate in favour of one or the other, but suggests that if 'traditional' trade unions are to respond to the rise in non-standard work, then they must reconsider how they prioritise and think about their functions in the contemporary labour market. Although newer trade unions have led the way in responding to non-standard workers, 'traditional' trade unions benefit from an institutional memory, credibility, and organisational structures which are invaluable. If they were to take on solidaristic tasks, which involve a financial commitment such as acting as an employee mutual, then 'traditional' trade unions tend to have greater financial means than newer trade unions. This is particularly the case amongst general unions that cover a number of different sectors where risks and financial burdens could be shared. Finally, 'traditional' trade unions often have links with established political parties which may give them greater political influence. Changing trade union behaviour is undeniably difficult. It involves thinking about the language used in recruiting non-standard (women) workers, encouraging the visibility of non-standard (women) workers as branch officers, workplace representatives, and national officers, and involving them in policy development. Recent campaigns launched by the TUC to recruit young workers suggest that there is a willingness to change.[90] This chapter takes a first tentative step in that regard by calling for a new research agenda which places the challenges for trade unions surrounding non-standard work, and work in the gig economy, within the context of the feminisation of work. Against this background, future work should test this hypothesis by considering, in more detail, the gendered nature of trade union responses to non-standard work and comparing their responses with non-traditional trade unions, and other grass-roots organisations, to consider lessons that could be learnt in this regard.

[90] See the TUC's WorkSmart model aimed at young workers: 'A Career Coach that Works for Everyone' (*WorkSmart*) www.getworksmart.co.uk/ accessed 17 November 2018.

8

A Socio-Legal History of the Coalition of Immokalee Workers

MANOJ DIAS-ABEY*

> How was a grassroots organisation with a limited budget, based in a poor backwater in South Florida, whose members could barely afford dietary basics, going to convince corporate executives in suburban Los Angeles to forgo profits by volunteering to pay a penny per pound more for the tomatoes that went into their salsa and salads?[1]

I. Introduction

The Coalition of Immokalee Workers (CIW) is part of a growing body of labour organisations[2] in the United States that have abandoned a broken labour law system, and instead engage in forms of social movement activity – public communication, alliance building, and political mobilisation – to make gains for workers. The most visible of these organisations are worker centres, which now number over 200 across the country,[3] but there are several other types of non-traditional labour organisations as well. Traditional unions are also engaging with these strategies; 'social movement unionism' and 'community unionism' are often presented

* Lecturer in Law, University of Bristol Law School. The author wishes to thank Laura Germino, Steve Hitov, and Sean Sellers for agreeing to be interviewed; Adriana Zicky for excellent research assistance; Neil Fligstein for a very helpful conversation about strategic action field theory; and finally, Tonia Novitz and Hila Shamir for reading and commenting on an earlier draft of this chapter.

[1] B Estabrook, *Tomatoland: How Modern Industrial Agriculture Destroyed Our Most Alluring Fruit* (Kansas City, Andrew McMeel Publishing, 2011) 111.

[2] Although the CIW does not identify as a labour organisation – it refers to itself as a human rights organisation – it is analytically useful to categorise it as such, because organisations like the CIW may point a way forward for the labour movement. However, it is not a 'labor organization' for the purposes of the National Labor Relations Act of 1935, 29 USC §§ 151–69 (2012) or the Labor Management Reporting and Disclosure Act of 1959, 29 USC §§ 401–531 (2012).

[3] JR Fine, 'New Forms to Settle Old Scores: Updating the Worker Centre Story in the United States' (2011) 66 *Relations industrielles/Industrial Relations* 604.

as paths to union revitalisation.[4] There is, however, something qualitatively different between unions that are beneficiaries of the 'New Deal' era legal reforms,[5] and non-traditional labour organisations that are often animated by the absence of these protections. Moreover, these organisations seek to serve and organise those that the New Deal compact intentionally left out: African-Americans and racialised workers.[6] Currently, there is no widely accepted way of studying these organisations and their successes, and failures. Some favour using traditional economic analysis to assess their impact,[7] whilst others stress the sociological aspects of these organisations' work.[8] Other scholars prefer to examine the work of these organisations through analytical paradigms rooted in governance and regulatory studies.[9] Some of the most insightful writing on this new face of the labour movement takes a case study approach, which provides rich detail of their various functions.[10]

The CIW is not a traditional labour organisation because it does not bargain with employers on behalf of its members, and it rarely attempts to partner with government agencies to encourage them to enforce statutory labour standards. Instead, the CIW has developed a private regulatory system called the Fair Food Program (FFP) which governs labour conditions on tomato farms in Florida. By enlisting large corporate entities that purchase tomatoes from Florida – mainly fast food chains and supermarkets – to obtain their tomatoes from growers complying with a series of labour standards set out in a private code of conduct (Code of Conduct), the CIW has leveraged the enormous buying power of entities at

[4] See, eg, A Tattersall, *Power in Coalition: Strategies for Strong Unions and Social Change* (Ithaca, ILR Press/Cornell University Press, 2010); K Voss and R Sherman, 'Breaking the Iron Law of Oligarchy: Union Revitalization in the American Labor Movement' (2000) 106 *American Journal of Sociology* 303. Cf JF McAlevey, *No Shortcuts: Organizing for Power in the New Gilded Age* (New York, Oxford University Press, 2016).

[5] Although, as many authors point out, the labour relations framework has been a mixed blessing for the labour movement and unions – see, eg, CL Tomlins, *The State and the Unions: Labor Relations, Law, and the Organized Labor Movement in America, 1880–1960* (Cambridge, Cambridge University Press, 1985).

[6] See, eg, P Frymer, *Black and Blue: African Americans, the Labor Movement, and the Decline of the Democratic Party* (Princeton, Princeton University Press, 2007).

[7] See, eg, KA Elliott and RB Freeman, 'White Hats or Don Quixotes? Human Rights Vigilantes in the Global Economy' in RB Freeman, J Hersch and L Mishel (eds), *Emerging Labor Market Institutions for the Twenty-First Century* (Chicago, University of Chicago Press, 2005) 47.

[8] See, eg, CF Rosado Marzán, 'Worker Centers and the Moral Economy: Disrupting through Brokerage, Prestige, and Moral Framing' (2017) *University of Chicago Legal Forum* 409.

[9] See, eg, M Amengual and J Fine, 'Co-enforcing Labor Standards: The Unique Contributions of State and Worker Organizations in Argentina and the United States' (2017) 11 *Regulation & Governance* 129; C Estlund, *Regoverning the Workplace: From Self-Regulation to Co-Regulation* (New Haven, Yale University Press, 2010).

[10] R Milkman and E Ott (eds), *New Labor in New York: Precarious Workers and the Future of the Labor Movement* (Ithaca, ILR Press/Cornell University Press, 2014); R Milkman, J Bloom and V Harro (eds), *Working for Justice: The LA Model of Organizing and Advocacy* (Ithaca, ILR Press/Cornell University Press, 2010); J Fine, *Worker Centres: Organizing Communities at the Edge of the Dream* (Ithaca, ILR Press/Cornell University Press, 2006).

the top of the supply chain. The CIW was able to pressure these entities to join the FFP by banding together with sympathetic allies and applying social movement pressure to its targets. Pursuing similar tactics to the United Farm Workers in the 1960s and 1970s, this pressure came in multiple forms, including organising protest marches, initiating consumer boycotts, demanding the closure of outlets on university campuses, and proposing shareholder resolutions designed to embarrass management. Farm workers had input in drafting the provisions in the Code of Conduct and, as a result, the Code comprehensively regulates conditions such as wages, sexual harassment, and occupational health and safety. Most importantly, the FFP requires buyers to pay 1 penny more per pound for all tomatoes purchased,[11] resulting in a 20–35 per cent wage increase for farm workers.[12] Tomato growers have been motivated to join the FFP so that they can continue selling their produce to the large corporate buyers that are FFP members. In practice, the FFP has proven to be effective because it maintains a strong focus on worker education, provides an avenue for workers to complain without fear of reprisal, contains a thorough auditing mechanism performed by an institution independent from growers, and applies meaningful sanctions on employers that are non-compliant.[13]

The CIW has received a string of accolades that recognise its success in transforming the working conditions of farm workers on Florida's tomato fields. These include a Global Citizen Award from the Clinton Global Initiative in 2014, a Presidential Medal in 2015, and most recently in 2017, a MacArthur 'Genius' Fellowship for one of its founders, Greg Asbed. The CIW started in 1993 as a loose collective of farm workers and advocates who came together with the aim of ending the deteriorating labour conditions of farm workers in Immokalee, Florida. It initially had some success – in the autumn of 1995, for example, the CIW organised a five-day general strike which managed to reverse a unilateral wage cut implemented by one of the largest tomato growers in the area – although a broader transformation of the labour situation in Florida proved to be elusive.[14] In the span of 25 years, the

[11] Although 'one penny more' is the catch cry with which the CIW is most commonly associated, in actual fact, the FFP requires growers to pay differing premiums for different types of tomatoes – the premiums range from 1 cent to 4.6 cents more per pound of tomato depending on the type of tomato – Interview with S Hitov, General Counsel, Coalition of the Immokalee Workers (Washington DC, 12 February 2018).

[12] S Greenhouse, 'In Florida Tomato Fields, a Penny Buys Progress' *The New York Times* (New York, 24 April 2014) www.nytimes.com/2014/04/25/business/in-florida-tomato-fields-a-penny-buys-progress.html accessed 16 December 2018.

[13] See, eg, M Dias-Abey, 'Justice on our Fields: Can "Alt-Labor" Organizations Improve Migrant Farm Workers' Conditions' (2018) 53 *Harvard Civil Rights-Civil Liberties Law Review* 167; G Asbed and S Hitov, 'Preventing Forced Labor in Corporate Supply Chains: The Fair Food Program and Worker-Driven Social Responsibility' (2017) 52 *Wake Forest Law Review* 497; JJ Brudney, 'Decent Labour Standards in Corporate Supply Chains: The Immokalee Workers Model' in J Howe and R Owens (eds), *Temporary Labour Migration in the Global Era: The Regulatory Challenges* (Oxford, Hart Publishing, 2016) 351.

[14] See, eg, SL Marquis, *I Am Not a Tractor! How Florida Farmworkers Took on the Fast Food Giants and Won* (Ithaca, ILR Press/Cornell University Press, 2017) 25–26.

CIW went from a seemingly hopeless political project to one of the United States' most celebrated, new labour organisations. This chapter seeks to make sense of the CIW's remarkable rise by looking back at its history and asking how it managed to navigate around quiescent legal institutions, powerful industry structures, and an indifferent public.

In order to answer this question, this chapter provides a contextual account of how the CIW took action and why it succeeded, all the while foregrounding the role of law.[15] The conventional wisdom is that state law offered no assistance to farm workers in Florida, so the CIW devised a novel private solution (the corollary of this analysis is that we should no longer see state regulation as a terrain of struggle).[16] There are reasons to be critical of this historiography (and the conclusion that it leads to) because we can never be entirely free of law, even when some of the rules that we depend upon fail us. Appraising the CIW's history shows that the law was heavily implicated in its rise, because the CIW drew heavily on legal discourse and processes at various points. I argue that the CIW relied upon the law, broadly understood, in three main ways. First, as significant attention was being devoted to the problem of labour trafficking in the national and international arenas in the late 1990s, the CIW was able to intervene in public debates and suggest that the most durable solution was to be found in addressing deteriorating labour conditions on farms. Secondly, the CIW made use of public attention on trafficking to motivate fast food chains and supermarkets, which were wary of the material and reputational harm that was caused by being linked to human rights abuses in their supply chains, to take responsibility for farm working conditions. Thirdly, the CIW contributed in several important ways to the federal government's prosecution of crew leaders who engaged in labour trafficking, which conferred a measure of social prestige on the CIW and allowed it to convince other actors of its strategy. My approach in this chapter is to analyse key moments in the CIW's history and ask: how were law and legal processes involved in the CIW's strategy for achieving labour rights for farm workers? This question is a pertinent one, because the risk of eliding the role of law in the CIW's story is that it limits the full range of resources that other labour organisations, hoping to replicate the CIW's success, may consider available.

[15] This chapter draws on a case study method to appraise broader transformations in the US labour movement. We can only understand how new labour organisations have come to exercise influence by studying important cases in detail. As many have noted, the case study method is particularly useful for drawing descriptive inferences, and since our aim is to understand how new labour organisations operate, it is an effective methodology. For some key writing on the case study method, see, eg, B Flyvbjerg, 'Five Misunderstandings About Case-Study Research' (2006) 12 *Qualitative Inquiry* 219; J Gerring, 'What is a Case Study and What is it Good For?' (2004) 98 *American Political Science Review* 341; RE Skate, *The Art of Case Study Research* (Thousand Oaks, SAGE, 1995).

[16] This analysis, for example, is reflected in Susan Marquis's book-length treatment of the CIW's history. Marquis states: '[The CIW's success] … shows the need for, and the power of, novel solutions in those policy areas where the nature of government may mean the solution cannot come through government mechanism. Government do many things well, but they cannot solve every societal problem': Marquis, *I Am Not A Tractor!* (n 14) 222.

Narrating the CIW's history with a view to uncovering the role of law requires a method and, in the next section, I outline the theoretical framework that I draw upon: namely, field theory. The section that follows examines how the CIW operated in five key fields – the labour relations field, the anti-trafficking field, the fast food field, the supermarket field, and the tomato industry field – and how it drew upon the discursive and symbolic power of law in each of these arenas. The final section analyses how the law undergirded the CIW's strategy at crucial moments. I conclude this chapter with some brief comments about how labour organisations may be able to draw on the law to achieve their objectives.

II. Field Theory to Make Sense of the Sprawl of History

There are many ways to tell the story of the CIW's emergence from a position of relative weakness to one of strength. The approach that I take in this chapter is to describe how the CIW purposefully interacted with key actors, setting in motion a series of interconnected events, which had the outcome of creating a new system of labour governance for farm workers in Florida.[17] My objective is to set out an historical narrative that draws out relevant insights about how labour organisations, armed with imagination and resolution, can transform the dynamics of labour relations in particular industries. I make use of an important theoretical tool from the discipline of sociology – field analysis – to achieve this end.

Field analysis is a popular analytical framework and methodological tool that seeks to explain social action by focusing on *meso*-level domains in which actors orient their actions to each other.[18] It is a way of understanding the social world which, in the words of Pierre Bourdieu, 'thinks *in terms of relations*'.[19] Moreover, it is also a technique that can be applied to particular empirical situations to trace the chain of casual connections that constitute social action. I draw particularly on a variant of field analysis pioneered by sociologists, Neil Fligstein and Doug

[17] To reconstruct this socio-legal historiography, I have used a variety of techniques, including reviewing archival material (old newspaper articles, campaign pamphlets, transcripts of public hearings, etc), reading secondary material written on the CIW, and conducting semi-structured interviews with key players in the organisation (Laura Germino, co-founder of the CIW and mainly responsible for the CIW's anti-trafficking work; Steve Hitov, CIW's General Counsel; and Sean Sellers, formerly of the Fair Food Standards Council and Student/Farmworker Alliance).

[18] See, eg, P Gastón, 'Contention Across Social Fields: Manipulating the Boundaries of Labor Struggle in the Workplace, Community, and Market' (2018) 65 *Social Problems* 231; E Barman, 'Varieties of Field Theory and the Sociology of the Non-Profit Sector' (2016) 10 *Sociology Compass* 442; N Fligstein and D McAdam, *A Theory of Fields* (Oxford, Oxford University Press, 2012); JL Martin, 'What is Field Theory?' (2003) 109 *American Journal of Sociology* 1; P Bourdieu and LJD Wacquant, *An Invitation to Reflexive Sociology* (Chicago, University of Chicago Press, 1992) 94.

[19] Bourdieu and Wacquant, *Reflexive Sociology* (n 18) 96.

McAdam, which explains the problematique of collective action by synthesising insights from the social movement, economic sociology, and organisational theory literatures.[20] While relying primarily on Fligstein and McAdam's model of fields – which they call 'strategic action fields' to emphasise the agency of actors and the contingency of behaviour that creates social transformation – I also rely on the work of a number of other scholars who have developed Fligstein and McAdam's conceptual apparatus to better understand change in the social world.[21] It is necessary to explicate some of its key features before I can proceed to apply this analytical framework to the situation of the CIW.

Turning first to providing a working definition of a field: it is an arena of social life where individual and collective actors struggle for control, while sharing an understanding of what is at stake.[22] The stakes in a field include the purpose of the field, the relationship between actors, and the rules regulating acceptable behaviour.[23] Ultimately, determining whether a field exists is an empirical matter to resolve.[24] This chapter explains the CIW's rise through the operation of five distinct, but overlapping, fields: a labour relations field, an anti-trafficking field, a fast food field, a supermarket field, and a tomato industry field. It is possible to describe each of these as distinct fields, because they contain actors who vie for supremacy within each of these arenas, while being aware of each other and operating in accordance with rules understood by them all. These fields are overlapping because certain actors are concurrently prominent players in a number of fields. The fact that the fields are overlapping means that shifts in one can reverberate across others and create system-wide changes.

A set of common understandings and rules govern fields. The common understandings include the purpose of the field, the distribution of power and resources between parties, and expectations about how each other should behave.[25] We can think of these rules as a complex amalgam of norms, practices, and processes that are supported by power and legitimacy.[26] While formal, written law is an important aspect of the field's governance, legal and cultural logics interact in numerous ways, including in determining how written laws are operationalised in a particular field. As a number of socio-legal scholars have pointed out, the law is not only a tool of domination, but under the right conditions can be utilised instrumentally

[20] Fligstein and McAdam, *A Theory of Fields* (n 18).

[21] I am less interested in Bourdieu's conception, since it is focused more on the reproduction of fields than on the change that occurs within them – for a critical discussion of Bourdieu's contribution to field theory, see especially, C Calhoun, 'Habitus, Field, and Capital: The Question of Historical Specificity' in C Calhoun, E LiPuma and M Postone, *Bourdieu: Critical Perspectives* (Chicago, University of Chicago Press, 1993) 61.

[22] Fligstein and McAdam, *A Theory of Fields* (n 18).

[23] ibid 9.

[24] Bourdieu and Wacquant, *Reflexive Sociology* (n 18) 100.

[25] Fligstein and McAdam, *A Theory of Fields* (n 18).

[26] S Falk Moore, 'Law and Social Change: The Semi-Autonomous Social Field as an Appropriate Subject of Study' (1973) 7 *Law & Society Review* 719.

by less powerful actors.[27] While these common understandings and rules are not static, they are often durable.

As Fligstein and McAdam point out, shared understandings do not indicate that the actors see the distribution of power and resources within the field as legitimate.[28] *Contention* is a central aspect of fields, because actors take individual and collective action to disrupt fields and change the power relations within them. *Incumbents*, usually endowed with greater resources and interpretive frames that favour the status quo, will succeed in having their dominant position reaffirmed. However, *challengers* can, and often do, manage to shift fields in alternative directions. Field analysis is, at its heart, a theory of social change. While field members have a fairly wide degree of latitude to act in ways that benefit them, their structural positions within the field and the accepted rules of the field often constrain their agency.

Even the most stable fields do not remain stable forever. The most common way for change to take place within a field is as a result of an exogenous shock emanating from another, since weaker actors will not find it easy to overcome the structural limitations engendered by their positions.[29] According to Fligstein and McAdam, an exogenous shock can take one of three forms: (1) entry into a field by external parties; (2) changes in a related field; or (3) through the occurrence of large and impactful events which create momentary crises.[30] This means that field changes occur as a result of something that comes from the outside. Pablo Gaston argues that the exogenous shock explanation of change does not account sufficiently for actors' agency – he finds that actors can actively manipulate the situation in one field with the objective of creating change in another (which Gaston calls 'cross-field manipulation').[31] Both dynamics – exogenous shock and intentional cross-field manipulation – are evident in the story of the CIW.

III. The Rise of the CIW

A. Challenging Labour Relations in Florida

The actors in the Florida labour relations field include tomato growers, farm workers, government bodies, and civil society actors. These actors are involved

[27] The literature on how weaker parties in society mobilise law in aid of their objectives is large. For some key sources, see especially GN Rosenberg, *The Hollow Hope: Can Courts Bring About Social Change?*, 2nd edn (Chicago, University of Chicago Press, 2008); SA Scheingold, *The Politics of Rights: Lawyers, Public Policy, and Political Change*, 2nd edn (Ann Arbor, University of Michigan Press, 2004); MW McCann, *Rights at Work: Pay Equity Reform and the Politics of Legal Mobilization* (Chicago, University of Chicago Press, 1994).

[28] Fligstein and McAdam, *A Theory of Fields* (n 18) 170.

[29] ibid.

[30] ibid.

[31] Gastón, 'Contention Across Social Fields' (n 18).

in determining how tomato farmers should engage with their workers. The government bodies include federal agencies that enforce various workplace standards (eg, Wage & Hours Division, and the Occupational Health and Safety Administration).[32] The National Labor Relations Board, which should be a key player in the labour relations field, does not feature prominently with respect to farm workers because the National Labor Relations Act of 1935 does not cover agricultural employees.[33] Farm workers in Florida rely heavily on legal service providers and farm worker advocacy organisations and, as a result, these organisations are important players in the Florida labour relations field.

Prior to implementation of the FFP, agricultural employers behaved as though they believed that the rights of farm workers could be violated with impunity, partially as a result of weak state enforcement.[34] While employers must abide by the limited federal and state workplace regulations that apply to them – limited because farm workers are not covered by significant parts of the federal Fair Labor Standards Act of 1938[35] – many employers do not comply because the risk of being caught by overburdened field officers is low.[36] Farming interests in the state have continued to exercise an outsized influence to ensure that statutory workplace standards will not be strengthened nor enforcement intensified.[37] Farm labour advocates who attempt to undertake private enforcement to fill the gap left by public regulators face a Sisyphean task. Of course, workers and their advocates do not share the view that their labour rights are violable, but their lack of power within the labour relations field means that they must often acquiesce.

Even among farm labour advocates, significant differences exist. The conflicts between two farm worker advocacy organisations – the CIW and the Migrant

[32] Government bodies in Florida only play a marginal role because there is no state department of labor (it was abolished in the early 2000s). While the State Attorney General has some oversight functions, she has mostly been inactive in enforcing labour standards: S Woodman, 'Florida Has Not Held an Employer Responsible for Violating the Minimum Wage Since 2011' *The Nation* (New York, 11 July 2016) www.thenation.com/article/florida-has-not-held-an-employer-responsible-for-violating-the-minimum-wage-since-2011/ accessed 21 December 2018.

[33] National Labor Relations Act of 1935, 29 USC § 152(3) (2012).

[34] Wage theft is rife in Florida and farm workers are particularly affected – see 'Wage Theft in Florida: A Real Problem with Real Solutions' (Research Institute on Social and Economic Policy, November 2010) acwttf.files.wordpress.com/2012/09/fact-sheet-wt-report.pdf accessed 22 December 2018.

[35] M Linder, 'Farm Workers and the Fair Labor Standards Act: Racial Discrimination in the New Deal' (1986) 65 *Texas Law Review* 1335.

[36] On the general dearth of federal labour inspectors, see, eg, M Dietz, D Levitt and E Love, 'Enforcement of Labor Standards' in M Reich, K Jacobs and M Dietz (eds), *When Mandates Work: Raising Labor Standards at the Local Level* (Berkeley, University of California Press, 2014) 229. On the limitations of federal labour enforcement in Florida, in particular, see, eg, R Greene, 'Advocates Don't Feel Labor Department is Ally' *The Miami Herald* (Miami, 2 September 2003) www.miamiherald.com/news/state/article1927846.html accessed 22 December 2018.

[37] Farming groups, such as the Florida Fruit and Vegetable Association, have been powerful advocates for the interests of farm employers, with influence in Washington and the state legislature since the 1940s: see, eg, C Hahamovitch, *No Man's Land: Jamaican Guestworkers in America and the Global History of Deportable Labor* (Princeton, Princeton University Press, 2011) 94.

Farmworker Justice Project (MFJP)[38] – about the correct strategy to assist farm workers, reveals that shared understandings are contested from multiple angles. MFJP, which is part of Florida Legal Services, is a legal aid provider that assists low-wage and vulnerable farm workers. MFJP services the farm worker population by trying to gain the attention of public labour inspectorates, or by filing private legal suits, sometimes in the form of class actions, to achieve legal remedies for its clients. For many years before the FFP commenced operation, the prevalent mode of contesting labour relations was to file private legal suits to achieve redress for individual workers who had experienced wage theft. In fact, two of the CIW's founders, Greg Asbed and Laura Germino, started their careers working as paralegals for a similar legal service provider, Florida Rural Legal Services.[39] Their frustration with the lack of impact of legal advocacy prompted Asbed and Germino, together with other members of the CIW, to devise the FFP. As the FFP started to become more prominent, tensions between the MFJP and CIW began to increase. Members of the MFJP questioned the effectiveness of the CIW's approach, going so far as to disparage the motivations of the group's leadership.[40] To understand how the CIW's vision of field transformation won out, it is necessary to examine nearby fields.

B. A Proximate Anti-Trafficking Field

As the issue of trafficking started to gain more traction in the 1990s, a national anti-trafficking field began to cohere and the CIW played a key role in this process. I argue that the CIW was able to strategically utilise prevalent discourses in this field to draw attention to the issue of farm working conditions in Florida where forced labour appeared to thrive. Equally important, I contend that the CIW was able to intervene in the public debate and argue that the problem of human trafficking could not be solved with additional prosecutions and harsher penalties, but that it required a preventative approach, which meant empowering workers and improving labour standards in industries affected by trafficking.

An anti-trafficking field had existed in the United States for many decades, primarily made up of federal and state authorities responsible for enforcing the patchwork of legal prohibitions on the books against slavery, forced labour, peonage, human smuggling, and aggravated sexual assault.[41] At the CIW's instigation, the anti-trafficking field, which had previously ignored the issue of forced labour, started to turn its attention to the problem of modern-day slavery on Florida's

[38] Recently renamed the Immigrant & Migrant Rights Project.

[39] Marquis, *I Am Not A Tractor!* (n 14) 10.

[40] 'Special Comment on the Lawsuit Filed Recently Against Burger King' (Coalition of Immokalee Workers, 13 September 2011) ciw-online.org/blog/2011/09/florida-legal-services-lawsuit/accessed 22 December 2018.

[41] JM Chacón, 'Misery and Myopia: Understanding the Failures of US Efforts to Stop Human Trafficking' (2006) 74 *Fordham Law Review* 2977.

farms. In 1992, the CIW discovered the existence of a trafficking operation through its contact with farm workers.[42] It started to investigate the matter when the US Department of Justice and the FBI initially showed limited interest, and it continued gathering information and collecting evidence for five years, even after law enforcement authorities became involved.[43] In 1997, after a lengthy trial, a crew leader and his associate were found guilty of 25 counts of enslavement, extortion, immigration and labour violations, and sentenced to 15 years in prison.[44] While the case was successfully prosecuted by the federal Department of Justice, it was brought only after the CIW had discovered the existence of the operation, applied pressure to prosecute, and provided vital evidence gathered through its own investigations.[45] Between 1997 and 2010, there were nine prosecutions involving forced labour on Florida's farms and the CIW participated, in some way, in most of them.[46] The horrors uncovered by these prosecutions prompted government officials to label Florida, the 'ground zero for modern day slavery'.[47] In one particularly egregious case, Miguel Flores and Sebastian Gomez were found to have kept a workforce of some 400 men and women, mostly indigenous Mexicans and Guatemalans, under armed guard and compelled them to work 10–12 hours each day harvesting tomatoes, six days per week, for as little as $20 per week.[48] As a result of these prosecutions, law enforcement authorities released more than 1,000 workers held captive.[49] These cases received significant coverage by the media, with stories placed prominently in publications such as the *St Petersburg Times*, the *Washington Post*, and the *New York Times*.[50]

[42] Marquis, *I Am Not A Tractor!* (n 14) 37–45.

[43] ibid.

[44] Department of Justice, 'Media Release: Miguel Flores and Associates Sentenced to 15 Years for Enslaving Migrant Workers' (Washington DC, 14 November 1997) www.justice.gov/archive/opa/pr/1997/November97/482cr.htm.html accessed 22 December 2018.

[45] Tom Perez, then at the Department of Justice, appointed Luis Cabeza deBaca, a civil rights prosecutor, to take charge of the case. This was one of deBaca's early forced labour cases. In 2009, deBaca was appointed Ambassador-at-Large to Monitor and Combat Trafficking in Persons by President Obama: Interview with Hitov (n 11).

[46] Due to the CIW's trusted status within the migrant farmworker community, it was able to receive information from workers and pass it on to the authorities, as well as provide support and reassurance to affected workers so that they could testify against their abusers. On occasion, the CIW also went undercover to gather evidence. See, eg, Asbed and Hitov, 'Preventing Forced Labor' (n 13) 502–4.

[47] J Bowe, 'Nobodies: Does Slavery Exist in America?' *The New Yorker* (New York, 21 April 2003) www.newyorker.com/magazine/2003/04/21/nobodies accessed 22 December 2018.

[48] S Sellers and G Asbed, 'The History and Evolution of Forced Labor in Florida Agriculture' (2011) 5 *Race/Ethnicity: Multidisciplinary Global Contexts* 29.

[49] ibid.

[50] See, eg, E Schlosser, 'A Side Order of Human Rights' *The New York Times* (New York, 6 April 2005) www.nytimes.com/2005/04/06/opinion/a-side-order-of-human-rights.html? accessed 22 December 2018; B Broadway, 'Churches Back Boycotts Over Migrant Workers' *The Washington Post* (Washington DC, 22 November 2003) www.washingtonpost.com/archive/local/2003/11/22/churches-back-boycotts-over-migrant-workers/3d2271c4-ae7b-4715-9a4c-d959995c00e7/?utm_term=.447e3364f777 accessed 22 December 2018; B Maxwell, 'Slavery Alive in Florida's Agricultural Industry' *St Petersburg Times* (St Petersburg, 3 July 2002).

At the turn of the century, the anti-trafficking field began to consider the enactment of specific legislation to facilitate greater prosecution of this conduct. Concurrently, spurred on by a desire to tackle transnational crime, the international community was engaged in the negotiation of a Trafficking Protocol under the auspices of the United Nations Office on Drugs and Crime.[51] While the international and national efforts mostly developed along parallel tracks, their paths frequently crossed. The US Congress passed the Trafficking Victims Protection Act of 2000[52] (TPVA) on 28 October 2000, amidst an extraordinary amount of attention on the issue of human trafficking in the preceding decade. The TPVA advanced a number of preventative measures, created new offences, and increased penalties to aid prosecutions, as well as providing for the protection of victims (eg, by the creation of a special T-visa for trafficked victims).[53] The CIW was involved in the TPVA's conception, drafting, and enactment.[54] Although President Bill Clinton signed the TPVA into law, the subsequent administration of George W Bush, keen to define 'compassionate conservativism', also expressed enthusiastic support.[55] Some have argued that genuine concern for the plight of trafficked victims intersected with the United States' post-September 11 preoccupation with securing its border with Mexico to create the perfect storm for a legislative intervention.[56] Others have pointed out that the national anti-trafficking discussion also relied upon anxieties about gender and sexuality.[57]

The passage of the TPVA saw a three-fold increase in the number of prosecutions undertaken by federal authorities,[58] with the then-Attorney General, John Ashcroft, announcing in 2001 that fighting trafficking would be a major priority for the Department of Justice.[59] The CIW made use of the national attention to make a compelling case for why the solution to the problem – at least with respect to forced labour – lay in improving the labour conditions of farm workers. Both the TPVA and the Trafficking Protocol take a criminal law approach to the issue of labour trafficking, which sees trafficking as an exceptional occurrence

[51] Which became the Protocol to Prevent, Suppress and Punish Trafficking in Persons, Especially Women and Children, supplementing the United Nations Convention against Transnational Organized Crime (adopted 15 November 2000, entered into force 25 December 2003) 2237 UNTS 319.

[52] Pub L No 106-386, 114 Stat 1464.

[53] H Shamir, 'A Labor Paradigm for Human Trafficking' (2012) 60 *UCLA Law Review* 76.

[54] Interview with L Germino, Founding Member, Coalition of Immokalee Workers (15 May 2018). See also, K Bales and R Soodalter, *The Slave Next Door: Human Trafficking and Slavery in America Today* (Berkeley, University of California Press, 2009) ch 3.

[55] W Chapkis, 'Soft Glove, Punishing Fist: The Trafficking Victims Protection Act of 2000' in E Bernstein and L Schaffner (eds), *Regulating Sex: The Politics of Intimacy and Identity* (New York, Routledge, 2005) 51, 59.

[56] N Sharma, 'Anti-Trafficking Rhetoric and the Making of a Global Apartheid' (2005) 17(3) *NWSA Journal* 88.

[57] Chapkis, 'Soft Glove, Punishing Fist' (n 55).

[58] Florida State University, Center for the Advancement of Human Rights, *Florida Responds to Human Trafficking* (2003) 25 www.northeastern.edu/humantrafficking/wp-content/uploads/Florida_Responds_to_Human_Trafficking.pdf accessed 22 December 2018.

[59] ibid.

that must be treated with penal sanction. However, the CIW saw forced labour on farms as driven by poverty and powerlessness, and therefore advocated for what labour law scholars such as Hila Shamir call a 'labour approach', which treats trafficking as a problem to be solved by transforming the underlying structure of labour markets.[60] Shamir's point is that in circumstances where work has become so degraded, unscrupulous traffickers are bound to act opportunistically. The labour approach sees trafficking as existing on a continuum: one end is characterised by low pay, dangerous working conditions, and limited worker power to seek remedies; and the other end, by workers forced to perform work under compulsion.[61] The CIW proposal to stamp out slavery in Florida was to transform the working conditions on fields growing one of Florida's major crops, tomatoes. This attitude characterised the CIW's approach right from the outset – as early as 2002, Germino, one of the CIW's founders, argued that, 'the solution … [to labour trafficking] … is attacking the root causes and modernizing agricultural labor relations so workers have more power'.[62]

Uniquely, the CIW also saw that if major purchasers of Florida's tomatoes could drive down prices through large volume purchases, then these same entities could also motivate farmers to eliminate forced labour.[63] Although the ultimate beneficiaries of forced labour were almost always larger businesses that purchased farmers' tomatoes, none were ever prosecuted.[64] Brandishing posters and placards featuring phrases, such as 'Taco Bell makes farm workers poor' and 'From the hands of a slave', the CIW made the public case for why fast food chains and supermarkets should be held responsible for failing to eradicate forced labour in their supply chains. The CIW was engaged in what the social movement literature calls 'reframing', which explains how actors present their vision for transformation in a way that is culturally resonant and socially convincing.[65] Sally Merry Engle reminds us that 'frames themselves are not ideas but ways of packaging and presenting ideas that generate shared beliefs, motivate collective action, and

[60] Shamir, 'A Labor Paradigm' (n 53).

[61] ibid. The continuum approach also accords with how workers subjectively experience coercion along a spectrum: D Brennan, 'Subjectivity of Coercion: Workers' Experiences with Trafficking in the United States' in P Kotiswaran (ed), *Revisiting the Law and Governance of Trafficking, Forced Labor and Modern Slavery* (Cambridge, Cambridge University Press, 2017) 134.

[62] M Maidenberg, 'Florida Employers Guilty of Slavery' (*LaborNotes*, 31 July 2002) www.labornotes.org/2002/07/florida-employers-guilty-slavery accessed 22 December 2018.

[63] Marquis, *I am not a Tractor!* (n 14) 45. This analysis is also shared by scholars who study the US tomato value chain: see, eg, G Gereffi, J Lee and M Christian, 'US-Based Food and Agricultural Value Chains and Their Relevance to Healthy Diets' (2009) 4 *Journal of Hunger & Environmental Nutrition* 357.

[64] United States Senate, Committee on Health, Education, Labor, and Pensions, *Hearing on Examining Ending Abuses and Improving Working Conditions for Tomato Workers*, 110th Cong 889 (15 April 2008) (testimony of Charlie Frost, Detective, Collier County Sherriff's Office).

[65] S Engle Merry, *Human Rights and Gender Violence: Translating International Law into Local Justice* (Chicago, Chicago University Press, 2006) ch 5; DA Snow and others, 'Frame Alignment Processes, Micromobilization, and Movement Participation' (1986) 51 *American Sociological Review* 464.

define appropriate strategies for action'.[66] The CIW was able to draw upon the national attention on combatting trafficking, together with the growing recognition that the agricultural sector in Florida was a site of forced labour, to give force to its claim for improving labour conditions.[67] Moreover, they had a convincing proposal for the means to achieve the elimination of forced labour on Florida's farms.

C. Taking the Fight to the Fast Food Companies

Even though the CIW proposed a labour approach to the problem of human trafficking, it was clear for them that pursuing the growers alone was not a feasible strategy for changing the working conditions on farms. Growers were facing increasing pressure from the purchasing practices of consolidated buyers. The unique insight of the CIW was that the real power to change labour conditions on farms lay with one of the big purchasers of Florida's tomatoes: the fast food chains. With the eating habits of Americans changing in recent decades, the food services sector (in which fast food is the biggest player) consumes a growing share of the tomatoes consumed.[68] By purchasing large volumes, fast food companies can dictate prices, product quality, and a variety of other conditions; Yum Restaurants!, McDonalds, Burger King, and a handful of other operators have the power to shape entire fresh produce sectors.[69] These companies depend upon Florida for its field tomatoes, because Florida supplies close to 90 per cent of America's needs during the winter months.[70] Based on its understanding of the structure of the tomato and fast food industries, and Florida's unique position as a major fresh produce supplier, the CIW decided to hold fast food companies responsible for farm working conditions. We can consider the dense network of horizontal and vertical relationships of production and exchange between tomato producers, fast food companies, and consumers as constituting a fast food field.

The CIW first targeted the fast food giant, Taco Bell, in 2000, by asking it to pay one penny more for each pound of round tomatoes purchased from

[66] Merry, *Human Rights and Gender Violence* (n 65) 136.

[67] The labour standards contained in the FFP are particularly effective in addressing labour trafficking. eg, the use of labour intermediaries is a major factor in the incidence of forced labour in domestic supply chains, and the FFP bans the use of labour contractors: see A Crane and others, 'Governance Gaps in Eradicating Forced Labor: From Global to Domestic Supply Chains' (2017) *Regulation & Governance*, doi:10.1111/rego.12162, 1–21.

[68] Oxfam America, *Like Machines in the Field: Workers Without Rights in American Agriculture* (March 2004) 28 www.oxfamamerica.org/static/media/files/like-machines-in-the-fields.pdf accessed 23 December 2018.

[69] ibid.

[70] Greenhouse, 'Florida Tomato Fields' (n 12).

Florida's farmers.[71] Taco Bell was an obvious choice of target because of its association with Mexican culture – its mascot is the iconic talking Chihuahua who exclaims in Spanish, '*Yo Quiero* Taco Bell!' (I want Taco Bell!).[72] At first, Taco Bell was unwilling to agree to the CIW's terms, citing the fact that the working conditions of its suppliers had little to do with the company. After a gruelling five-year campaign, Yum! Brands (which owned the Taco Bell chain) eventually capitulated. With further campaigning, the CIW was able to pressure McDonalds in 2007 to agree to its terms. Burger King and Subway followed suit in 2008, and Chipotle and Mexican Grill signed in 2012. Wendy's is the last of the five major fast food corporations not to have joined the FFP, and it is still (as of February 2019) the target of a wide-ranging campaign. The tactics that the CIW employed in its campaigns against the fast food companies included organising protest marches, calling for boycotts, staging hunger strikes, and proposing resolutions at shareholder meetings to pressure management. The boycotts, in particular, proved to be a potent tool in the modern era because of their ability to disrupt contemporary forms of capitalism, which Stuart Hall has argued is increasingly mediated by cultural meaning and knowledge.[73]

The CIW confronted these powerful corporations with sympathetic allies by its side, such as churches and student groups.[74] Students, for example, ran campaigns at close to 300 colleges, resulting in 25 schools, colleges, and universities either removing or preventing new Taco Bell restaurants from opening, or ending existing sponsorship agreements with the company.[75] The campaigns that the CIW waged from 2005 against the fast food sector contained two ingredients that social movement scholars have highlighted as essential to successful social change: repertoires of contention that are broad, creative, and impactful, and solidarity from networks of allies.[76]

Why did fast food companies ultimately bow to social movement pressure from the CIW and its allies? One reason is that the CIW ran a campaign that caused tangible commercial damage.[77] A company executive at Compass Group (a food service company), which signed on to the FFP in 2009, admitted in a

[71] Taco Bell is owned by Yum! Brands, which also owns Pizza Hut, KFC, A&W, and a number of other fast food brands.

[72] Marquis, *I am not a Tractor!* (n 15) 54.

[73] S Hall, 'Brave New World' [1988] (October) *Marxism Today* 24.

[74] J Lo and A Jacobson, 'Human Rights from Field to Fork: Improving Labor Conditions for Food-Sector Workers by Organizing Across Boundaries' (2011) 5 *Race/Ethnicity: Multidisciplinary Global Contexts* 61.

[75] D Campbell, 'Taco's Tomato Pickers on Slave Wages' *The Guardian* (London, 17 March 2003) www.theguardian.com/world/2003/mar/17/usa.duncancampbell accessed 23 December 2018.

[76] See, eg, SG Tarrow, *Power in Movement: Social Movements and Contentious Politics*, 3rd edn (Cambridge, Cambridge University Press, 2011).

[77] University campaigns succeeded in either removing existing or preventing new Taco Bell restaurants opening on 23 campuses. At Boise State University, the campaign prevented Taco Bell obtaining naming rights to a basketball stadium: see Marquis, *I Am Not a Tractor!* (n 14) 64.

rare moment of candour that the reason for the company's acquiescence was the disruption that the CIW threatened to its university operations.[78] We can only speculate about other motivations. Generally, an important reason why companies agree to social movement demands is fear of the damage that might be caused to their carefully cultivated brands.[79] This seems particularly apposite in the case of fast food companies, which value their reputations highly. The CIW's campaign also came at an opportune time. In the closing decades of the twentieth century, public opinion seemed to be turning against fast food. The libel case that McDonalds brought against two Greenpeace activists in 1990 turned out be a public relations disaster, because it showed the corporate chicanery necessary to maintain its public image.[80] In 2004, the premier of Morgan Spurlock's documentary, 'Super Size Me', brought further bad publicity. The CIW strategically called boycotts at a time of unprecedented interest in the fast food sector's impact on people's health, the environment, and animal rights. The CIW capitalised on the fast food sector's momentary weakness to draw attention to working conditions in its supply chains. It used the incidence of forced labour uncovered through the anti-trafficking prosecutions to further dramatise the situation.

D. Supermarkets Join the Fair Food Program

Besides fast food corporations, the other major customers of Florida's tomatoes are supermarkets. In 2008, Whole Foods voluntarily joined the FFP. Aimed at a niche, upwardly mobile urban market, Wholefoods seeks to distinguish itself on the basis of product quality, just treatment of animals, and environmentally sustainable practices. Its decision to join the FFP can be attributed to growing awareness about labour issues in product supply chains, the often forgotten pillar of ethical consumption.[81] Walmart's accession to the FFP in 2014 was more surprising, and potentially more transformative because Walmart also agreed to apply the FFP to its tomato growers in Georgia, South Carolina, and Virginia, in addition to its

[78] C Queen, Compass Group, 'Address' (United Nations Annual Forum on Business and Human Rights, Geneva, 18 November 2015) www.ciw-online.org/blog/2015/11/ffp-united-nations accessed 23 December 2018.

[79] Elliott and Freeman, 'White Hats or Don Quixotes?' (n 7). cf Tim Bartley and Curtis Child did not find that anti-sweatshop campaigns had a discernible impact on firms' reputations: T Bartley and C Child, 'Movements, Markets and Fields: The Effects of Anti-Sweatshop Campaigns on US Firms, 1993–2000' (2011) 90 *Social Forces* 425.

[80] E Schlosser, *Fast Food Nation: The Dark Side of the All-American Meal* (Boston, Houghton Mifflin, 2001) 245–49.

[81] See, eg, Whole Foods announced in 2015 that it would no long source products from suppliers that use prison labour: S Shemkus, 'Beyond Cheap Labor: Can Prison Work Programs Benefit Inmates?' *The Guardian* (London, 9 December 2015) www.theguardian.com/sustainable-business/2015/dec/09/prison-work-program-ohsa-whole-foods-inmate-labor-incarceration accessed 23 December 2018.

strawberry and apple suppliers.[82] But what motivated Walmart, a company that labour historian Nelson Lichtenstein has described as possessing a 'militant hostility to trade unionism',[83] to join a programme aimed at improving the lot of farm workers?

Some context is important to understand the evolving relationship between the FFP and prominent supermarket companies.[84] After World War II, the number of supermarkets in the United States exploded, transforming the way that Americans receive their food. It is estimated that 40,000 supermarkets (conventional supermarkets and 'hypermarkets' like the Walmart SuperCenters) are located around the country.[85] In the 1990s, there was a massive wave of consolidation in the industry and locally-based chains gave way to large regionally based and national monoliths.[86] Many of these consolidations were in response to Walmart's entry into the supermarket business and its rapid growth. Through a combination of bringing logistics such as purchasing, warehousing, distribution, and trucking in-house, using technological innovations to meticulously gather data on sales, keeping labour costs low, and leveraging its large purchasing volumes to obtain cheap prices from its suppliers, Walmart came to dominate the American retail sector more generally, and food retailing in particular.[87] Walmart now accounts for almost one-quarter to one-third of all grocery sales in the United States.[88] Within the supermarket field, which is made up of these regionally and nationally-based supermarket chains and their suppliers, there is fierce competition. This competition means that supermarkets compete on the basis of price, quality, and diversity.[89] According to Jason Konefal and his colleagues, the range and quality of fresh produce has become an especially important field of battle, and retailers have moved to using private labels as a way to 'advertise the quality of their products, but also to further diversify the marketplace for food and develop new market niches'.[90]

[82] G Gilbert, 'The Coalition of Immokalee Workers Takes Aim at Wendy's' (*In These Times*, 2 March 2015) inthesetimes.com/working/entry/17701/coalition_of_immokalee_workers_wendys accessed 24 February 2019.

[83] Nelson Lichtenstein describes in great detail the extreme steps taken by Walmart to defeat unionisation efforts amongst its distribution and retail workers: N Lichtenstein, *The Retail Revolution: How Wal-Mart Created a Brave New World of Business* (New York, Metropolitan Books, 2009) ch 5.

[84] The following supermarket chains are members of the FFP (indicates when they joined): Whole Foods Markets (2008), Trader Joe's (2012), Walmart (2014), Fresh Market (2015), and Ahold USA (2015).

[85] 'How Many Grocery Stores are in the United States?' (*FoodIndustry.com*, 23 April 2017) www.foodindustry.com/articles/how-many-grocery-stores-are-there-in-the-united-states accessed 23 December 2018.

[86] J Konefal and others, 'Supermarkets and Supply Chains in North America' in D Burch and G Lawrence (eds), *Supermarkets and the Agri-food Supply Chains: Transformation in the Production and Consumption of Foods* (Cheltenham, Edward Elgar, 2007) 268.

[87] Lichtenstein, *The Retail Revolution* (n 83).

[88] HS James Jr, MK Henrickson and PH Howard, 'Networks, Power and Dependency in the Agrifood Industry' in HS James Jr (ed), *The Ethics and Economics of Agrifood Competition* (Dordrecht, Springer, 2013) 99.

[89] Konefal and others, 'Supermarkets and Supply Chains' (n 86).

[90] ibid, 278.

With this background in mind, it is possible to posit four hypotheses as to why Walmart joined the FFP. The most obvious explanation is that the FFP offered a relatively inexpensive way for Walmart to launder its reputation. Charity has long been a part of corporate public relations strategy, which likely explains why Walmart controls one of the country's largest philanthropic foundations.[91] Secondly, Walmart's 'just-in-time' procurement practices means that it has little room for disruption in its supply chains. Labour strife on farms can cause disruption, and thus, from Walmart's perspective, pacifying workers with a relatively small increase in wages might have provided it with a way to insure against this risk.[92] Thirdly, joining the FFP might have offered Walmart with an opportunity to appease a growing segment of its consumer base that is no longer primarily motivated by price alone.[93] The fourth, and perhaps most intriguing hypothesis, is that the prevalence of forced labour on farms was a situation that Walmart's management could no longer openly countenance. Bethany Moreton has shown how Evangelical Christianity was strategically invoked at several points in Walmart's history to further its corporate strategy, and the existence of forced labour in its supply chains likely contradicted Walmart's professed piety.[94] In all likelihood, the real attraction of the FFP was a combination of factors – while eliminating the risk of disruption in its supply chain, the FFP allowed Walmart to burnish its Christian credentials and also appeal to a portion of its customers that cares about ethical consumption.

E. Tomato Industry Field

The growing number of fast food and supermarket companies joining the FFP could not make improvements for workers until the CIW obtained the cooperation of the growers to implement the conditions of employment set out in the Code of Conduct and to pass on the wage premium to workers. Growers were initially wary of the FFP for two main reasons. First, even though the wage premium was being provided by buyers further upstream, growers would still incur costs to implement some of the FFP's terms.[95] Secondly, and more importantly, accession

[91] Lichtenstein, *The Retail Revolution* (n 83) 209–15.

[92] A sub-field called 'supply chain risk management' provides important insights for companies seeking to manage a variety of risks in their supply chains (environmental, industrial, organisational, etc): see, eg, W Ho and others, 'Supply Chain Risk Management: A Literature Review' (2015) 53 *International Journal of Production Research* 5031.

[93] Walmart has recently launched a range of organic products under its Great Value store brand: J Sturgeon, 'Organic Groceries Go Discount as Walmart Canada Rolls Out New Label' *Global News* (Toronto, 16 December 2015) globalnews.ca/news/2404387/organic-groceries-go-discount-as-walmart-canada-rolls-out-new-label accessed 23 December 2018.

[94] B Moreton, *To Serve God and Wal-Mart: The Making of Christian Free Enterprise* (Cambridge, Mass., Harvard University Press, 2009).

[95] eg, Pacific Tomato Growers reported that the company spent $5,000 on shade tents, and $50,000 for an improved drinking water system, in addition to wage costs for the time spent on waiting (which was previously unpaid): Greenhouse, 'Florida Tomato Fields' (n 12).

to the FFP meant that the growers would need to share power with workers, a state of affairs to which they were unaccustomed. In the early days of the CIW's struggle, in response to a request for a wage increase, a grower tellingly remarked: 'The tractor does not tell the farmer how to run his farm.'[96] This statement encapsulates how the tomato growers saw their workforce: as a factor of production, rather than living and breathing humans with their own needs and desires. In 2005, the CIW marked its first victory with Yum! Brands joining the programme, but it would not be until 2010 that the first grower would agree to implement the FFP.[97]

Growers' compliance with the FFP ultimately depended on a set of unique dynamics in the tomato industry field. Initially, the growers insisted that implementation was a matter for buyers to resolve with the CIW. The growers cited practical and legal impediments to implementing the FFP and argued that they could not be held responsible for the instances of slavery uncovered, because growers did not directly employ the farm workers (workers were mostly employed through labour contractors).[98] They remained unmoved by the demands of buyers – even an entreaty by the National Restaurants Association was unsuccessful. In fact, the Florida Tomato Growers Exchange (Exchange), an industry group made up of tomato growers in Florida, threatened its members with US$100,000 fines if they cooperated with the CIW.[99] The continued revelations regarding forced labour on Florida's fields, however, changed the calculus for the growers. On 20 December 2008, an article in the *Fort Meyer News* named the two largest tomato growers in Florida, Six L's (now Lipmans Produce) and Pacific Tomato Growers, as direct beneficiaries of labour trafficking.[100] In 2010, Publix, Florida's largest grocery chain, refused to purchase tomatoes from Florida until it could be assured that slaves did not pick their tomatoes.[101] This proved to be the turning point which split the united front of the growers. Shortly after, Pacific Tomato Growers left the Exchange and agreed to implement the FFP. A few weeks later, Six L's signed. In late 2010, the Exchange surrendered and entered into an agreement with the CIW, which extended the protections to include a complaint resolution process, workplace health and safety committees, and a process for

[96] United States Senate, Committee on Health, Education, Labor, and Pensions, *Hearing on Examining Ending Abuses and Improving Working Conditions for Tomato Workers*, 110th Cong 889 (15 April 2008) (testimony of Benitez, Co-Founder of the Coalition of the Immokalee Workers).

[97] During the five-year period in which the growers refused to cooperate, the wage premium that the buyers provided sat in escrow accounts undistributed to workers.

[98] United States Senate, Committee on Health, Education, Labor, and Pensions, *Hearing on Examining Ending Abuses and Improving Working Conditions for Tomato Workers*, 110th Cong 889 (15 April 2008) (testimony of Reggie Brown, Executive Vice-President, Florida Tomato Growers Exchange).

[99] Greenhouse, 'Florida Tomato Fields' (n 12).

[100] A Bennett Williams, 'Immokalee Family Sentenced for Slavery' *Fort Myers News-Press* (20 December 2008), cited in Marquis, *I Am Not a Tractor!* (n 14) 90–1.

[101] Marquis, *I Am Not a Tractor!* (n 14) 93.

educating farmworkers on their rights under the Code of Conduct.[102] As a result of this agreement, the Code of Conduct has been in place since the 2011–2012 growing season.

F. A New Labour Relations Paradigm

The CIW's proposal for reforming the labour relations field ultimately triumphed, overtaking the MFJP's more limited vision of strategic employment litigation to assist the migrant farm worker community. The CIW did not implement its vision because it suddenly became a dominant player in the labour relations field, able to wield its power to compel other parties to agree to its demands. Nor did the CIW manage to influence state institutions to enact new laws, and therefore, utilise the coercive power of law to change the behaviour of parties on farms. Instead, the CIW had to employ a softer kind of power 'to induce cooperation by appealing to and helping create shared meanings and collective identities'.[103] One of the key ways in which the CIW was able to do this was by amassing 'symbolic capital', a term that Pierre Bourdieu has used to describe the reputation and prestige of actors,[104] which it then deployed to convince other parties to follow its vision.

The CIW gained symbolic capital primarily through its anti-trafficking work. This provides a useful way to understand how an organisation lacking in the usual accoutrements of power can nevertheless convince others to follow its path. Symbolic capital, like other forms of capital in Bourdieu's conception, can be gained and lost – it is a quantity that is accretive, relational and, above all else, likely to persuade. When the CIW was organising work stoppages and hunger strikes in its early days, it did not possess much in the way of symbolic capital. However, its stature grew through its participation in trafficking prosecutions throughout the 1990s and 2000s. Part of the reason for this was that participation in formal state processes, like court actions, conferred a measure of legitimacy and authority, which other actors began to notice. In recognition of the CIW's important role in the anti-trafficking field, it received numerous awards, including the recognition of Germino by the US State Department as a 'Trafficking in Persons Hero'.[105] On the occasion of the CIW receiving the Robert F Kennedy Memorial Centre for Human Rights Award, in 2003, the *Palm Beach Post* observed that the award recognised

[102] 'About CIW' (*Coalition of Immokalee Workers*, 2018) ciw-online.org/about accessed 23 December 2018.

[103] Fligstein and McAdam, *A Theory of Fields* (n 18) 46.

[104] See, especially, P Bourdieu (R Terdiman tr), 'The Force of Law: Toward a Sociology of the Juridical Field' (1987) 38 *Hastings Law Journal* 805; P Bourdieu, *The Logic of Practice* (Richard Nice tr, Stanford, Stanford University Press, 1980) ch 7.

[105] 'Slavery in the Fields and the Food We Eat' (*Coalition of Immokalee Workers*, N.d) ciw-online.org/wp-content/uploads/12SlaveryintheFields.pdf accessed 23 December 2018.

the CIW's 'growing national impact'.[106] Simply put, the CIW's growing prestige was a key dynamic in how it managed to convince other labour relations actors to implement its vision of justice on farms. The extent to which the CIW's vision has taken hold today in the labour relations field is summed up in a revealing quip made by Gerardo Chavez, another founder of the CIW: '[W]e are the new department of labour.'[107]

IV. Uncovering the Role of Law

The CIW's pursuit of improved working standards for Florida's tomato farm workers has primarily been a political struggle. Finding little support for new laws or better enforcement among state institutions, the CIW politically campaigned for a private regulatory system to govern working conditions. However, at key points in the CIW's struggle, the law proved to be a crucial resource. The above analysis has traced how the CIW participated in legal processes and drew upon legal discourses in the various, overlapping fields in which it was involved. This is a story that often does not get told with respect to the CIW. This does not mean that the law accounts for all of the CIW's successes. Other factors were clearly in play. For example, it is no coincidence that the CIW's campaign for the FFP took flight at the same time that the anti-globalisation movement started to focus attention on multinational corporations as sources of human rights abuse, 'adbusting' began to heighten our awareness of the perils of unbridled consumption, and Naomi Klein's 'No Logo' – perhaps the zeitgeist of the era – exhorted people to put away their credit cards and pick up placards instead.[108] However, we should not be too quick to ignore the role of law, even if it is only the symbolic and discursive power of the law that should concern us.

For the CIW, the law proved to be an important resource that it could use in its struggle for fair working conditions. Events in the anti-trafficking field, in which the CIW was a key participant, proved vital in several respects. At one level, the increased attention on anti-trafficking at the international and national levels was a political opportunity to which the CIW responded. But equally, the CIW shaped the direction of the anti-trafficking movement by pressuring the Department of Justice to prosecute crew leaders running forced labour operations. Here we have the deliberate cross-field manipulation that Gaston argues is so vital to how social movement actors affect change.[109] Law proved to be the tool that allowed this manipulation. In his seminal work on the pay equity campaigns of the 1970s and

[106] D Moffett, 'Slavery? In Florida? In 2003? Yes' *The Palm Beach Post* (Palm Beach, 23 November 2003) http://ciw-online.org/blog/2003/11/pbpedslavery/ accessed 23 December 2018.
[107] G Chavez in *Food Chains* (S Rawal dir, Screen Media Films, 2014).
[108] N Klein, *No Logo* (New York, Picador, 2000).
[109] Gastón, 'Contention Across Social Fields' (n 18).

1980s, Michael McCann attempted to lay bare the central role played by law.[110] He found that law 'was a complex repertoire of discursive strategies and symbolic frameworks that structure ongoing social intercourse and meaning-making activity among citizens'.[111] We can begin to disaggregate how the CIW drew upon the discursive and symbolic power of anti-trafficking laws to frame and give authority to its political campaigns.

First, the ongoing prosecutions of farm crew leaders in Florida throughout the 1990s and 2000s highlighted just how pervasive these practices were in agriculture. It also made clear the extent to which general labour conditions had deteriorated. For the CIW's friends and allies in the student and church movements, this evidence was too compelling to ignore and, as a result, the CIW could count on the support of a broad cross-section of the community to press its claims. It also provided the CIW with a cudgel to bludgeon the fast food companies and supermarkets, which claimed to deplore forced labour while reaping its benefits. The companies, of course, had pre-existing corporate codes of conduct that prohibited products made with slave labour, but the CIW's campaign posed a question that they could not ignore: could they prove that there was no forced labour in their supply chains?[112] The discursive and symbolic qualities of the law were crucial in raising public consciousness, mobilising support for the CIW, and putting its targets on the back foot.

Secondly, the CIW's participation in the prosecutions conferred a measure of prestige on a grassroots organisation that had previously enjoyed little clout, at least in the eyes of company decision-makers based in glass-panelled corporate headquarters, many thousands of kilometres away. If law enforcement agencies and government lawyers were engaged in dialogue with the CIW, how could corporate executives continue to evade and ignore the farm worker organisation? Participation in legal processes also gave the CIW influence to convince state labour agencies and other farm worker advocates about the merits of the FFP. This has resulted in a remarkable situation in Florida currently, where state institutions openly acknowledge that the agricultural sector is mistreating farm workers in contravention of the law, but are happy for an under-resourced civil society actor to shoulder the burden of changing the situation.

It is necessary to sound a note of caution about drawing overly optimistic conclusions from the CIW story, which also has a bearing upon the broader relationship between law and social movements. In the first instance, the law's malleability is a two-sided coin. While the law can be utilised strategically to achieve broadly progressive ends, it can also work in the other direction. For example, scholars have pointed out how anti-trafficking laws and discourses have

[110] McCann, *Rights at Work* (n 27).

[111] ibid 282.

[112] Interview with S Sellers, Director of Strategic Partnerships, Worker-Driven Social Responsibility Network (Sarasota, Florida, 15 February 2018).

been deployed to obscure violent forms of border enforcement,[113] the criminalisation of sex work,[114] and even to support deeply problematic forms of international intervention.[115] Furthermore, the law in the CIW's story is not an innocent bystander – it has constructed the conditions that oppress farm workers. Listing the various laws that render farm workers vulnerable is beyond the scope of this chapter, but suffice to say that immigration rules permitting certain forms of entry and barring others, judicial decisions that treat workers differently depending on their migration status, and the legal exclusion of certain industries from labour law protections, all play a role. The foregoing does diminish the capacity of actors to draw strategically upon the law, but it should cause us to pause before simplistically extolling its virtues.

V. Conclusion: Law's Promise?

In this chapter, I have provided an historical account of the CIW's emergence as a powerful actor in the Florida farming sector, emphasising the role of law. This is important because, at key moments, the CIW drew upon the symbolic and discursive power of anti-trafficking law to press its political claims for governing labour relations to better protect farm workers. However, the CIW did not only passively respond to the legal opportunities it found – it actively created and shaped those opportunities by encouraging US government authorities to take labour trafficking seriously and prosecute contractors engaging in this deplorable conduct. The CIW's story demonstrates that the law can be mobilised by workers in a variety of ways to envision and present political demands, and that other labour organisations, both new and old, may be able to learn important lessons from it. As we have seen time and time again, those consigned to the margins often develop the tools for resistance that become propitious for others on a later day. The importance of understanding the precise relationship between new labour movements, and the law, cannot be overstated if we are to realise a world where labour has a fair stake.

For labour law scholars, examining how new forms of labour associations are utilising law in their struggle for better working conditions invites us to think about productive ways in which our discipline may be able to develop. Labour law was a concession granted to insurgent labour movements in the early

[113] See, eg, S Plambech, 'Between "Victims" and "Criminals": Rescue, Deportation, and Everyday Violence Among Nigerian Migrants' (2014) 21 *Social Politics* 382.

[114] See, eg, J Halley and others, 'From the International to the Local in Feminist Legal Responses to Rape, Prostitution/Sex Work, and Sex Trafficking: Four Studies in Contemporary Governance Feminism' (2006) 29 *Harvard Journal of Law & Gender* 335.

[115] See, eg, P Kotiswaran, 'Beyond Sexual Humanitarianism: A Postcolonial Approach to Anti-Trafficking Law' (2014) 4 *UC Irvine Law Review* 353.

twentieth century, and the political compromise that ensued created a legal framework for employers and workers to bargain over how the benefits of economic production were to be distributed (and, in a more limited way, production organised).[116] Unions and workers relied upon this legal framework to press their claims for better wages and conditions, and to gain more control over their working lives. The collapse of this system in particular sectors of the economy means that workers may need to look elsewhere to make meaningful improvements in their lives. It is not surprising that we have started to see the appearance of new forms of labour organisation which draw upon alternative legal resources to promote workers' welfare. This invites labour law scholars to study, more broadly, the laws that labour movements rely upon, as well as their symbolic and discursive aspects. This chapter, which adopts a socio-legal lens to uncover how one particularly successful new labour organisation used legal discourses and processes to achieve its ends, contributes in a modest way to this project.

[116] See, eg, J Fudge and E Tucker, *Labour Before the Law: The Regulation of Workers' Collective Action in Canada, 1900–1948* (Toronto, Oxford University Press, 2001); KE Klare, 'Judicial Deradicalization of the Wagner Act and the Origins of Modern Legal Consciousness, 1937–1941' (1978) 62 *Minnesota Law Review* 265.

9

Comment

Changing Collective Representation and Action to Meet the Challenges – Historical Lessons and Contemporary Learning

TONIA NOVITZ*

In each of the three chapters in this section, contemporary challenges are raised regarding the role of collective representation and collective action alongside their appropriate regulation. Such challenges include changes in the nature of the workforce, which is now feminised (Zahn), more likely to have a migrant component (Dias-Abey), flexibilised and precarious (Vergis). Questions arise as to the most desirable ways in which to represent these emergent forms of labour, particularly in the context of technocratic legislation which regulates trade union membership and activities. More fundamentally, Fotis Vergis and Rebecca Zahn both ask (albeit in different ways) normative questions regarding the functions that trade unions should serve and which could be recognised through legal mechanisms. Manoj Dias-Abey poses the more difficult question regarding how normative and legal change can take place: who are the actors, what forms of collective action makes a difference and how can law assist or obstruct effective representation? This brief comment considers three issues: first, how much is changing in the twenty-first century labour markets; secondly, what adjustments could be made to collective forms of representation and action; and, thirdly, when making regulatory choices what lessons can we learn from labour histories. It seems that there are enforcement issues and an international dimension that will need to feature in any consideration of the need for change and its regulatory aspects. We can anticipate an ongoing learning process in this context.

* Professor, University of Bristol.

I. Changes Apparent in the Twenty-First Century Labour Market

It was predicted that software would be unable to correct for the change of dates from 1999 to 2000. At one minute past midnight on 1 January 2000, we were entering a new millennium in which banking, financial and other communication systems might collapse – one article posited the possibility that all ATM machines in the United States (US) would stop working.[1] Less transpired than was anticipated, in part because work was done previously to eliminate some of the dangers.[2]

This is not to say that the twenty-first century world stayed the same. The global food crisis of 2006 indicated that trade systems were not working effectively,[3] as did the beginning of the global financial crisis the following year, which led on to a sovereign debt crisis affecting public spending and wage growth.[4] We are now in a digitalised society, in which computer and 4G mobile phone usage is extensive across the world, enabling cross-border telecommunications services and other forms of 'gig' working,[5] with the potential threat not just of job outsourcing, but job replacement by computerised functions.[6] Further, in response to the financial crisis, the costs of labour were reduced so as to protect business interests and government budgets, by extending temporary, agency, part time and zero hours work in both the private and public spheres.[7] Legislative protection

[1] Marshall Brain, 'How the Year 2000 Problem Worked' *HowStuffWorks.com* (1 April 2000) computer.howstuffworks.com/y2k1.htm accessed 17 January 2019.

[2] See also 'Millennium Bug Fails to Bite' *The Guardian* (London, 4 January 2000) www.theguardian.com/technology/2000/jan/04/y2k accessed 17 January 2019; K Rutledge et al, 'Y2K Bug' *National Geographic* (21 January 2011) www.nationalgeographic.org/encyclopedia/Y2K-bug/ accessed 17 January 2019.

[3] Wheat prices rose suddenly by 50% and rice by 70%, while food prices overall had risen by 75% between 2005 and 2007. See P McMichael, 'A Food Regime Analysis of the "World Food Crisis"' (2009) 26 *Agricultural Human Values* 281. Further, 'trade events provide an explanation of how a tighter world food situation rapidly turned into a full-blown crisis', as discussed in D Headey, 'Rethinking the Global Food Crisis: The Role of Trade Shocks' (2011) 36 *Food Policy* 136.

[4] CM Reinhart and KS Rogoff, 'From Financial Crash To Debt Crisis' (2010) NBER Working Paper No. 15795 www.nber.org/papers/w15795 accessed 7 January 2019; J Carmassi, D Gros and S Micossi, 'The Global Financial Crisis: Causes and Cures' (2009) 47 *Journal of Common Market Studies* 977. For the impact on labour markets see A Koukiadaki and L Kretsos, 'Opening Pandora's Box: The Sovereign Debt Crisis and Labour Market Regulation in Greece' (2012) 41 *Industrial Law Journal* 276; K Armingeon and L Baccaro, 'Political Economy of the Sovereign Debt Crisis: The Limits of Internal Devaluation' (2012) 41 *Industrial Law Journal* 254, 255–56, 261–63.

[5] V De Stefano, 'The Rise of the "Just-In-Time Workforce": On-Demand Work, Crowdwork and Labour Protection in the "Gig-Economy"' (2016) 37 *Comparative Labor Law & Policy Journal* 471.

[6] See A Korinek and J Stiglitz, 'Artificial Intelligence and Its Implications for Income Distribution and Unemployment' (December 2017) NBER Research Paper www.nber.org/chapters/c14018.pdf accessed 7 January 2019, who challenge the inevitability of this prediction.

[7] C Kilpatrick and B De Witte (eds), 'Social Rights in Times of Crisis in the Eurozone: The Role of Fundamental Rights' Challenges' (2014) Working Paper EUI LAW 2014/05 http://cadmus.eui.eu/handle/1814/31247 accessed 7 January 2019.

of individual workers was given a more limited ambit, amended or repealed,[8] while collective bargaining systems (especially in Europe, where sectoral bargaining had been effective) were dismantled or at least significantly modified so that wages and terms and conditions could be determined at the level of the enterprise or even the workplace.[9] Moreover, corporate entities determined to make profits in volatile markets sought to remake themselves, through subsidiaries, mergers and divisions across borders, and through the use of franchising arrangements.[10]

As Zahn observes, in this context we can observe the 'feminisation' of work. Of course, women have been entering the labour market in ever increasing numbers since the 1970s,[11] but twenty-first century developments have a particular flavour linked to the financial crisis and arguably the enabling through digitalisation of 'gig' forms of work. Initially, women were among those most affected by the emergency measures taken by governments and employers to address the financial crisis. They were more likely to work in the public sector, where budgetary costs led to loss of jobs and a stark reduction of terms and conditions (including pension reforms).[12] Further, they were more likely to be on temporary, agency, part time or other forms of insecure contract and immediately, during the financial crisis, were more likely to lose their jobs. However, as the experience tapered from crisis to austerity, employers restructured so that male jobs in 'standard employment relationships' (SER) declined, part time and flexible labour provided by women was encouraged and family breadwinners (whether male or female) found themselves under-employed, struggling to bring in sufficient income.[13] In this sense, Zahn is correct when she points to 'feminisation' having a double

[8] eg, regarding status of workers covered by employment law protections and rights to protection from dismissal. See T Novitz, 'Changes in Employment Status under Austerity and Beyond: Implications for Freedom of Association' (2016) 39 *Dublin University Law Journal* 27.

[9] See S Clauwaert, I Schömann and Z Rasnača, 'The Crisis and National Labour Law Reforms: A Mapping Exercise' (2012) ETUI Working Paper 2012.04 www.etui.org/Publications2/Working-Papers/The-crisis-and-national-labour-law-reforms-a-mapping-exercise accessed 7 January 2019; A Koukiadaki, I Távora and M Martínez Lucio, *The Transformation of Joint Regulation and Labour Market Policy in Europe During the Crisis: Comparative Project Report* (Brussels, ETUI, 2014); K Ewing and J Hendy, *Reconstruction After the Crisis: A Manifesto for Collective Bargaining* (Liverpool, Institute of Employment Rights, 2013); F Rocha, G Feigl, S Leonardi, L Tomev and C Triafantafillou, *The New EU Economic Governance and its Impact on National Collective Bargaining Systems* (Noisy-le-Grand, Institut de recherches économiques et sociales, 2014).

[10] D Weil, *The Fissured Workplace: Why Work Became So Bad for So Many and What Can Be Done to Improve It* (Cambridge, Mass., Harvard University Press, 2014). For recent appreciation of these corporate objectives in an EU context, see *Commission Proposal for a Directive Amending Directive (EU) 2017/1132 as Regards Cross-Border Conversions, Mergers and Divisions* COM(2018) 241 final.

[11] See Zahn, this volume.

[12] A Rafferty and J Rubery, 'Gender, Recession and Austerity in the UK' in M Karamessini and J Rubery (eds), *Women and Austerity* (Abingdon, Routledge, 2013) 145–65; also J Rubery, 'Public Sector Adjustment: The Threat to Gender Equality' in D Vaughan-Whitehead (ed), *Public Sector Shock: The Impact of Policy Retrenchment in Europe* (Cheltenham/Geneva, Edward Elgar/ILO, 2013).

[13] J Heyes, M Tomlinson and A Whitworth, 'Underemployment and Well-being in the UK before and after the Great Recession' (2017) 31 *Work, Employment and Society* 71.

meaning: 'the increased labour market participation of women and the proliferation of forms of employment historically associated with women, that is jobs that are part time, temporary, poorly paid and lacking benefits and collective forms of representation'.[14]

The gig economy is emblematic of the so-called flexibility that parents are seeking, whereby digital platforms enable someone to offer services when they are available around other caring responsibilities.[15] These arguably still respond to women's needs more than men, in that societal conventions mean that more of the former have caring responsibilities. The result is that, around such responsibilities, women may be more likely to opt for an hour's work here and there on 'Amazon Turk' or a few hours as a driver for Uber. The question is what the costs of such flexibility can and should be; and how collective representation and action could be utilised to prevent what we are seeing as increasingly exploitative conduct in which hirers pay less than the national minimum wage and provide unregulated hours without access to paid holidays.[16]

Another way in which to cut labour costs is through utilising other cheaper workers, namely a migrant workforce, which is vulnerable to forms of deportation and less likely to complain of ill-treatment. Dias-Abey points to use of such labour in an agricultural context, in which geographical isolation and language barriers combine to create a vulnerable population. So vulnerable, in fact, that accusations of trafficking and modern slavery are rife. There is a growing literature which exposes how pressure from lead firms in global supply chains to make profits (adding value) at each stage of the picking, processing and sales stages, leads to a radical undervaluing of the labour of the workers involved. Real wages have declined and terms and conditions worsened in the agricultural sector globally, while food has never been cheaper.[17] Temporary migrant labour[18] has also been used to reduce labour costs in fields such as care[19] and construction[20]

[14] Zahn, this volume.

[15] J Prassl, *Humans as a Service: The Promise and Perils of Work in the Gig Economy* (Oxford, Oxford University Press, 2018) 78.

[16] For discussion of the gig economy case law in the UK, such as *Aslam v Uber BV* [2017] IRLR 4 see K Bales, A Bogg and T Novitz, '"Voice" and "Choice" in Modern Working Practices: Problems With the Taylor Review' (2018) 47 *Industrial Law Journal* 46. For a broader perspective, see A Aloisi, 'Commoditized Workers: Case Study Research on Labor Law Issues Arising from a Set of On-Demand/Gig Economy Platforms' (2015) 37 *Comparative Labor Law & Policy Journal* 653.

[17] See WB Gould IV, 'Some Reflections on Contemporary Issues in California Farm Labour' (2017) 50 *UC Davis Law Review* 1243; M Dias-Abey, 'Justice on our Fields: Can 'Alt-Labor' Organizations Improve Migrant Farm Workers' Conditions' (2018) 53 *Harvard Civil Rights-Civil Liberties Law Review* 167; L Medland, 'Misconceiving 'Seasons' in Global Food Systems: The Case of the EU Seasonal Workers Directive' (2017) 23 *European Law Journal* 153.

[18] J Howe and R Owens (eds), *Temporary Labour Migration: The Regulatory Challenges* (Oxford, Hart, 2016).

[19] N Yeates, 'Global Care Chains' (2004) 6 *International Feminist Journal of Politics* 369; N Yeates, 'Global Care Chains: A State-of-the-Art Review and Future Directions in Care Transnationalization Research' (2012) 12 *Global Networks* 135. See also for an extension of this approach, A Stewart, *Law and Justice in Global Markets* (Cambridge, Cambridge University Press, 2011).

[20] G Meardi, A Martin and M Lozano Riera, 'Constructing Uncertainty: Unions and Migrant Labour in Construction in Spain and the UK' (2012) 54 *Journal of Industrial Relations* 5.

internationally. This phenomenon can be understood as a key feature of localised circular migrant labour schemes, but also more systemically as a feature of 'trade in services' (the latter giving a gravitas to exploitative practices, which seems to place them beyond question).[21]

II. Adjustments to Collective Representation and Action

These developments seem to be transforming labour markets and the nature of work. Currently, the relative scale of gig economy work remains small,[22] but the attractiveness of flexibilisation for certain employers is immense. 'Informal' or semi-entrepreneurial work – whether platform-based or not – appears to sit outside normal regulation by employment law and trade union representation. A threat (whether real or imagined) of replacement by undervalued migrant labour arguably feeds into contemporary nationalism too.[23] Such developments shape expectations of both employers (in terms of how much they need to offer in exchange for labour) and those who do the work for them (in terms of what will be offered). The scale of abuse still remains relatively small, but that is not to say that there will not be expansion. Just like the potential 'millennium bug' of 1 January 2000, the best plan may be to take action, so that this becomes less likely. Like the authors in this section of the book, my suggestion would be to consider the scope for collective representation and action to operate in a preventative way.

Women are now more likely to be trade union members than men, as Zahn observes, in part due to public sector unionism. However, they are less represented in the everyday cut and thrust of trade union business in the private sector, which is still male dominated and declining.[24] She also recognises that more may need to be done to represent those working in the informal (and gig) economy to represent the interests of women in work. In doing so, she points to the range of potential functions of trade unions as famously identified by Keith Ewing in 2005: individual

[21] T Novitz, 'Evolutionary Trajectories for Transnational Labour Law: Trade in Goods to Trade in Services?' (2014) 67 *Current Legal Problems* 239.

[22] eg, in the UK it was estimated in 2016 that only 900,000 workers were on zero hours contracts (less than 6% of the working population). See Pyper and Brown, House of Commons Briefing Paper, *Zero-Hours Contracts* (April 2017) http://researchbriefings.parliament.uk/ResearchBriefing/Summary/SN06553 accessed 7 January 2019.

[23] Discussed in T Novitz, 'Collective Bargaining, Equality and Migration: The Journey to and from Brexit' (2018) 46 *Industrial Law Journal* 109; also T Novitz, 'Freedom of Association: Its Emergence and the Case for Prevention of its Decline?' in J Bellace and B ter Haar (eds) *Research Handbook on Business, Labour and Human Rights Law* (Edward Elgar, 2019 forthcoming).

[24] Zahn cites DS Cobble, *Gender Equality and Labour Movements: Towards a Global Perspective* (Solidarity Center, 2013).

and collective representation; regulation and rule-making; government and public administration functions; and provision of commercial and social services, potentially also supporting 'partnership' in industrial relations.[25] She suggests ways in which representation and regulation could be extended from a pay, hours and holidays agenda (as is standardly accepted under, for example, Schedule A1 of the Trade Union and Labour Relations (Consolidation) Act 1992 (UK)) to reflect more closely the preoccupations of women as 'atypical' workers, including job segregation, flexibility and social and equality issues. To this list Vergis adds the educational role of trade unions, and again reminds us of the importance of reaching beyond the economic objectives of collective representation to non-economic values, offering scope for learning, personal development and dignity.[26]

Dias-Abey discusses the ways in which conventional forms of trade unionism in the agricultural sector, such as a five day strike led by the Coalition of Immokalee Workers (CIW) in 1995 had little impact; nor did its litigation regarding wage theft (a strategy to which Zahn notes trade unions have had increasing recourse). Whereas, Dias-Abey observes that the CIW contribution to prosecution of labour trafficking won the union greater authority and status, which can be understood as 'symbolic capital'.[27] More importantly, the creation of a private regulatory scheme, the Fair Food Program (FFP) appealed to leading fast food chains and supermarkets to boost (or, as Dias-Abey puts it, 'launder') their reputation, while achieving significant flow-on benefits for workers hired by the growers of the produce.[28] There are echoes in Dias-Abey's analysis of the normative issues raised by Vergis. The link of trade union action to individual as well as collective human dignity is made tangible in the trafficking sphere of human rights concerns. Further, the importance of active participation, education and self-determination arises in relation to the operation and monitoring of the FFP.

III. Regulatory Lessons from the Past Taken into the Present

It is important in planning for the future that we take due account of the past. Indeed, all three contributions to this part of the book do so, offering a historical perspective on female participation in trade union organisation (Zahn),

[25] KD Ewing, 'The Function of Trade Unions' (2005) 34 *Industrial Law Journal* 1 cited by Zahn, this volume.
[26] Vergis, this volume.
[27] Dias-Abey, this volume.
[28] Dias-Abey, this volume.

past strategies for collective action in the agricultural field (Dias-Abey) and the contemporary uses of a Hegelian construct of an honourable life (Vergis). No one is advocating simply a return to nineteenth century 'service unions' which provided friendly benefits at a time when it was illegal for trade unions to engage in collective bargaining or strike. Rather, a historical trajectory reminds us of what certain statutes represent in terms of legal gains for collective worker representation and action, despite their limitations. Gains for workers through legal means may be incremental, obtained layer upon layer. As such, it is suggested here that they need not be abandoned in pursuit of new strategies, but rather used as foundations upon which we can build. Although, that said, some further construction is essential.

Extreme casualisation and flexibility are not only features of segments of the twenty-first century labour market, but were evident at other historical junctures. For example, workers would wait at 'stands' around the docks hoping for selection for ad hoc unloading work from the local foremen.[29] It was in reaction to the precarity of such work that collectively negotiated dock schemes were created and endorsed by the International Labour Organization (ILO).[30] What is alarming is that the modes of collectively bargaining security are currently unravelling under a series of commercial preoccupations prioritising trade and competition law, such that the minimal forms of protection once offered to workers are under threat.[31] Returning to Ewing's trade union functions, the importance of collective representation becomes clear, especially the ability to have recourse to large scale industrial action by union federations. Further, the government function of trade unions, mobilising in the political sphere (whether national or international) to preserve basic protections for workers remains essential. In this sense, the older standard functions of trade unions continue to be relevant.

The problem with simply advocating a return to the past is that the mainstream larger trade unions tend to provide only very limited support for the concerns of women – or, indeed, migrant worker concerns – in collective bargaining. These problems are well documented in the United Kingdom (UK), from the Grunwick dispute onwards.[32] A recent example of such a union's reluctance to engage with

[29] P Turnbull and D Sapsford, 'Hitting the Bricks: An International Comparative Study of Conflict on the Waterfront' (2001) 40 *Industrial Relations: A Journal of Economy and Society* 231; S Davies, CJ Davies, D de Vries, L Heerma van Voss, L Hesselink and K Weinhauer (eds), *Dock Workers: International Explorations in Comparative Labour History, 1790–1970* (Abingdon, Routledge, 2017).

[30] ILO Convention No. 137 'concerning the social repercussions of new methods of cargo handling in docks'.

[31] See J Hendy and T Novitz, 'The Holship Case' (2018) 47 *Industrial Law Journal* 315, discussing the impact of *Holship Norge AS v Norsk Transportarbeiderforbund* Case E-14/15 [2016] 4 CMLR 29.

[32] Led by female migrant workers (notably Jayben Desai) challenging low wages and exploitative and degrading terms and conditions. For useful resources on the Grunwick dispute, see 'More About Grunwick' *Grunwick 40* https://grunwick40.wordpress.com/about accessed 17 January 2019; 'The Grunswick Dispute' *Striking Women* www.striking-women.org/module/striking-out/grunwick-dispute accessed 17 January 2019.

the equality concerns of female members was arguably *Allen v GMB*.[33] Sue Ledwith attributes this phenomenon to 'male trade unionism' which can 'trace its origins back to the closed shop of the craftsman' involving 'control over the supply and price of labour'.[34] Even just placing equal opportunities on the bargaining agenda of an established trade union will not work, given a decline in bargaining and a lack of prioritisation by officials within the organisational framework.[35] Yet, as Zahn and Nicole Busby have observed in their *Dangerous Women* blog,[36] an alternative is to look back at the autonomous organising even in the nineteenth century, which offered the first spontaneous female opposition to employer's use of sweated labour in conditions dangerous to the health, safety and well-being of workers. They cite, as did Beatrice and Sidney Webb, the match girl strike of 1888, where workers assisted by Annie Besant formed a trade union and embarrassed their employer, Bryant and May.[37]

Ledwith sees as vital women's 'collective initiatives', which could then be brought into the mainstream. However, those working with migrant workers suggest that the process of 'inclusion' could be a dangerous one where it does not also engage with the need for empowerment.[38] It is such empowerment which Vergis is seeking, and which Dias-Abey considers is at least partially realised in the less conventional organisational strategies of the CIW case. These are more responsive to workers' needs and less to the conventional preoccupations of a trade union's bargaining agenda. The match girl strike also had a broad appeal to narratives of Christian decency (akin perhaps to some of Walmart's concerns in the CIW context), was linked to a broader movement for female emancipation and fitted with emergent journalistic and social concerns with sweated labour.

There is difficulty finding space for bottom-up movements in a system of labour regulation conducted by monolithic legislation, such as the National Labour Relations Act in the US (which forms the backdrop to the CIW activities) or the Trade Union and Labour Relations (Consolidation) Act 1992 (UK), which recently blocked the attempt of the Independent Workers Union of Great Britain (IGWB) to represent casualised zero hours Deliveroo workers.[39] Current regulatory models

[33] [2008] EWCA Civ 810 CA.

[34] S Ledwith, 'Gender Politics in Trade Unions: The Representation of Women Between Exclusion and Inclusion' (2012) 18 *Transfer* 185, 187.

[35] ibid 190–94; see also M Martínez Lucio and R Perrett, 'The Diversity and Politics of Trade Unions' Responses to Minority Ethnic and Migrant Workers: The Context of the UK' (2009) 30 *Economic and Industrial Democracy* 324, 333–34.

[36] N Busby and R Zahn, 'A Dangerous Combination?' *Dangerous Women* (20 June 2016) http://dangerouswomenproject.org/2016/06/20/womens-trade-unionism accessed 17 January 2019.

[37] B Webb and S Webb, *The History of Trade Unionism* (London, Longmans, Green & Co., 1911) 388–89.

[38] Martínez Lucio and Perrett, 'The Diversity and Politics of Trade Unions' Responses to Minority Ethnic and Migrant Workers' (n 35) 341–42.

[39] Independent Workers' Union of Great Britain (IGWB) and RooFoods Limited TA/ Deliveroo, Central Arbitration Committee, 14 November 2017 (TUR1/985(2016)).

for the enabling and constraint of trade union organisation and activity may play into the maintenance of embedded trade union structures. However, the good news perhaps is that mobilisation by the IGWB seems to be prompting other unions to act on behalf of gig economy workers, with the GMB now taking on the role of 'individual representation' for Amazon delivery drivers to claim for them minimum pay and entitlement to holiday pay,[40] a job which had been previously left to the local Citizens Advice Bureau to attempt.[41]

Also, just as Dias-Abey strikes a note of caution at the end of his chapter (about the dangers of collective campaigning on trafficking), so too we have to be wary of historical myths associated with bottom-up organising. Such organising may need complementary pressures to be truly effective, including an international dimension. For example, the story of the match girls strike is not as simple a tale of successful spontaneous female mobilisation as it might seem. Bryant and May went on to secure a reputation as a good employer, which had agreed to the demands of the workers. However, for the next ten years, this employer continued to hide cases of phosphorous bone damage (so-called 'phossy' jaw), paying company doctors to give false diagnoses and causes of death, supported by the Inspector of Factories until, finally, under pressure from the newspapers, the Women's Trade Union League and then in Parliament, they were exposed and the legislature intervened (but only in 1910).[42] Over 20 years of injury to the health of workers had followed the initial strike; we want something more for the CIW. So the work of the FFP which makes it successful is not just the fact of mobilisation through diverse avenues but, as Dias-Abey says, the concrete aspect of worker education that it delivers (in line with the learning Vergis advocates), and also that it 'provides an avenue for workers to complain without fear of reprisal, contains a thorough auditing mechanism performed by an institution independent from growers, and applies meaningful sanctions on employers who are non-compliant'.[43] So learning about effective mechanisms for enforcement and the role that collective representation and action can play in this context is also of importance.

Further, what was important in the context of my two historical examples, the dock schemes and the phosphorous matches, was not only local action but international mobilisation. Workers' representatives fought within the ILO to

[40] S Butler and R Smithers, 'Amazon Delivery Firms Face Legal Action over Workers' Rights' *The Guardian* (London, 4 June 2018) www.theguardian.com/technology/2018/jun/04/amazon-delivery-firms-face-legal-action-over-workers-rights accessed 7 January 2019.

[41] See the situation highlighted through a BBC undercover documentary in Bristol in 2016: 'Amazon Drivers 'Work Illegal Hours'' *BBC News* (London, 11 November 2016) www.bbc.co.uk/news/uk-england-37708996 accessed 17 January 2019. See also the work of the Citizens' Advice Bureau which sought to address the issues: Citizens' Advice Bristol, 'None of the Freedom, All of the Risk' (Bristol, 7 March 2018) www.bristolcab.org.uk/none-freedom-risk accessed 17 January 2019.

[42] Narrated in LJ Satre, 'After the Match Girls' Strike: Bryant and May in the 1890s' (1982) 26 *Victorian Studies* 7.

[43] Dias-Abey, this volume.

establish the dock work measures that are currently under review and will no doubt need to do so again under the Standards Review Mechanism.[44] Even for the match girls, what seems to have steered the UK legislative approach was international trade union and employer lobbying on the issue of white phosphorous. A number of conferences convened by the International Association of Labour Legislation from 1905 onwards led to a treaty signed by several European States in 1906, which the UK then followed by signing in 1908.[45]

There are reflexive processes at play here. Here we can return again to the emphasis that Vergis places on learning, which may not just be personal to the worker, but a collective exercise for trade unions of all shapes and sizes, nationally and internationally. The past has regulatory lessons for us, but also we have to be alert to selective retellings and the ways in which present challenges offer us potential to explore alternatives. We could do with new ways to hold collective representatives to account and to make their actions effective and enforceable. We also need to consider additional methods to link and campaign across borders, perhaps addressing the trade rules which are shaping the relevance of international labour standards, rather than focusing only on the latter. This would bring into play further critical reflection on development and sustainability alongside other labour related issues.[46]

Collective bargaining and collective action is not a panacea; nor is the national and international legislation achieved by past mobilisation. They offer us a starting point for reflection, on which these three chapters build and construct additional options. This is not necessarily a matter of stark alternatives. We may wish to preserve traditional functions of trade unions and the forms of regulation that enable their activities while, as these three authors suggest, developing a multiplicity of tools to achieve further objectives that address the intricacies and dynamics of our twenty-first century labour markets.

[44] Discussed as suitable for review at: Standards Review Mechanism, 'SRM TWG Working Paper 1: Defining the Programme of Work' *International Labour Organization* www.ilo.org/wcmsp5/groups/public/---ed_norm/---normes/documents/genericdocument/wcms_449869.pdf accessed 17 January 2019; Standards Review Mechanism, 'Technical Note 5.3: Outdated Instruments Concerning Dockworkers' *International Labour Organization* www.ilo.org/global/standards/international-labour-standards-policy/WCMS_521947/lang--en/index.htm accessed 17 January 2019.

[45] Satre, 'After the Match Girls' Strike' (n 42) 29–30.

[46] For a beginning, see the ILO initiative on the 2015 United Nations Sustainable Development Goals: 'Decent Work and the 2030 Agenda for Sustainable Development' *International Labour Organization* www.ilo.org/global/topics/sdg-2030/lang--en/index.htm accessed 17 January 2019.

10

Comment

Collectivism and Trade Unions (Past, Present and Future) and the New World of Work

NICOLA SMIT*

I. Introduction

The chapters in Part B of this book adopt a socio-legal historical approach to consider lessons learnt from the past to solve both old and new problems in a future, often described as 'the new world of work', that has been experienced by many for some time.[1] Employment characterised by continuity, security and stability has indeed become the exception rather than the norm.

When thinking about collective labour law the backdrop that inevitably takes centre stage is the recognition and protection of freedom of association (as an enabling right), the right to organise, the right to strike and voice and representation. All of these notions, principles and rights are important in the new world of work. It may even be argued (having regard to the cracks displayed in the social contract, the lack of social cohesion and solidarity and the fact that the 'crisis of liberal democratic institutions is indeed a crisis of collective labour law')[2] that

* Dean and Professor of Labour and Social Security Law, Stellenbosch University, South Africa.

[1] See J Fudge and R Owens, *Precarious Work, Women, and the New Economy: The Challenge to Legal Norms* (Oxford, Hart Publishing, 2006) 3 as cited by Zahn (this volume) who points out that the 'increase in precarious or non-standard work undermines labour law and labour institutions, which have been created around the concept of standard employment relationships' has now been replaced with a 'feminisation of work'. Further explanation is required in that: '"Feminisation" in this case has a double meaning, referring both to the increased labour market participation of women and the proliferation of forms of employment historically associated with women, that is, jobs that are part time, temporary, poorly paid, and lacking benefits and collective forms of representation' (Zahn, this volume).

[2] See generally A Bogg, R Dukes and T Novitz, 'Introduction: Contemporary Issues in Collective Labour Law' (2017) 46 *Industrial Law Journal* 1, 4.

these protections and instruments are more important than ever before.[3] In fact, the public good arising from collectivism and trade unions are in need of renewed recognition and improvement. The 'new' world of work infers that the actors, script and the stage have undergone significant changes (most of them to the detriment of collectivism and trade unions)[4] in the last decades. Labour law will arguably have to come up with a new 'big idea' to reclaim significance and social impact.[5]

II. Re-discovering the Value of Collective Labour Law and Institutions

In his chapter, Fotis Vergis sets out to rediscover the 'value and substance of the concept of labour itself, and the objective of the mechanisms to ensure its protection from coercion and abuse of power' by 'going back to the conceptual roots of the idea of labour protection'.[6] The shift in paradigm that has contributed to labour market deregulation and alignment of labour regulation and work to the new market conditions,[7] results in a choice for labour law: 'to resist, adapt or be reinvented

[3] See especially ibid 5: '... reports of the death of collective labour law have been greatly exaggerated. Indeed, there has never been a more urgent need for these debates to be at the very centre of our discipline'. The debates referred to by Bogg, Dukes and Novitz focus on issues included in a special edition of the journal, including the role of the law in helping to shape society, on social and economic fronts; the reconsideration of the normative and conceptual notions of 'individual' and 'collective' in labour law; and the response of labour law and, in particular, rules pertaining to representation and voice to a deepening divide between the needs of different groups of workers. Most of these issues are covered to some degree by the chapters in Part B of this volume.

[4] See H Arthurs, 'Concluding Remarks to the Roundtable on Re-Imagining Forms and Approaches to Workplace Representation' (2017) 20 *Canadian Labour & Employment Law Journal* 269. Arthurs states that 'current arrangements for protecting workers' rights and interests are inadequate'. He continues that this is the case 'measured by almost any metric coverage of the social safety net, union density, the incidence of strikes, job tenure, the labour share of GDP, income inequality, labour's power, workers' moral and material interests have been devaluated over recent decades and are at risk of further devaluation.'

[5] But see Arthurs (ibid 269–70) who uses an auto-sector metaphor of Thompson, to show that labour law reform in the recent past often resulted in a Taurus ('a modest adaptation of and improvement in existing arrangements') rather than a Tesla (representing 'a transformative change in the deep structures of society and economy'). Arthurs adds a third paradigm, namely the Tucker which was apparently a 'radical 1948 car' that represented 'state-of-the-art automotive engineering and design', but was never built – according to legend – because of the big three auto companies' conspiracy to discredit Tucker. Arthurs describes the Tucker as having metaphoric significance for labour law reform: 'Innovation in labour law and policy is hard to come by because those who control the present system play hardball: they use their considerable political influence, economic power and vested legal rights to preserve the *status quo*. Hence, in Mark Thompson's terms, a Taurus is the best we are likely to get, seldom a Tesla, let alone a Tucker.' This comment will attempt to show that having regard of the new world of work and the apparent failure of collectivism and trade unions to respond to it, a Tucker is exactly what is needed.

[6] See Vergis, this volume.

[7] Vergis, this volume, speaks of a 'radical departure from familiar norms, structures and their certainties' in reference to the term that is sometimes used, namely 'disorganised capitalism'.

and embedded on new norms and structures'.[8] Another dimension of this shift in paradigm involves the role of trade unions during this transition. Vergis states that trade unions 'essentially conceded to a purely economic understanding of their role' and by 'accepting a shift away from their role as the embodiment of collective negotiation power … it is possible that Trade Unions contributed to disillusion',[9] which ultimately is signified in the low levels of union membership and density discernible across the world. Vergis therefore raises the possibility that trade unions 'lost their "*representational credibility*"[10] in the eyes of individual workers and their position in the collective imaginary as social and political, as well as economic, actors'. It is well-known that trade union density and membership have steadily decreased in the recent past[11] and structural and social reasons contributed to such incidence.

Because individuals are part of society and inherently display at least three dimensions, namely 'as persons, as bourgeois citizens (members of a particular societal configuration and the classes therein), and members of a particular political community, a particular polity', any economic system, including its structures, cannot be defined and regulated without reference to the individual and the collective dimensions of society. Vergis submits that the functions of collective labour law structures correspond to considerations connected to these dimensions, in other words, as instruments in the service of social, democratic and political values and objectives, as a catalyst of social re-embedding of the 'market economy' and as the vehicle of market democratisation. It is significant that Vergis shows that trade unions and the relevant collective labour law mechanisms 'become incubators of civic virtues'.[12] It would be difficult to deny that socially just societies require 'conscious, engaged citizens' and collective participation in labour law institutions, such as trade unions, educate and prepare individuals to take up such role.[13] This fundamental truth remains valid even in a changed world of work.

[8] ibid.

[9] ibid.

[10] Vergis (ibid) refers to R Hyman, 'Trade Unions and the Disaggregation of the Working Class' in M Regini (ed), *The Future of Labour Movements*, 2nd edn (London, Sage, 1994) 150.

[11] See G Mundlak, 'We Create Spots from Which We Shine to Others: Organizing as a Bridging Practice between Distinct Meanings of Association' (2017) 38 *Comparative Labor Law & Policy Journal* 291, 298.

[12] Vergis, this volume.

[13] See also K Ewing and J Hendy, 'New Perspectives on Collective Labour Law: Trade Union Recognition and Collective Bargaining' (2017) 46 *Industrial Law Journal* 23. The authors refer to an earlier work where they set out 'the reasons for rebuilding collective bargaining, which it referred to as the Four Pillars of collective bargaining' (KD Ewing, J Hendy and C Jones, *A Manifesto for Labour Law: Towards A Revision of Workers' Rights* (Liverpool, The Institute of Employment Rights, 2006)). In summary, collective bargaining was shown as 'amongst the principal means of achieving (i) workplace democracy, (ii) social justice, (iii) economic efficiency and (iv) the fulfilment of the UK's relevant international legal obligations, consistent with the rule of law' (footnotes omitted). Considering the widespread ratification of the relevant ILO Conventions concerning collective bargaining and freedom of association, the object in (iv) would certainly be true for any country and not only the UK.

Rebecca Zahn's contribution[14] explores aspects that are in synergy with the 'idea of systemic democratisation and overcoming contemporary boundaries' mooted by Vergis.[15] Zahn considers the gig economy and the feminisation of work having regard of lessons from the past. From the perspective of workers in the gig economy, she postulates that 'many of the successful efforts at organising non-standard workers … have been undertaken by "non-traditional" trade unions and other forms of grassroots organisations'.[16] The lesson being that traditional collectivism and trade unions' strategies to recruit, register and represent members are not suitable (in an unchanged fashion) in the new world of work. Why is it that traditional unions have been unsuccessful in organising non-standard workers where they did in fact set out to do so?[17]

Vergis explains that trade unions by being conscious of the 'social interconnectivity of interests, break the walls that delimit their traditional function within the workplace or the confines of the labour market, to connect with their broader communities, in pursuit of wider social objectives'.[18] Manoj Dias-Abey's contribution, however, illustrates that in some contexts trade unions have not been able to transform themselves sufficiently, which has resulted in labour organisations abandoning 'a broken labour law system' and, in its place, these labour organisations have engaged in 'forms of social movement activity – public communication, alliance building, and political mobilisation – to achieve gains for workers'.[19] There is synergy in the submissions of Zahn and Dias-Abey in that it appears that traditional trade unions will have to significantly reimagine themselves in order to effectively respond to the new world of work. Even though unions may also engage with the same strategies as utilised by labour organisations, Dias-Abey indicates that non-traditional labour organisations often focus on 'outsiders', including African-Americans; to this could be added marginalised workers in the informal economy and other generic non-standard workers. This development underlines the concern that the traditional institutional arrangements developed to establish and protect labour standards are insufficient to the urgent need for relevant (ie local, contextual and embedded) labour protection. In addition, it may be asked whether international labour and social security conventions with their focus on the formal sector, whilst ignoring the inherent complexity and nature of the informal sector, are able to meet the needs of non-standard workers and those working in the informal economy.

The underlying question with regard to the International Labour Organization (ILO), the primary international labour standard setting institution, relates

[14] Vergis, this volume.

[15] See ibid.

[16] Zahn, this volume.

[17] It must be acknowledged that in many sectors there may be little incentive for a trade union to attempt to extend its membership base due to costs and challenges involved.

[18] Footnotes omitted from quote.

[19] Dias-Abey, this volume.

to a more fundamental question, namely whether the tripartite structure is still appropriate and relevant[20] when in many countries, in particular the developing world, trade unions are marginalised and their impact minimal.[21] The pertinent question whether the traditional ILO structure should move towards including non-governmental organisations (NGO) and/or 'non-traditional' workers' organisations and giving them a voice is related. Although this may raise problems of legitimacy and representivity, the fact that it may be challenging should not mean that it should not be considered or pursued. It seems implicit that those who have been able to successfully organise and mobilise on behalf of non-standard workers should be serious contenders for a seat at such reinvented structure. It therefore appears that other than the structure of the standard-setting ILO, one must also reconsider the current collective bargaining structures, including its role players, purpose and the nature of outcomes of bargaining or mobilising.

Zahn sets out the 'exponential growth in work in the so-called gig economy',[22] which primarily is understood to comprise of two main forms of work that is 'crowd work' and 'work on-demand via app'. Workers in the gig economy is justly seen as a continuation of the rise in non-standard forms of work and Zahn fittingly states that there has been little evidence of attempts at comprehensive reform of the 'classical' labour law model based on employers, trade unions and the State. Clearly, it must be noted that this 'classical' labour law model hides the challenges posed to trade unions by non-traditional work from the beginning of time.[23] The rise of new forms of work in the new world of work has simply 'added an extra layer of complexity to the challenges facing trade unions and has injected a sense of urgency into the debate on how trade unions should respond to the rise'.[24] One response has been for trade unions to resort to litigation; a response

[20] See M Weiss, 'Re-Inventing Labour Law?' in G Davidov and B Langille (eds), *The Idea of Labour Law* (Oxford, Oxford University Press, 2011) 46: 'In short: in spite of the dramatic changes in work reality, there is no reason to question the need for labour law as such. As far as the core assumptions are concerned on which labour law is based, I see no need for a change of paradigm. This, of course, does not mean that the structure of the field can remain as it is'.

[21] See also ibid 47: 'Bargaining for employees who do not belong to the core group of trade union members leads to difficult problems of representativity. In short: satisfying collective representation of interests for people in new work forms cannot be provided by traditional trade union and bargaining structures.' Although Weiss believes that diversity of interests within the workforce must be adapted to, he is not convinced that 'extending the scope of the full amount of labour law application on economically dependent self-employed' might not lead to 'de-legitimacy of labour law' (ibid 48). With regard to the informal economy, see N Smit and E Fourie, 'Extending Protection to Atypical Workers, Including Workers in the Informal Economy in Developing Countries' (2010) 26 *International Journal of Comparative Labour Law and Industrial Relations* 43.

[22] See Zahn, this volume.

[23] Zahn (ibid) refers to the description of 'non-standard work' by the Webbs as 'casual workers with no skills who are *chiefly the daughters, wives and widows of these men who turn to labor of this kind*'.

[24] ibid.

which departs from previous strategies of unions.[25] The larger role that constitutional law and fundamental rights has played over the last decades and the decline in union membership and density contributed to this new approach, which of course contradicts a traditional collective *laissez faire* model.[26] Although regulation of work has become more State driven (since the regulatory role of collective bargaining has receded) these regulations are often efficiency-driven rather than fairness-based and Zahn suggests that it is therefore not surprising that working patterns of those engaged in low-paid precarious work have not changed substantially. Zahn argues for unions to 'confront problems that women workers have struggled with for decades' and that the successful 'reaching out to non-standard workers' will also 'enhance the effectiveness of industrial relations law and practice by broadening unions' representational base'.[27] Distinct from other writers who prioritise the regulatory function of unions, Zahn submits that the service function of trade unions has to date responded most successfully to non-standard workers and should therefore not be devalued as it 'hinders trade unions in identifying and placing matters of concern to these workers centre-stage'.[28]

[25] See also A Bogg and KD Ewing, 'The Continuing Evolution of European Labor Law and the Changing Context for Trade Union Organizing' (2017) 38 *Comparative Labor Law & Policy Journal* 211. Bogg and Ewing state that 'it is a grave analytical error to assess union organizational strategies divorced from the wider structures of legal norms at both the national *and* transnational levels': at 226. They highlight the fact that cases, such as *R (UNISON) v The Lord Chancellor* [2015] WLR 370, show 'the perils of litigation as a strategy' and that 'judicial review [in the UK] provided an important strategic opportunity for the trade union movement to prevent the erosion of rights that had already been secured through Parliamentary action. It is important to acknowledge how this strategy of "politics through law" was highly dependent upon the norms and institutions of European Union law and European Human Rights law'. Litigation depends on norms and standards; rarely, does litigation create new labour standards.

[26] Bogg and Ewing (ibid 228–29) highlight other limitations of 'law as a new form of political engagement for trade unions' including: the expense involved; the uncertainty of the outcome and the time-consuming nature thereof; adverse legal decisions may provide 'a legal legitimation for an unjust set of arrangements'; legal argumentation is usually limiting and technical in scope of discourse, an egalitarian strategy of protecting the integrity of the 'floor of rights' for all workers, trade unions often prioritise 'collective over individual justice …, which struggled to translate easily into a judicial forum … reflected in judicial discomfort'; and judicial deference in judicial review by its very nature limits what litigation as strategy can achieve. Re-regulation having regard of new market conditions and the rise of a human rights approach in the workplace may bring important benefits, but of course a rights-based approach often requires litigation to effect implementation.

[27] Zahn, this volume.

[28] See, eg, Ewing and Hendy, 'New Perspectives on Collective Labour Law' (n 13) 37 who, while not denying the importance of all functions, focus on the regulatory aspect and note that when trying to rebuild a regulatory collective bargaining system challenges, including that of resisting employers, remain: 'This brings us back to the question of power, and the coercive power of the State in particular, to be reclaimed as a force for good rather than as the enemy as it has been seen by some workers for almost two generations. In the modern legal climate a system of regulatory collective bargaining needs to anticipate that power and harness it in a productive manner' (footnote omitted). The authors argue for the extension of collective bargaining not only through 'the expansion of horizontal measures for sectoral standard setting' but also for 'deepening vertical enterprise based trade union activity, vertical in the sense that the trade union role should be embedded from the cloakroom to the boardroom': at 42. This requires fusion between the regulatory collective bargaining model and the representative collective bargaining model 'based on the enterprise or parts thereof, created and operated by labour law techniques'.

Trade unions have not been successful mobilising non-standard workers and promoting collective bargaining among non-standard workers such as temporary workers, temporary agency workers and dependent self-employed have proven challenging. Studies show that even where non-standard workers have fundamental rights in theory, they may not be able to exercise them in practice.[29] There are several reasons for this state of affairs and it seems apparent that in the case of most unions that have a wide membership base, mobilising and promoting collective bargaining under non-standard workers will represent challenges due to economies of scale and other organisational hurdles. Nevertheless, having regard of the facts that more than 60 per cent of the world's employed population are in the informal economy and that non-standard work is steadily increasing,[30] it is necessary for trade unions to show a willingness to be adaptable in different contexts so that they may be flexible enough to prioritise the needs of a particular group of workers at a specific point in time in order to obtain 'representational credibility'. This may encourage non-standard workers (and society at large) to recognise the public good of collectivism and the importance of supporting trade unions (and other labour organisations) to uphold the notion of collectivism, while accepting (and trusting) that although their divergent needs may not always be the primary or immediate concern of a union, that the union will be responsive.[31] In this sense, one is talking about a Tesla, rather than a Tucker.[32] As a start, trade union strategies and collective bargaining regulations should not 'impose obstacles that disproportionately affect, or prevent, the exercise of collective rights by non-standard workers'[33] and must show a willingness to be reinvented in the changed world of work.

Dias-Abey describes the emergence and success of the Coalition of Immokalee Workers (CIW) as a non-traditional organisation that does not bargain with employers on behalf of its members and that rarely partners with government agencies in improving enforcement of statutory labour standards. Rather, it developed a private regulatory system, the Fair Food Program (FFP), which 'governs labour conditions on farms' by 'enlisting large corporate entities … that purchase their tomatoes from Florida … to obtain their tomatoes from growers complying with a series of labour standards' that are contained in a private code of conduct.[34]

[29] See ILO, *Non-standard Employment around the World Understanding Challenges Shaping Prospects* (ILO, Geneva, 2016) 234ff.

[30] See ILO, *Women and Men in the Informal Economy: A Statistical Picture* (ILO, Geneva, 2018). Two billion workers (61.2%) are in informal employment according to this report.

[31] See more about the building blocks necessary for social change below.

[32] See n 5.

[33] See V De Stefano, 'Non-Standard Work and Limits on Freedom of Association: A Human Rights-Based Approach' (2017) 46 *Industrial Law Journal* 185, 206. De Stefano argues that a human rights-based approach to decent work 'calls for a revision of existing restrictions and limits to collective rights'. He concludes in the current economic landscape such approach is 'pivotal to ensure that the weakest parts of the workforce, and especially non-standard workers, who may be particularly subject to the employers' managerial prerogatives, are not denied effective access to fundamental labour rights and protection of human dignity at the workplace'.

[34] Dias-Abey, this volume.

Dias-Abey shows how CIW used a topical public debate on labour trafficking to make use of the public attention to mobilise fast food chains and supermarkets 'wary of the material and reputational harm that was caused by being linked to human rights abuses in their supply chains' to take responsibility for farm working conditions and obtained 'social prestige' by contributing to the federal government's prosecution of crew leaders engaged in labour trafficking. The success of this strategy may be attributed to 'reframing'. In other words, 'how actors present their vision for transformation in a way that is culturally resonant and socially convincing'.[35] In particular, CIW utilised two essential building blocks for social change, namely 'repertoires of contention that are broad, creative and impactful' and 'solidarity from networks of allies'. The principles of fair labour standards in supply chains and ethical consumption significantly contributed to supermarkets joining the FFP. CIW effected social change by employing 'a softer kind of power "to induce cooperation by appealing to and helping create shared meanings and collective identities"'.[36] Dias-Abey observes that CIW was able to do so 'by amassing "symbolic capital", which it then deployed to convince other parties to follow its vision'.[37] The questions that arise are why trade unions have seemingly not been able to employ similar strategies successfully, and whether the success of CIW (one case study but it could be considered to be representative of more) indicates that non-traditional representational organisations for workers are better suited to cater for specific categories of workers, in particular but not limited to, non-standard workers.

Trade union representivity and 'representational credibility' appear to have become even more important in the globalised world of work where networks and multi-national actors frequently are relevant. Guy Mundlak offers a perspective on different meanings for freedom of association (on the side of labour), and implicitly influence, within the context of 'social bargaining' (that include state wide pacts as well as sector- and occupational-based bargaining) and 'enterprise bargaining' that is conducted within the domain of a single employer.[38] For success in the non-standard work sphere, it appears as if something between social, enterprise and network bargaining and persuasive influence has become relevant. Added to this, for collective bargaining to survive, it appears necessary to reimagine the current

[35] ibid.

[36] ibid.

[37] ibid.

[38] Mundlak, 'We Create Spots from Which We Shine to Others' (n 11). 'Social bargaining is based on the power of trade unions that have historical and political standing. Bargaining is conducted with employers' associations, sometimes with the involvement of the state. The trade unions interact with the political sphere directly and are viewed as "social partners" to the regulation and coordination of the labor market and other aspects of the welfare state. By contrast, enterprise bargaining is based on the power trade unions accumulate at the shop floor. The trade union's impact on the political order is indirect and based on political endorsement of favoured parties, but to a much lesser extent on formalized participation in policymaking.' As described above, CIW was successful without any direct bargaining with employer or employers' associations.

models to extend to new hybrid models of collectivism involving non-traditional role players and extending to subjects other than traditional terms and conditions of employment and social benefits.

III. What are the Lessons, If Any, to be Learnt From the Past?

The chapters of Vergis, Zahn and Dias-Abey cover the wide spectrum from labour law and industrialised and early Fordist economies to post Fordist and the gig economy. The authors contemplate whether the original conceptual roots of labour protection in a time where neither labour nor labour law was considered a commodity can still be relevant and useful in the new world of work. The chapters reflect on whether the normative content of classic labour law and collective labour law institutions should be overhauled or reinvented or whether something more moderate could suffice. One viewpoint is that a 'slight shift in our perception' of collective labour law, and consequently our use thereof and approach to it could be sufficient. Another perspective is that a 'conscious conceptual shift' should take place when thinking about the purpose of trade unions. The third perspective shows that non-traditional labour organisations 'both challenges and breathes new life into labour law's project' whilst acknowledging the importance of law as underpinning to these new ventures.

The past has taught us that without social justice[39] no person can be free and secure. It is because of conditions of labour that involved 'injustices, hardship and privation to large numbers of people' that threated the peace and harmony of the world that the ILO adopted its founding constitution. The representative and regulatory structures that were adopted and introduced internationally and nationally, and that were successfully utilised for almost a century are now in need of urgent reimagination. Too many workers do not enjoy decent work while being unrepresented by a collective body and too few successful attempts at being responsive to their plight are observable. The social impact of collectivism and trade unions as we know it – although important – has become negligible when one considers all work rather than the traditional 'male breadwinner' notion of work.

The changed world of work demands a new 'big idea', for collectivism and trade unions to continue to give effect to the old and proven values and rationale for (collective) labour law protection in the era of the fourth industrial revolution.

[39] See the Preamble to the ILO Constitution: 'Whereas universal and lasting peace can be established only if it is based upon social justice'.

PART C

Advancing Theoretical Models to Respond to the New World of Work

11

Employment Regulation and Working Time Through the Lens of a Regulatory Space Approach

CRISTINA INVERSI*

I. Introduction

Labour law is an essential component of what constitutes the regulation of employment relations. This chapter places its role and purpose in an analytical framework that is useful for a broader understanding of employment regulation. Regulatory theories can be useful for the theorisation of labour law, as they contribute to the discussion and to the intrinsic multidisciplinary and holistic approach of the subject. The framework proposed in this chapter and the insights of regulatory theories may be useful as both an analytical and methodological tool for approaching the study of labour law. First, I introduce my theoretical approach and focus on regulatory theory, using the concept of regulatory space.[1] Secondly, I put forward an analytical framework, organised according to levels and dimensions of regulatory activity.[2] In the framework, levels represent the spaces where regulation is formed and enforced (international, national, or workplace), whereas the dimensions represent the way in which regulation is created – through the formal legal process, through negotiations (mandated or voluntary), or through unilateral decisions. Finally, as an example of the framework's application, I focus on an analysis of the spaces of regulation in the area of working time, with examples from the European context and, in particular, the United Kingdom (UK).

* Lecturer in Employment Law, Alliance Manchester Business School, The University of Manchester.

[1] Regulatory space theory was first elaborated by L Hancher and M Moran, 'Organizing Regulatory Space' in L Hancher and M Moran (eds), *Capitalism, Culture, and Economic Regulation* (Oxford, Clarendon Press, 1989) 271.

[2] The analytical framework is discussed in more depth in C Inversi, LA Buckley and T Dundon, 'An Analytical Framework for Employment Regulation: Investigating the Regulatory Space' (2017) 39 *Employee Relations* 291.

The present chapter thus illustrates how the application of an analytical approach to regulatory analysis could enhance a multidisciplinary theoretical and methodological understanding of the study of labour law.

II. Regulatory Space: New Perspectives for Researching Labour Law

In the current world of work – particularly with the emergence of new forms of labour organisation that are supported by the use of new technologies and changes in business models – investigating regulatory processes and actors at multiple levels is essential for understanding current legal issues and phenomena. In particular, recent investigations that have focused on the new realities of work (ie, new jobs facilitated by online platforms like crowd working or work on demand) are putting regulatory failures, strategies, forms of adaptation, and resistance in the regulation of employment under the spotlight.

The approach adopted by my proposed analytical framework is necessarily multidisciplinary – in their analysis of regulatory models, many academics have highlighted that it is fundamental to take various forms and sources of regulation into account which, for example, might be legal or collectively negotiated, at national or supranational levels.[3]

Building on an existing regulatory framework, that extends traditional legal understandings of employment regulation,[4] my aim is to illustrate the application of this analytical tool using the example of working time regulation, to move beyond a narrow view of regulation as primarily a legal matter. The framework specifically recognises the importance of taking a broader perspective to the issue of employment regulation, and is therefore able to capture the variability created by the transformation of work, as well as its historical contextualisation across both work and societal spaces.[5] More particularly, I adopt and use the institutional theory of regulatory space[6] to describe the processes and actors that shape employment regulation. A regulatory space perspective contributes to the analysis of reflexive law strategies, by looking at the relationship between labour law

[3] See, for instance, P Berg, G Bosch and J Charest, 'Working-Time Configurations: A Framework for Analyzing Diversity across Countries' (2014) 67 *Industrial and Labour Relations Review* 805; and in an empirical application of the framework, see Eurofound, *Working Time Developments in the 21st Century: Work Duration and its Regulation in the EU* (Luxembourg, Publications Office of the European Union, 2016).

[4] Inversi, Buckley and Dundon, 'Analytical Framework for Employment Regulation' (n 2).

[5] T Dundon and others, 'Employer Occupation of Regulatory Space of the Employee Information and Consultation (I&C) Directive in Liberal Market Economies' (2014) 28 *Work, Employment & Society* 21.

[6] Hancher and Moran, 'Organizing Regulatory Space' (n 1).

and other self-regulatory mechanisms, and considering the agency of regulators.[7] Thus, when looking at the regulation of employment, the central aim is not to leave aside the power dynamics between actors, as they are useful to assess both the production and the effective application of regulation.

Regulatory space theory enhances debates around the role and purpose of labour law within the areas of work and employment. It requires investigation of the role of other regulatory sources, such as negotiated or unilateral forms of regulation, as well as the roles of actors and their agency. It also engages with legal pluralist theory by considering the legal order as a container of 'multiple rules of recognition that lead to the order containing multiple, unranked, legal sources'.[8]

The metaphor of regulatory space evokes the idea that regulation is a matter of contestation between actors, building on Paul Edwards's theory of 'structured antagonism' as an inherent feature of the employment relationship.[9] Actors have agency and capacity to 'occupy' and contest a specific regulatory domain. This space-occupation process and its outcomes can be unevenly distributed, reflecting existing power relations and the variable ability of actors to mobilise resources and information.[10] The regulatory space approach is not just interested in unveiling the 'geography' of actors occupation, but also has a fundamental historical perspective: regulatory processes are not just situated in space, but also in time, and are therefore contingent on historical, institutional and economic factors.

Given these characteristics, such an approach should be favoured over a classic industrial relations one, which has been criticised for not taking into account the overall institutional context in which regulation is shaped and re-shaped, as well as largely neglecting the historical interactions between a broader range of actors, besides trade unions and employers.[11] Indeed, from a multidisciplinary perspective, assessing the historical evolution of regulation requires a combination of legal and institutional analysis, and could assist in moving beyond legal approaches based purely on labour market considerations, which have a tendency to underemphasise conflicts of interest between regulatory actors.[12]

The regulatory space approach requires us to take actors' agency into account, by analysing actions and strategies, and the capacity of such actors to mobilise

[7] For an account on 'Reflexive Law', see R Rogowski and T Wilthagen (eds), *Reflexive Labour Law: Studies in Industrial Relations and Employment Regulation* (Deventer, Kluwer Law and Taxation, 1994).

[8] See NW Barber, 'Legal Pluralism' in *The Constitutional State* (Oxford, Oxford University Press, 2010) 145.

[9] PK Edwards, *Conflict at Work: A Materialist Analysis of Workplace Relations* (Oxford, Blackwell, 1986).

[10] For an empirical investigation, see Dundon and others, 'Employer Occupation of Regulatory Space' (n 5).

[11] R MacKenzie and M Martínez Lucio, 'The Colonisation of Employment Regulation and Industrial Relations? Dynamics and Developments over Five Years of Change' (2014) 55 *Labor History* 189.

[12] R Dukes, *The Labour Constitution: The Enduring Idea of Labour Law* (Oxford, Oxford University Press, 2014).

resources and power, competencies, and cooperation. In particular, the use and management of information is a key factor to consider in assessing actors' regulatory agency. Regulatory space theory claims that, in both decision-making and enforcement processes, actors do not necessarily follow an immutable and hierarchical structure, as they can adopt bargaining or cooperation strategies, as well as threats or customary assumptions.[13] Going beyond consideration of the law as the fundamental object and outcome of regulation, a regulatory space approach encompasses other formal and informal sources of regulation created by the continuous and dynamic process of adaptation and counterbalance that happens between actors over time and space.

Although legal systems require a rigid and structured hierarchy of sources to function, a broader perspective on regulation outlines the difficulties in finding a coherent and immutable structure within regulatory systems, as regulatory space is complex and fragmented, influenced by the features just outlined above (time, space and actors' agency).

The regulatory space approach, in particular, assists with moving beyond a labour market narrative based on a 'regulation versus deregulation' dichotomy, which tends to simplify regulatory discussions around the presence and removal of labour protections. In fact, regulatory space is populated by a wide range of actors, and subject to a continuous process of adaptation and change of strategy, instruments and agendas.[14] This is especially the case when space is ceded from formal institutional control to voluntarist, unilateral or mandated negotiated forms of regulation. In this respect, the literature often simplifies the characterisation of market economies as being bifurcated between liberal (those which have a tendency to adopt more de-regulatory strategies) and coordinated (which, in contrast, appear to be more rule-bound and 'regulated').[15] By taking a regulatory space approach, though, it is incorrect or, at the very least, simplistic to talk about mere 'deregulation'. Talking about 'deregulation' is useful in explaining one step of the regulatory process. However, characterising changes in law and labour market norms as 'deregulation' does not illuminate the necessary outcomes or further developments required to fill the 'gaps' left for other regulatory sources and actors. Indeed, "deregulation" often paradoxically involves the development of a more intricate web of systematic regulation by state bodies, which is needed to develop, control and administer delegated regulation.[16] Furthermore, use of the term 'deregulation' seems to suggest a quantitative removal of rules, towards a 'simplification' of legal requirements and administrative burdens.

[13] Hancher and Moran, 'Organizing Regulatory Space' (n 1).

[14] M Martinez Lucio and R MacKenzie, 'Unstable Boundaries? Evaluating the "New Regulation" within Employment Relations' (2004) 33 *Economy and Society* 77.

[15] G Esping-Andersen and M Regini (eds), *Why Deregulate Labour Markets?* (Oxford, Oxford University Press, 2000).

[16] See C Scott, 'Analysing Regulatory Space: Fragmented Resources and Institutional Design' [2001] (Summer) *Public Law* 329.

This interpretation appears insensitive to the complexities of regulation, at least in terms of its functions, regulatory instruments and processes.[17] The regulatory literature argues that deregulation necessarily entails a continuous process of re-regulation, and cannot be reduced to the simple removal and minimisation of rules.[18] Through the lens of regulatory space, the de-regulatory process is the starting point for further formal or informal processes of regulation: when there is a ceded space, created by the absence or the removal of legal provisions, or through the derogation of powers enacted by law itself, processes of space occupation occur between actors, in order to colonise and influence a specific area. In these cases, the law can cede space to voluntarist and unilateralist processes, shifting decision-making power from the centre (the state, supranational or national authority), to the periphery (ie, employers or workplace actors more broadly).

III. The Analytical Framework for Employment Regulation

Acknowledging the need for a theoretical approach to consider spaces and power relationships, my proposed framework therefore takes regulatory actors, sources, and processes into account. In particular, the framework consists of three dimensions which represent regulatory mechanisms. The dimensions are identified in 'law', 'negotiated forms of regulation', and 'unilateralism'.

The proposed framework, illustrated in Table 1 below, aims to take account of the broader socio-economic and political aspects of regulatory activity, thus advancing a more dynamic and fluid interpretation of employment regulation. The table includes examples of regulatory sources relating to the specific dimensions and levels (ie, international, national, and workplace spaces) where they might apply in practice. It could be used as both a methodological and analytical instrument, thereby allowing us to conceptualise employment regulation in a holistic manner. Furthermore, it might offer a useful tool for comparative studies because of its multidisciplinary emphasis upon the institutional context of regulation.

The framework expands upon previous theorisations and attempts to improve our understanding of the role of key actors' interests in employment regulation, by exploring a combination of different regulatory dimensions.[19] Three main regulatory levels, which are useful in identifying where regulation takes place, have been identified: these are the international, the national, and the workplace.

[17] R MacKenzie and M Martinez Lucio, 'The Realities of Regulatory Change: Beyond the Fetish of Deregulation' (2005) 39 *Sociology* 499.

[18] G Majone (ed), *Deregulation or Re-regulation? Regulatory Reform in Europe and in the United States* (London, Pinter, 1990).

[19] Berg, Bosch and Charest, 'Working-Time Configurations' (n 3); Inversi, Buckley and Dundon, 'Analytical Framework for Employment Regulation' (n 2).

By combining an analysis of dimensions and levels, the proposed framework does not aim to present a static representation of the nature of regulation, but to stress the complexities and the fragmentation of employment regulation. As a simplified illustration, Table 1 is not able to capture the dynamic nature of regulation or the contingent overlaps between sources and levels in which regulation takes place. These features can be further investigated through empirical analysis and research.

Table 1

	Law	**Negotiated Regulation – Codetermination**	**Negotiated Regulation – Voluntarism**	**Unilateralism**
International Level	*International Laws*: ILO Conventions (etc) *EU Law:* EU Human Rights; Regulations; Directives; Recommendations; Policies; Soft Law (etc)	European Works Councils	Collective bargaining (EU level)	Regulation by transnational agents (ECB, IMF)
National Level	Constitutional provisions; Acts; Case Law; Statutory instruments (etc)	Statutory collective bargaining	Social Partnership Collective bargaining	Corporatist regulation; Regulation by Managerial or Union associations
Workplace Level	Codes of Practices; Customs	Board level representation; Company Law; Workers' buy-out	Decentralised collective bargaining (workplace); Non-union voice; Employment contract	Managerial prerogative Human Resource Management Conflict

The model proposed by Peter Berg, Gerhard Bosch and Jean Charest identified three ideal regulatory models that described different national configurations (unilateral, negotiated, and mandated configurations, corresponding respectively to the United States, Swedish, and French regulatory approaches).[20] However, the

[20] Berg, Bosch and Charest, 'Working-Time Configurations' (n 3).

authors highlighted that the definition of ideal models was for didactic purposes only and, in reality, pure models did not exist because regulation always entailed complexities and combinations of different configurations. Using these categories, and with further adjustments,[21] my proposed analytical framework attempts to explain and illustrate the 'mixed' regulatory models that have been defined, but not developed, in previous work. The three dimensions (legal, negotiated, and unilateral) are regarded as complementary and fluid elements of regulatory activity. Furthermore, their role in the regulatory space changes according to context in time and space (ie, the historical moment and the national jurisdiction).

A. Law

The first and foremost consideration of the role that labour law has in the regulation of employment derives from Otto Kahn-Freund's work, who contends that 'the principal purpose of labour law is to regulate, to support and to restrain the power of management and the power of organised labour'.[22] In traditional theories, labour law is seen as the result of power battles and struggles between a variety of social actors, who have different needs, interests and beliefs.[23] However, in accordance with a pluralist approach, labour law is but one of the sources of employment regulation for consideration in legal and regulatory research.

Law within the regulatory space assumes a facilitative function and, importantly, a proceduralist dimension, precisely due to its capacity to generate hierarchies and organised systems.[24] We tend to consider labour law as coordinating a system of sources in a hierarchical structure, with the purpose of regulating the employment relationship in its entirety. However, as commonly accepted in legal pluralist theory, the structure and supposed hierarchies that it sets up are not without inconsistencies.[25] As outlined earlier, and stressed by the framework proposed, putting law at the centre of analysis when talking about employment regulation may be over-simplistic. The generalisation and abstraction of legal reasoning may impede the investigation of not immediately legally relevant issues (and regulatory processes) at company or industry level. This could undervalue the complex web of formal and informal processes that are undertaken by regulatory actors in order to mediate, moderate and influence legal regulation.[26]

[21] For a practical application, see Eurofound, *Working Time Developments* (n 3).

[22] O Kahn-Freund, *Labour and the Law* (London, Stevens, 1972).

[23] B Hepple, 'Factors Influencing the Making and Transformation of Labour Law in Europe' in G Davidov and B Langille (eds), *The Idea of Labour Law* (Oxford, Oxford University Press, 2011) 30.

[24] B Morgan and K Yeung, *An Introduction to Law and Regulation: Text and Materials* (Cambridge, Cambridge University Press, 2007).

[25] Barber, 'Legal Pluralism' (n 8).

[26] A Fox, *Beyond Contract: Work, Power and Trust Relations* (London, Faber 1974); T Dundon and D Rollinson, *Understanding Employment Relations* (2nd edn, London, McGraw-Hill Higher Education, 2011).

The proposed approach requires that we take account of the limitations of legal regulation, including by directing greater attention to the so-called 'design failures' which might be responsible for a variety of issues, including the creation of unclear and vague regulations, and lack of coordination and coherence within the regulatory system, potentially increasing the rigidity or the structural inability to adapt to regulatory challenges and changing environments.[27] Legal uncertainty can also cede space to other actors for regulatory occupation and self-regulation. The analysis of regulatory loopholes and limitations is extremely important for examining the institutional shaping of responsibilities and accountabilities of regulatory actors.

B. Negotiated Regulation

In relation to the negotiated dimensions of regulation, the present analysis adopts a number of adaptations which have been made to the original framework.[28] Therefore, 'negotiated regulation' is sub-divided into two variants which describe mandated (or statutory) processes of negotiation on one side, and voluntarist instruments of decision-making between regulatory actors on the other. In different national institutional settings, these variations occur according to the role that the law assumes in supporting them.

Mandated forms of regulation that are supported and created by the law can be found in codetermination (with the classical example being the German model of codetermination in industrial relations)[29] or statutory forms of information and consultation. In these cases, the law creates some space for self-regulation in favour of industrial relations actors; for instance, by compelling employers to inform and consult their employees on specific employment subjects, giving participatory rights to employees, and delegating some areas of regulation to mandatory negotiations.

At the other end of the spectrum of mandated forms of negotiated regulation, the framework considers forms of negotiation and regulation that can be the result of a voluntarist process between labour market actors. Collective bargaining exemplifies the voluntarist dimension of negotiations as, historically, it represents the willingness of employers and trade unions to engage 'in the autonomous creation of norms governing the relations of third parties', rather than to enter into purely contractual relationships.[30]

Labour law can assume the role of supporting and facilitating voluntary agreements between parties, by providing a minimum floor of rights for workers, and

[27] Esping-Andersen and Regini, *Why Deregulate* (n 15) 31.

[28] Inversi, Buckley and Dundon, 'Analytical Framework for Employment Regulation' (n 2).

[29] See, for instance, M Behrens, 'Germany' in C Frege and J Kelly (eds), *Comparative Employment Relations in the Global Economy* (Abingdon, Routledge, 2013) 206.

[30] Dukes, *Labour Constitution* (n 12) 12.

establishing principles of non-derogation to those minimum standards (as occurs, for instance, in health and safety regulations, and in relation to minimum wages). However, voluntarism also includes other forms of regulation beyond collective bargaining: indeed, it can consist of regulation made through corporate or workplace processes. Voluntarism can encompass forms of Social Dialogue at European or national levels; dialogue may be voluntary (as in the Irish case for instance) or mandated, and more or less strictly regulated by the State (as in the case of the Italian 'Concertazione'). Voluntarism is also reflected at workplace level by instruments of employee-management dialogue and voice. Examples can be found in decentralised collective bargaining, non-union voice mechanisms, or individualised negotiations of employment terms and conditions.[31]

Both forms of negotiation, and their variants, can theoretically occur at many levels (supranational, national, local, sectoral, plant, or individual). Forms of information or participation can be outlined at international level, just as they can be implemented voluntarily at plant level. Similarly, collective bargaining may assume, or not (in relation to a specific institutional design), the same force as law; for instance, if it is applicable, the *erga omnes* effect, which extends the terms of collectively agreed regulation to non-organised workplaces within the area of employment covered by it.

C. Unilateralism

Unilateralism consists of regulation by the authority of a single body, typically imposed without negotiation. It represents an interesting dimension, and yet not an easy one to evaluate: unilateralism has a strong political and actor-centred characterisation, which often makes it difficult to conceptualise from a legal perspective. Unilateralism can be justified and reproduced by the legal framework, including through the principle of *ius variandi* typical of civil law systems and managerial prerogative, though it is often constrained by certain fundamental boundaries (such as the principle of *bona fidae*).

As a particular mode and process of regulating employment conditions, unilateralism potentially has a role in the analytical framework for assessing regulatory spaces. Space for unilateralism can be created by the legal framework, but also carved out by regulators acting individually in their own interest. As for the other dimensions, the impact of unilateralism can be studied both from protective and participative points of view.[32] In relation to the latter, the literature

[31] PJ Gollan, *Employee Representation in Non-Union Firms* (London, Sage, 2007); P Gunningle, J Lavelle and A McDonnell, 'Subtle but Deadly? Union Avoidance through "Double Breasting" among Multinational Companies' (2009) 16 *Advances in Industrial and Labor Relations* 51.

[32] W Sengenberger, 'Protection, Participation, Promotion: The Systemic Nature and Effects of Labour Standards' in W Sengenberger and D Campbell (eds), *Creative Economic Opportunities: The Role of Labour Standards in Industrial Restructuring* (Geneva, International Labour Office, 1994) 45.

about union avoidance, for instance, is useful in highlighting the extent to which managerial prerogative is used by employers to restrain the collective impact of trade unions or employee representative bodies in their efforts at influencing regulation.[33]

At an international level, unilateralism can be found where regulation is imposed by a superior authority embedded in the institutional setting, but external to the national democratic regulatory process. The role endorsed by the Troika (the European Commission, the International Monetary Fund, and the European Central Bank) in imposing austerity measures on the employment policies and laws of European Union (EU) Member States most affected by the economic crisis is an example of unilateralism at an international level, which then impacts upon the national level.[34]

At a national level, unilateralism can be found in an analysis of forms of corporatism and lobbying. The role of large firms and Transnational Corporations (TNCs) in influencing national regulations, through use of political power, resources, and lobbying, is outlined in a wide range of literature.[35] By having a place in the room of decision-making, TNCs can set standards and influence the political regulatory process by acting as government consultants or by lobbying ministers' offices. The literature provides examples of the role played by the American Chamber of Commerce, based in Ireland, in lobbying Irish civil servants and European government officials for the purpose of weakening the collective aspects of the Employee Information and Consultation Directive (Directive 2002/14/EC).[36]

Finally, I suggest that, at the workplace level, the role of Human Resource Management (HRM) (and managerial strategies) offers evidence of the unilateral imposition of practices and standards on employee working conditions. Keith Sisson argues that there seems to be a lack of interplay between legal regulation and the role of HRM.[37] From a participative point of view, it has been found that employers and managers often conceive of managerial strategies to avoid the collectivisation of workers – particularly in liberal market economies – thereby denying legitimate union recognition and representation.[38] Furthermore, case

[33] G Gall, T Dundon (eds) *Global Anti-Unionism* (London, Palgrave Macmillan, 2013).

[34] A Koukiadaki, I Távora and M Martinez Lucio (eds), *Joint Regulation and Labour Market Policy in Europe during the Crisis* (Brussels, European Trade Union Institute, 2016).

[35] C Crouch, *The Strange Non-Death of Neo-Liberalism* (Cambridge, Polity Press, 2011); M Martinez Lucio, 'Globalization, Organizations and Employment: the dynamics of degradation?' in M Martinez Lucio (ed), *International Human Resource Management: An Employment Relations Perspective* (London, Sage Publications, 2014) 17; P Almond and MC Gonzales Menendez, 'The Changing Nature of HRM, Organizational Change and Globalization' in M Martinez Lucio (ed), *International Human Resource Management: An Employment Relations Perspective* (London, Sage Publications, 2014) 37.

[36] Dundon and others, 'Employer Occupation of Regulatory Space' (n 5).

[37] K Sisson, 'In Search of HRM' (1993) 31 *British Journal of Industrial Relations* 201.

[38] G Gall and T Dundon (eds), *Global Anti-Unionism: Nature, Dynamics, Trajectories and Outcomes* (London, Palgrave Macmillan, 2013).

studies conducted at the workplace level, and focused on the unilateral regulation of working time arrangements in the workforce, seem to link the dominant position of employers in negotiations with the lack of structural economic power and institutional support afforded to workers and unions.[39] Studies conducted at a workplace level also illustrate how the lack of structural economic power and institutional support for workers and unions enables employers to take a de facto dominant position in negotiations, which can result in the unilateral imposition of working conditions.[40]

IV. The Analytical Framework Applied to Working Time

This section illustrates how the case study of working time regulation can be analysed through the lens of the regulatory framework, with the aim of outlining different dimensions and spaces of regulation. It also critically assesses aspects of current UK regulation in the area of working time.

The concept of working time is defined here by three main sub-meanings, which are discussed in the broader employment and sociological literature.[41] This definition tries to look at the different definitions of working time, going beyond the unitary model adopted by the legal approach, which focuses on the basic distinction between working time and rest time. In adopting a multi-dimensional definition, three key contributing aspects to the construction of the working time experience can be taken into account: time duration, which consists of the length of the working period; time organisation, which describes the working time schedule within a given period of work (this aspect is strongly linked with the distinction between 'social' and 'unsocial' hours of work[42]); and time utilisation, which considers the extent of working time spent in productive activity (or, more broadly, in work-related activity), and the intensity (pace, rhythm) of it.[43]

When it comes to regulatory issues, these three dimensions are strongly interconnected and need to be analysed as an overall system to develop a better picture of the experience of work and its impact on non-work life. Indeed, in modifying

[39] J Rubery, K Ward and D Grimshaw, 'The Changing Employment Relationship and the Implications for Quality Part-Time Work' (2005) 15 *Labour & Industry* 7.

[40] AJ Wood, 'Flexible Scheduling, Degradation of Job Quality and Barriers to Collective Voice' (2016) 69 *Human Relations* 1989.

[41] B Adam, *Time and Social Theory* (Cambridge, Polity, 1990); M Noon, P Blyton and K Morrell, *The Realities of Work: Experiencing Work and Employment in Contemporary Society* (4th edn, London, Palgrave Macmillan, 2013).

[42] Rubery, Ward and Grimshaw, 'Changing Employment Relationship' (n 39).

[43] Noon, Blyton and Morrell, *Realities of Work* (n 41).

one of these three aspects, it is possible to have side effects on the other aspects, which might frustrate the purpose of regulation: for instance, changes to the duration of work might increase work intensity (working time utilisation), or might include a re-allocation of working time across the day or week (working time organisation). As the next section shows, these three aspects are also often interconnected within legal norms, especially in relation to duration and organisation. While it might sometimes be difficult to analyse them separately, it is useful to deconstruct the overall definition of working time to see how regulation influences these three aspects, in order to better explain strategies and techniques of regulatory activity.

A. The Legal Dimension of Working Time Regulation

The role and limitations of statutory regulation in the area of working time have been outlined by Sangheon Lee and Deirdre McCann, who researched the capacity of workers to advance their preferences in relation to working time.[44] From a labour market perspective, the investigation of working time capabilities based on utilitarian analysis seems to suggest that workers have the power to voluntarily choose their working time; and therefore, that they should be considered responsible for their situation at work. However, to be responsible for one's choice, it is necessary to have the freedom or the possibility to choose.[45] In order to give workers the necessary freedom and, accordingly, the possibility of choosing and influencing aspects of their working time, law should be directed to providing an equal 'capability set',[46] which would include instruments such as freedom of choice, rights to information, as well as minimum working standards. In addition, law should also promote policies and social rights to support the influence of workers on working time regulation.[47]

From a regulatory space perspective, legal regulation should be orientated toward the creation of space for employee influence on working time issues, as the actual space available is limited by their subordinated position. Given the conflict between interests for flexibility (from employers) and the demand for accommodating preferences (from employees), scholars have further argued that setting

[44] S Lee and D McCann, 'Working Time Capability: Towards Realizing Individual Choice' in JY Boulin and others (eds), *Decent Working Time: New Trends, New Issues* (Geneva, International Labour Office, 2006) 65.

[45] See A Sen, *Development as Freedom* (Oxford, Oxford University Press, 1999) 824: 'Responsibility requires freedom … Without the substantive freedom and capability to do something, a person cannot be responsible for doing it'.

[46] J Browne, S Deakin and F Wilkinson, 'Capabilities, Social Rights and European Market Integration' in R Salais and R Villeneuve (eds), *Europe and the Politics of Capabilities* (Cambridge, Cambridge University Press, 2005) 205.

[47] Lee and McCann, 'Working Time Capability' (n 44).

highly standardised working hours, as established by statute, becomes extremely difficult.[48] While providing individual rights might be part of the solution, its effectiveness as a stand-alone strategy is questionable. Instead, I suggest that, beyond an analysis of substantive rules, the roles and interplay between collective actors and negotiators should be enhanced and further investigated in the regulatory literature.

i. Working Time, Employment Status and Labour Contracts

Within modern labour law, working time is linked to the nature of contractual relationships between the employer and employee. This is not just a matter of regulations limiting the number of hours or the timing of work activity, however, as the issue of working time regulation is implicitly included in the choice of a specific contractual instrument, and in the length of the contract.[49] For instance, the use of part-time, zero hours contracts, or job sharing, are ways of framing the temporal dimension of an employment relationship, within a pre-defined legal framework, which is prompted by the employer's decision to offer a specific contractual arrangement in line with the organisation's business strategy. Therefore, the legal regulation of working time must not be considered in a strict sense, as either the set of rules that regulate working experiences by limiting the working period, or as providing rest time and holidays (ie, The Working Time Regulations 1998, or WTR). Analysis must also consider the legal pattern that enables different contractual relationships for the purpose of working time flexibility. In this sense, working time is not just limited to the establishment of regulatory instruments for ensuring decent conditions of work, but also constitutes an element that differentiates forms of employment, and employment status or position.

ii. Duration, Organisation, and Utilisation

The regulation of working time duration and organisation is determined at international and national levels by provisions that, for instance, limit the length of the working day/week, provide for rest times and their length, give rights to annual paid holidays, etc. Further space is then allowed for decentralised forms of regulation at the industry or plant level, as well as at an individual level: in some cases, the regulation at lower levels can derogate, for better or worse, from legal provisions. However, derogation can only happen within the limits and according to the formal requirements outlined by law, where regulatory power and authority is ceded to other actors, who can occupy (or not) the space created by the legal mechanism. For example, the case of the individual opt-out laid down in regulation 5 of the WTR.

[48] Berg, Bosch and Charest, 'Working-Time Configurations' (n 3).

[49] A Supiot, *Beyond Employment: Changes in Work and the Future of Labour Law in Europe* (Oxford, Oxford University Press, 2001).

Regulation of working time duration is often accompanied by organisational aspects that, in some cases, can make provisions more 'flexible'. For instance, regulation 4 of the WTR, while imposing a working time limit of 48 hours for each seven-day period (including overtime), states that the reference period for calculating the average hours worked for the purpose of the limit is set at 17 weeks (and the starting day for the calculation can be voluntarily agreed by the employer and the employee, or their representatives). This provision includes both aspects of duration and organisation, as it provides for a ceiling on working time duration but, at the same time, the regulations allow for a flexible distribution of working hours over the 17 weeks of the reference period. This mechanism provides an example of the ceding of space from the legal instrument to voluntarily agreed provisions that affect the organisation of working time.

Provisions about working time utilisation are more difficult to find within the legal regulatory dimension. An interesting discussion, however, is reflected in analysis of national and European case law, and from the connection between the regulation of hours and pay. Measuring the pace of working activity can find its regulatory dimension in the evaluation of remuneration for time spent at work. Pay could indeed be differentiated on the basis of the different utilisation of working time. The case of on-call workers is particularly interesting. In *Rossiter*[50] and *Hughes*,[51] the Employment Appeal Tribunal (EAT) considered and referred to work intensity to evaluate pay rates for workers during their on-call time. In *Rossiter*, the EAT held that work intensity should not be considered as a factor determining the level of remuneration under the National Minimum Wage (NMW). While this reasoning is in line with the aims of the WTR, and the Working Time Directive[52] (WTD),[53] it has been challenged by the decision in *Hughes*, and by the recent position of the CJEU in *Tyco*.[54] These decisions contemplate the possibility of differentiating pay according to the nature of working activity, and the notion of working time (for instance, time spent on-call, or travelling between home and work, could be considered working time but, at the same time, it could be excluded from the application of the NMW).

With this brief analysis, I have shown how working time utilisation can become an interesting element in the evaluation of workers' conditions, through

[50] *Burrow Down Support Services Ltd v Rossiter* [2008] ICR 1172 (*Rossiter*).

[51] *Hughes v Jones (t/a Graylyns Residential Home)* [2008] UKEAT 0159_08_310 (3 October 2008) (*Hughes*).

[52] Directive 2003/88/EC of the European Parliament and of the Council of 4 November 2003 concerning certain aspects of the organisation of working time [2003] OJ L299/9.

[53] L Rodgers, 'The Notion of Working Time' (2009) 38 *Industrial Law Journal* 80.

[54] *Federación de Servicios Privados del sindicato Comisiones obreras (CC.OO.) v Tyco Integrated Security SL and Tyco Integrated Fire & Security Corporation Servicios SA* (Court of Justice of the European Union, C-266/14, 10 September 2015). For commentary on *Tyco*, see D McCann, 'Travel Time as Working Time: Tyco, the Unitary Model and the Route to Casualisation' (2016) 45 *Industrial Law Journal* 244.

the link between working time regulation and pay regulation. Further, it assists us to understand how regulatory arenas can connect and combine different sources of regulation to adapt regulation to present challenges.

B. Negotiation of Working Time Regulation

Although the UK law on working time cedes multiple spaces for collective bargaining, the negotiation process is actually not underpinned by law, as the British tradition is historically one of voluntarism, rather than mandated negotiation. The gap of knowledge in this field (for instance, concerning the role of European Works Councils in addressing issues of working time regulation) is particularly interesting. It is important to remember, however, that codetermination or institutionally supported collective bargaining in the UK are not common regulatory instruments, even if there is increased attention to this form of regulation, especially where driven by EU law.[55]

At the other end of the spectrum, voluntarist negotiation, in the form of collective bargaining and individual negotiations, still represents one of the most important sources of regulation in the area of working time. British tradition has historically assigned a prominent role to sectoral collective bargaining. Until the 1980s, when policies of decentralisation had the effect of restricting the coverage of sectoral-level collective agreements, it represented the primary mechanism for regulating basic working hours, overtime, shift work *premia*, and annual paid holidays.[56]

The WTD and subsequent British legislation provide a new balance between statutory and voluntary sources of regulation: in many provisions of the European and national regulations, considerable space is allocated for voluntary regulation, both at a national and regional level. Collective and workforce agreements can derogate from and modify regulations in the area of night work, daily and weekly rest periods and breaks, weekly limits on working time, and the reference period.[57] However, scholars have outlined how falling levels of employee representation in the UK may be the reason for a rather inflexible application of working time standards by collective agreements, and for greater use of forms of individual negotiations.[58]

[55] See, for instance, Directive 2009/38/EC of the European Parliament and of the Council of 6 May 2009 on the establishment of a European Works Council or a procedure in Community-scale undertakings and Community-scale groups of undertakings for the purposes of informing and consulting employees [2009] OJ L122/28.

[56] S Deakin and GS Morris, *Labour Law*, 6th edn (Oxford, Hart Publishing, 2012).

[57] Working Time Regulations 1998, reg 23(b).

[58] C Barnard, S Deakin and R Hobbs, 'Opting Out of the 48-Hour Week: Employer Necessity or Individual Choice? An Empirical Study of the Operation of Article 18(1)(b) of the Working Time Directive

i. Duration, Organisation, and Utilisation

An important provision of the WTD, and the WTR, which leaves considerable space for voluntarist (individual) negotiation is the possibility of 'opting out' of the 48-hour weekly limit on working time duration.[59] In the empirical research conducted by Catherine Barnard, Simon Deakin and Richard Hobbs,[60] the findings from employer surveys revealed that the opting-out instrument was preferred to other forms of derogation, such as the option of classifying employees as occupying 'managerial positions' (with autonomous decision-making power) and then applying the 'unmeasured working time' provisions in regulation 20 of the WTR. The opt-out instrument was considered preferable to the derogations provided by regulation 20 of the WTR, as the latter left too much room for judicial interpretation, and thus legal regulatory intervention. In this case, voluntary regulation was possibly preferred over the worker being (unilaterally) classified under regulation 20 of the WTR, due to the fear of judicial action.

The voluntarist nature of the 'opting-out' procedure is particularly noteworthy. Indeed, the CJEU criticised the UK regulations on the basis that this provision did not provide the necessary degree of freedom for employees to make a voluntary choice and individually opt-out of the 48-hour limit (regulation 5 of the WTR).[61] Employee freedom of choice might be at risk, especially if the contractual arrangement is pre-defined by the employer, and the opt-out clause is implicitly proposed as a condition for obtaining the job.[62] In this respect, we can see how the voluntarist nature of opting-out can turn into unilateral regulation, especially if one of the parties to the contract does not have the freedom to choose or the 'strength' to negotiate.

C. Unilateralism

As foreshadowed above, the unilateral aspect of regulation deals with the power of managers to shape and direct employee working time, but also with workers' ability to resist employers' regulation or impose their preferences. The literature on working time regulation has stressed how employer-led models have increasingly been able to shape, and tailor, regulatory solutions by adopting unilateral

in the UK' (2003) 32 *Industrial Law Journal* 223; R Rogowski, 'Implementation of the EU Working Time Directive in the United Kingdom' in J Barbier, R Rogowski and F Colomb (eds), *The Sustainability of the European Social Model: EU Governance, Social Protection and Employment Policies in Europe* (Cheltenham, Edward Elgar, 2015) 231.

[59] According to reg 5 of the WTR, the validity of opting out is conditioned by the presence of an individual written agreement between the employer and the employee, which can last for a precise or indefinite period of time, and which is terminable by the worker with a written notice.

[60] Barnard, Deakin and Hobbs, 'Opting Out of the 48-Hour Week' (n 58).

[61] *United Kingdom v Council of the European Union* (C-84/94) [1996] ECR I-5755.

[62] IT Smith and A Baker, *Smith and Wood's Employment Law*, 10th edn (Oxford, Oxford University Press, 2010).

approaches rather than voluntarist ones.[63] This section provides a brief outline of how unilateralism is exercised in the area of working time as an instrument for creating effective working time regulation. This model, it is argued, can be supported by the institutional environment and by legislation.

i. Duration, Utilisation, and Organisation

Unilateralism finds spaces to regulate both the duration and the organisation of working time, but appears to have a stronger, more prominent role when considering the organisation of working schedules and the rhythms of production at company/workplace level. In particular, the literature shows a prevalence for unilateralist practices and strict managerial control in decisions on worker schedules, and a failure to consistently take employee preferences, requests, or needs into account.[64]

Unilateralism has a prominent role in the regulation of working time duration and organisation in the UK. It has been linked to use of the opting-out clause made available by the WTR, which has been used extensively in the British context.

In looking at the future of regulation, it has been argued that the existence of opt-out provisions could undermine the stimulus to modernise working time.[65] From a regulatory space perspective, however, removal of this provision alone will not be sufficient to enable development of a complete framework for working time regulation: the challenge of employee representation is also inherently linked with the attempt to modernise working time arrangements, as is the challenge of eroding unilateralism by providing basic support for collective action or voluntarist negotiation.[66] Simply removing a legal norm that gives considerable space to the unilateral power of employers would be ineffective, if not supported by complementary regulatory restructuring in favour of more collaborative forms of regulation, such as co-determination or voluntarism. At the same time, basic limits on working time duration would not be sufficient to guarantee worker health and wellbeing, as the influence of employers over work utilisation (such as an increase in the rhythm of work over a shorter period of time) could counterbalance the positive protections achieved through statutory rights.

V. Conclusion

This chapter has outlined a theoretical approach, and an analytical framework, that try to capture the complexity of multilevel regulation (across three main

[63] Rubery, Ward and Grimshaw, 'Changing Employment Relationship' (n 39).

[64] JR Henly and SJ Lambert, 'Unpredictable Work Timing in Retail Jobs: Implications for Employee Work-Life Conflict' (2014) 67 *ILR Review* 986; Wood, 'Flexible Scheduling' (n 40).

[65] Barnard, Deakin and Hobbs, 'Opting Out of the 48-Hour Week' (n 58).

[66] ibid.

levels: supranational, national, and workplace) and the varieties of regulatory mechanisms, with a view to enhancing our understanding of regulatory processes and the role of labour law. The framework goes beyond a traditional understanding of regulation as purely a legal matter: it encompasses other means of regulation as negotiated forms of regulation and unilateralism.

To illustrate the application of the theoretical approach, this chapter has applied the analytical framework to the area of working time. I argue that the framework can be used as an analytical and methodological tool to enhance the research and theorisation of labour.

My analysis has focused on the regulation of working time to illustrate the limits of an isolated analysis of the 'legal space' of regulation. In doing so, I have considered and illustrated how labour law can contribute to shaping and creating spaces for other regulatory dimensions and actors. In conclusion, my contribution sustains a legal pluralist approach and argues for a greater appreciation of dimensions and spaces (levels) of regulation, outside the legal hierarchies of sources, which can contribute to the material regulation of employment in the realities of work.

12

Re-Systematising Labour Law: Beyond Traditional Systems Theory and Reflexive Law?

ALYSIA BLACKHAM*

I. Introduction

Reflexive law has an enduring place in the theory of labour law, having featured prominently in the work of leading labour law scholars.[1] Grounded in systems theory, reflexive law offers a key means of moving beyond command and control regulation,[2] to consider how law interacts with other social systems.[3] Systems theory, as developed by Niklas Luhmann, argues that the world is composed of

* Associate Professor and Australian Research Council Discovery Early Career Research Fellow, Melbourne Law School, the University of Melbourne, Australia. This research was funded by the Australian Government through the Australian Research Council's *Discovery Projects* funding scheme (project DE170100228). The views expressed herein are those of the author and are not necessarily those of the Australian Government or Australian Research Council. I am grateful to Miriam Kullmann and Ania Zbyszewska, who had a formative role in the development of this chapter; and Ralf Rogowski, who provided insightful comments and critiques on an earlier version.

[1] See, eg, B Hepple, 'Enforcing Equality Law: Two Steps Forward and Two Steps Backwards for Reflexive Regulation' (2011) 40 *Industrial Law Journal* 315; R Rogowski, *Reflexive Labour Law in the World Society* (Cheltenham, Edward Elgar, 2013); C Barnard et al, 'Reflexive Law, Corporate Social Responsibility and the Evolution of Labour Standards: The Case of Working Time' (Working Paper, Cambridge, December 2004); S Deakin and R Rogowski, 'Reflexive Labour Law, Capabilities and the Future of Social Europe' in R Rogowski et al (eds), *Transforming European Employment Policy: Labour Market Transitions and the Promotion of Capability* (Cheltenham, Edward Elgar, 2011); C Barnard et al, 'Capabilities and Rights: An Emerging Agenda for Social Policy?' (2001) 32 *Industrial Relations Journal* 464; W Njoya, 'Employee Ownership in the European Company: Reflexive Law, Reincorporation and Escaping Co-Determination' (2011) 11 *Journal of Corporate Law Studies* 267; W Njoya, 'Job Security in a Flexible Labor Market: Challenges and Possibilities for Worker Voice' (2011–12) 33 *Comparative Labor Law & Policy Journal* 459.

[2] P Zumbansen, 'Law After the Welfare State: Formalism, Functionalism, and the Ironic Turn of Reflexive Law' (2008) 56 *The American Journal of Comparative Law* 769, 791.

[3] G Teubner, 'Substantive and Reflexive Elements in Modern Law' (1983) 17 *Law & Society Review* 239.

social subsystems, each of which is autopoietically closed but cognitively open. Law, in this view, is one social sub-system, with its own system of self-referential and self-constituting communication. One system cannot influence, control, or determine other systems: instead, systems might occasionally 'irritate' each other. Law therefore cannot control the economy, labour market or organisations: it can only irritate other social systems to effect change. For Luhmann, then, the focus is on self-referential communications *within* systems, rather than any input-output relation between them.

In seeking a more inclusive theory of labour law, reflexive law seems an obvious option to consider, as it encompasses a wider range of regulatory techniques and actors than that envisaged by traditional and direct state regulation. That said, while reflexive law has been influential in labour law scholarship, and offers significant advantages over a focus on direct regulation, it appears to be built on unstable foundations. Systems theory, which has been the bedrock of reflexive law theory, arguably has a number of fundamental theoretical limitations, which limit its usefulness and applicability to a labour law context. This, then, should cause concern if systems theory is seen as the basis for labour law theorising through reflexive law.

In this chapter, I outline the prevailing limitations of systems theory, and how they might undermine labour law theorising, drawing on a case study of United Kingdom (UK) equality law scholarship. I map the difficulties of applying reflexive law to the UK context, and consider whether this might be related to the theoretical critiques of systems theory and reflexive law. I argue that, while the critiques of systems theory and reflexive law have weight, developing critical systems theory scholarship means that the theories still have much to offer labour law theorising.

II. Systems Theory

According to systems theory, law and other social areas occupy discrete, closed, self-referencing and self-reinforcing autopoetic systems.[4] Legal autopoiesis applies self-referentiality to the legal sphere, arguing that 'the reality of law consists of a multitude of circular processes'.[5] For Gunther Teubner, circularity of the legal system also suggests its closure.[6] Autopoiesis therefore seeks to map circular relationships, assess their internal dynamics and evaluate external interactions.[7]

[4] See N Luhmann, *Law as a Social System* (F Kastner et al trs, Oxford, Oxford University Press, 2004).

[5] G Teubner, 'Introduction to Autopoietic Law' in G Teubner (ed), *Autopoietic Law: A New Approach to Law and Society* (Berlin, Walter de Gruyter, 1988) 1.

[6] ibid 2.

[7] ibid 1.

Operational closure of systems means that they cannot communicate directly with each other. Each social system creates its own world view and ways of knowing: this might mean that 'world-views in different subsystems are thoroughly incompatible on the basis of their cognitive assumptions'.[8] Communication between systems has to be 'translated' to fit within systems' own communicative processes. Social systems have *communication* as their basic element, not human beings,[9] though humans belong to the environment of the system.[10]

As Teubner recognises, characterising systems as operationally closed but cognitively open sounds paradoxical.[11] However, the underlying assumption of systems theory seems to be that legal autopoiesis has the potential to render the legal system more responsive to social reality:[12] as Teubner explains, a 'radical closure of the system – under certain conditions – means its radical openness', arguing that the more closed and autonomous the legal system becomes, the more open it is to other influences.[13] Rather than a relationship of direct or linear influence, though, law and social systems are subject to 'mutual interference' as they 'share the same world of meaning' and the elements of the systems are 'essentially similar'.[14]

Central to systems theory, therefore, is the idea that the legal system, in its functional logic, does not follow or remain beholden to moral considerations or political power structures. The legal system only obeys its own legal specifications, meaning that only law can produce law. On the flipside, however, law can only govern society by governing itself[15] or, potentially, 'irritating' other systems through an 'external stimulation of internal self-regulating processes which, in principle, cannot be controlled from the outside'.[16]

III. Reflexive Law

Systems theory therefore posits the (non-legal) results of legal change as being fundamentally uncertain. This 'problem with regulation' can be depicted as a black box, as each (sub)system 'knows the input and the output of the other, but the internal processes that convert inputs to outputs remain obscure'.[17] Autopoiesis therefore requires labour law to embrace reflexive regulatory techniques.[18]

[8] G Teubner, *Law as an Autopoietic System* (Z Bankowski ed, A Bankowska and R Adler trs, Oxford, Blackwell, 1993) 62.

[9] Teubner, 'Introduction to Autopoietic Law' (n 5) 3.

[10] N Luhmann, *Social Systems* (J Bednarz Jr tr, Stanford, Stanford University Press, 1995) chs 6, 7.

[11] Teubner, 'Introduction to Autopoietic Law' (n 5) 2.

[12] ibid.

[13] ibid.

[14] Teubner, *Law as an Autopoietic System* (n 8) 88–89.

[15] ibid 82.

[16] G Teubner, 'Autopoiesis in Law and Society: A Rejoinder to Blankenburg' (1984) 18 *Law & Society Review* 291, 298.

[17] ibid 299–300.

[18] S Deakin, 'Law as an Autopoietic System' (1997) 26 *Industrial Law Journal* 89, 90–91.

Reflexive law focuses attention on the limits of law and legal regulation, self-regulation in other systems,[19] and the regulatory capacities of the legal system itself.[20] It seeks to understand legal and social change, including by mapping the relationship between changes in law and changes in society, and between legal and social structures.[21] The role of reflexive law theory is therefore to help scrutinise the link between legal autopoiesis and societal regulation.[22]

Reflexive law scholarship is based on the idea 'that regulatory interventions are most likely to be successful when they seek to achieve their ends not by direct prescription, but by inducing "second-order effects" on the part of social actors'.[23] Law should not command change: rather, law reform should 'irritate' other systems to promote and stimulate self-regulation.[24] Law, then, 'becomes a system for the coordination of action within and between semi-autonomous social subsystems'[25] through 'enforced or stimulated self-regulation'.[26] Thus, reflexive law seeks regulation 'without the unintended and undesirable side-effects associated with substantive law'.[27] It therefore has significant implications for the design of regulation that is aimed at bringing about social change,[28] and moves legal interventions beyond 'simple "command and control"'.[29] Applying reflexivity to law is assumed to improve the effectiveness of legal interventions.

For Ian Ayres and John Braithwaite, reflexive law can be achieved through the 'enforcement pyramid', where escalating government regulation reinforces market self-regulation.[30] Regulation should commence at the base of the pyramid, starting with 'restorative dialogue', information, persuasion and voluntary agreement.[31] If these voluntary measures fail, regulation can become increasingly interventionist; it is the prospect of more interventionist measures that makes voluntary measures effective,[32] and encourages firms to self-regulate.[33]

[19] Rogowski, *Reflexive Labour Law in the World Society* (n 1) 32.

[20] See especially Teubner, *Law as an Autopoietic System* (n 8) ch 5.

[21] Teubner, 'Substantive and Reflexive Elements in Modern Law' (n 4) 242, 257.

[22] Teubner, *Law as an Autopoietic System* (n 8) 65.

[23] C Barnard and S Deakin, 'In Search of Coherence: Social Policy, the Single Market and Fundamental Rights' (2000) 31 *Industrial Relations Journal* 331, 341.

[24] R Rogowski and T Wilthagen, 'Reflexive Labour Law: An Introduction' in R Rogowski and T Wilthagen (eds), *Reflexive Labour Law: Studies in Industrial Relations and Employment Regulation* (Deventer, Kluwer Law and Taxation Publishers, 1994) 7.

[25] Teubner, 'Substantive and Reflexive Elements in Modern Law' (n 4) 242.

[26] C McLaughlin, 'Equal Pay, Litigation and Reflexive Regulation: The Case of the UK Local Authority Sector' (2014) 43 *Industrial Law Journal* 1, 4.

[27] P Capps and HP Olsen, 'Legal Autonomy and Reflexive Rationality in Complex Societies' (2002) 11 *Social & Legal Studies* 547, 551.

[28] Deakin and Rogowksi, 'Reflexive Labour Law' (n 1) 230.

[29] Hepple, 'Enforcing Equality Law' (n 1) 320.

[30] I Ayres and J Braithwaite, *Responsive Regulation: Transcending the Deregulation Debate* (Oxford, Oxford University Press, 1992).

[31] Hepple (n 2) 321.

[32] ibid 322.

[33] Ayres and Braithwaite, *Responsive Regulation* (n 30) 4.

IV. Reflexive Law in Labour and Equality Law Scholarship

Reflexive law has played a prominent role in labour and equality law scholarship in the UK and European Union (EU). However, studies of equality law in particular are increasingly doubting the capacity for reflexive law (or, at least, what has been described as 'reflexive law') to protect vulnerable groups from discrimination. This research increasingly demonstrates the possible limits of 'reflexive' regulation in practice.

For example, Christopher McCrudden identifies a number of potential problems with using reflexive regulation to recast equality law in the UK.[34] More generally, McCrudden puts forward three critiques of reflexive law: that it fails to recognise the role of conflicting political and economic interests and power, by depoliticising regulatory failure; that deliberation on *how* to implement certain values can undermine core values themselves; and that reflexive law has certain institutional requirements that must be in place for deliberation to succeed. Focusing on this third critique, McCrudden argues that the pre-conditions for effective reflexive regulation are not in place in the UK: namely, an obligation on firms to examine what they are doing (such as through the need to gather and review data on their workforce); that firms consider alternatives designed to shift patterns of inequality, and that this be reviewed by an external body; and a requirement to engage with other stakeholders. A reflexive approach to equality law is unlikely to be successful in this context. Instead, there is a risk of falling into 'non-regulation' or 're-regulation' by the courts.[35]

Bob Hepple also uses reflexive law and the enforcement pyramid to model and critique UK equality law.[36] In his study of equality law enforcement, Hepple outlines a number of reforms in the Equality Act 2006 and Equality Act 2010 that move towards reflexive law, including the creation of a single Equality and Human Rights Commission (EHRC) with extensive enforcement powers, and the extension of the Public Sector Equality Duty (PSED) to all protected grounds. However, Hepple also identifies reforms that undermine this trend towards reflexive regulation, including limits to the EHRC's enforcement powers and budget, and removing any engagement requirement from the PSED.

In considering the potential advantages and disadvantages of reflexive regulation in the field of equality law, Hepple argues that there is a risk that reflexive law 'ignores or underestimates' the role of power, particularly the institutional power held by corporations and public bodies. To address these power disparities, Hepple

[34] C McCrudden, 'Equality Legislation and Reflexive Regulation: A Response to the Discrimination Law Review's Consultative Paper' (2007) 36 *Industrial Law Journal* 255, 263.

[35] ibid.

[36] Hepple, 'Enforcing Equality Law' (n 1).

reinforces the importance of engagement, which might include information, consultation, participation and collective bargaining.[37] If meaningful engagement is not present, then

> the disadvantage of the reflexive regulation model is that it may simply serve to legitimate or rubber-stamp the exercise of corporate and institutional power unless individuals and groups affected by their actions have the legal power to compel engagement, and the enforcement agency has the power to ensure that agreements uphold the values of the legislation and, where necessary, to impose deterrent sanctions.[38]

Hepple concludes, however, that these engagement mechanisms are not adequately in place in the UK, and are entirely absent from the statutory provisions of the Equality Act 2010. Thus, 'reflexive law' (at least, as it has been effected through the Equality Act 2010) is unlikely to be successful in Britain.[39] This may reflect the fact that politicians and policy-makers do not actually grasp what 'reflexive law' entails or, if they do, 'chose to ignore' it: thus, 'grand theories such as that of reflexive regulation may have little impact on the actual development of legal enforcement'.[40] The application of 'reflexive law' as a means of modelling legal and policy change may be confined to academic commentators seeking 'signs of a model of reflexive regulation'.[41] More generally, the problem with 'reflexive regulation' is that it 'can mean all things to all people. No one can decide in advance what use different political groups will make of it'.[42] In the case of equality law in the UK, 'reflexive regulation' has been used to undermine legal protection for vulnerable groups.

Sandra Fredman also uses reflexive law to critique the PSED and its requirement to have 'due regard' to equality issues,[43] questioning whether this '[reflects] a fundamental ambivalence as to the importance of equality, deferring to public authorities' view as to what priority equality deserves' or whether it could be given 'a more positive interpretation, regarding it as an instance of "reflexive law"'.[44] Fredman concludes that, while the 'due regard' standard has the potential to be reflexive, it is not working that way in practice. Relying on judicial review for enforcement of the PSED puts courts in a difficult position: they must both look to the substance of organisational decision-making, to ensure consideration of equality issues is not just proceduralism or 'box-ticking'; but, equally, a focus on substance not form makes it difficult to create a stable set of legal principles with predictable outcomes. For Fredman, this is the 'paradox' of using judicial review to enforce the PSED:

> On the one hand, the role of courts is to supply a stable set of principles capable of guiding decision making without resort to litigation. On the other hand, the more settled

[37] ibid 322.
[38] ibid 323.
[39] ibid 332.
[40] ibid 334.
[41] ibid.
[42] ibid.
[43] S Fredman, 'The Public Sector Equality Duty' (2011) 40 *Industrial Law Journal* 405.
[44] ibid 418.

> the principles, the more scope there is for mere procedural compliance and the less space is left for flexible decision making.[45]

Thus, relying on established legal mechanisms (such as judicial review) for the enforcement of potentially reflexive tools (such as the 'due regard' standard) is unlikely to prompt cultural change and mainstream equality.[46] As Fredman concludes,

> the "due regard" standard falls well short of the requirements for truly reflexive law, which would require a carefully modulated system of internal and external drivers, with judicial review as a last, not first resort. Without a duty to take action, the risk of proceduralism is difficult to overcome.[47]

The impact of the due regard standard, then, may be no better than command and control regulation. This reflects the difficulty of implementing reflexive regulatory techniques in practice.

Colm McLaughlin uses reflexive law as a theoretical framework to examine the implementation of collective agreements around equal pay in the UK local authority sector.[48] Drawing on qualitative interviews, including with senior human resources representatives from local authorities in England and union representatives, McLaughlin identifies three potential issues with the implementation of reflexive law in the equal pay context. First, he questions the extent to which unions can effectively challenge existing power relations in the collective bargaining process, given the divergent interests of their members.[49] This becomes particularly apparent in the equal pay context, where there are potential 'winners' (often women) and 'losers' (often men). Secondly, McLaughlin identifies potential contradictions and tensions between equal pay litigation and collective bargaining. In the context of equal pay, 'the law operates less as a default than a norm with potentially overriding effect, and collectively agreed settlements have no such protection from challenge via litigation'.[50] This sets the stage for conflict between collectively negotiated solutions on the one hand, which attempt to balance competing interests, and litigated outcomes based on individual rights on the other. Thirdly, McLaughlin identifies a need for 'effective bridging mechanisms between the legal sphere and the organisational sphere',[51] particularly given local actors may not have the expertise or capacity to effectively bargain over equal pay. Overall, then, McLaughlin's study 'highlights that reflexive approaches do not always deliver the outcomes intended by parliament, and that the tribunals and litigation have also played an important role in delivering fairness and justice for some

[45] ibid 420.
[46] ibid 424.
[47] ibid 427.
[48] McLaughlin, 'Equal Pay, Litigation and Reflexive Regulation' (n 26).
[49] ibid 26–27.
[50] ibid 26.
[51] ibid 27.

very low paid women'.[52] This reinforces the need for statutory minima or rights to supplement or reinforce collectively negotiated solutions. Equally, though, these statutory minima or rights might serve to undermine or challenge the process of reflexive regulation. For McLaughlin, this is the 'ambiguous role of litigation, which may act as a catalyst to self-regulation in some instances while undermining it in others'.[53]

In my own study of age discrimination law in the UK, I use reflexive law to both critique and normatively model potential changes to equality law.[54] I argue that reflexive law is a useful theoretical framework for two reasons: first, it helps to explain why age discrimination law has had limited impact on organisational practice, despite ten years of operation; and, secondly, it helps to shift the focus of academics and policy makers toward more creative regulatory interventions, as an alternative to a focus on command and control regulation.[55]

While recognising these theoretical benefits, however, I also identify a worrying tendency in my empirical research for reflexive law to be confused with soft or non-law. As I map in that study, the focus of UK governments in relation to equality law (and age discrimination law in particular) has been primarily on 'restorative dialogue', information and persuasion,[56] which form the base of the enforcement pyramid and the default form of intervention in a reflexive law model.[57] I find that the UK government's focus on education and persuasion has not resulted in concrete organisational change: this is an 'irritation' that has not worked. I argue, however, that this is understandable from a theoretical standpoint, as reflexive law requires more than just dialogue to achieve change: there must also be increasingly interventionist action where dialogue and self-regulation fail. In the context of equality law, however, interventionist actions are being increasingly undermined by government reforms, which have made individual enforcement more difficult, and reduced the power and resources of the EHRC.

My study, then, illustrates the fundamental problems of relying on reflexive law to overcome a deregulatory governmental agenda.[58] Indeed, 'reflexive law' appears to have become a means and theoretical justification for furthering governments' retreat from social and employment regulation. I conclude, then, that

> the use of a reflexive law [theoretical] framework may condone and enhance the push for deregulation and a withering away of governmental responsibility, rather than

[52] ibid 28.

[53] ibid 3.

[54] A Blackham, *Extending Working Life for Older Workers: Age Discrimination Law, Policy and Practice* (Oxford, Hart Publishing, 2016).

[55] ibid 227.

[56] J Macnicol, 'The Age Discrimination Debate in Britain: From the 1930s to the Present' (2005) 4 *Social Policy and Society* 295, 298.

[57] J Braithwaite, *Restorative Justice and Responsive Regulation* (Oxford, Oxford University Press, 2002) 30.

[58] *cf* Ayres and Braithwaite, *Responsive Regulation* (n 30).

> providing a way out of the deregulation/regulation divide. … reflexive law should be used with a degree of caution and scepticism.[59]

These concerns with the use of reflexive law are not limited to equality law: Catherine Barnard, Simon Deakin and Richard Hobb's empirical study of working time in the UK concludes that reflexive law is insufficiently developed in the UK, meaning relying on voluntary measures to promote organisational change is highly problematic. In the context of working time, the 'high hopes' of reflexive law have not been borne out:[60] statutory limits on working time have been easily avoided by employers, the culture of long working hours has not shifted, and working time regulations are not seen by employers as promoting efficiency. Thus, a reliance on self-regulation and multi-level and decentralised deliberation has been ineffective in practice.

These studies illustrate that there is a growing body of research that doubts the effectiveness of 'reflexive law' in the context of UK labour and equality law.[61] This may reflect the limited or imperfect adoption or implementation of reflexive principles in regulation. Indeed, as Lizzie Barmes argues, innovative regulatory techniques have been overlaid onto existing legal rules, conveying inconsistent and poorly articulated messages to organisations.[62] It is possible that reflexive regulatory techniques will be more successful in other labour law contexts, such as occupational health and safety,[63] though even these contexts experience challenges in implementation.[64] Alternatively (or additionally) it may reflect the particular limitations of the UK labour law context, where there are few mechanisms in place for engagement to moderate the power of organisations and public bodies. Reflexive law may be more successful in other national regulatory contexts, where stronger traditions of social dialogue and corporatism are built into the regulatory structure.

Problematically, these studies may reveal more fundamental problems with attempting to use reflexive regulation in practice. As Hepple notes, this may be because legislators do not or will not engage with the ideas of reflexive law. Equally, 'reflexive law' may be used as a convenient label to justify and legitimise a de-regulatory push. Potentially, though, this may also reveal that reflexive law,

[59] Blackham, *Extending Working Life for Older Workers* (n 54) 228.

[60] Barnard et al, 'Reflexive Law, Corporate Social Responsibility and the Evolution of Labour Standards' (n 1) 35.

[61] Though, of course, other scholars find reflexive law to be more compelling: see, eg, Rogowski, *Reflexive Labour Law in the World Society* (n 1).

[62] L Barmes, 'Equality Law and Experimentation: The Positive Action Challenge' (2009) 68 *Cambridge Law Journal* 623, 635; D Ashiagbor, 'Evaluating the Reflexive Turn in Labour Law' in A Bogg, C Costello, A Davies and J Prassl (eds), *The Autonomy of Labour Law* (Oxford, Hart Publishing, 2015) 143.

[63] Rogowski, *Reflexive Labour Law in the World Society* (n 1) 38; T Wilthagen, 'Reflexive Rationality in the Regulation of Occupational Safety and Health' in R Rogowski and T Wilthagen (eds), *Reflexive Labour Law – Studies in Industrial Relations and Employment Regulation* (Deventer, Kluwer Law and Taxation Publishers, 1994).

[64] Wilthagen, 'Reflexive Rationality' (n 63).

and the systems theory it is grounded in, are divorced from the reality of regulation, such that achieving truly reflexive regulation in practice is prohibitively difficult.

V. Critiques of Systems Theory

As McCrudden argues, no system of regulation is perfect;[65] equally, no theory of labour law or regulation is perfect. However, the repeated problems identified with the implementation of reflexive law in the UK necessitate consideration of whether there are more fundamental problems associated with reflexive law, and the systems theory on which it is based. Indeed, systems theory has been criticised on a number of grounds, potentially reducing its persuasiveness as a basis for labour law theorising. Some of these critiques have been foreshadowed in the equality law literature above. Below, I synthesise the key critiques of systems theory, focusing on three areas: (1) the relative autonomy of legal systems and inter-systemic interactions, (2) the place and role of humans, bodies and agency in the context of legal systems, and (3) problems related to normativity. These critiques may provide additional explanations for some of the difficulty in applying reflexive law in the UK context.

A. Autonomy of Legal Systems

First, it is questionable whether law's operations can be classified as a closed system, separate from society and other social systems: indeed, 'it is highly debatable whether any social system can be closed'.[66] It is arguable that law's content can only come from beyond law. For Sidney Post Simpson and Ruth Field,

> law is not and cannot be an autonomous subject. No system of thought, except possibly pure mathematics, can be isolated, kept within previously determined categories, and re-main healthy or effective. This is peculiarly true of the law, which reflects and embodies in its substance the institutions of the community. Law without social content or significance … is law without flesh, blood or bowels.[67]

The content and substance of law is derived from 'the facts of social life'; and critiques of law and its effectiveness should be grounded in assessing how well the law achieves social ends, which are not derived from law itself.[68]

[65] McCrudden, 'Equality Legislation and Reflexive Regulation' (n 34) 262.

[66] AL James, 'An Open or Shut Case? Law as an Autopoietic System' (1992) 19 *Journal of Law and Society* 271, 275. See also SP Simpson and R Field, 'Law and the Social Sciences' (1946) 32 *Virginia Law Review* 855, 862.

[67] Simpson and Field, 'Law and Social Sciences' (n 66) 862.

[68] ibid.

Internally-driven legal critiques, grounded in legal theory, 'can be directed to nothing more significant than the logical symmetry of the legal system'.[69] Thus, for Adrian L. James, 'law, by its very nature, is a *social* institution and the environment in which it "exists" is a *social* environment'.[70] Key normative legal concepts, such as 'justice', are moral and social constructs.[71] Law is also inextricably linked with other social institutions, like Parliament, 'so that the nature, shape, and content of law, as well as its external representations such as the machinery of the courts, are determined of necessity by its parameters, both social and institutional'.[72] James therefore argues that law is an inherently *open* system, which is influenced and changed by its environment and, in turn, creates pressure for social change.[73]

Relatedly, it is arguable that by focusing on the internal self-reproduction of legal systems, systems theory pays too little attention to the impact and social influence of legal norms.[74] This inwardly focused orientation neglects the study of the empirical impact of law. In contrast, Hubert Rottleuthner makes 'a plea for a nonreductionist, "multiple," and empirically oriented sociology of law'.[75] In this approach, 'one could try to answer the question of how legislative, administrative, or court decisions come into existence, of how statutes and their interpretations are changed, and what impact they have'.[76]

To better recognise the dynamism or porosity of boundaries between systems, Thomas E. Webb uses complexity theory as an alternative systems theory to critique autopoiesis. This theory has a different understanding of boundaries, seeing them as contingent, emergent, and interfacing.[77] For Webb, systems can only be understood in the context of interaction, not alone or in isolation.[78] Boundaries are context dependent, rather than 'hard' or fixed,[79] and can be the subject of competing accounts and disagreement.[80] Boundaries are therefore better seen as 'flexible facilitator[s]' that help distinguish systems, rather than confining or restricting.[81] Webb's critique of autopoiesis offers an alternative understanding of systems theory that may better represent law and the legal system, and its relationship with other social systems.

[69] ibid.
[70] James, 'An Open or Shut Case?' (n 66) 275.
[71] ibid 275.
[72] ibid.
[73] ibid.
[74] H Rottleuthner, 'A Purified Sociology of Law: Niklas Luhmann on the Autonomy of the Legal System' (1989) 23 *Law & Society Review* 779, 790–91; *cf* M King, 'The "Truth" about Autopoiesis' (1993) 20 *Journal of Law and Society* 218, 230.
[75] Rottleuthner, 'A Purified Sociology of Law' (n 74) 794.
[76] ibid 790.
[77] TE Webb, 'Exploring System Boundaries' (2013) 24 *Law and Critique* 131, 133.
[78] ibid.
[79] ibid 135.
[80] ibid 139.
[81] ibid 145.

B. Humans, Bodies and Agency

Second, systems theory replaces a theoretical focus on autonomous individuals with a focus on communicative processes. Systems theory effectively claims that the legal system can 'operate without agents',[82] because human beings are considered to be 'bearers' of the system, rather than participants in the system.[83] Autopoiesis is therefore a non-humanist theory, and only observes systemic communications, not human actions.[84] While humans are seen as part of the *process* of communication, they are not its cause or origin.[85]

This theoretical focus on communicative processes, not individuals, carries a number of risks. First, it may underestimate the capacity of individuals to determine, affect and critique social systems.[86] In some situations, unintended consequences are better attributed to individual agency rather than systems: individuals act within and are part of society,[87] and can be powerful agents of change. Recognising the agency of individuals, and their ability to construct and respond to legal change, helps to explain the potential for legal reform to have unintended consequences.[88]

To some extent, of course, reflexive law does speak to agency: in its focus on 'structuring mechanisms for self-regulation', rather than commanding specific results,[89] and internal communicative processes, reflexive law can empower people (individually or collectively) to be active participants in the regulatory environment. Thus, reflexive law does not ignore agency, as it acknowledges that some agency resides in parties to collective employment and labour relations, and accounts for particularity and a need for local solutions (as opposed to state or centralised solutions).

Going further, though, David E. Van Zandt argues that there is a need to refocus on actors, and sees law as a complex collection of individual decisions about whether to invoke or avoid the power of the state.[90] For Van Zandt, it is *people* employing 'the legal system and its legal rules to accomplish tasks in the real world'.[91] It is the actors, as users of the legal system, who breathe life into the law, and their decisions that shape law.[92] In this view, autopoiesis just complicates our

[82] Capps and Olsen, 'Legal Autonomy and Reflexive Rationality' (n 27) 552.
[83] ibid 554–55.
[84] A Philippopoulos-Mihalopoulos and TE Webb, 'Vulnerable Bodies, Vulnerable Systems' (2015) 11 *International Journal of Law in Context* 444, 445.
[85] ibid 446.
[86] See, eg, James (n 67) 276.
[87] Capps and Olsen, 'Legal Autonomy and Reflexive Rationality' (n 27) 552–58.
[88] E Mertz, 'Conclusion: A New Social Constructionism for Sociolegal Studies' (1994) 28 *Law & Society Review* 1243, 1246–47.
[89] Teubner, 'Substantive and Reflexive Elements in Modern Law' (n 3) 251.
[90] DE Van Zandt, 'The Breath of Life in the Law' (1991–92) 13 *Cardozo Law Review* 1745, 1754.
[91] ibid 1756–57.
[92] ibid 1757. Van Zandt in particular refers to judges, lawyers, legislators, as well as (potential) litigants and other users of the legal system.

conception of law, and has little to offer.[93] However, in the context of labour law, a focus on individuals alone is insufficient, and ignores the collective and relational aspects of work. Thus, in this context, collective, community or relational responses may be more appropriate than what Van Zandt proposes. Equally, though, traditional systems theory may underestimate the importance of community.[94]

Secondly, autopoiesis tends to ignore the material or corporeal,[95] making it a 'bodyless' theory. Since the underlying notion of being 'human' is normatively male,[96] systems theory remains gendered, even if it is framed in neutral language. Contrary to this 'bodyless' approach, then, critical and feminist scholars have called for the incorporation of the body into law, as embodiment is seen as having a direct effect on people's lived experiences.[97] In this view, meaning (in life and law) comes from corporeality, and recognition of the body allows the legal system to appreciate some of its limits.[98] In seeking to enrich systems theory, then, Andreas Philippopoulos-Mihalopoulos and Webb see vulnerability (a key quality of a living body) as a constant of autopoiesis,[99] which is ever-present and cannot be ignored.[100] For these authors, a recognition of vulnerability opens up new communicative possibilities,[101] and allows for the theoretical development of autopoiesis.[102] Thus, while ignoring the human and vulnerable may undermine and stultify the development of systems theory, it appears possible to extend systems theory to encompass vulnerability.[103]

Thirdly, systems theory's theoretical focus on communication, rather than autonomous individuals, might minimise consideration of power disparities and create inequality of communicative opportunities.[104] Systems theory has been criticised for its limited focus on the distribution of power, particularly in the context of labour law, where power is especially unevenly distributed. Systems theory does not consider how power is distributed or redistributed, and has no normative content in relation to the balancing of power between employers and workers.[105] Hugh Collins therefore argues that reflexive law 'runs counter to the traditional spice of labour law': traditionally, labour lawyers have seen 'the world

[93] ibid 1758.

[94] J Nedelsky, 'Reconceiving Autonomy: Sources, Thoughts and Possibilities' (1989) 1 *Yale Journal of Law and Feminism* 7.

[95] Philippopoulos-Mihalopoulos and Webb, 'Vulnerable Bodies' (n 84) 452.

[96] ibid 453.

[97] ibid.

[98] ibid 454.

[99] ibid 456.

[100] ibid 457.

[101] ibid 456.

[102] ibid 458.

[103] See also Philippopoulos-Mihalopoulos's extended 'reading' of Luhmann, which positions it in post-modern thought: A Philippopoulos-Mihalopoulos, *Niklas Luhmann: Law, Justice, Society* (London, Routledge-Cavendish, 2010).

[104] Philippopoulos-Mihalopoulos and Webb, 'Vulnerable Bodies' (n 84) 451.

[105] Though Luhmann does offer a theory of power as a 'communication medium': N Luhmann, *Trust and Power* (Cambridge, Polity, 2017).

in terms of interest groups, capital and labour, and conspiracies [of employers], competing in the workplace and in the legislature for the advancement of self-interest' and their comparative position.[106] Reflexive law moves the object of analysis from interest groups to 'communication systems', meaning that it 'translates political and economic battles into problems of communication between social systems'.[107] Thus, systems theory and reflexive law tend to make labour law appear less combative than it would be seen in a traditional view, and mask battles over power and the allocation of resources.

C. Normativity

Third, systems theory (and, therefore, reflexive law) is concerned with legal *process*, not legal *substance*.[108] Systems theory lacks its own normative element – indeed, it was never intended to provide a normative theory,[109] let alone a normative theory of legal change.[110] Autopoiesis is not directed towards creating a better society or values – it is about taking a particular perspective to describe communication,[111] and to describe society as it is.[112]

While the absence of normative content is not seen as a limitation by systems theory scholars, it raises more concern among labour law scholars generally. For Diamond Ashiagbor, for example, a lack of normative content in reflexive law would leave labour law 'untethered from the sort of distributive or redistributive goals that characterise state regulation of employment relations'.[113] As Ashiagbor contends, law must have normative content: if reflexive law is to steer the ordering of other systems, what goals will it pursue?[114] It is this normative content which must be derived from somewhere (else).

That said, Ashiagbor argues that reflexive law may have some normative content, and tends towards an 'alliance' with neoliberalism, given its focus on the market and state as separate systems, the de-centring of the state, and its failure to consider power relations.[115] Thus, by failing to adopt a normative position,

[106] H Collins, 'Reflexive Labour Law: Studies in Industrial Relations and Employment Regulation Ralf Rogowski Ton Wilthagen' (1998) 61 *The Modern Law Review* 916, 920.

[107] ibid.

[108] Rogowski and Wilthagen, 'Reflexive Labour Law' (n 24) 7; Teubner, 'Substantive and Reflexive Elements in Modern Law' (n 3) 255.

[109] Van Zandt, 'The Breath of Life in the Law' (n 90) 1760.

[110] That said, some scholars have argued that reflexive law, at least, is a normative theory. For Barnard et al, reflexive law offers normative guidance on the appropriate form of governance, focusing on multi-level and decentralised deliberation: Barnard et al, 'Reflexive Law, Corporate Social Responsibility and the Evolution of Labour Standards' (n 2) 2.

[111] Philippopoulos-Mihalopoulos and Webb, 'Vulnerable Bodies' (n 84) 448.

[112] ibid 449.

[113] Ashiagbor, 'Evaluating the Reflexive Turn in Labour Law' (n 62) 125.

[114] ibid 134.

[115] ibid 132. See also H Arthurs, 'Corporate Self-Regulation: Political Economy, State Regulation and Reflexive Labour Law' in B Bercusson and C Estlund (eds), *Regulating Labour in the Wake of Globalisation: New Challenges, New Institutions* (Oxford, Hart Publishing, 2008) 28–29.

but suggesting a form of proceduralism that minimises direct state intervention, reflexive law and systems theory may (indirectly) adopt a normative position.[116] Further, it is unclear how reflexive law and systems theory can be reconciled with minimum standards of employment or general prohibitions of discrimination, which are major regulatory advances of the post-war era: both would appear to be unreflexive forms of command and control regulation.[117] There may, then, also be a need for fundamental rights, in addition to reflexive regulation.[118]

It may therefore be timely to consider a 'normative turn' in systems theory, to further promote and develop a critical systems theory as it applies to law.[119] The obvious means of pursuing this might be to overlay other theories, which have normative content, onto systems theory and reflexive law. Indeed, some authors have added a normative element to systems theory to increase its usability (such as justice[120] or critical race theory[121]).

VI. Conclusion: The Ongoing Relevance of Systems Theory and Reflexive Law

In sum, then, there is a growing school of scholarship that seeks to enrich and extend systems theory, including through critical normative scholarship,[122] an expanded focus on complexity and the dynamism of systems,[123] and renewed recognition of vulnerability.[124] These ideas have potential to develop and enhance systems theory and reflexive law as they apply to labour law. Given labour law is fundamentally about power and its (re)distribution, this shift and expansion in reflexive thinking could address the potential mismatch in focus between reflexive law and labour law.

Thus, it is clear that labour law has something to learn from its 'reflexive turn'. As Michael King notes, a systems approach may 'be able to offer some sobering thoughts on the capacity of law to regulate the behaviour of other systems' and, for all its limitations, still represents 'a considerable advance on the simple input-output models of previous critical and socio-legal theories'.[125] Further,

[116] Though, as Deakin and Rogowski note, this link between means and aims 'is not inevitable': Deakin and Rogowksi, 'Reflexive Labour Law' (n 1) 232–33.

[117] See, more generally, the discussion of values and rights in Philippopoulos-Mihalopoulos and Webb, 'Vulnerable Bodies' (n 84) 448–49.

[118] See, eg, Barnard and Deakin, 'In Search of Coherence' (n 23) 343–44.

[119] A Fischer-Lescano, 'Critical Systems Theory' (2012) 38 *Philosophy & Social Criticism* 3.

[120] AJ Colangelo, 'A Systems Theory of Fragmentation and Harmonization' (2016) 49 *New York University Journal of International Law and Politics* 1.

[121] S Sargent, 'Transracial Adoption in England: A Critical Race and Systems Theory Analysis' (2015) 11 *International Journal of Law in Context* 412.

[122] Fischer-Lescano, 'Critical Systems Theory' (n 119).

[123] Webb, 'Exploring System Boundaries' (n 77).

[124] Philippopoulos-Mihalopoulos and Webb, 'Vulnerable Bodies' (n 84).

[125] King, 'The "Truth" about Autopoiesis' (n 74).

as Collins has noted, a positive aspect of systems theory is that it makes scholars and others more attuned to the difficulties and complexities of enacting effective regulation.[126] For Ashiagbor, the benefit of reflexive law is that it 'nudges legal scholars away from the over-preoccupation with "old governance" measures', including statutes, directives and rule enforcement.[127]

However, as Ashiagbor points out, the relevance of reflexive law and systems theory to labour law going forward must be assessed against three related questions.[128] First, is reflexive law *descriptively* appropriate for understanding existing regulatory interventions? The answer, at least in the UK studies described above, appears to be no (for now). Secondly, is reflexive law *normatively* the right approach for labour law? (And, relatedly, does reflexive law condone and reinforce a neoliberal turn?) Thirdly, is reflexive law *empirically* an effective approach to regulation? It is arguable that the studies described above show that reflexive law has never been perfectly implemented in UK equality law; this makes it difficult to answer this third question with any certainty. Ashiagbor's third question, then, might become: is it possible to ever perfectly implement reflexive law in the UK context, such that it can be empirically evaluated?

This chapter concludes, then, with more questions than answers. Systems theory and reflexive law have substantial potential to illuminate the difficulty of labour regulation, and the risks of unintended consequences as a result of legal intervention. The challenge going forward, though, is to develop a critical systems theory tailored to labour law, which emphasises the dynamism of systems; engages with the centrality of people, vulnerability and power; and lends law normative content. This would be a more inclusive systems theory, particularly in positing people, in all their diversity and vulnerability, as a central focus. We are reaching a critical juncture in systems theorising, where there is growing potential and need for theory to be developed and expanded to be more inclusive and better reflect the realities and demands of labour law.

Even with this theoretical development, however, it still appears difficult to translate systems theory and reflexive law into practical regulatory interventions. The apparent failure of 'reflexive law' in the context of UK equality law flags the practical and regulatory challenges of implementing theory in practice, and the need for systemic change to make reflexive interventions effective. While this may reflect the non-engagement or mis-understandings of policy makers with regulatory theory, it could equally reveal the national limitations of the UK context, which is ill-prepared for a reflexive turn. Reflexive law, if implemented improperly, runs a substantial risk of 'non-regulation' or 're-regulation':[129] the very risks it is trying to overcome. Failed reflexive law, then, is just as bad – if not worse – at achieving impact than command and control regulation.

[126] Collins, 'Reflexive Labour Law' (n 106).
[127] Ashiagbor, 'Evaluating the Reflexive Turn in Labour Law' (n 62) 143.
[128] ibid.
[129] McCrudden, 'Equality Legislation and Reflexive Regulation' (n 34) 263.

Despite the theoretical potential of reflexive law and systems theory, it should therefore be used with caution in some national contexts, particularly where there are few mechanisms in place for engagement to moderate the power of organisations and public bodies. The disjunction between reflexive theory and reflexive practice reflects a gulf between academic scholarship and policy: perhaps another example of systems that cannot directly communicate. This explanation would be cold comfort to those who experience discrimination or occupy a vulnerable position in the labour market. More needs to be done to work to translate theoretical regulatory benefits into practical outcomes.

13

Argumentative Strategies in the Defence of Labour Law: The Promises of Republican Theory

ANJA ELEVELD*

I. Introduction

Labour law is in crisis. According to Guy Davidov and Brian Langille, labour law 'is attacked for impeding efficiency, flexibility and development; vilified for reducing employment and for favouring already well-placed employees over less fortunate ones; and discredited for failing to cover the most vulnerable workers and workers in the "informal sector"'.[1] For them, a way of 'solving' this crisis is to look for a solid foundation for labour law in political philosophy. While Amartya Sen's capability approach has been a popular one among labour lawyers,[2] more recently, they have also considered the (neo-Roman) republican theory of non-domination as a foundation of labour law.[3] 'Arbitrary power' is a key concept in

* Assistant Professor, Faculty of Law, Vrije Universiteit Amsterdam.

[1] G Davidov and B Langille, 'Understanding Labour Law: A Timeless Idea, a Timed-Out Idea, or an Idea Whose Time has Now Come?' in G Davidov and B Langille (eds), *The Idea of Labour Law* (Oxford, Oxford University Press, 2011) 1.53.

[2] eg, N Busby, *A Right to Care? Unpaid Work in European Employment Law* (Oxford, Oxford University Press, 2011); S Deakin, 'The Contribution of Labour Law to Economic and Human Development' in G Davidov and B Langille (eds), *The Idea of Labour Law* (Oxford, Oxford University Press, 2011) 156; R Del Punta, 'Labour Law and the Capability Approach' (2016) 32 *International Journal of Comparative Labour Law and Industrial Relations* 383; J Fudge, 'Labour as a "Fictive Commodity": Radically Reconceptualizing Labour Law' in G Davidov and B Langille (eds), *The Idea of Labour Law* (Oxford, Oxford University Press, 2011) 120; A Goldin, 'Global Conceptualizations and Local Constructions of the Idea of Labour Law' in G Davidov and B Langille (eds), *The Idea of Labour Law* (Oxford, Oxford University Press, 2011) 69; B Langille, 'Labour Law's Theory of Justice' in G Davidov and B Langille (eds), *The Idea of Labour Law* (Oxford, Oxford University Press, 2011) 101; A Supiot, *Beyond Employment: Changes in Work and the Future of Labour Law in Europe* (Oxford, Oxford University Press, 2001).

[3] A Bogg, 'Republican Non-Domination and Labour Law: New Normativity or Trojan Horse' (2017) 33 *International Journal of Comparative Labour Law and Industrial Relations* 391; K Breen, 'Non-Domination, Workplace Republicanism, and the Justification of Worker Voice and Control' (2017) 33

this republican theory of non-domination, as developed by Philip Pettit and Frank Lovett. According to Pettit and Lovett, relationships between citizens (ie, social justice), and between citizens and the state (ie, political legitimacy), should be guided as much as possible by the ideal of freedom as non-domination.[4] Pettit defines 'freedom as non-domination' as the absence of arbitrary power which amounts to a lack of control experienced by individuals subject to the exercise of power.

As explained further in Section III, this approach – at first sight – seems to fit well with the widely supported idea that labour law serves to minimise the vulnerabilities of employees who are subordinated to and dependent on an employer.[5]

However, notwithstanding the popularity of these discussions, I do not believe that labour law is in need of a *foundation* in political philosophy. While contemporary political philosophical concepts of social justice and political legitimation are usually based on the viewpoints of 'rational actors', according to the post-foundationalist view (which I endorse), 'any social objectivity is ultimately political'.[6] This means that these concepts are necessarily contingent; they confirm existing constellations of power and knowledge in which the force of rational argumentation dominates. Regarding the prominence of 'power relations', from a post-foundational stance, the republican concept of 'arbitrary power' would only be acceptable as describing one particular form of power. To illustrate using Michel Foucault, whose work is more in line with post-foundationalism, power is not something that you possess in the sense that the employer *has* the power to influence the employee. Instead, Foucault refers to power as a dynamic totality of force relations between individuals, groups, institutions, and the state that both enables and constrains a subject's range of options. Unlike Pettit and Lovett's concept of power, Foucault's work thus points to forms of agent-less power.[7] Moreover, his work suggests that the exercising of power cannot originate in a specific subject – say, the employer – as the latter's subjectivity is itself constituted

International Journal of Comparative Labour Law and Industrial Relations 419; D Cabrelli and R Zahn, 'Theories of Domination and Labour Law: An Alternative Conception for Intervention?' (2017) 33 *International Journal of Comparative Labour Law and Industrial Relations* 339; G Davidov, 'Subordination vs Domination: Exploring the Differences' (2017) 33 *International Journal of Comparative Labour Law and Industrial Relations* 365; V Mantouvalou, 'Life After Work: Privacy and Dismissal' (2008) LSE Law, Society and Economy Working Papers 5/2008 www.lse.ac.uk/law/working-paper-series/2007-08/WPS2008-05-Mantouvalou.pdf accessed 1 July 2018.

[4] F Lovett, *A General Theory of Domination and Justice* (New York, Oxford University Press, 2010); P Pettit, *Republicanism: A Theory of Freedom and Government* (Oxford, Oxford University Press, 1997); P Pettit, *On the People's Terms: A Republican Theory and Model of Democracy* (Cambridge, Cambridge University Press, 2012).

[5] H Arthurs, 'Labour Law After Labour' in G Davidov and B Langille (eds), *The Idea of Labour Law* (Oxford, Oxford University Press, 2011) 13; G Davidov, 'Re-matching Labour Laws with their Purpose' in G Davidov and B Langille (eds), *The Idea of Labour Law* (Oxford, Oxford University Press, 2011) 179.

[6] C Mouffe, *The Democratic Paradox* (London, Verso, 2000) 21.

[7] For a comparison of the concept of power and domination in republican theory and Foucault's work, see also C McBride, 'Freedom as Non-domination: Radicalisation or Retreat? (2015) 18 *Critical Review of International Social and Political Philosophy* 349.

by power relations. For Foucault, then, power is always present, both ontologically and as an enabling and constraining force.

From the viewpoint of post-foundationalism, I fully agree with Bob Hepple, according to whom 'labour law is not an exercise of applied ethics, [but] the outcome of struggles between different social actors and ideologies, of power relationships'.[8] In my opinion, however, labour lawyers should not refrain from political philosophical analyses altogether. Instead, as a coherent theory and as a provider of a convincing language, political philosophy might be very useful in those political struggles and social policy debates.[9] As Chantal Mouffe argues, with regard to John Rawls' (political philosophical) theory of justice, this theory should be understood as *one* interpretation that belongs to a struggle between different justice discourses; the most that a justice theory can do is provide us with the language to articulate different interpretations of the ideals of liberty and equality.[10] Likewise, a coherent theory, such as the republican theory of freedom of non-domination, including its specific conception of domination and power, can be regarded as an interpretation of the core ideas of justice and equality, to be used in the political struggle between different justice discourses.

In general, the influence of labour lawyers on these and other policy reforms has been marginal. Amongst other things, this has been due (in my view) to the lack of an appropriate and convincing language based on a coherent normative theory offering a counterweight to economic discourses based on neoliberal thought and its emphasis on deregulation. In this respect, I agree with Langille that the guiding idea of 'rebalancing the inequality of bargaining power' is too thin for a normative theory; in particular, because it does not tell us *why* the inequality of bargaining power should be balanced.[11] The same is true for concepts such as 'subordination' or 'vulnerability', which are popular among labour lawyers. Without a coherent theory, it is not clear why we should compensate for subordination or why we should initiate legislation to protect vulnerable workers. Moreover, stressing the 'subordinate' and 'vulnerable' role of workers (decoupled from any theory) in debates on labour law reforms is also at risk of essentialising workers in these roles.[12]

The aim of this chapter is to examine how the republication theory of non-domination may serve as the source of a coherent theory, and of a persuasive

[8] B Hepple, 'Factors Influencing the Making and Transformation of Labour Law in Europe' in G Davidov and B Langille (eds), *The Idea of Labour Law* (Oxford, Oxford University Press, 2011) 30.

[9] *cf* Rorty's statement that '[p]hilosophical problems are anything other than transient tensions in the dynamics of evolving contingent vocabularies': R Rorty, *Consequences of Pragmatism: Essays, 1972–1980* (Minneapolis, University of Minnesota Press, 1982) 217.

[10] C Mouffe, 'Rawls: Political Philosophy Without Politics' (1987) 13 *Philosophy and Social Criticism* 105, 120–21.

[11] Langille, 'Labour Law's Theory' (n 2) 111.

[12] On the risk of essentialising vulnerability, see L Peroni and A Timmer, 'Vulnerable Groups: The Promise of an Emerging Concept in European Human Rights Convention Law' (2013) 11 *International Journal of Constitutional Law* 1056, 1071.

language, to justify the use of labour law regulations in political struggle and policy debates. However, before considering republican theory, I will first argue why Sen's capability approach should be rejected as a source for the defence of labour law (Section II). Following this discussion, I turn to the advantages of republican theory (Section III) and then, as a point of contrast, examine the arguments against using the theory of non-domination as a justificatory theory for labour law (Section IV). The final section contains the main conclusions (Section V).

II. Sen's Capability Approach as a Foundation of Labour Law: Langille's Argument

In this section, I will explain why Sen's capability approach is not adequate to function as a 'foundation' of labour law. For this purpose, I will focus on Langille's arguments in its favour.[13] First, however, I will set out some of the key tenets of Sen's capability approach. Initially, Sen formulated the capability approach as a response to Rawls's theory of justice. According to Sen, Rawls's theory is too focused on a fair distribution of goods, without taking into account the capability of individuals to use these goods in an advantageous way. For example, a handicapped person will need more, and other, goods in order to enjoy the right to freedom of movement compared to a person who is not handicapped. Further, Sen's capability approach dictates that the subjective well-being of all persons in a society should be enhanced. This can be achieved when persons have a capability set that gives them 'real' or effective freedom to choose between various forms of life. Increasing subjective well-being thus implies that society ought to maximise the set of capabilities that will enhance individual freedom to lead a valuable life.

Langille provides two reasons as to why the capability approach should be preferred over the traditional justification of labour law (ie, that it compensates for the unequal bargaining position of employees). In the first place, a negative morality (ie, 'to compensate') is replaced by a positive morality (ie, 'maximizing freedom'). In the second place, Sen's capability approach dissolves the difficult relationship between, on the one hand, the protection of the employee and, on the other hand, the interests of the market; an approach that characterises traditional thinking in the field of labour law. For example, Sen's capability approach, according to Langille, results in labour law being viewed as an instrument that regulates and encourages the use of human capital which will, ultimately, lead to the increase of human freedom via economic growth and individual welfare.

[13] Langille 'Labour Law's Theory' (n 2).

There are three objections to this argument. First, the promotion of human capital in and through labour law does not necessarily enhance the capability set of all people. Take, for example, the reconciliation of work and family life. From a human capital perspective, labour law should facilitate the combination of work and care activities. However, while a human capital perspective might reject (very) long-term maternal or parental leave (since this would essentially result in a waste of human capital), the right to very long-term maternal or parental leave enhances the capability set, as it accommodates people who value time spent on care activities over, for example, the possession of a second car. In my opinion, Langille confuses human capital and human capabilities, which for Sen are two entirely different things.[14]

Secondly, the question can be raised as to whether a labour law discourse which follows Langille's interpretation of Sen's capability approach is able to distinguish itself from the economist discourse based on neoliberal thought. According to Langille's interpretation, then, the ultimate goal of labour law is to encourage the development of human capital, which is the same goal that underscores the economist discourse based on neoliberal thought.

The third objection is not so much related to Langille's specific deployment of Sen's capability approach, but to the capability approach itself. Where the capability approach seeks to enhance the effective freedom of individuals to lead valuable lives, it raises a question as to whether this approach permits the increase of freedom for one person (eg, the employer) at the expense of another (eg, the employee), or vice versa. What this shows is that by focusing explicitly on *individual* capabilities, Sen's capability approach barely takes into account the fact that people live and work in *social* relationships.[15] This raises the question as to how a theory that focuses on *individual persons* can be used to justify labour law, which regulates a specific *relationship between at least two persons* (ie, employment relations). In the literature, it has therefore been argued that Sen's capability approach fails to sufficiently address issues of power and domination.[16] Sen acknowledges this, but he believes that this is not an insurmountable problem, since the capability approach is only interested in the actual ability or power to act, irrespective of whether this person is dependent upon the goodwill of other persons to do the things s/he wants to do. Nevertheless, Sen admits that a theory of domination – such as the republican theory of freedom as non-domination – would add to his capability approach, without undermining it.[17]

[14] H Dean, 'Critiquing Capabilities: The Distractions of a Beguiling Concept' (2009) 29 *Critical Social Policy* 261, 261–62; A Sen, *Development as Freedom* (Oxford, Oxford University Press, 1999).

[15] See also L Barclay, 'The Importance of Equal Respect: What the Capabilities Approach Can and Should Learn from Human Rights Law' (2016) 64 *Political Studies* 385.

[16] P Pettit, 'Symposium on Amartya Sen's Philosophy: 1 Capability and Freedom: A Defence of Sen' (2001) 17 *Economics and Philosophy* 1.

[17] A Sen, *The Idea of Justice* (Cambridge, Mass., Harvard University Press, 2009) 304–9.

III. The Republican Theory of Non-domination and Labour Law

In this section, I will examine how republican theory can serve as a source for the articulation of arguments in defence of labour law in social policy discourses. Republican political philosophy comprises different strands, with the work of Pettit[18] and Lovett[19] having become popular in recent years, including among labour lawyers. In addition, labour lawyers have been exploring the scholarly work of workplace republicans.[20] The last subsection contains my main conclusions.

A. Pettit: Freedom as the Absence of Arbitrary or Uncontrolled Interference

'Freedom as non-domination' is the guiding idea in Pettit's version of republican theory. The republican conception of freedom should be distinguished from the one proposed by liberal thinkers, such as Isaiah Berlin,[21] who accepts the possibility of arbitrary or – in his later work – uncontrolled interference with freedom. In this liberal view, then, the only condition for freedom as non-interference is that a powerful person or group of persons does not interfere *in practice*. By contrast, the republican conception of freedom acknowledges that, even though a person – say, a benevolent dictator or slaveholder – abstains from interfering in the lives of their citizens or slaves, s/he can interfere whenever s/he wants to do so. The difference between a liberal and a republican conception of freedom can also be illustrated by Kurt Pärli's recent study on the phenomenon of 'presenteeism' in modern workplaces.[22] His study provides evidence that sick employees continue working – despite the presence of sick leave regulations – because they fear repercussions in terms of, for example, their career prospects should they call in sick. A liberal might argue that such employees exercise freedom of choice, because their employer does not interfere in their decision to call in sick or go to work; whereas for a republican, such as Pettit, this is not

[18] Pettit, *Republicanism* (n 4); Pettit, *On the People's Terms* (n 4).

[19] Lovett, *General Theory* (n 4).

[20] R Dagger, 'Neo-Republicanism and the Civic Economy' (2006) 5 *Politics, Philosophy & Economics* 151; I Gonzáles-Ricoy, 'The Republican Case for Workplace Democracy' (2014) 40 *Social Theory and Practice* 232; N Hsieh, 'Rawlsian Justice and Workplace Republicanism' (2005) 31 *Social Theory and Practice* 115; N Hsieh, 'Workplace Democracy, Workplace Republicanism, and Economic Democracy: Workplace Democracy – Why Not?' (2008) 8 *Revue de Philosophie Économique* 57.

[21] I Berlin, *Four Essays on Liberty* (London, Oxford University Press, 1969). However, also note the similarities between republican theory and 'the liberalism of fear': eg, J Shklar, 'The Liberalism of Fear' in S Hoffmann (ed), *Political Thought and Political Thinkers* (Chicago, University of Chicago Press, 1998) 3.

[22] K Pärli, 'Presenteeism, Its Effects and Costs: A Discussion in a Labour Law Perspective' (2018) 34 *International Journal of Comparative Labour Law and Industrial Relations* 53.

the case and, instead, it is suggested that these employees have acted preemptively on an expectation of how their employer might behave. The employees thus adjust their behaviour to accord with the *arbitrary* or *uncontrollable* power of the employer.[23]

In short, for Pettit, a person who is subjected to the exercise of arbitrary power will not be able to: (1) enjoy free choice, or (2) make proper plans for the future. In addition, this person will (3) have a reduced sense of their personal dignity.[24] This is why Pettit defines 'freedom as non-domination' as the absence of arbitrary or uncontrolled interference.

Based on this idea of freedom as non-domination, Pettit distinguishes between, on the one hand, 'social justice' which imposes demands on horizontal relations between citizens and, on the other hand, 'legitimacy' which imposes demands on vertical relations between the citizenry and the state. According to Pettit, 'social justice' means that

> citizens should be guaranteed resources and protections in the same range of choices – the basic liberties – on the basis of public laws and norms and up to the limit dictated by the eyeball test; [meaning that] absent timidity, each should be able by local standards to look others in the eye without reason for fear or deference.[25]

Hence, Pettit's theory of social justice involves a rather loosely formulated equal distribution of basic liberties, such as the freedom to associate and the freedom to change occupation and employment, for example. In addition to these fundamental labour rights, Pettit's theory of social justice justifies rules that coordinate employment relations. As Pettit argues, the distribution of basic liberties is conditioned upon co-exercisable and co-satisfying constraints,[26] which rule out choices that individuals cannot perform individually or at the same time, and choices which are harmful or counterproductive. These choices have to be reconstituted by social (and legal) rules. For example, whereas the choice to start a company that exceeds a one-person company can neither be performed individually, nor at the same time, it could be argued that labour law (eg, the regulation of the employment contract) gives this choice an entrenched status.

A third justification for labour law follows from the *resourcing* of basic liberties. Pettit proposes three kinds of policy programmes to achieve a satisfying resourcing of basic liberties: (1) infrastructure programmes such as education, a court system, and ecological policies; (2) an insurance programme that provides people with social security, judicial security, or a basic income; (3) insulation programmes, which offer special protections in relationships characterised by asymmetries of power, such as the relationship between the employee and employer. While the

[23] While Pettit has, in recent years, changed the term 'arbitrary power' to 'uncontrolled power', I will use them interchangeably in this chapter. See further Pettit, *On the People's Terms* (n 4) 58.

[24] ibid 88–90.

[25] ibid 297–98.

[26] ibid 103.

latter insulation programmes are of particular importance for labour law, Pettit – unfortunately – only provides a few examples, such as 'screening in various options for the weaker' party (eg, legalising employee unionisation), 'screening out various options for the stronger' party (eg, dismissal law), and creating new opportunities for the weaker party (eg, unemployment benefits).[27] Thus, in relation to labour relationships, insulation programmes may provide the weaker party with legal instruments to strengthen its position in the relationship with the stronger party, or provide legal instruments to weaken the position of the stronger party in relationship to the weaker party, or provide general protection to the weaker party. Nonetheless, Pettit's republican approach to social justice shows that the republican theory of non-domination does not merely justify so-called negative rights (which place a duty on the other party not to interfere with the rights bearer), but also positive rights (which place a duty on the other party – the state – to provide for goods or special protections).

In vertical relations between the citizenry and the state, Pettit's version of the republican theory of non-domination requires that state power be exercised legitimately. As further explained in Section C, workplace republicans use Pettit's idea of the legitimacy of the state to justify a workers' democracy. This is why I also briefly examine Pettit's analysis of state legitimacy. According to Pettit, the social order is 'illegitimate insofar as it … is sustained independently of what citizens think'.[28] Republican theory, therefore, requires citizens to be able to control the state in an individual and effective way. Pettit's argument on state legitimacy is first and foremost supportive of traditional democratic constitutions. Yet, in his opinion, the 'threat of domination' may still arise in the discretion enjoyed by the (democratic) state. Acknowledging that – also within a democratic constitution – it is impossible to control all discretionary spaces, Pettit holds that discretionary oversight requires citizens to remain vigilant, socially connected, and politically active (ie, 'resistance prone') in such a way that the political institutions serve the common good rather than the interests of particular groups.[29] As such, Pettit justifies both 'input democracy' and 'output democracy'.

B. Lovett's Contribution: External Rules and Exit Costs

Lovett's theory of non-domination has added, in particular, to Pettit's account of social justice in horizontal relations. Lovett has argued that in: (1) social relations characterised by a (2) dependence of one party on the other, which can be calculated by *high exit costs*, (3) a high imbalance in the distribution of power will – unless this relationship is constituted by effective external rules – result in

[27] ibid 115.
[28] ibid 141.
[29] ibid 174, 225–28.

the exercise of arbitrary power over the dependent party. According to Lovett's normative theory, these relations of domination should be minimised.

While the term 'exit costs' is, in my opinion, a valuable addition to the republican theory of non-domination, since it helps to clarify why (additional) protective legislation is needed, the relationship between exit costs, external rules, and the exercise of arbitrary power is more complex than Lovett seems to assume. This can be illustrated by the case of migrant domestic workers in the United Kingdom (UK). Under previous UK law, migrant workers who desired to work in a private household had to apply for a work permit which was tied to the particular household where s/he had secured work.[30] Hence, the exit costs were quite high for a migrant domestic worker: ending the work relationship implied that his/her working permit would be withdrawn and that s/he would have to leave the UK. As such, high exit costs clearly contributed to bad working conditions for migrant domestic workers and many cases involving the abuse of migrant domestic workers were reported.[31] This example illustrates – in conformity with Lovett's theory – a narrow relationship between exit costs and arbitrary power. Yet, it also shows – according to Lovett – that the presence of external rules (eg, UK labour law) does not necessarily prevent the exercise of arbitrary power, because people may simply be afraid to invoke such rules.

In my opinion, the problem with Lovett's contribution is, above all, his mechanical treatment of exit costs and external rules. People may refrain from invoking rules, because they are – for different reasons – afraid to do so. In addition, rules may be contradictory or unclear.[32] Instead, I argue that low exit costs, combined with the presence of external effective rules, are factors that *contribute* to a decrease in the risk of (rather than securing the absence of) the exercise of arbitrary power, including asymmetrical power relations. This is a better fit with Pettit's republican theory.[33]

C. Workplace Republicans and Workers' Control

While it is not difficult to see how Pettit's account of social justice could be applied to the employer-employee relationship, it is more challenging to conceive of how Pettit's account of state legitimacy could be applied in this context. Political

[30] Immigration Rules, pt 5, paras 159A–159H.

[31] V Mantouvalou, 'What Is to Be Done for Migrant Domestic Workers? in B Ryan (ed), *Labour Migration in Hard Times* (Institute of Employment Rights, 2013) https://ssrn.com/abstract=2386947 accessed 1 July 2018.

[32] For a discussion on Lovett's reification of rules, see A Eleveld, 'Rules and the Reduction of Arbitrary Power in Workfare Relationships: A Critical Assessment of Republican Theory' (Seminar, 'Normative Perspectives on Working Welfare Recipients', VU University Amsterdam, 4 November 2016).

[33] Lovett is not consistent in his approach to the *working* of (legal) rules. See also Breen, 'Non-Domination' (n 3) 424, 431 fn 39.

philosopher, Elizabeth Anderson, provides an interesting justification for transferring the republican theory of state legitimacy to the workplace. As she points out, corporate law and labour law created 'the infrastructure for capitalism. It is a public good provided by the state. As such, its structure is properly subject to evaluation and control by democratic processes'.[34] In revealing the connection between state democracy, public goods, and the firm, Anderson thus justifies a 'workers' democracy'.

This republican perspective on workers' democracy has been elaborated by scholars such as Richard Dagger, Iñigo Gonzáles-Ricoy, and Nien-hê Hsieh in two important ways.[35] First, they have interpreted protective rules such as international labour standards, and professional and craft standards, as 'workplace constitutionalism', which offer a basic protection to employees (compare insulation programmes) *and* – at the same time – function as rules that limit the scope of discretion afforded to the manager or employer. Accordingly, these rules reduce the ability of the employer or manager to make decisions in an arbitrary way.[36]

Yet, workplace republicans also acknowledge that managerial power will never be entirely limited by legislation such as safety standards, minimum wage rates, and working time legislation. There will always be scope for discretion, enabling the employer or the manager to instruct the employee on *when* s/he has to work (eg, overtime), on *where* s/he has to work, and on *how* s/he has to perform his/her work. Therefore, workplace republicans have also argued for a workers' democracy, which permits employees to influence and control these discretionary spaces. How should this workers' control over the remaining discretionary space look like, according to workplace republicans? While Hsieh has argued for the institutionalisation of employee participation in decision-making procedures,[37] González-Ricoy has proposed a 'genuine' workplace democracy that does not simply seek to constrain managerial discretion, but that is aimed at reducing its arbitrary exercise 'by granting workers a binding say both over the firm's decisions and their enforcement'.[38] Hsieh and González-Ricoy thus both emphasise the workers' voice in decision-making processes (ie, 'input democracy'). However, recall that Pettit in his justification of state legitimacy referred to the value of input democracy *and* 'output democracy'. Transferred to a workplace context, this seems to imply that Pettit's republican theory not only requires worker participation in decision-making procedures, but also scope for worker contestation of bad decisions and majority decisions that have a negative impact on specific workers (ie, 'output democracy').

[34] E Anderson, 'Equality and Freedom in the Workplace: Recovering Republican Insights' (2015) 31 *Social Philosophy & Policy* 48, 64.

[35] See above n 20 for relevant literature.

[36] But see Lovett, *General Theory* (n 4) 96, who makes a distinction between discretionary power (ie, constrained by rules, etc) and arbitrary power (ie, not constrained by rules, etc).

[37] Hsieh, 'Workplace Democracy' (n 20).

[38] González-Ricoy, 'The Republican Case' (n 20) 247.

D. Republican Theory, Labour Law, and Argumentative Strategy

In the previous sections, I have sought to demonstrate that republican theory provides a substantive theory which tells us *why* we need employment law that protects the weaker party in employment relations (mostly the worker). To summarise:

1. Pettit's version of republican theory – that is, based on the idea of freedom as non-domination – teaches us that social justice requires the equal distribution of basic liberties. Hence, the justification of fundamental labour rights.
2. However, as Pettit argues, additional rules are needed where choices are not co-exercisable and co-satisfying, such as the choice to start a company that exceeds the size of a one-person company. Hence, the need for coordinating labour law regulations.
3. In asymmetrical relationships, such as the employer-employee relationship, an equal distribution of basic liberties is insufficient to attain the goal of freedom as non-domination. In these relationships, protective labour law (and social security law) and/or workplace constitutionalism are called for.
4. Regarding the fact that labour law is a public good provided by the state, which enables capitalist production, this structure should be subject to evaluation and control by democratic processes. This implies that managerial discretion needs to be put under the scrutiny of a workers' democracy which, as Pettit's account of state legitimacy suggests, should enable worker participation in decision-making processes ('input democracy') *and* the possibility of challenging managers' decisions ('output democracy').

As such, a republican justification of (protective) labour law regulations may be able to compete with neoliberal thought that justifies the de-regulation of employment relations.[39] While neoliberal policy discourses will probably endorse the first two points above, discussion will focus on the third and fourth points. However, since these latter points, like neoliberal thought, are based on the ideal of freedom *and* on a coherent political theory, which also offers persuasive concepts (eg, 'arbitrary power', 'exit costs', and 'effective external rules'), the justification of labour law grounded in republican theory will – at least for neoliberals – not be easy to rebut.

IV. Critiques on Deployment of the Republication Theory of Non-domination as a Foundation of Labour Law

To date, various labour lawyers have referred to or discussed the republican theory of non-domination as a foundation of labour law. In 2016, a conference

[39] See P Mirowski and D Plehwe (eds), *The Road from Mont Pelèrin: The Making of the Neoliberal Thought Collective* (Cambridge, Mass., Harvard University Press, 2009).

was dedicated to the significance of the republican theory of non-domination for labour law. The conference papers, published in a 2017 themed issue of the *International Journal of Comparative Labour Law and Industrial Relations*,[40] varied in their valuation of the republican theory for labour law. In this section, I examine three points of critique drawn from these papers, which are relevant to the purpose of this contribution: (A) Republican objections to the employment contract; (B) coverage of republican theory that is viewed as too broad; and contrastingly (C) coverage of republican theory that is viewed as too narrow.

A. The Republican Theory of Non-domination Objects to the Employment Contract (Because it Establishes Relations of Domination)

Alan Bogg expresses his concerns regarding the republican conceptualisation of the labour contract. In the past, (radical) republicans have been rather critical of the employment contract (or 'wage labour'), as it would subject workers to the domination of employers.[41] Quoting from Pettit's seminal book, *Republicanism*,[42] Bogg ascribes a radical view on the employment contract to Pettit. According to Bogg, incorporating Pettit's republican theory as a normative foundation of labour law could invite in a 'Trojan horse' that justifies, and entrenches, the neoliberal deregulation of labour relations.

Is it true that Pettit would be opposed to the employment contract, because of its dominating effects (ie, the legalisation of a relationship of subordination)? In support of Bogg's remarks, it could be argued that the employment contract is a special form of contract in which one party – the employee – voluntarily trades away a part of his/her freedom. The employee, then, agrees to work under the authority of the employer who – as a result – has the authority to decide where, when, how, etc, the employee performs his/her work. To put it differently, the employment contract provides the employer with authority over the employee that s/he would not have had if the parties had concluded a different kind of contract (ie, not an employment contract). Hence, it could be concluded that the employment contract results in a considerable reduction of freedom on the part of the employee, which would be contrary to Pettit's ideal of freedom as non-domination.

[40] See Bogg, 'Republican Non-Domination' (n 3); Breen, 'Non-Domination' (n 3); Cabrelli and Zahn, 'Theories of Domination' (n 3); Davidov, 'Subordination vs Domination' (n 3).

[41] Anderson, 'Equality and Freedom' (n 34).

[42] Pettit refers to a situation in which 'individual contracts of employment are wrested from workers under the specter of destitution and … they put the employer in a position of domination relative to employees': Pettit, *Republicanism* (n 4) 142, quoted in Bogg, 'Republican Non-Domination' (n 3) 406.

However, as regards Pettit's (and Lovett's) aim to minimise uncontrolled or arbitrary power, I do not share Bogg's concerns. First, it is hard to imagine how the absence or repeal of employment contracts would reduce the risk (for the people lacking the means of production) of being subjected to the arbitrary power of those who possess the means of production (eg, Pettit's insistence on rules that reconstitute choices which are not co-exercisable and co-satisfying). Secondly, and related to the first point, an employment contract makes a work relationship more predictable and therefore less arbitrary (eg, Lovett's insistence on effective external rules). Thirdly, employment regulations referred to in the employment contract set boundaries on the exercise of the employer's discretionary power (eg, workplace constitutionalism and Pettit's insulation programmes). Fourthly, the employment contract ideally contains rules aimed at the resourcing of basic liberties, as a result of which the weaker party will be protected against exercises of arbitrary power (eg, Pettit's insulation programmes).

In sum, Pettit's (and Lovett's) republican theory provides a justification of the employment contract, as it *regulates* power relations between employees and employers. For them, the employment contract not only legalises a relationship of subordination, it also limits the exercise of one party's power (usually the employer) over the other party (usually the employee), and it makes this relationship more predictable.

B. The Republican Theory of Non-domination is Too Broad to be a Justificatory Theory for Labour Law

According to Davidov, Pettit's republican theory is not useful as a foundation of labour law, since his definition of arbitrary power – 'that the decision can be made "without reference to the interests, or the opinions of those affected"'[43] – would cover all economic relations where parties act in their own interests, and is therefore too broad.

I do not agree with this point of critique. Recall that for Pettit, rules may be called for to reconstitute choices in horizontal relations which are not co-exercisable or co-satisfying. As such, republican theory justifies, amongst other things, legal rules regulating economic relations. We could call these rules 'negative rules' that protect individuals from interference in their freedom. In this respect, it could indeed be argued that Pettit's republicanism justifies a broad range of legal regulations, including laws regulating economic relations. Yet, in addition to these negative rules, Petit formulates positive rules designed for relationships where the equal distribution of basic liberties and coordination rules are not sufficient to meet the general requirements of freedom as non-domination. These rules (insulation programmes) serve to protect the weaker party and seem

[43] Pettit, *Republicanism* (n 4) 55, quoted in Davidov, 'Subordination vs Domination' (n 3) 376.

to be urgent, above all, in relationships where people will not easily invoke legal rules, because 'triggering them can have costs of its own'. For example, as Pettit argues, 'the employees who complain to an inspector about working conditions may find that they consequently get all the rougher jobs'.[44] This shows that Pettit justifies protective (positive) measures only in (personal) relationships where one party is dependent on the other party, and where the first party may fear high personal costs if s/he seeks to protect him/herself from the arbitrary inference of the other party, such as the employer-employee relationship. In other words, Pettit's republican theory does not justify protective *positive* measures in all possible economic relations.

Secondly, regarding the purpose of this chapter, it could be argued that the broad coverage of a justificatory theory, instead of a weakness, is an advantage as it will – like neoliberal thought – appeal to many people. Indeed, republican theory may even justify labour law reforms that benefit employers in particular. Consider, in this respect, the example of the employers' obligation in the Netherlands to pay wages during the first two years of sickness. While the employer is not allowed to dismiss the sick employee during the first two years of sickness, s/he will not be able to exit his/her relationship with the employee. In particular, where the employer lacks economic power, the employer may feel that s/he is the one who is subject to the whims of the other contracting party (employee). In this case, the republican language of power imbalance, dependency, exit costs, and arbitrary power could be used to defend employers' interests to reduce the period that the employer is obliged to pay wages to the sick employee, arguing that this period should be covered by sickness insurance. This shows that a republican justification of labour law reforms may appeal to both employees and employers, which would make republican theory more attractive as a justificatory theory in social policy discourses.

C. The Republican Theory of Non-domination Only Justifies a (Small) Part of Labour Law

In addition to the critique that the republican theory of non-domination is too broad, it is argued that republican theory justifies only a small part of labour law. David Cabrelli and Rebecca Zahn (and Davidov) conclude that the theory of non-domination is, in the end, 'too selective' to be used as a general justification of labour law, because of its sole focus on domination.[45] Davidov further argues that republican theory does not cover the situation where the employer exercises *non-arbitrary* power because, even where the employer has to consider the views

[44] Pettit, *On the People's Terms* (n 4) 115.

[45] Cabrelli and Zahn, 'Theories of Domination' (n 3) 361. See also Davidov, 'Subordination vs Domination' (n 3) 378.

and interests of the employees (eg, co-determination rules), 'at the end of the day the decision is still taken by the employer'.[46] In the same vein, Keith Breen refers to the 'residual decision-making rights by managers [that] cannot be eliminated altogether [by] state-sanctioned regulations, collective bargaining agreements, contracts and well-defined job descriptions'.[47]

Is it true that republican theory only justifies a small part of labour law? In my opinion, the analysis of republican theory in previous sections does not support this conclusion. To repeat, regarding the fact that almost all employment law regulations serve to: (1) regulate the employment relationship under conditions where choices are not co-exercisable and co-satisfying; (2) constrain the discretionary scope of managers or employers;[48] (3) resource basic liberties in an asymmetrical relationship; and/or (4) provide procedural protections to employees, it could be concluded that republican theory can serve to justify most (or even the entire field) of labour law. The critique that republican theory is too broad (see Section IV(B)) seems more to the point.

Notwithstanding these justifications for (procedural) employment law, Davidov problematises the fact that (workplace) republicanism does not cover *non-arbitrary* exercises of power. Assuming that he does not question 'authority relations' and 'hierarchical structures', which – as Breen admits – are required within companies,[49] I believe that both Davidov's and Breen's hesitance is rooted in their focus on 'input democracy'. In their opinion, aside from the presence of co-determination or other democratic procedures, it is the manager who normally decides. However, as I mentioned in the previous section, Pettit's conceptualisation of republican democracy covers both 'input' and 'output democracy'. What counts for Pettit – in the context of the state – is that the people can *effectively* control the discretionary space of the state. Translated in a workplace context, this means that a decision is – by definition – non-arbitrary, as workers have been able to influence or control the decision before it was taken *and* they are able to contest the final decision. From this, it follows that even where workers have been able to influence or control a decision *ex ante* (input democracy), a decision may still count as arbitrary or uncontrollable, unless workers are able to contest decisions *ex post* (output democracy).

Indeed, as Pettit argues in the context of the state, 'input democracy' does not necessarily lead to just decisions. Acknowledging the need to control the discretionary spaces of state officials, and the problem of majority tyranny, he argues for civic vigilance as an additional way of controlling government (ie, 'output democracy'). Transferring Pettit's republican theory to the workplace, this would imply that the institutionalisation of workplace democracy should be complemented

[46] Davidov, 'Subordination vs Domination' (n 3) 377.

[47] Breen, 'Non-Domination' (n 3) 427.

[48] Applying Lovett's version of the republican theory of non-domination to labour law, Cabrelli and Zahn also conclude that it would justify certain policy areas of labour law, such as minimum wage laws, equal pay laws, and working time regulations: Cabrelli and Zahn, 'Theories of Domination' (n 3) 350.

[49] *cf* Breen, 'Non-Domination' (n 3) 436.

by a similar vigilance of workers, and a willingness to contest managers' bad decisions or majority decisions that have a negative impact on specific workers. Pettit's defence of output democracy might also justify the institutionalisation of instruments not mentioned by workplace republicans, such as whistle blowing procedures.[50] These kinds of procedures will be particularly necessary in situations where a manager simply ignores participatory institutions, and/or where workers' resistance increases repression.[51]

All in all, the republican focus on 'input' *and* 'output' democracy advances a flexible approach to labour law regulation and, as such, it offers a (discursive) foundation for a broad range of substantive and procedural labour law regulations.

V. Conclusion

According to Cabrelli and Zahn, the terminology of the theory of non-domination

> is particularly unsettling for the adherents of the neoliberal ideology; if a social and legal order – such as labour law – is legitimate and truly liberal insofar as it secures non-coercion in the lives of its employee citizens, then according to the neoliberal approach, the theoretical account of social justice as an absence of domination should be difficult to rebut.[52]

This connects with my argument that labour lawyers are in need of a coherent theory that provides a language enabling them to compete with dominant discourses based on neoliberal thought and which justify the de-regulation of employment relations. As I have argued, republican theory should be preferred over the celebrated capability approach because, unlike the latter approach, the republicans discussed in this chapter genuinely take the power relations underlying labour relations into account. In addition, republican theory offers a coherent theory, and a convincing language (eg, 'exit costs', 'arbitrary power', 'effective external rules'), in the defence of employment law regulations and procedures that protect workers and that foster both input and output democracy in the workplace.

To repeat, as a post-foundationalist, I do not believe in 'foundations' of labour law, nor in foundations of anything else. I also agree with other criticisms that republican theory fails to take account of agentless and structural forms of power relations.[53] Still, neoliberals – who dominate current social policy discourses – will find it simpler to argue against political philosophies that consider these structural forms of power relations (eg, Marxism), than the republican idea of freedom as non-domination.

[50] See Eleveld, 'Rules and the Reduction of Arbitrary Power' (n 32).

[51] R Hodson, *Dignity at Work* (Cambridge, Cambridge University Press, 2001).

[52] Cabrelli and Zahn, 'Theories of Domination' (n 3) 355–56.

[53] ibid 359; Bogg, 'Republican Non-Domination' (n 3) 414; Breen, 'Non-Domination' (n 3) 430; Davidov, 'Subordination vs Domination' (n 3) 383–85. See also Mc Bride, 'Freedom as Non-domination' (n 7).

14

Anti-Authoritarian Employment Relations? Labour Law from an Anarchist Perspective

ANDREA IOSSA*

I. Introduction

This contribution aims at initiating a discussion about the possibility of conceiving labour law from the perspective of anarchism. The impetus for this endeavour is found in the observation that the two traditional expressions of authority in the labour market, namely the state and the employer, are vanishing due to the ideological stance of the economic orthodoxy that has prevailed in the last 30 years. In the context of extreme flexibilisation of labour markets and the precariousness of employment that neoliberal policies have produced, the authority of state law in protecting employment and social rights has been constrained, and the employer has abdicated from a managing role in running the business. Labour law struggles in understanding this evolution. Therefore, a radical critique of labour law itself is needed to set forth new ideas for discussing radical changes. However, this contribution does *not* aim to list rules and precepts to be applied to any potential work-related situation in an imaginary anarchist society. Rather than present a rulebook on anarchist social organising, the ambition here is to shed new (anarchist) light on the contemporary discussions on work and labour law so as to move it forward.

If it is true that, in the current socio-economic context, the authority of the state and the employer vanishes, the question is: why not look to the ideas of those who sought the abolition of authoritarianism from society; that is, the anarchists?

* Postdoctoral fellow, Faculty of Law, Lund University. I would like to thank the editors of this volume for their accurate comments. The final text has also benefitted from the careful reading and precious feedback provided by César Rosado Marzán and Judy Fudge. Finally, I am grateful to Filip Dorssemont and to the other participants of a seminar that he arranged on 17 April 2018, during my three-month research visit at the Université Catholique de Louvain, which was sponsored by the Louvain Global College of Law. There, I had the opportunity to present this work and receive valuable comments. The usual disclaimer applies.

Anarchism is a socio-political theory (and praxis) aimed at dismantling and eradicating from society any authoritarian social relations. A basic principle of anarchism concerns the 'rejection of external authority, whether that of the state, the employer, or the hierarchies of administration and of established institutions like the schools and the church'.[1] Yet anarchism is a very wide social, political, and philosophical spectrum in which several streams, traditions, and movements coexist.[2] Since the aim of this contribution is not to explore anarchism as a kaleidoscope of political experiences, the analysis is conducted by considering anarchist theory unitarily through the recognition of its recurrent and common features; that is, questioning the legitimacy of any hierarchical organisations and rejecting a society based on authoritarian relationships.[3] The 'principle of authority' represents the thread of the discussion, observed in its expressions in the labour field; ie, as the grounding principle of the employment relationship and the rationale of the regulatory intervention of the State limiting the authority of the employer.[4]

Eventually, this may respond to what Judy Fudge has defined as the 'analytical problem' that 'plagues the contemporary debate about the role of labour law; a specific form of regulation at a particular moment in time has come to be seen as *the* form, rather than *a* form, of labour law'.[5] In order to preserve its role of protecting labour, labour law needs to re-invent itself.

The chapter evolves as follows: first, the classical expressions of authority in the labour market (ie, the employer and the state) are discussed as constitutive elements of labour law itself. Secondly, their evolution is analysed in relation to the emergence of neoliberalist ideology and the ensuing flexibilisation of the labour market. This discussion stresses the metamorphoses that the expressions of authority in labour law have undergone, including the forms that the employer's authority acquires in the so-called 'gig economy'. Thirdly, against that evolution, anarchist perspectives are explored. This section presents anarchist arguments on authority, law, and workplace to provide a basis for reflecting upon the nature and function of labour law. Finally, the last section concludes by highlighting the potential relevance of an anarchist perspective in discussing and reflecting upon the possible evolution of labour law towards emancipatory and liberating regulatory forms.

[1] C Ward, *Anarchism: A Very Short Introduction* (Oxford, Oxford University Press, 2004) 3.

[2] See the global and historical overview outlined in L van der Walt and M Schmidt, *Black Flame: The Revolutionary Class Politics of Anarchism and Syndicalism* (Edinburgh, AK Press, 2009). See also R Kinna, *Anarchism: A Beginner's Guide* (Oxford, Oneworld, 2005).

[3] P Kropotkin, 'Modern Science and Anarchism' in RN Baldwin (ed), *Kropotkin's Revolutionary Pamphlets: A Collection of Writings by Peter Kropotkin* (first published 1927, New York, Dover, 1970) 145, 158.

[4] The presence of limits to the authority of the employer, including rules set by collective bargaining, distinguishes the understanding of authority within the labour law field from a philosophical take conceptualising 'authority' as an absolute power of an agent over a patient not limited by any intermediate rule or compromise, see A Kojève, *The Notion of Authority* (London, Verso, 2014) 8–9.

[5] J Fudge, 'Labour as a "Fictive Commodity": Radically Reconceptualizing Labour Law' in G Davidov and B Langille (eds), *The Idea of Labour Law* (Oxford, Oxford University Press, 2013) 121 (emphasis in original).

II. The Principle of Authority in Labour Law

A. The Authority of the Employer in the Employment Relationship

In the classical understanding of labour law, the employer is the 'legal entity that exercises the entrepreneurial power of control and direction over the working activity'.[6] The employer is thus the subject of the employment relationship, and has the right to allocate and direct the work within the company; that is, managerial prerogative.[7] The employment relationship as a socio-economic relationship, which emerged from the Industrial Revolution, is grounded in this form of subordination expressed by the 'power of control' of the employer, meaning the 'exercise of power in which there is control not only over what but also over how and when work must be done'.[8] Accordingly, Otto Kahn-Freund conceptualised the firm as 'an absolute monarchy'[9] in which the power is distributed in favour of the employer.

The application of technology to production has strengthened the employer's power over the worker. As long as the worker preserved a unique 'craftsman' knowledge necessary for the production of certain goods, the authority of the employer was restrained.[10] The employer needed the knowledgeable worker as part of the enterprise. The introduction of Taylorist and Fordist methods of industrial organisation brought about the standardisation of mechanisms in the use of machines.[11] The simplification of training made workers interchangeable, while increasing the employer's power as the only holder of knowledge in industrial organisation.[12] Consequently, the authoritarian nature of the employment relationship was augmented.

The socio-economic relationship of employment has received legal translation through the form of the contract. This implicitly means that the two subjects of the employment contract – the employer and the employed – are equal parties free to negotiate the conditions of the exchange. Yet this scheme reproduces, in the employment realm, the scheme of an exchange between two commodities: money

[6] L Corazza and O Razzolini, 'Who is an Employer?' in MW Finkin and G Mundlak (eds), *Comparative Labor Law* (Cheltenham, Edward Elgar, 2015) 135.

[7] See M Rönnmar, 'The Managerial Prerogative and the Employee's Obligation to Work: Comparative Perspectives on Functional Flexibility' (2006) 35 *Industrial Law Journal* 56, 61.

[8] B Veneziani, 'The Evolution of the Contract of Employment' in B Hepple (ed), *The Making of Labour Law in Europe: A Comparative Study of Nine Countries Up to 1945* (London, Mansell Publishing Limited, 1986) 65. See also J Prassl, *The Concept of the Employer* (Oxford, Oxford University Press, 2015) 27.

[9] O Kahn-Freund, 'Legal Framework' in A Flanders and HA Clegg (eds), *The System of Industrial Relations in Great Britain: Its History, Law and Institutions* (Oxford, Basel Blackwell, 1954) 49.

[10] See also KVW Stone, *From Widgets to Digits: Employment Regulation for the Changing Workplace* (Cambridge, Cambridge University Press, 2004) 22.

[11] B Settis, *Fordismi: Storia politica della produzione di massa* (Bologna, Il Mulino, 2016).

[12] AD Flanders, 'The Internal Social Responsibilities of Industry (1966)' in *Management and Unions: The Theory and Reform of Industrial Relations* (London, Faber and Faber, 1970) 135.

and labour.[13] This disguises the real and concrete control of the employer over the worker under the 'free will' of the parties.[14] What the liberal state interprets as a contract freely entered into by the two parties is, instead, 'a command under the guise of an agreement'.[15] The contractual exchange means that 'the employee surrenders control over a large part of [his/her] life'.[16] Therefore, although deemed as a contractual relationship, the employment contract '[i]n its inception it is an act of submission'.[17] The original idea behind the emergence of labour law is hence to achieve a more just social relationship through normative intervention aimed at recovering the freedom of the worker annulled in the action of employment.[18] From an anarchist point of view, however, the outcomes are disappointing.

B. The Authority of the State and the Function of Labour Law

As a 'technique for the regulation of social power',[19] labour law constitutes the expression of the authority of the state, whose main purpose is 'to regulate, to support and to restrain the power of management and the power of organised labour'.[20] The 'invention' of labour law was a response to the need for a supreme regulatory institution (the state) to regulate the socio-economic relationship that emerged from the Industrial Revolution. Yet the legal regulation of relationships in the sphere of economic production is not just a prerogative of contemporary times. Bruno Veneziani illustrates how certain types of contracts for the commission of *opera* (product or service) were already present in Roman Law, and Medieval Law, to distinguish these activities from serfdom.[21]

The terms of the legal transposition of the socio-economic relationship necessarily changed when the economic system changed. The emergence of the capitalist firm placed the provision of *opera* into the framework of 'dependency and control'.[22] The notion of labour law emerged on this basis, engaging with the worker's subordination to the employer, which was an integral feature of the industrial mode of production.

[13] J Fudge and E Tucker, *Labour Before the Law: The Regulation of Workers' Collective Action in Canada, 1900–1948* (Toronto, University of Toronto Press, 2004) chs 6 and 11. See also O Kahn-Freund, 'Introduction' in K Renner, *The Institutions of Private Law and their Social Functions* (London, Routledge & Kegan Paul Limited, 1949) 28.

[14] Lord Wedderburn, 'Labour Law: From Here to Autonomy?' (1987) 16 *Industrial Law Journal* 1, 5.

[15] Kahn-Freund, 'Introduction' (n 13) 28.

[16] Flanders, 'Internal Social Responsibilities' (n 12) 132.

[17] O Kahn-Freund, *Labour and the Law*, 2nd edn (London, Stevens, 1977) 18.

[18] B Langille, 'Labour Law's Theory of Justice' in G Davidov and B Langille (eds), *The Idea of Labour Law* (Oxford, Oxford University Press, 2013).

[19] Kahn-Freund, *Labour and the Law* (n 17) 14.

[20] ibid 15.

[21] Veneziani, 'Evolution of the Contract of Employment' (n 8) 32.

[22] ibid 64.

Under pressure from workers' movements, which developed to fight for better working conditions, the state took on the role of remedying the imbalance of the employment relationship.[23] Thus, labour legislation – which regulates the relationship between private parties – is enacted by the state to protect weaker subjects.[24] Accordingly, Hugo Sinzheimer locates labour law at the intersection between private and public law.[25] In this respect, the authority of the state is expressed in the task of intervening in the private law dimension of employment and mitigating the 'freedom of contract' between the parties through protective labour law legislation.[26]

Yet labour legislation has also served the purpose of 'codifying' the employment relationship, so as to preserve the authority of the employer. Albeit mitigated, the paradigm of subordination in employment is the cornerstone of labour law. Rather than functioning as an emancipatory factor, labour law incorporates a new subject of the capitalist economic system into the legal system – the worker – who is 'free' to enter into a voluntary contract to renounce their freedom during the time of work.[27] Thus, labour law plays a functional role in the maintenance and reproduction of the capitalist system by ensuring that production is made and carried within the scheme of the subordinated employment relationship.[28] Ultimately, labour law does not remedy the asymmetry of the employment relationship, rather it re-states the power and authority of the employer over the employee.[29]

III. Authority Lost: From Neoliberal Thinking to the 'Gig Economy'

A. The Neoliberal State and Labour Law

The protective stance of labour law legislation has followed a parabola that ascended in the years after 1945, when the bases for the welfare state were set in

[23] T Ramm, '*Laissez-faire* and State Protection of Workers' in B Hepple (ed), *The Making of Labour Law in Europe: A Comparative Study of Nine Countries Up to 1945* (London, Mansell Publishing Limited, 1986).

[24] The original understanding of social rights, which included employment rights, was indeed grounded in the positive action that the State undertakes in order to ensure certain standards of living for its citizens: see TH Marshall, *Citizenship and Social Class* (Cambridge, Cambridge University Press, 1950) 14.

[25] O Kahn-Freund, 'Hugo Sinzheimer 1875–1945 (1976)' in R Lewis and J Clark (eds), *Labour Law and Politics in the Weimar Republic* (Oxford, Blackwell, 1981) 73, 75.

[26] M Freedland, 'Otto Kahn-Freund, the Contract of Employment and the Autonomy of Labour Law' in A Bogg and others (eds), *The Autonomy of Labour Law* (Oxford, Hart Publishing, 2015) 35.

[27] A Blackett, 'Emancipation in the Idea of Labour Law' in G Davidov and B Langille (eds), *The Idea of Labour Law* (Oxford, Oxford University Press, 2011); J Heyes and I Clark, 'The State and Employment Relations' in K Townsend and A Wilkinson (eds), *Research Handbook on the Future of Work and Employment Relations* (Cheltenham, Edward Elgar, 2011) 73.

[28] Fudge, 'Labour as a "Fictive Commodity"' (n 5) 123.

[29] R Hyman, *Industrial Relations: A Marxist Introduction* (London, Macmillan, 1975) 24.

many European countries, and which reached its highest point in the 1970s, in conjunction with the widespread global economic crisis.[30] In recent decades, this parabola has moved downward, not because of a lack of legislative intervention, but rather because of reforms undertaken globally that have tended to disempower the protective role of labour law.

The descent of that protective tendency corresponds with the ascent of neoliberal ideology. Arising as a philosophical movement that rejected an understanding of individual rights based upon natural law,[31] the neoliberal movement became political when it started critiquing those collectivistic and planned forms of political economy (socialist and social-democratic) which positioned the state in a leading role.[32] Instead, in the state's action and in its administrative machine, neoliberal thinking sees a threat to the freedom of individuals that must be constrained. In the economic sphere, neoliberals have called for a drastic marginalisation of the state, which they argue should abstain from any intervention that could alter the free functioning of the market, including in the spheres of employment and welfare.[33]

Later, the idea of a 'minimal State'[34] became popular amongst the political elites of the Western world as the linchpin of a political project opposed to socialism and social-democracy. The neoliberal vision of a society composed only of single individuals, and of a political economy based exclusively on private enterprise, has been adopted by a number of influential Western states (ie, the Reaganian United States (US) and the Thatcherian United Kingdom (UK)) and by world financial institutions (ie, the International Monetary Fund and the World Bank), which have influenced politics globally and steered the process of development in several countries following decolonisation and the end of the Cold War.[35]

The adoption of economic reforms based upon a neoliberal agenda has re-shaped the relationship between the state and the market.[36] In legal terms, the central position attributed to the market as the driving force of the economy

[30] This path is well-designed in the historical classification outlined in the contributions included in B Hepple and B Veneziani (eds), *The Transformation of Labour Law in Europe: A Comparative Study of 15 Countries, 1945–2004* (Oxford, Hart Publishing, 2009). See also S Giubboni, 'The Rise and Fall of EU Labour Law' (2018) 24 *European Law Journal* 7.

[31] See A Zimmerman, 'Jurisprudencia libertaria: Aspectos filosófico-legales del trabajo libertario de Friedrich Hayek y Robert Nozick' (2013) 10 *Revista de Economía y Derecho* 99.

[32] RS Turner, 'The "Rebirth of Liberalism": The Origins of Neo-Liberal Ideology' (2007) 12 *Journal of Political Ideologies* 67.

[33] TA Knutsen, 'Should Liberals Sometimes Prefer Dictatorships to Democracies? A Closer Look at the Hayek Thesis' (2016) 23 *Democratization* 375.

[34] The definition of the 'minimal State', also known as 'the night-watchman state', refers to a State that refrains from any interventions or interferences in the lives of its citizens, including the collection of taxes: see R Patterson, 'The Minimal State v The Welfare State: A Critique of the Argument between Nozick and Rawls' (2005) 9 *Southern Cross University Law Review* 167.

[35] D Harvey, *A Brief History of Neoliberalism* (New York, Oxford University Press, 2005) 39. On neoliberal reform in developing countries, see F Wanderley, 'Between Reform and Inertia: Bolivia's Employment and Social Protection Policies Over the Past 20 Years' (2009) 148 *International Labour Review* 253–67.

[36] J Peck, *Constructions of Neoliberal Reason* (Oxford, Oxford University Press, 2010) 16.

translated into the renewed relevance of freedom of contract and individual legal entities.[37] In a neoliberal state, the law operates to enhance the market, in order to boost economic efficiency and rationality which become, in turn, the criteria for assessing law's success. Individual (economic) freedoms, private property, and free enterprise are the top-rank values that the legal framework seeks to protect.[38] Paradoxically, the authority of the state is exercised to protect the autonomous functioning of the market from the authority of the state itself.[39]

The primacy given to private business by neoliberal ideology has meant the privatisation of economic sectors traditionally within the public domain (ie, energy, telecommunication, public transport, etc – but also schools and hospitals). This has limited the direct role of the state in regulating the labour market.[40] The free market creed has led neoliberals to put the dismantling of the trade union institution on its agenda – deemed a 'monopoly' restraining the functioning of the labour market, and responsible for unemployment and economic stagnation.[41] In accordance with the ideals of individualism, freedom of trade union association has to be deemed an individual freedom, namely as freedom *not* to associate.[42] The coordinated and centralised systems of industrial relations have to be dismantled; collective bargaining must be decentralised to the company level – or eliminated in favour of individual negotiations.[43] The labour market shall be flexible, and ready to adjust wages and employment conditions to economic contingencies. Wage flexibility is identified as the factor that fosters competition between companies and, eventually, raises labour productivity.[44] The narrative of labour market flexibility as the engine of economic development, through competition, has meant

[37] Harvey, *Brief History of Neoliberalism* (n 35) 64.

[38] AH Villmoare and PG Stillman, 'The Neoliberal State's Janus Faces of Law' (2014) 65 *Studies in Law, Politics and Society (Special Issue: Law and the Liberal State)* 31.

[39] DS Grewal and J Purdy, 'Introduction: Law and Neoliberalism' (2014) 77 *Law and Contemporary Problems* 1–23.

[40] KVW Stone, 'Flexibilization, Globalization, and Privatization: Three Challenges to Labour Rights in Our Times' in B Bercusson and C Estlund (eds), *Regulating Labour in the Wake of Globalisation: New Challenges, New Institutions* (Oxford, Hart Publishing, 2008) 122.

[41] Lord Wedderburn, 'Freedom of Association and Philosophies of Labour Law' (1989) 18 *Industrial Law Journal* 8; G Gall, R Hurd and A Wilkinson, 'Labour Unionism and Neo-Liberalism' in G Gall, A Wilkinson and R Hurd (eds), *The International Handbook of Labour Unions: Responses to Neo-Liberalism* (Cheltenham, Edward Elgar, 2011); C Crouch, *The Strange Non-Death of Neo-Liberalism* (Cambridge, Polity Press, 2011). For other examples of neoliberal reforms hitting the trade unions, see RL Madrid, 'Labouring Against Neoliberalism: Unions and Patterns of Reform in Latin America' (2003) 35 *Journal of Latin American Studies* 53.

[42] Wedderburn, 'Freedom of Association' (n 41) 10.

[43] L Baccaro and C Howell, 'A Common Neoliberal Trajectory: The Transformation of Industrial Relations in Advanced Capitalism' (2011) 39 *Politics & Society* 521. For further national cases, see, inter alia, R Cooper and B Ellem, 'The Neoliberal State, Trade Unions and Collective Bargaining in Australia' (2008) 46 *British Journal of Industrial Relations* 532; B Amable, 'The Political Economy of the Neoliberal Transformation of French Industrial Relations' (2016) 69 *ILR Review* 523; CJ Fernández Rodríguez, R Ibáñez Rojo and M Martínez Lucio, 'Austerity and Collective Bargaining in Spain: The Political and Dysfunctional Nature of Neoliberal Deregulation' (2016) 22 *European Journal of Industrial Relations* 267.

[44] See the example of neoliberal reform of the labour market adopted in New Zealand: see PS Morrison, 'Deregulation of the New Zealand Labour Market' (2004) 59 *GeoJournal* 127–36.

the abatement of employment protection. Under neoliberal influence, the grounds for individual dismissals have been widened and employment protection diminished (recent examples in Europe are the 2015 Italian *Jobs Act* and the 2016 French *Loi Travail*). According to a neoliberal perspective, the original idea of labour law is undermined, and the employment contract 'is but one contract among many, to be governed by common principles of "freedom of contract" and the general law'.[45]

The self-proclaimed anti-statist stance of the neoliberal movement is translated into policies of labour market deregulation and decentralisation that leave workers at the mercy of market forces and employer authority. This pattern has been replicated with authoritarian labour market reforms that have reinforced the authority of the employer in the employment relationship, and in the workplace.[46]

B. Labour Market Flexibility and the Invisible Employer

In 1987, Lord Wedderburn observed the progressive shifting from the classical concept of the employment relationship based upon dependent labour, towards new forms of labour relations in which the 'subordination' of the worker was masked as 'autonomy' by virtue of the type of contract signed between the parties. He noted that the shift was due to 'a rapid fragmentation of the labour market, especially by the growth of myriad, so-called "a-typical" or "marginal" relationships', including 'the worker part-time, casual, temporary, lump labour, homeworker, outworker, or the subcontractor'.[47] In his view, this undermined the autonomy of labour law in regulating labour relations by blurring the contours of a traditional concept such as the one of the 'employer'.[48]

Several forms of atypical and flexible contracts have been introduced in the labour market in the last few decades. The variety of contracts differs from country to country; however, no country has been immune. In this regard, it is interesting to compare two articles written by the sociologist Arne Kelleberg, almost ten years apart. In 2000, he described the world of employment as increasingly consisting of non-standard relations, including part-time and short-term jobs, contract work, temporary agency work, and 'contingent work'; that is, 'work arrangements that were conditional on employers' needs for labor and thus lacked an attachment between employer and worker'.[49] In 2009, Kalleberg recognised nonstandard employment (named 'precarious work'[50]) as the 'dominant feature' in almost all

[45] Wedderburn, 'Freedom of Association' (n 41) 9.

[46] See also A Bogg, 'Beyond Neo-Liberalism: The Trade Union Act 2016 and the Authoritarian State' (2016) 45 *Industrial Law Journal* 299.

[47] Wedderburn, 'Labour Law' (n 14) 6.

[48] ibid 21–22.

[49] AL Kalleberg, 'Nonstandard Employment Relations: Part-Time, Temporary, and Contract Work' (2000) 26 *Annual Review of Sociology* 341, 354.

[50] AL Kalleberg, 'Precarious Work, Insecure Workers: Employment Relations in Transition' (2009) 74 *American Sociological Review* 1.

economic sectors.[51] In his view, the precariousness of employment produced risk-shifting from the employer to the employee.[52] Precarious jobs, therefore, entail the subversion of traditional roles.

Two extreme examples of how the employer's role is shifting are, for instance, 'zero-hours contracts' in the UK, and the so-called 'job-voucher' (*buoni-lavoro*) in Italy. The zero-hours contract is a well-established reality of the UK labour market. Simon Deakin defines it as 'essentially a contract or arrangement under which an employer agrees to pay for work done but makes no commitment to provide a set number of hours of work per day, week or month'.[53] Minimal contractual obligations arise on the employer's side, and they are not compelled to integrate the worker into the company by distributing working hours on a regular basis.[54] In the case of 'job-vouchers', no contractual obligations exist at all. The voucher constitutes a hyper-flexible form of payment for occasional labour through a ticket that can be purchased in a tobacco shop. The progressive deregulation of the limits to its operation (originally it provided only for subjects at the margins of the labour market or 'at risk of social exclusion', such as students, migrants, and domestic workers) led to a boom in use.[55] In 2016,[56] it became the most diffused form of flexible employment in the Italian labour market.[57]

The mutuality of the employment contract disappears in the case of both zero-hours contracts and job-vouchers. Through resort to forms of atypical and hyper-flexible employment, exposure to the labour law (and social security) regime is almost annulled: no obligations for the employer; no protection for the worker. Yet subordination persists, as does the employer's authority, albeit under a different form. The 'employer' of labour is transformed into a 'consumer' of labour. No managerial prerogatives are required to perform this activity. Conversely, the authority of the state, as represented by labour law legislation, vanishes due to the scarce – if not null – protection ensured by the labour law regime to these forms of employment. The employer decides the forms and modalities of work performance, without the obligations of an employment contract.

These features also appear in the so-called 'gig economy'.[58] In these forms of work, the economic production (usually a service, such as transportation,

[51] ibid 17.

[52] ibid 8.

[53] S Deakin, 'New Forms of Employment: Implications for EU Law – The Law as It Stands' in R Blanpain and others (eds), *New Forms of Employment in Europe* (Alphen aan den Rijn, Wolters Kluwer, 2016) 47.

[54] ibid 48.

[55] See A Zilli, 'L'inclusione sociale attraverso i voucher per prestazioni di lavoro accessorio' in M Brollo, C Cester and L Menghini (eds), *Legalità e rapporti di lavoro: Incentivi e sanzioni* (Trieste, EUT, 2016).

[56] The job-voucher instrument was cancelled, in 2017, as result of a campaign pursued by the main Italian trade union CGIL, which collected signatures for proposing a referendum to repeal them.

[57] See M Fana, D Guarascio and V Cirillo, 'La crisi e le riforme del mercato del lavoro in Italia: Un'analisi regionale del Jobs Act' (2016) 5 *Argomenti* 26.

[58] See V de Stefano, 'The Rise of the "Just-in-Time Workforce": On-Demand Work, Crowdwork, and Labor Protection in the "Gig-Economy"' (2016) 37 *Comparative Labor Law & Policy Journal* 471, 474.

home-delivery, cleaning, etc) is organised through use of digital platforms as a means of linking the subjects involved in the economic exchange. The client and the service performer are connected through an app on which both are signed up. The company running the app claims that it performs only the role of the 'intermediary', and not of the employer, by connecting the service performer and the client who are the parties in the exchange. Yet this picture has been rejected by the EU Court of Justice which, instead, has recognised the platform Uber as a transport company rather than a digital service.[59]

In other legal disputes, the courts have detected elements of an employment relationship based on the exercise of a power to monitor and control by the company. The UK Employment Tribunal acknowledged (and the Employment Appeal Tribunal confirmed)[60] that drivers are part of the business run by Uber.[61] This conclusion was reached by ascertaining that Uber exercises its power of control over drivers through a set of actions that include discretion in selecting drivers, obligations for drivers to accept rides, the unquestionable decision of the route that the driver has to follow, and the fare that must be charged. Using a similar analysis, the US District Court of North California concluded that drivers are Uber's 'presumptive employees', as they render services to Uber which, in turn, exercises control over them.[62] The Court explained that Uber prohibits drivers from picking up passengers outside the app, or that it selects drivers and inspects their cars. Moreover, the Court pointed to the fact that the actual profit made by Uber derives from the revenue generated by the rides performed by workers, rather than from the software and its widespread diffusion. *Contra*, a decision of the Fair Work Commission in Australia recognised certain elements of autonomy that would exclude the conditions of Uber's drivers from the scope of employment subordination, as currently formulated by employment law, such as the ability to log-off from the app at any time and the possession of fundamental tools such as the car and phone.[63] The autonomy of workers in deciding when to work was also the element upon which an Italian court (Turin) denied the claim of subordination advanced by six riders providing meal home-delivery services for the platform, Foodora. According to the Court, employment subordination can only exist when the worker is exposed to the managerial powers of the employer expressed through specific orders and supervisory activities.[64] Thus, the fact that the digital platform does not perform the managerial prerogative of allocating shifts and tasks – which in the 'gig economy' tend to be self-decided by the workers – and only monitors whether the delivery is successfully completed, means that such workers are qualified as 'self-employed'.

[59] Case C-434/15 *Asociación Profesional Élite Taxi v Uber Systems Spain, SL* (ECJ, 20 December 2017).

[60] *Uber BV v Aslam* [2018] ICR 453. This decision was appealed by Uber to the Court of Appeal (Civil Division), which dismissed the appeal with a 2-1 majority: *Uber BV v Aslam* [2018] EWCA Civ 2748.

[61] *Aslam v Uber BV* [2017] IRLR 4.

[62] *O'Connor v Uber Technologies, Inc*, 82 F Supp 3d 1133 (ND Cal 2015).

[63] *Kaseris v Rasier Pacific VOF* (2017) 272 IR 289.

[64] Tribunale di Torino, sez. V Lavoro, case n. 778/18 (7 May 2018).

In light of the preceding discussion, forms of work such as those apparent in the 'gig economy' represent an evolution in the practices of employer authority. Rather than disappearing, workforce management has been elevated to the 'next level', and now operates through an algorithm.[65] The business is firmly organised by platform companies via management strategies that aim at making production as lean as possible. Even the allocation of shifts and hours of work is a task performed by the workers themselves, which they do by logging into the app, and signing up for certain shifts. Yet control over the practices of production and its standardisation persist.[66] The digital companies style their workers as self-employed individuals who directly contract with the clients, with the platform simply facilitating this act of contracting. However, the reality is that these workers are not in fact free to negotiate the terms of the contract or the service that they provide. They have to accept the conditions unilaterally imposed by the platforms. Ultimately, in the lean business of the 'gig economy', the exploitation of labour reaches its extreme: those moments in which workers are unproductive, such as when cars are empty, or food has been delivered, are eliminated from the production process.[67] Labour can be put on stand-by and used only when it is deemed productive. In this sense, the 'gig economy' realises what the anarchist writer Colin Ward foresaw in 1995 – that 'capital has achieved its object which was to eliminate labour'.[68]

IV. Anarchism and Labour Law

A. Anarchism and Authority

Despite the nuances distinguishing different approaches, the refusal of authoritarian relationships is an element that all anarchist thinkers and anarchist practices share. Although the view of an anarcho-individualist, such as Max Stirner, differs from the view of an anarcho-communist, such as Pëtr Kropotkin,[69] they converge on considering autonomy from coercion and the liberation of free individuals as the values of an anarchist society.

The anarchist spectrum can be divided into two macro-approaches: a political anarchism, orientated towards direct action and mass organising, and a philosophical

[65] MA Cherry, 'Beyond Misclassification: The Digital Transformation of Work' (2016) 37 *Comparative Labor Law & Policy Journal* 577, 597.

[66] See also de Stefano, 'Rise of the "Just-in-Time Workforce"' (n 58) 476.

[67] J Prassl and M Risak, 'Uber, Taskrabbit, and Co: Platforms as Employers? Rethinking the Legal Analysis of Crowdwork' (2016) 37 *Comparative Labor Law & Policy Journal* 619, 625.

[68] C Ward, 'The Factory We Never Had (1995)' in C Wilbert and DF White (eds), *Autonomy, Solidarity, Possibility: The Colin Ward Reader* (Oakland, AK Press, 2011) 187.

[69] Max Stirner rejected any form of political or social organisation and moral obligation that could impose constraints on the freedom of the individual. Instead, Piotr Kropotkin and the anarchist communists (as well as the anarcho-syndicalists) believe in the free association of individuals into collective organisations.

anarchism, engaged in the intellectual problematisation of political legitimacy. Yet anarchist thinkers are often directly engaged in social activism. For instance, Pierre-Joseph Proudhon, Mikhail Bakunin, and Errico Malatesta (to recount the most famous examples) divided their activities between intellectual analysis and the organising of social movements amongst the working class and farmers.[70] However, what best defines anarchism is its 'scepticism towards authority'.[71] In a nutshell, 'anarchism is a doctrine that aims at the liberation of peoples from political domination and economic exploitation by the encouragement of direct or non-governmental action'.[72]

The ultimate value for anarchists is the freedom of the individual, which is expressed by their autonomy, but which conflicts with the authority exercised by social, political, and economic power.[73] In philosophical anarchism, 'authority' is defined as '*a form of domination*' that 'involves the capacity of one party to exercise control over another party'.[74] Further, authority is 'a dominative social power that is binding and content-independent, necessarily involving recognition and submission by its subjects, which uses coercion even if it is not defined by it'.[75] Coercion and domination are two constitutive elements of the principle of authority: the power of one party in a social relationship to force the other party to adopt certain behaviour. The employment relationship can be easily conceptualised in these terms.

The anarchist vision of society implies the persistence of certain (non-authoritarian) authorities which, however, are put into question and required to demonstrate their legitimacy.[76] While refusing authoritarian forms of socio-political relationships, anarchism accepts and fosters authority 'from below' as legitimised by the free and voluntary collective association of individuals.[77] A free and voluntary decision that legitimises the authority of a collective of individuals does not curtail the autonomy of the individual, rather it seeks to amplify it.

The basic tenet of anarchism is to question any form of authority and any duties that the individual is subjected to in society. For philosophical anarchism, the rejection of authority is an intellectual exercise that implies seeking moral (and ethical) legitimacy for any individual action imposed by social and legal rules.[78]

[70] Kinna, *Anarchism* (n 2) 10–11.

[71] P McLaughlin, *Anarchism and Authority: A Philosophical Introduction to Classical Anarchism* (London, Routledge, 2016) 29.

[72] Kinna, *Anarchism* (n 2) 3.

[73] RP Wolff, *In Defense of Anarchism* (Berkeley, University of California Press, 1998) 18–19.

[74] McLaughlin, *Anarchism and Authority* (n 71) 54 (emphasis in original).

[75] M Egoumenides, *Philosophical Anarchism and Political Obligation* (New York, Bloomsbury Academic, 2014) 39.

[76] For instance, the anarchists do not challenge parental authority as such: see McLaughlin, *Anarchism and Authority* (n 71) 33.

[77] RT De George, 'Anarchism and Authority' in JR Pennock and JW Chapman (eds), *Anarchism* (New York, New York University Press, 1978) 91.

[78] See M Huemer, *The Problem of Political Authority: An Examination of the Right to Coerce and the Duty to Obey* (Houndmills, Palgrave Macmillan, 2013). This might sound similar in socialist anarchist and anarcho-capitalist thinking. Yet the tools and solutions are very different.

But the political stream of anarchism firmly believes that 'inegalitarian and hierarchical social structures [make] freedom impossible'.[79] The aim of anarchism is to overthrow artificial hierarchical structures that exploit, coerce, and dominate, which have been created through ideas instilled 'by minorities of priests, military chiefs and judges, all striving to establish their domination, and of scientists paid to perpetuate it'.[80] For Bakunin, '[t]he freedom of individuals is by no means an individual matter. It is a collective matter, a collective product. No individual can be free outside of human society or without its cooperation'.[81] Therefore, in anarchist thinking, freedom is an individual value, to be achieved, and exercised collectively.

B. Anarchism and the Law

The primary object of the anarchist critique is the state which, through its normative power (ie, the laws that it enacts), claims legitimate authority.[82] Anarchists believe that the principle of authority is entrenched in the political principle on which the state is built, thus conflicting with the social principle on which an anarchist society must be grounded.[83]

In anarchism, the state is rejected as an artificial construction and as the expression of the ruler class. Anarchism denies and contests the Hobbesian theory of the social contract entered into by free individuals to remedy their state of nature by creating a supreme authority – the state – to channel the individualistic and violent human nature into forms of political representation.[84] From an anarchist perspective, the state does not hold legitimacy to rule, since it has been imposed rather than self-imposed by the individuals over which it rules.[85] Accordingly, anarchists question the obligation to obey the law, whose authority 'stems from the fact that the sovereign has willed it, not because it corresponds to the laws of nature or principles of natural justice'.[86]

Anarchists reject the metaphysical origin of law implied by social contract theory and, instead, focus on its anthropological and historical origins.[87] Law is the expression of social relationships established in society, and often the

[79] van der Walt and Schmidt, *Black Flame* (n 2) 47.
[80] P Kropotkin, 'Anarchism: Its Philosophy and Ideal' in RN Baldwin (ed), *Kropotkin's Revolutionary Pamphlets: A Collection of Writings by Peter Kropotkin* (first published 1927, New York, Dover, 1970) 114, 123.
[81] M Bakunin, 'Three Lectures to Swiss Members of the International' in RM Cutler (ed), *The Basic Bakunin: Writings, 1869–1871* (New York, Prometheus, 1992) 39, 46.
[82] McLaughlin, *Anarchism and Authority* (n 71) 82.
[83] C Ward, 'Anarchism as a Theory of Organisation (1966)' in C Wilbert and DF White (eds), *Autonomy, Solidarity, Possibility: The Colin Ward Reader* (Oakland, AK Press, 2011) 47.
[84] A Carter, *The Political Theory of Anarchism* (first published 1971, London, Routledge, 2010) 15.
[85] Egoumenides, *Philosophical Anarchism* (n 75) 40.
[86] Carter, *Political Theory of Anarchism* (n 84) 22.
[87] Kropotkin, 'Modern Science' (n 3) 175.

expression of the will of the dominant class, which crystallises its dominant position in society through law.[88] For Bakunin, the inherently violent nature of law,[89] which requires coercive enforcement to remedy disobedience, does not fulfil the ideal aim of justice, but rather perpetrates the domination of exploited classes.[90] Kropotkin affirms that the force of law and the force of capital have evolved hand in hand.[91] The legal system is conceived in a way that supports and reproduces the economic system in which it is generated, by creating and protecting those legal institutions that preserve the socio-economic relationships on which such a system is based.[92]

Rather than hierarchical and centralised forms of socio-political organisation (such as the state or the capitalist company), anarchists believe in horizontal and decentralised forms of collective organisations in which the social principle is expressed through the free, voluntary, and egalitarian association of individuals.[93] The rejection of a hierarchical form of political organisation does not automatically renounce any form of organisation. The most important distinction that anarchists make concerns the divide between 'state' and 'society'. For anarchists, the state is *a* form of societal organisation. Accordingly, state and government are different entities: the state is a historically contextualised form of socio-political organisation; whereas government, meant as the entity governing social relationships, can assume different forms – also non-authoritarian – of organising society.[94]

The anarchist vision of the state might sound similar to the critique advanced by neoliberals. Yet anarchists envision a society of collectively organised individuals, rather than the society of atomised individuals promoted by neoliberals. The anarchist vision implies that free individuals shall associate voluntarily with the intention of self-governing aspects of socio-political and economic life. The social contract assumes the form of the voluntary decision to share the common burden of self-government. In the words of Kropotkin:

> The anarchists conceive a society in which all the mutual relations of its members are regulated, not by laws, not by authorities, whether self-imposed or elected, but by mutual agreements between the members of that society and by a sum of social customs and habits – not petrified by law, routine, or superstition, but continually developing and continually readjusted in accordance with the ever-growing requirements of a free life stimulated by the progress of science, invention, and the steady growth of higher ideals.[95]

[88] P Kropotkin, 'Law and Authority' in RN Baldwin (ed), *Kropotkin's Revolutionary Pamphlets: A Collection of Writings by Peter Kropotkin* (first published 1927, New York, Dover, 1970) 195, 196.

[89] Carter, *Political Theory of Anarchism* (n 84) 42.

[90] Bakunin, 'Three Lectures' (n 81) 57–58.

[91] Kropotkin, 'Law and Authority' (n 88) 207.

[92] See A Pannekoek, *Workers' Councils* (first published 1948, Oakland, AK Press, 2003) 14–15.

[93] See C Ward, 'Anarchist Sociology of Federalism (1992)' in C Wilbert and DF White (eds), *Autonomy, Solidarity, Possibility: The Colin Ward Reader* (Oakland, AK Press, 2011).

[94] On these distinctions, see Carter, *Political Theory of Anarchism* (n 84) 28–29.

[95] Kropotkin, 'Modern Science' (n 3) 157.

Therefore, the anarchist vision takes the idea of 'living law' to the extreme and considers the law as an evolving set of rules that is constantly re-negotiated by members of the polity, and which develops according to societal advancements.

The organisations that anarchists favour are based on the 'principle of federalism', which requires freely entered contracts by individuals, and federations between collective organisations.[96] In legal terms, the contract is the legal lynchpin of an anti-authoritarian society, not based on the vertical and authoritarian relationship between the citizens and the state. The original status of a free and voluntary contract would also imply the absence of any enforcement mechanisms, as the individuals would be aware and respectful of the self-assumed obligations that free choice implies.[97] In opposing the idea of a society organised vertically on the basis of a (fictious) contract between rulers and citizens, Proudhon indicates – in the contract between peers – the foundation of an anarchist society grounded in self-government, mutualism, and federalism.[98] Thus, self-government shall be based on a system of contracts that replace the system of state laws.[99] Based on a voluntary exchange and reciprocity, rather than on coercion, these contracts would enhance unity and solidarity by providing a structure to the horizontal organisation of production and the collective satisfaction of needs.[100]

The employment contract, as we know it, does not fit within this category as it is not concluded between free peers. For Bakunin, the authority of socio-economic power derives from the fact that individuals are not born free in society, but rather in conditions that oblige them to enter into unbalanced contracts, such as the employment one.[101] As for labour legislation, in 1913, Kropotkin observed how it – although adopted under the guise of a protective instrument – constituted a tool compelling the worker to perform compulsory working hours, and to keep selling their labour, thus exposing them to the employer's authority.[102]

C. Anarchism and the Workplace

In light of the above discussion, a question arises: if anarchists refuse to accept an economic system based on the subordinated employment relationship, how do they envisage the socio-economic dynamics established around production? The anarchist does not aim at eliminating work or abolishing industrial production.

[96] R Graham, 'The Role of Contract in Anarchist Ideology' in D Goodway (ed), *For Anarchism: History, Theory, and Practice* (London, Routledge, 1989) 156–57; WH George, 'Proudhon and Economic Federalism' (1922) 30 *Journal of Political Economy* 531, 534.

[97] See Graham, 'Role of Contract' (n 96) 165.

[98] J Jennings, 'Rousseau, Social Contract and the Modern Leviathan' in D Boucher and P Kelly (eds), *The Social Contract from Hobbes to Rawls* (London, Routledge, 2004) 130.

[99] P-J Proudhon, *General Idea of the Revolution in the Nineteenth Century* (JB Robinson tr, first published 1923, New York, Haskell House Publishers, 1969) 206.

[100] ibid, also cited in Graham, 'Role of Contract' (n 96) 153.

[101] Bakunin, 'Three Lectures' (n 81) 46.

[102] Kropotkin, 'Modern Science' (n 3) 175–76.

The goal of anarchism is rather to replace the vertical and authoritarian organisation of the capitalist company with a horizontal relationship, in which production is managed and directed by a self-organised collective of workers, who share decision-making power on an equal footing.

On the means and strategies to achieve this aim, anarchists have different ideas: Proudhonian mutualism based on workers' cooperatives and small owners differs from the revolutionary road proposed by Bakunin, who advocates the collectivisation of property through a revolutionary overturning of the capitalist system.[103] Similarly, the anarcho-syndicalists' stance to achieve power through general strikes[104] differs from the scientific approach of Kropotkin, who envisioned a world of labour without distinctions between intellectual and manual work, and free from wage labour.[105]

Despite such differences, again, some common features can be found: for anarchists, the spheres of labour and production must be organised around the collective organisation of trade unions (or workers' councils) and guided by the principles of cooperation, direct action, workers' autonomy and control, and the decentralisation of production.[106] Tom Cahill outlines the 'five qualities' on which anarchist economic organisation is grounded: it must be '(1) decentralised, (2) egalitarian, (3) self-managing and empowering, (4) based on local needs and (5) supported by other autonomous units in a non-hierarchical fashion'.[107]

The ownership of the means of production is key in this regard. The anarchist opposes private property and considers it 'theft';[108] but the dispossession and accumulation of property by the state would only entail a different form of exploitation. Anarchist economic production would instead be grounded in collective ownership[109] and workers' control.[110] Socio-economic organisation would be left to the trade unions and economic production to cooperatives.[111] These two forms of organisation constitute the cornerstone of the anarchist view on labour and employment based upon mutualism and reciprocity; that is, on solidarity.

[103] On this distinction, see van der Walt and Schmidt, *Black Flame* (n 2) 84–85.

[104] See R Rocker, *Anarcho-Syndicalism: Theory and Practice*, 6th edn (first published 1938, Oakland, AK Press, 2004); FF Ridley, *Revolutionary Syndicalism in France: The Direct Action of Its Time* (first published 1970, Cambridge, Cambridge University Press, 2008).

[105] See P Kropotkin, *The Conquest of Bread and Other Writings* (Cambridge, Cambridge University Press, 1995); Graham, 'Role of Contract' (n 96) 163–64.

[106] C Ward, 'The State (1988)' in C Wilbert and DF White (eds), *Autonomy, Solidarity, Possibility: The Colin Ward Reader* (Oakland, AK Press, 2011) 17.

[107] T Cahill, 'Co-Operatives and Anarchism' in D Goodway (ed), *For Anarchism: History, Theory, and Practice* (London, Routledge, 1989) 244.

[108] The obvious reference is to Proudhon's classical work, *What is Property?* (1840).

[109] On this point, Bakunin opposed Proudhon. Whereas the latter claimed the maintenance of small ownership, Bakunin claimed the complete and total collectivisation of land and property: see M Bakunin, 'On Cooperation' in RM Cutler (ed), *The Basic Bakunin: Writings, 1869–1871* (New York, Prometheus, 1992) 151, 153.

[110] Cahill, 'Co-Operatives and Anarchism (n 107) 242.

[111] Yet some anarchist movements question the role of trade unions as the product of a capitalist system, created in order to collaborate with the employers: see van der Walt and Schmidt, *Black Flame* (n 2) 138; Rocker, *Anarcho-Syndicalism* (n 104) 59.

In order to combat the accumulation of capital and the ensuing authoritarian forms of employment, Kropotkin proposed to decentralise production, which would be carried out in small workshops, and to reject the theory of division of labour, which is at the basis of an authoritarian organisation of the company.[112] In his view (Kropotkin talks about the 'integration of labour'), by blurring the distinctions between workers – between the tasks that they perform, and between the knowledge that they possess – production and labour can be re-organised on non-authoritarian bases.[113] For Proudhon, the cooperative and the union represent instruments that workers have for self-organising their labour, even in complex industries, or in factories where a certain kind of 'managerial organisation' would be required.[114] On a macro-scale, trade unions would constitute the supreme form of anarchist organisation in the economy, acting as 'labour cartels' on different scales: a union (or workers' councils) in the workplace tasked with organising production within the factory or workshop; a federation of unions responsible for organising the total production of a country; and a confederation of federations positioned to build cooperation between countries.[115]

This anarchist vision of workplace organisation might surely sound utopian. However, it provides a basis for exploring alternatives to the dominant neoliberal logic. In this sense, researchers in critical management studies seek, in the anarchist alternative, new perspectives for managing and organising complex structures for the benefit of individual freedom.[116] As for concrete anarchist experiences of re-organising production and the economy at large, history only provides us with ephemeral attempts. Examples are the dramatic experience of the Paris Commune in 1871, and the anarchist insurrection that occurred in some regions of Spain, in particular, Catalonia and Aragon, during the 1936–1939 civil war.[117]

Yet, in the maze of the capitalist system, several non-authoritarian experiences have emerged in the attempt to democratise the economy and to carry out production outside the authoritarian structure of the company. For instance, workers' cooperatives constitute the backbone of social movements that have arisen to achieve more democratic control over economic production and business

[112] M de Geus, 'Peter Kropotkin's Anarchist Vision of Organization' (2014) 14 *Ephemera. Theory & Politics in Organization* 859, 868–69.

[113] P Kropotkin, *Fields, Factories and Workshops* (first published 1899, London, Swan Sonnenschein & Co, 1901) 5–6.

[114] Proudhon, *General Idea of the Revolution* (n 99) 216.

[115] Rocker, *Anarcho-Syndicalism* (n 104) 63.

[116] For an overview, see T Swann and K Stoborod, 'Did You Hear the One About the Anarchist Manager?' (2014) 14 *Ephemera: Theory & Politics in Organization* 591; see also P Reedy, 'Impossible Organisations: Anarchism and Organisational Praxis' (2014) 14 *Ephemera: Theory & Politics in Organization* 639, 652.

[117] For the Paris Commune experience, see D Gluckstein, 'Workers' Councils in Europe: A Century of Experience' in I Ness and D Azzellini (eds), *Ours to Master and to Own: Workers' Councils from the Commune to the Present* (Chicago, Haymarket Books, 2011). For the Spanish experience, see A Souchy, 'Workers' Self-Management in Industry' in S Dolgoff (ed), *The Anarchist Collectives: Workers' Self-Management in the Spanish Revolution, 1936–1939* (New York, Free Life Editions, 1974).

organisation.[118] An illustrative example is the movement of cooperatives (*empresas recuperadas*) that emerged in Argentina in the aftermath of the 2001 economic crisis, through which workers at risk of losing their jobs occupied factories, and recovered the business by re-organising production on anti-authoritarian and horizontal bases.[119] Empirical studies on these experiences illustrate how these cooperatives work through collective decision-making. The workers' cooperatives have put in place a horizontal management system based on a general assembly, in which all workers participate and have the right to vote. The general assembly then elects a more restricted directive council that runs the operations of the business, but which is constantly accountable to the general assembly.[120] The inevitable tendency towards the reproduction of authoritarian forms of management is offset by a wide prerogative granted to each worker to demand information about business decisions, and to contest them on behalf of the collective of workers.[121] The need to maintain certain standards of productivity has, however, pushed the workers' cooperatives to adopt internal rules that include discipline sanctions. Here, managerial authority is substituted with *self*-discipline, which is *self*-imposed by a collective of workers, and which is the ultimate decision-maker as well as beneficiary.[122] Collective organising and solidarity are thus the principles upon which non-authoritarian forms of employment are based.

Collective self-organising, and solidarity between peer workers, represent the core of attempts 'from below' where workers in the 'gig economy' have engaged to achieve recognition and better working conditions. For instance, in the Italian city of Bologna, a collective of riders working for food delivery digital platforms established the Riders' Union; an autonomous rank-and-file union that organises campaigns to create awareness around the poor working conditions and precarity of gig workers.[123] In May 2018, the Riders' Union succeeded in signing a 'Charter of the fundamental rights of digital work in the urban context' (*Carta dei diritti fondamentali del lavoro digitale nel contesto urbano*) with the municipality, the major trade unions, and two local digital platforms for food delivery.[124]

[118] M Vieta, 'The Stream of Self-Determination and *Autogestión*: Prefiguring Alternatives Economic Realities' (2014) 14 *Ephemera: Theory & Politics in Organization* 781, 795.

[119] See International Labour Office, *Job Preservation Through Worker Cooperatives: An Overview of International Experiences and Strategies* (2014) www.ilo.org/actrav/info/pubs/WCMS_312039/lang--en/index.htm accessed 29 December 2018.

[120] See, for instance, M Atzeni and P Ghigliani, 'Labour Process and Decision-Making in Factories under Workers' Self-Management: Empirical Evidence from Argentina' (2007) 21 *Work, Employment and Society* 653. See also the documentary written by Naomi Klein: *The Take* (Avi Lewis dir, Barna-Alper Productions & National Film Board of Canada, 2004) www.youtube.com/watch?v=3-DSu8RPJt8 accessed 29 December 2018.

[121] Atzeni and Ghigliani, 'Labour Process and Decision-Making' (n 120) 663.

[122] ibid 667. However, the authors stress that the disappearance of managerial authority would expose the workers to the discipline imposed by market forces.

[123] R Ciccarelli, 'Avanti Riders! Oggi la prima assemblea nazionale dei ciclo-fattorini a Bologna' *Il Manifesto* (15 April 2018) https://ilmanifesto.it/avanti-riders-oggi-prima-assemblea-nazionale-dei-ciclo-fattorini-a-bologna/ accessed 29 December 2018.

[124] 'Bologna, il 31 maggio la firma della carta sui rider: "E'il primo accord europeo sul delivery food"' *La Repubblica.it* (Bologna, 25 May 2018) https://bologna.repubblica.it/cronaca/2018/05/25/news/bologna_carta_rider-197310179/ accessed 29 December 2018.

The Charter sets, inter alia, the right of workers to be properly and correctly informed about the terms of their contract; the right to a fair and decent hourly wage; the right to receive compensation for night work, work during holidays, and work in adverse atmospheric conditions; and the right to collective action in the form of collectively withdrawing from work.[125]

Further examples reflecting the anti-authoritarian experience of workplace organisation include the movement of so-called 'Platform cooperativism', which proposes an alternative economic model based upon a different use of technology to oppose the narrative and practices of 'platform capitalism'; that is, the business model operated by the digital companies of the 'gig economy'.[126] Platform cooperativism includes a wide array of different experiences that range from taxi driver cooperatives owned by unions, to media service cooperatives owned by workers, to other experiences in which the figures of producer and user blend in an attempt to use the available technology to organise the production of digital services horizontally.[127] The minimum common denominator of these experiences is an ideological view proposing a solidaristic model, based upon collective ownership, small-business, decent pay and fair working conditions, income security and workers' involvement in business-related decisions[128] – all principles ascribable to the anarchist tradition.

V. Anti-Authoritarian Employment Relations?

What contribution to labour law and labour law scholarship can be derived from anarchism? Primarily, the anarchist view permits a radical critique of the foundations and function of labour law. Labour law, rather than being praised as a protective tool, is questioned as the means through which labour exploitation is perpetrated. From an anarchist perspective, the idea of protecting the worker *within* the subordination of employment simply fails. For anarchism, there is no liberation in this – rather, it is the codification of the authority of the employer. Secondly, an anarchist perspective challenges the bilateral conception of the employment relationship. Following anarchist principles, workplaces can be organised horizontally, by and through a collective of workers (thus *self*-organised). This questions the capitalist company as the only possible mechanism for economic organisation, and necessarily involves discussion of questions related to private property,

[125] The Charter text (in Italian) is available at Comune di Bologna, 'Firmata a Bologna la "Carta dei diritti fondamentali dei lavoratori digitali nel contest urbano"' (*Iperbole*, 31 May 2018) www.comune.bologna.it/news/firmata-bologna-la-carta-dei-diritti-fondamentali-dei-lavoratori-digitali-nel-contesto-urbano accessed 29 December 2018.

[126] F Pasquale, 'Two Narratives of Platform Capitalism' (2016) 35 *Yale Law & Policy Review* 309.

[127] T Scholz, *Platform Cooperativism: Challenging the Corporate Sharing Economy* (New York, Rosa Luxembourg Stiftung, 2016) www.rosalux-nyc.org/platform-cooperativism-2/ accessed 29 December 2018.

[128] ibid 18–19.

political organisation, and socio-economic inequalities. Thirdly, the anarchist perspective argues against the assumption that the worker must work to produce profit for the benefit of the employer. Horizontal and self-managed economic organisations, such as cooperatives, would instead redistribute earnings amongst the workers themselves.[129]

Overall, anarchism offers a radical perspective to counter the radical changes that the realm of labour, work, and employment have undergone with the contemporary neoliberal socio-economic dynamic. The economic power accumulated by multinational companies has become political power, and therefore requires a political response. As advocated by Ruth Dukes, the globalisation of the economy does not modify the foundations of labour law.[130] Examining past experiences, ideas, and concepts to understand the contemporary dynamics of labour markets is not a nostalgic exercise, not does it imply an antiquated or conservative view. Dukes provides an example of how this approach can be used effectively with her conceptualisation of the 'labour constitution'; an approach based upon the work of Kahn-Freund and Sinzheimer. However, in looking to the past, one must remain focused on the present socio-economic reality.

The dynamics of economic globalisation marginalise the state from its role as the protective authority of employment. The transnational scope of capital allows multinational companies to escape the strictures of national labour laws.[131] Labour market flexibility subverts the traditional elements of the employment relationship, without eradicating the subjugation of workers to the authority of the employer, but instead by producing new forms of authority and dependency,[132] and atomising the workforce into 'micro-labour'.[133] The forms of work produced by the 'gig economy' demolish the foundations of labour law as we know it, and highlight the shortcomings and contradictions of a legal understanding of work grounded on the contract of employment. Given this, we ought to reflect upon whether the current form of labour law still manages to effectively capture the socio-economic reality of work in Western societies. The socio-economic conditions in which the contract of employment emerged are fundamentally altered. Technological change renders the legal protection of work, channelled through the contract of employment, at risk of disappearing entirely.

[129] See B Jossa, *L'impresa democratica: Un sistema di imprese cooperative come nuovo modo di produzione* (Roma, Carocci, 2008).

[130] R Dukes, *The Labour Constitution: The Enduring Idea of Labour Law* (Oxford, Oxford University Press, 2014). See also A Iossa, 'Collective Autonomy in the European Union: Theoretical, Comparative and Cross-Border Perspectives on the Legal Regulation of Collective Bargaining' (Doctoral thesis, Lund University, 2017).

[131] Inter alia, J Fudge and G Mundlak, 'Justice in a Globalizing World: Resolving Conflicts Involving Workers' Rights Beyond the Nation State' in Y Dahan, H Lerner and F Milman-Sivan (eds), *Global Justice and International Labour Rights* (Cambridge, Cambridge University Press, 2016).

[132] See also G Davidov, *A Purposive Approach to Labour Law* (Oxford, Oxford University Press, 2016) 116.

[133] Cherry, 'Beyond Misclassification' (n 65) 598.

Consequently, labour law needs to be reinvented and disentangled from the subordinated employment relationship, and from its constitutionalised expression. The image of the worker as a wage-earner is obsolete. The protection of workers' dignity must transcend the distinction between employed and unemployed, as it is within the contradictions of this distinction that exploitation takes place.[134] If legal subordination fades away, the reality of the economic dependence of workers emerges and demands renewed attention towards addressing the socio-economic nature of subordination in the realm of work.[135] New forms of labour law need to emerge 'from below' with the aim of democratising the economy by democratising workplaces. Although utopian, the anarchist perspective challenges us to re-think labour law and the entire economic system in which it was conceived. The success of certain cooperative experiences, such as the Mondragon Cooperatives, relies upon the relationship that horizontal forms of economic organisation build with the surrounding community.[136] Whilst not explicitly informed by anarchism, those experiences tell us that anti-authoritarian employment relations can emerge from the downfalls and pitfalls of capitalism to revolutionise the basis of the economic system. Emancipatory labour policies must be as radical as neoliberal policies of labour market flexibilisation; however, instead, they ought to be directed at empowering workers by challenging the authority of the subjects that exploit labour. Ultimately, the socio-economic evolution requires labour law to evolve as well, with a call for labour lawyers to move beyond the current parameters of labour law to imagine innovative solutions that keep its role and struggle alive.

[134] See M Denning, 'Wageless Life' (2010) 66 *New Left Review* 79–97. See also R Ciccarelli, *Forza lavoro: Il lato oscuro della rivoluzione digitale* (Roma, DeriveApprodi, 2018), who suggests grounding worker protection in the right to existence, thus moving beyond protection ensured only via employment.

[135] See H Arthurs, 'Labor Law as the Law of Economic Subordination and Resistance: A Thought Experiment' (2013) 34 *Comparative Labor Law & Policy Journal* 585. See generally, N Countouris, *The Changing Law of the Employment Relationship: Comparative Analyses in the European Context* (first published 2007, Abingdon, Routledge, 2016) 62. A spark for reflecting upon the socio-economic, rather than legal, nature of subordination is evident in the case law of the European Court of Justice: see, eg, Case C-413/13 *FNV Kunsten Informatie en Media v Staat der Nederlanden* (ECJ, 4 December 2014).

[136] See A Latinne, *The Mondragon Cooperatives: Workplace Democracy and Globalisation* (Cambridge, Intersentia, 2014).

15

Challenging Labour Law's 'Productivity' Bias Through a Feminist Lens: A Conversation

ANIA ZBYSZEWSKA* AND SUPRIYA ROUTH**

I. Introduction

The changing nature of work, work relations, composition of labour markets, and the new global division of labour have challenged lawyers to think beyond standard employment and related regulatory models, and beyond the jurisdictional spaces of traditional labour law. A common analytical feature of the various efforts to 'stretch' labour law to encompass an ever-increasing range of work activities, and extend legal protections to the people who carry them out, is the claim that these activities can be viewed through the lens of economically *productive* 'employment-like' relationships.[1] This approach tends to make sense, given labour law's historic constitution and related normative goals. Labour law regimes, as they were variously institutionalised after the industrial revolution, especially during the post-World War II period, pertained to and, indeed, standardised, particular forms of waged work carried out with the purpose of producing goods or services in the formally organised economy. The focus in legal scholarship on work's productive, economic contribution has stemmed partly from the fact that one

* Assistant Professor, Department of Law and Legal Studies, Carleton University. We would like to thank Emily Grabham and Nicole Busby, as well as Miriam Kullmann and Alysia Blackham, for their valuable comments on this chapter. Some ideas presented in this chapter also appear in the following article: A Zbyszewska, 'Regulating Work with People and "Nature" in Mind: Feminist Reflections' (2018) 40 *Comparative Labor Law and Policy Journal* 9.

** Assistant Professor, Faculty of Law, University of Victoria, Canada. Arguments offered in this chapter have received a more comprehensive treatment in the article: Supriya Routh, 'Revisiting Social Reproduction: Migrant Care Workers And Their Entitlements in Canada' (2019) 35:2 International Journal of Comparative Labour Law and Industrial Relations 1.

[1] See S Routh, 'Embedding Work in Nature: The Anthropocene and Legal Imagination of Work as Human Activity', for a discussion of how varied perspectives of labour law either explicitly or implicitly accept an employment-centric economic exchange as foundational for any regulatory (re)imagination: (2018) 40 *Comparative Labor Law and Policy Journal* 129.

of labour law's historic functions, at least in the context of capitalist economies, has been to facilitate some (however limited) re-balancing of bargaining power between workers and owners, employers and employees, and re-distribution (however incomplete) of the gains achieved in the process of production, which, in capitalism, is so asymmetrically structured.[2]

Similarly, the pursuit of humanisation of subordinated labour through a plethora of legal standards intended to render work safer, more dignified, and more adaptable to workers' needs, has historically been secured through claims about the benefits of such rights *also* for enterprise productivity and economic efficiency. Rights to occupational health and safety, rest periods, leisure and time away from work, are all exemplary here.[3] Moreover, given the limited possibilities for securing a livelihood outside of paid employment or of accessing various social entitlements and drawing rights, it is unsurprising that the notion of paid work as an essential aspect of human life, a route to self-actualisation and personal development, and a key aspect of active, meaningful citizenship has become a common refrain in labour law theorising in relation to both rights *to*[4] and *at* work.

Seen in this light, the approach of troubling labour law's boundaries and seeking to extend them to encompass once excluded forms of work on the basis that they are analogous to those that had been within the scope of protection, not least because they make economic and productive contributions, questions the discipline's assumptions while maintaining some fidelity to its original normative and political goals, and modes of justification. And yet, viewed through the lens of some recent critical scholarship on work, work encroachment, or alternative forms of valuation on the one hand, and the predictions of the end of work (the disappearance of many jobs due to digitisation or, at least, the impossibility of full employment) on the other hand, this approach may have some limitations.[5] For one, even if it has the potential to accept more of the plethora of employment-like activities in which people engage to make a living (or a life) under labour law's

[2] The notion that of labour law's key historic functions has been to act as a countervailing force to counteract the inequality of bargaining power is broadly accepted in labour law scholarship: P Davies and M Freedland, *Kahn-Freund's Labour and the Law*, 3rd edn (London, Stevens, 1983). More recently, scholars have reframed this function around the notion of non-domination; namely, this law's role in minimisation of the domination exerted by an employer over an employee: D Cabrelli and R Zahn, 'Critical Republican Political Theory and Labour Law' in H Collins, G Lester, and V Mantouvalou (eds), *Philosophical Foundations of Labour Law* (Oxford, Oxford University Press, 2018).

[3] As are, indeed, the more contemporary rights to work-family reconciliation, maternity and parental leaves, and other accommodations for care provision.

[4] On the treatment of the 'right to work' see, V Mantouvalou (ed), *The Right to Work: Legal and Philosophical Perspectives* (Oxford, Hart Publishing, 2015).

[5] See, ie K Weeks, *The Problem with Work. Feminism, Marxism, Antiwork Politics, and Postwork Imaginaries* (Durham, Duke University Press, 2011); D Frayne, *The Refusal of Work. The Theory and Practice of Resistance to Work* (London, Zed Books, 2015); J Ferguson, *Give a Man a Fish. Reflections on the New Politics of Distribution* (Durham, Duke University Press, 2015). All three books provide an excellent overview of longer term debates problematising work and productivism in mainstream and leftist thinking.

protective umbrella, in emphasising the *economically productive* nature of these activities, we might risk reducing their actual value and much wider-reaching *social* contributions. This is especially the case for forms of work that are associated with care and domestic labour, as well as other work associated with the process of reproducing and sustaining life and social bonds. In so doing, such an approach also risks reifying paid, productive work – a mode of market exchange – as a central and necessary aspect of people's lives. As such, it may inadvertently play into and reproduce the economic, productivity, and growth-orientated discourses that dominate the mainstream (neoliberal) policy of today, but which have also long been present in certain strands of leftist or, as Guy Standing recently called it, 'labourist' thinking about work.[6]

With this critical contention as our common vantage point – beyond which we partly disagree – our reflection here aims to revisit some ways in which feminist labour lawyers have critically engaged in debates on recognising, valuing and protecting various forms of work, including those that have been traditionally marginalised or entirely excluded from labour law's scope. We are especially interested in probing the extent to which these critical contributions have also managed to challenge the implicit (if unintentional) productivism underlying labour law as a discipline and a regulatory field. To account for our points of agreement and disagreement, as well as our varying perspectives, we adopt a conversational format; taking turns to respond to each other's reflections. As such, and at the risk of indulgence, rather than attempt a comprehensive review, our conversation below evolves organically around our research interests and perspectives, and in continuation of conversations we have had in the past.

We begin, in Section II, by highlighting efforts by feminist scholars in particular to shift labour law's narrow focus (Zbyszewska), and by reflecting also on the possible limitations of this scholarship (Routh). In Section III, we move to consider some complementary and alternative ways in which unpaid and paid forms of domestic and care work could be valued and justified as worthy of legal protection. While the notion of public good might be a useful tool in reconceptualising labour and expanding the scope of labour law (Routh), we also reflect on some of its limitations and consider ways in which they might be overcome (Zbyszewska). Ultimately, we conclude that an (organisational and regulatory) approach which emphasises the *social* significance/value of work, its contribution to the long-term sustainability and the social reproduction of communities is a more promising one in so far as recognition and protection of care and domestic work is concerned. At the same time, we acknowledge the need for this work's redistribution, so as to challenge the gendered, classed, and racialised ways in which it is currently organised both locally and globally, and re-emphasise the importance of spaces of freedom from work.

[6] G Standing, 'Left Should Stop Equating Labour with Work' (2018) *Social Europe* (23 March), available at www.socialeurope.eu/why-work-not-labour-is-ecological-imperative accessed on 14 January 2019.

II. Work, Production and Social Reproduction – Feminists Challenge Labour Law

A. Zbyszewska

One of the key challenges to labour law's exclusionary scope and productivity focus has come from its feminist critics, who have shown that legal norms have been central to demarcating and maintaining the boundary between the domains of family and work, and the sites of home and workplace.[7] A key contribution of this scholarship has been to question the neutrality of standard labour law norms, revealing them instead to be devised with male, unencumbered workers in mind, and as such implicated in the exclusion or marginalisation of women from standard employment, and the reproduction of gendered (as well as classed, racialised, heteronormative) assumptions about what counts as labour or work, which forms of work are valued, how work ought to be organised, and who deserves voice and protection.[8]

The 'discovery' of work-family conflict and the 'crisis' of care that have accompanied women's mass entry into labour markets from the 1970s on, especially in industrialised 'western' economies, have provided particularly fertile ground for this critique. At the same time, re-regulation of labour markets and the decline of trade unions, together with the progressive erosion of standard employment and the 'feminisation' of work, which have paralleled these processes, have left no doubt that traditional labour law norms have always been a product of time, place, and particular social, political, and economic settlements.[9] With this recognition, labour law's gendered (exclusionary) scope and the importance of adapting it to new realities have been accepted in mainstream scholarship, and in policy. And yet, despite significant regulatory adaptation, feminist scholars have shown, time and again, that these efforts have been too often instrumental and limited, rather than transformative, in so far as reconceiving labour law norms to

[7] For a good summary discussion of this wide-ranging feminist project see J Fudge, 'Feminist Reflections on the Scope of Labour Law: Domestic Work, Social Reproduction, and Jurisdiction' (2014) 22 *Feminist Legal Studies* 1; see also, J Conaghan and K Rittich, *Labour Law, Work, and Family: Critical and Comparative Perspectives* (Oxford, Oxford University Press, 2005).

[8] Among others, N Busby, *A Right to Care?: Unpaid Work in European Employment Law* (Oxford University Press, 2011); J Conaghan, 'Work, Family, and the Discipline of Labour Law', in J Conaghan and K Rittich (eds), *Labour Law, Work and Family: Critical and Comparative Perspectives* (Oxford, Oxford University Press, 2005) 19; J Conaghan and K Rittich, 'Introduction: Interrogating the Work/Family Divide', in J Conaghan and K Rittich (eds), *Labour Law, Work and Family: Critical and Comparative Perspectives* (Oxford, Oxford University Press, 2005) 1; S Fredman, *Women and the Law* (Oxford, Oxford University Press, 1997); J Fudge and R Owens, *Precarious Work, Women, and the New Economy: The Challenge to Legal Norms* (Oxford, Hart Publishing, 2006); A Zbyszewska, *Gendering European Working Time Regimes: The Working Time Directive and the Case of Poland* (Cambridge, Cambridge University Press, 2016); L Hayes, *Stories of Care: A Labour of Law* (London, Palgrave MacMillan, 2017).

[9] Fudge, 'Feminist Reflections' (n 7).

encompass and reflect its more diverse subjects, and the various sites where work takes place.[10]

Moreover, as Judy Fudge has observed in relation to how our discipline has addressed labour law's scope, even the more expansive intellectual efforts to re-consider the law's limitations and its potential have been reluctant to let go of its exclusion of *unpaid* household and care labour.[11] While casting the latter as labour for the purpose of regulation might be regarded as an inappropriate intrusion into bonds of love or private obligations, and could signify an effective commodification of these sorts of activities (if one function of labour law is to decommodify work), such questioning of labour law's jurisdiction is ultimately necessary to illuminate the structural dependence of paid work on unpaid work activities. As Fudge urges, such exclusion can be seen as a normatively valid choice only if we ignore that the separation of social reproduction (mainly women's unpaid labour within the household and in relation to care) from the realm of activity, was a historically contingent construction that labour law helped to maintain.[12]

The concept of social reproduction, as developed in feminist political economy, has been an important element in the theoretical toolkit that feminist labour law scholars use to unravel labour law's narrative. Social reproduction refers to the process of the daily and generational maintenance of the working population, but it is also necessary for the maintenance of economic, cultural and social bonds.[13] Variously theorised in feminist literature, social reproduction typically involves three aspects: biological reproduction, reproduction of labour power, and social practices connected to care, socialisation and fulfilment of human needs.[14] Crucially, feminist political economists such as Antonella Picchio, and many others, have shown not only that social reproductive work has been always entwined with what is considered productive activity, but also that the latter has always relied on it.[15] In the 'western' world, the historical splitting of labour

[10] S Fredman, 'Women at Work: The Broken Promise of Flexicurity' (2004) 33 *Industrial Law Journal* 299; Fudge and Owens, *Precarious Work, Women, and the New Economy* (n 8); V Schultz, 'Feminism and Workplace Flexibility' (2010) 42 *Connecticut Law Review* 1203; K Rittich, 'Families on the Edge: Governing Home and Work in a Globalized Economy' (2010) 88 *North Carolina Law Review* 1527; N Busby, 'The Evolution of Gender Equality and Related Employment Policies: The Case of Work-family Reconciliation' (2018) 18 *International Journal of Discrimination and the Law* 104; Zbyszewska, *Gendering European Working Time Regimes* (n 7); A Zbyszewska, 'Active Aging Through Employment: A Critical Feminist Perspective on Polish Policy' (2016) 32 *International Journal of Comparative Labour Law & Industrial Relations* 449.

[11] Fudge, 'Feminist Reflections' (n 7).

[12] ibid.

[13] K Bezanson and M Luxton (eds), *Social Reproduction: Feminist Political Economy Challenges Neoliberalism* (Montreal-Kingston, McGill-Queens University Press, 2006); I Bakker and R Silvey (eds), *Beyond States and Markets: The Challenges of Social Reproduction* (Abingdon, Routledge, 2008).

[14] I Bakker and S Gill (eds), *Power, Production and Social Reproduction* (Basingstoke, Palgrave Macmillan, 2003) 23.

[15] A Picchio, *Social Reproduction: The Political Economy of the Labour Market* (Oxford, Oxford University Press, 1992); K Rittich, *Recharacterizing Restructuring: Law Distribution and Gender in Market Reform* (New York, Kluwer, 2002).

into these two types – an outcome of the interplay of political, technological, and ideological developments – occurred during the transition from agrarian feudal societies to industrial ones.[16] It not only became physically more challenging to reconcile paid work in manufacturing and other industrial enterprises with the already gender-coded work of care,[17] but the subordination of social reproduction and its assignment to the sphere of private responsibility was also tied to the maximisation of profits.[18] Thus, capitalism drew the boundary between the two particularly sharply, although to some, albeit much more limited, extent this division also existed in state socialist countries.[19]

As feminist lawyers contend, the law played a crucial role in enacting and institutionalising this process of separation, and simultaneously became marked by it.[20] While the labour law regimes that developed out of the social crises and ruptures that accompanied the industrial revolution resulted from negotiated social (class-based) settlements, these regimes and the legal norms within them nonetheless referenced a very particular model and organisation of work, enabled only by the institutionalisation of parallel 'reproductive bargains',[21] to use Ruth Pearson's term, or gender contracts.[22] As such, even if these 'new' regimes instituted better systems of redistribution, representation, and protection for some working people, they were based on an explicitly gendered division of labour. Even if not all men's and women's actual practices and realities of work and life fit these models, their normative power was decisive in reproducing the separation of social reproduction (care especially) as something that is primarily, though not exclusively, confined to the private sphere of the home and family;[23] a domain not belonging to labour law.

The historic and ongoing misrecognition and undervaluing of the contributions (including economic) women (and some men too) make through their unpaid and paid affective and physical labour of maintaining lives, households, and communities, women's economic dependency and insecurity, their exclusion from or disadvantage in labour markets and social life are among some of the key artefacts and consequences of these particular policy choices. Thus, if we are to reconceive labour law's subjects and domains, we must address also the interdependence of production and social reproduction, as well as the role of law in

[16] Picchio, *Social Reproduction* (n 15); L Leete, 'History and Housework: Implications for Work Hours and Family Policy in Market Economies' in L Golden and D Figart (eds), *Working Time: International Trends, Theory and Policy Perspectives* (New York, Routledge, 2000) 233.

[17] Leete, 'History and Housework' (n 16).

[18] Picchio, *Social Reproduction* (n 15).

[19] Zbyszewska, *Gendering European Working Time Regimes* (n 8).

[20] J Fudge and B Cossman, 'Introduction' in B Cossman and J Fudge (eds), *Privatization, Law and the Challenge to Feminism* (Toronto, University of Toronto Press, 2002) 3.

[21] R Pearson, 'Renegotiating the Reproductive Bargain: Gender Analysis of Economic Transition in Cuba in the 1990s' (1997) 28 *Development And Change* 671.

[22] On the concept of 'gender contract': B Pfau-Effinger, 'The Gender Contract and Part-time Paid Work by Women: A Comparative Perspective' in S Duncan (ed), Spatial Divisions of Patriarchy in Western Europe. (1994) 26 *Environment And Planning A (Special Issue)* 1355.

[23] S Moller Okin, *Justice, Gender, and The Family* (New York, Basic Books, 1989).

ascribing value to certain forms of work and not others. Feminist lawyers have called for the recognition of caregiving as the basic human process that must be recognised, valued, and properly accommodated, and have proposed that the law should either recognise a 'right to care'[24] or even that we should reconsider a range of key labour law norms with a worker/caregiver – or an encumbered subject – as a normative baseline.[25] Ultimately, however, like feminist political theorists,[26] feminist lawyers also call for the *redistribution* of care work and other work of social reproduction among women and men and a range of institutions. This is in view of the fact that everyone who wishes to should be able to partake in and reap the mutual-benefits of the care relation,[27] while retaining the possibility of making meaningful choices about taking part in a range of social and economic activities without forfeiting their (relational) autonomy and freedom to do otherwise.[28]

B. Routh

The International Labour Organization (ILO) developed a legal instrument for domestic workers entitled Decent Work for Domestic Workers Convention and Recommendation in 2011, which constitutes formal international legal recognition of domestic work as an economically productive activity. While the Convention needs to be ratified by ILO member-states in order to be enforceable in their respective jurisdictions, the significance of the Convention lies in the general willingness of the ILO tripartite constituents to adduce formal recognition of widespread work, performed primarily by women workers. The justification offered for recognising domestic work as valuable work is that it contributes *to the global economy* (Preamble to Convention 189). Domestic work is valuable – and therefore wage-worthy – because domestic work produces future market participants.[29] Conceptually, therefore, the ILO Convention allows domestic workers a share of market efficiency.

In its economic logic, the ILO Convention recognises that by exchanging their labour through the market (prominently, by means of an employment relationship, although not limited to it), market participants (workers) indirectly connect domestic workers to the market in an economic exchange relationship. Arguably, then, because of efficient outcomes of the market exchange, market returns of a

[24] Busby, *A Right to Care* (n 8).

[25] Conaghan and Rittich, 'Introduction: Interrogating the Work/Family Divide' (n 8); J Fudge, 'The New Dual Earner Gender Contract: Work-life Balance or Working-time Flexibility?' in J Conaghan and K Rittich (eds), *Labour Law, Work and Family: Critical and Comparative Perspectives* (Oxford, Oxford University Press, 2005); Zbyszewska, *Gendering European Working Time Regimes* (n 8).

[26] N Fraser, *The Fortunes of Feminism* (London, Verso, 2013).

[27] Busby, *A Right to Care* (n 8).

[28] J Nedelsky, *Law's Relations: A Relational Theory of Self, Autonomy, and Law* (Oxford, Oxford University Press, 2011).

[29] A Blackett, 'Introduction: Regulating Decent Work for Domestic Workers' (2011) 23 *Canadian Journal of Women and the Law* 1, 1–5.

worker's labour should include economic returns for the domestic worker who was instrumental in creating that market-exchangeable labour. While this is the normative justification that seems to be the force behind the legal recognition of domestic work through the ILO instruments, more immediately, the ILO Convention is concerned with direct market exchange for domestic work, that is, paid domestic work through an employment relationship.

Feminist legal scholars have generally praised the ILO Convention for opening the domestic private space to public legal scrutiny.[30] The idea that domestic work is eventually market-productive has received international validation in formal legal terms, albeit to a limited extent.[31] It is true, as you noted above, that dissociating social reproduction from economic productivity of the market produces a distorted picture of economic reality. It is also true that if market-determined wages must be the only basis for taking cognisance of social reproduction, there is reason to argue that such wages include the share of home (domestic) workers. However, this conceptual framework tightly binds the value of home-work to market interaction and exchange. And since markets are spaces of private exchange, the logic of domestic work – including care work – remains bound to private self-interest-based relationships.

In fact, it is this self-interest-based private (market) exchange that many feminist legal scholars seek to exploit to substantiate their argument. When they adapt the social reproduction literature to demonstrate inadequacies of labour law, feminist legal scholars often point out that segregating the home as a private domain and, thereby, attributing domestic interactions solely to love and emotion hides the economic exchanges of the domestic sphere.[32] That domestic work is the precursor to economic productivity of the market is indeed a helpful critical reflection of the social reproduction scholarship. This critical reflection has successfully problematised the false division between economically productive

[30] ibid 11–14. Also see A Blackett, 'The Decent Work for Domestic Workers Convention and Recommendation, 2011' (2012) 106 *The American Journal of International Law* 778; E Albin and V Mantouvalou, 'The ILO Convention on Domestic Workers: From the Shadows to the Light' (2012) 41 *Industrial Law Journal* 67.

[31] The ILO Convention 189 by recognising domestic work such as cleaning; cooking; washing and ironing clothes; caring for children, elderly, sick, and pets; gardening; securing the house; and driving for family business, in fact, recognises these socially reproductive activities. However, by recognising these activities only when performed through a direct employment relationship and not when these are performed without pay, Convention 189 only partially recognises the market productivity social reproduction. Although the Convention recognises the value of domestic work, it does so when it is performed through private market exchange (ie, the domestic work market). See Convention concerning decent work for domestic workers (Entry into force: 05 Sep 2013), available at www.ilo.org/dyn/normlex/en/f?p=NORMLEXPUB:12100:0::NO:12100:P12100_INSTRUMENT_ID:2551460:NO accessed 14 January 2019.

[32] For example see J Fudge, 'Labour as a 'Fictive Commodity: Radically Reconceptualizing Labour Law' in G Davidov and B Langille (eds), *The Idea of Labour Law* (Oxford, Oxford University Press, 2011) 120, 134; Fudge, 'Feminist Reflections' (n 7); Blackett, 'The Decent Work' (n 30); E Albin and V Mantouvalou, 'The ILO Convention on Domestic Workers' (n 30); also see S McGrath and J DeFilippis, 'Social Reproduction as Unregulated Work' (2009) 23 *Work, Employment & Society* 66, 68–69.

market-employment and emotion-driven domestic work. The aim of these feminist scholars, then, seems to be justifying the economic productivity of domestic work including care work.

Picchio, the political economist you cited earlier, emphatically articulates this ambition: 'Housework is the *production* of labour as a commodity, while waged work is the *exchange* of labour. To be exchanged, labour must be produced; and to be used in the production of other commodities, labour must be produced and exchanged.'[33] However, replicating this Marxian logic of 'exchange value' in the context of labour exchange is somewhat problematic. That labour as a commodity is unique is not disputed. According to this logic, when labour that is produced by a home worker is exchanged in the market, it should be the home worker who is the primary beneficiary of the market return for the exchange. This, however, is inconsistent with the autonomy, agency, and freedom of the worker who is actually undertaking the exchange of her labour (which was produced at home). This is so because this logic ignores the decision-making capacity of the market-participating worker and instead places the homeworker as the owner (ie, master and decision-maker) of the workers' labouring capacity. Thus, this perspective constructs a mechanical notion of 'worker' devoid of freedom and agency, and merely an embodiment of a homeworker's labour.

In any case, on the basis of the above reasoning, Picchio critiques the liberal market-logic as applied to wages, which takes into account only economic production, thereby ignoring social reproduction through housework.[34] She argues for a socio-historically determined wage concept that is able to take into account social reproduction at home. While applying this market-logic to wages may be a valid critique of the wage system taken in isolation, linking social reproduction to market exchanges subsumes social and historical processes into the market space. Although it is true that housework remains unrecognised in a market-based supply-demand logic, the proper place, it would seem, to take cognisance of house work is social relationships rather than market exchanges.

Linking social reproduction to market exchanges ends up conceding substantial justificatory ground for valuing domestic and care work to market exchanges. This manner of justifying wages for house work (or care work) goes against the stated objectives of a strand of feminist activism that sought to dissociate wages for house work from any market-based justification, including the contribution to market productivity: 'For our aim is to … price ourselves out of the market, for housework and factory work and office work to be "uneconomic."'[35] If 'extricat[ing] a portion of their lives from capital's logics and purposes' was an aspiration of the feminist movement for returns on housework,[36] that aspiration is only undermined by linking housework to that of the economic productivity of the market.

[33] Picchio, *Social Reproduction* (n 15).
[34] ibid 1–5, 20–21, 121.
[35] N Cox and S Federici, *Counter-Planning from the Kitchen: Wages for Housework, A Perspective on Capital and the Left* (Brooklyn, New York Wages for Housework Committee, 1976) 14.
[36] Weeks, *The Problem with Work* (n 5) 136.

In this linkage of social reproduction to market production, Noah Zatz sees only a reinforcement of the market-logic as applied to domestic work, rather than any reformulation of the justification to apply to housework.[37] Through her proposal on universal basic income, political theorist Kathy Weeks seeks to overcome this market-logic driven approach to domestic work by dissociating basic income from work altogether. By doing so, she hopes to overcome 'the notion that waged work is the only legitimate means of access to even a minimal standard of living'.[38] Citing Ailsa McKay and Jo Vanevery approvingly, Weeks notes:

> Whereas the demand for wages for housework intended to expose the dependence of waged work on household-based relations of reproduction, the demand for basic income entails … 'an implicit recognition that all citizens contribute to society in a variety of ways,' including contributions 'that may or may not have monetary value or even be measurable'.[39]

Her advocacy for universal basic income is also supported by her perception of obscurity in the difference between work and non-work (or production and reproduction).[40]

C. Zbyszewska

Weeks's critique of the (unintentional) productivism inherent in the feminist equivalence between unpaid house and care work (social reproductive labour) and paid forms of labour is one with which I am also in agreement. Some feminist engagements with/around work have tended to embrace work without sufficiently questioning its problematic aspects, such as its tendency to colonise life at the expense of other things, or its imbrication in neoliberal policy or capitalist relations[41] given that, as Weeks observes, 'living for and through work renders subjects supremely fit for capitalist purposes'.[42]

However, to characterise the feminist conceptualisation of social reproduction, or its application by feminist legal scholars, as one that *always* conflates domestic, and especially care work, with market-orientated reproduction of labouring bodies does not do justice to the richness of the concept or its subsequent development. As Weeks notes, the early Marxist feminist articulations of social reproduction indeed fell into this trap.[43] Yet, it is important to recall that feminists

[37] ND Zatz, 'The Impossibility of Work Law' in G Davidov and B Langille (eds), *The Idea of Labour Law* (Oxford, Oxford University Press, 2011) 234.

[38] Weeks, *The Problem with Work* (n 5) 146.

[39] ibid 143.

[40] ibid 142.

[41] N Fraser, 'Feminism, Capitalism, and the Cunning of History' in *Fortunes of Feminism: From State-Managed Capitalism to Neoliberal Crisis* (London, Verso, 2013).

[42] Weeks, *The Problem with Work* (n 5) 12.

[43] ibid.

have celebrated work in part because it can provide an escape from the normative and cultural limitations of life in the private domain.[44] Indeed, for the autonomist feminist movement, to which you have already referred, to call housework 'work' worthy of a wage was a step towards its *refusal*, and refusal also of the role that (Fordist) capitalism assigned to women.[45] Similarly, the manoeuvre of exposing the structural dependencies between productive and social reproductive activities, and subordination of the latter in capitalist economies, was an essential stepping stone in developing a much more nuanced notion of what social reproduction entails.

Accordingly, most articulations of social reproduction go beyond biological reproduction of people (labour power) or their daily regeneration through care, provisioning and housework. Instead, they encompass also the reproduction of sociality, communities, human bonds, etc.[46] Likewise, feminist theorising on social reproduction has sought its recognition not simply because of its economic contributions but as one of the *conditions of possibility*, to use Nancy Fraser's term, for any productive (economic) activity,[47] capitalist or otherwise and, indeed, life itself. So, as you already pointed out through reference to Silvia Federici and autonomous feminists, feminists have questioned the false distinctions between different types of labour, paid and unpaid, that capitalist relations engender and which labour law has tended to reproduce. Thus, concepts such as total social organisation of labour (TSOL)[48] or the notion of 'life's work',[49] among others, try to encompass the interconnections and the fluidity of the boundary between productive and social reproductive activities, and capture better the realities of people's lives between the public and private domains, as these domains have been constructed.[50]

Similarly, feminist lawyers have also engaged this concept in a more nuanced way than simply to make the case for equating work of care and housework with 'standard' labour because of the former's contribution to production. Questioning how and why we value some work activities and not others,[51] and why some deserve protection while others are excluded fully or in part from labour law's protective scope, is not the same as relinquishing the justification for valuing or protecting care and domestic work to the logic of the market.

[44] ibid; A Gorz, *Paths to Paradise: On the Liberation from Work* (London, Pluto Press, 1985).

[45] S Federici, 'Wages against Housework' in *Revolution at Point Zero: Housework, Reproduction, and Feminist Struggle* (Oakland, CA, PM Press, 2012).

[46] Bakker and Gill, *Power, Production* (n14); Bezanson and Luxton, *Social Reproduction* (n 13).

[47] N Fraser, 'Behind Marx's Hidden Abode: For an Expanded Conception of Capitalism' in P Deutscher and L Lafont (eds), *Critical Theory in Critical Times: Transforming the Global Political and Economic Order* (New York, Columbia University Press, 2017) 141.

[48] M Glucksmann, 'Why Work? Gender and the "Total Social Organization of Labour"' (1995) 2 *Gender, Work and Organization* 63.

[49] K Strauss and K Meehan, *Precarious Worlds: Contested Geographies of Social Reproduction* (Athens, University of Georgia Press, 2015).

[50] ibid.

[51] See ie, D Alessandrini, *Value Making in International Economic Law and Regulation: Alternative Possibilities* (Abingdon, Routledge, 2016) for an excellent feminist discussion of past and current debates on this issue.

On the contrary, feminist scholars have often been critical of the latter logic, especially in relation to privatisation of public services, neoliberal employment policy and labour market regulation.[52] For example, we have often critically assessed various policy and legal innovations seeking to 'accommodate' social reproductive labour within the current legal regimes (eg, reconciliation of work and family policies) on the basis of their apparent instrumentality (ie, interests of increasing employment rates or fertility rates) rather than *genuine* recognition that care work is an essential human activity, not least because it contributes to both economic and social development (but not only for that reason).[53] Indeed, not all forms of care work can be justified on the basis of their productive contribution through reproduction of labour power. Elder care or care for those who are unlikely to ever enter labour markets because of capability issues or for other reasons are some such examples. As Lydia Hayes notes in her study of the home-care sector in the United Kingdom, these forms of care work should be instead grounded in the meaning of community and public (state or community, not individual) duty.[54]

III. Towards Better Valuation and Other Justifications for Regulating Paid and Unpaid Care and Domestic Work

A. Routh

Indeed, as your last point makes plain, justification for cognisance of care work must be found outside of the market. I would urge, in fact, that all domestic and care work should be justified on an alternative basis – beyond a market exchange logic. Unlike Weeks, however, I do not subscribe to the notion that since *everyone is presumed to contribute to society*, social contribution through work is an irrelevant consideration for a universal basic income – a way in which she proposes to value contributions. Although it might be true that every individual in a society does *something*, it is an overstatement to assert that every individual makes a positive social contribution for the sustenance and evolution of the society. For example, as a logical extension of Hayes's reflection you cited above, it could be argued that there are always individuals in a society who may not be able to contribute – either in the market space or the social space. Thus, the analytical strategy of conflating work with any activity is unhelpful in situating the significance of domestic work in society, and it somehow diminishes the contribution of domestic workers by equating it with *any other* activity.

[52] See (n 8, n 13).
[53] See (n 10).
[54] Hayes, *Stories of Care* (n 8) 67–68.

Although this is not the space to do so, it is indeed possible to develop an account of work with reference to society rather than subsuming work into any other activity. What, however, is important is to develop a public account of domestic work, in contrast to private relationship-based domestic work. Both in the legal regime proposed by the ILO and, to a large extent in my view, in the feminist agenda of linking market-wage to domestic work, domestic work (including care work) is conceptualised through private exchange-based economically productive market relationships. While Weeks dissociates domestic work from the market, she does not develop a public account of work or, indeed, any account of work.

The market space functions on the logic of private self-interested exchange. While admittedly this is true of a neoliberal market space, it is not untrue of other quasi-capitalist or non-capitalist market spaces either. Although capital may not be involved, or its role may be limited, the market still exists for facilitating private exchanges. One of the ways that the neoliberal market space differs from others is that market participants are seen as narrowly self-interested, isolated individuals.[55] Domestic work, including care work, which is seen as social *reproduction*, cannot primarily be about *self-interested* or *private* exchange. While for unpaid domestic work the primary motive is perhaps diametrically opposite to that of self-interested private exchange, even in the context of paid domestic work workers regularly perform activities that go far beyond the *contractual private exchange* and are characterised by emotions including love and empathy.

Domestic work is not primarily a private exchange also because it is in the social, that is, *public interest* to see that children, elderly, and all other citizens have flourishing lives.[56] The diverse resources and circumstances necessary for such flourishing lives are generated *inter alia* through domestic work performed at home. From a domestic worker's perspective, it would therefore be improper to conceptually attribute production of market exchangeable labour without taking into account their motivations. While it may be true that many domestic workers see their work as indirectly market-productive, many might also perceive their contribution beyond the market and into the broader realm of society.

Of course, as you noted already, feminists do recognise contributions of social reproduction beyond the market, indicating the three broad aspects of social reproduction as biological; labour power; and practices of care, socialisation, and fulfilment of human needs.[57] Yet, while this recognition posits a diversified account of social reproduction when considered in isolation, when it is linked (ie, any component of the above three) to market exchange, the 'production of

[55] See eg, A Sen, *The Idea of Justice* (New York, Allen Lane, 2009) 174–78; also see, E Ostrom, *Governing the Commons: The Evolution of Institutions for Collective Action* (New York, Cambridge University Press, 1990) 1–25.

[56] A Sen, *Development as Freedom* (New York, Alfred A Knoph, 1999) 292–97; also see generally M Nussbaum, *Creating Capabilities: The Human Development Approach* (Cambridge, Mass & London, UK, The Belknap Press of Harvard University Press, 2011).

[57] Bakker and Gill, *Power, Production* (n 14); Bezanson and Luxton, *Social Reproduction* (n 13).

labour' subsumes its other aspects. If the emphasis of social reproduction remains production of market exchangeable labour, it is then the market that judges the quality (ie, characteristics) of marketable labour. Neoliberal markets increasingly demand humanistic, social, cultural, linguistic, and emotional qualities from workers beyond their mere skillsets as workers.[58] Thus, love, empathy, altruism, patience, and trustworthiness are also qualities that the market demands of a good worker.

The social perspective, instead, would entail that domestic work be seen as a component of the public relationship between domestic workers and society. Domestic workers discharge not a private obligation of care, but a public obligation of facilitating social well-being and sustenance, thereby promoting conditions for flourishing lives of each individual member of society. In this exchange (or interaction) between domestic workers and society, it is incumbent on the state (ie, various instrumentalities of the state) and non-state civil society to take cognisance of domestic workers' social contribution, and thereby reciprocate in furthering domestic workers' flourishing lives. Regulation of domestic work – or labour law – then should be conceptualised with reference to the worker-society relationship, instead of the employer-employee relationship. The normative goal of such regulation should be the promotion of flourishing lives of workers.

In this manner of (re-)conceptualising regulation pertaining to work, domestic workers' legal entitlements should primarily be a state responsibility, although non-state actors may also contribute towards fulfilling such legitimate entitlements. Centralising this social relationship as the basis of legal regulation of work does not, however, dismiss private market exchanges; it only recognises limitations of the market in taking account of efforts not resulting in economic production. While markets are *per se* significant for efficient private exchanges, markets too should be seen as components of society because of their capacity to promote human interaction and generate wealth for society.[59] While markets sometimes may be able to compensate workers (including domestic workers) for their technical skills (that is, if there are no other market imperfections, which itself is a contentious issue), they are unable to take into account the emotional components of labour rendered by such workers. It is this vacuum that society needs to fill through legal regulation when domestic work is performed through a formal private exchange. When domestic work is not performed through private exchange relationships (for example, when it is unpaid), it is primarily society that needs to reciprocate through legal entitlements of domestic workers.

[58] See eg, British Council et al, 'Culture at Work: The Value of Intercultural Skills in the Workplace', available at www.britishcouncil.org/sites/default/files/culture-at-work-report-v2.pdf accessed 28 May 2018; also see A R Hochschild, 'The Managed Heart: Commercialization of Human Feeling' in J O'Brien (ed) *The Production of Reality: Essays and Readings on Social Interaction*, 5th edn (Los Angeles, Sage, 2011) 320–25; also J Payne, 'Emotional Labour and Skill: A Reappraisal' (2009) 16 *Gender, Work and Organization* 348; also A Argandona, 'Beyond Contracts: Love in Firms', (2011) 99 *Journal of Business Ethics* 77.

[59] Sen, *Development as Freedom* (n 56) 116–24.

B. Zbyszewska

I partly agree with you that casting society and the public sphere as the appropriate domain within which to locate domestic and care (paid and unpaid) work's contribution is indeed an important step. As already noted, in both western countries and in former state socialist ones, the state has historically played a residual role in managing social reproduction and stepping in to mediate the crises and tensions to which it is prone. At the same time, however, the state has hardly been neutral, as it has in various ways 'retaine[d], and … hardened, a kernel of normative, sexist ideology, by which the social, economic, and political costs of caregiving are born by women'.[60] Accordingly, feminists have been both critical of the state's role but also located demands for recognition and redistribution, including by way of socialisation, of this work vis-à-vis the state.

Thus, swapping what you call the private, market-logic and productivity driven justification (even though I am not entirely in agreement that all feminist proposals really entail this) for one solely based on the notion that care and domestic work contributes to public good, wellbeing and flourishing is also not without problems. There is a danger, for example, that such a justification could slip into an *expectation* that such work be carried out, or that it becomes a duty or a public obligation that takes on a coercive character. This, in some ways, would not be distinct from the implicit duty to participate in gainful employment as a matter of one's social citizenship and obligations – a duty that has been extended by neoliberal policies to the unemployed and welfare or social benefit recipients through increasingly punitive and compulsory 'workfare' programs or in-work conditionality[61] – that the more critical engagements in and around work have problematised.

To illustrate this problem with respect to care and socially reproductive labour, take a literary example that has been in popular imagination for some time, Margaret Atwood's *The Handmaid's Tale*,[62] which shows a society, that she calls Gilead, wherein social reproductive (reproductive and domestic) labour becomes demanded (with refusal constituting a death sentence) of women capable of carrying it out (because they are fertile or young, for example) precisely on the basis of public good, as in continuation and renewal of the society befallen by infertility. While in Atwood's dystopia, care work and domestic contributions are valorised and elevated, women of Gilead are also stripped of their autonomy; they are slaves.

This is of course a very drastic illustration, and a fictional one. However, there are also real precedents we can draw on that are subtler, yet equally problematic.

[60] Hayes, *Stories of Care* (n 8) 198.

[61] J Millar and F Bennett, 'Universal Credit: Assumptions, Contradictions and Virtual Reality' (2017) 16 *Social Policy & Society* 169; J Peck, *Workfare States* (New York, The Guildford Press, 2001); A Daguerre and D Etherington, *Workfare in 21st century Britain: The Erosion of Rights to Social Assistance*, Working Paper, ESRC, 2014 http://workfare.org.uk/images/uploads/docs/Workfare_in_21st_century_Britain-Final.pdf accessed 10 January 2019.

[62] M Atwood, *The Handmaid's Tale* (Vintage, original publication 1985).

In Poland, a jurisdiction I am familiar with, for instance, the concept of Mother Poland has been historically used to elevate and valorise unpaid care work but also the work of reproducing cultural, linguistic, and national values during times when those were threatened.[63] Women charged with these responsibilities were socially elevated, but as this 'work' was carried out in the private sphere, domesticity and traditional gender roles were being reproduced, as was women's material dependence on men. The state socialist period saw the erosion of the traditional family model as women were encouraged to take on paid work. But the notion of Mother Poland has persisted, and contemporary Polish governments, such as the now governing populist-traditionalist Law and Justice (PiS), have deployed this notion time and again. The recently introduced pro-natalist policy of granting families significant social transfers for child support to encourage child bearing is one example of how unpaid care can be valorised while, at the same time, women are instrumentalised.

Moreover, to return to a point that Weeks makes (as many feminists have done), it is also important not to romanticise domestic and care work as emotion driven and thus somehow always and inevitably enjoyable.[64] While these sorts of work, care especially, are likely to be fuelled by emotion and empathy, they (whether paid or not) can also be monotonous and joyless, and can be a source of similar frustrations that befall alienated (paid) labour. And yet, it is precisely this notion that care and domestic work are emotion-driven, altruistic, and *natural* (to women) that has contributed to their instrumentalisation and devaluation, regardless of whether they are carried out of love or obligation, or for pay.

Thus, public recognition, valuation and organisation of social reproductive labour is important, and as Donatella Alessandrini's work on employer of last resort suggests, it might indeed carry the possibility, in the long term, of transforming the institution of 'wage labour' and the meaning of 'work' away from the ideology of 'work as worth' to one that concentrates on the question of how we organise activities we value in life.[65] At the same time, it is essential to think also about the sorts of approaches that simultaneously challenge the gendered and often racialised dynamics that characterise socially reproductive labour, both paid and unpaid. I am not sure that the notions of public good and wellbeing, as you articulate them, can do that alone. Thus, feminist calls for not just valuation and protection but also *better redistribution* of this work between women and men and social institutions (thus, socialisation of some of this work when it is unpaid) more adequately respond to this problem. Weeks's call for universal basic income, but also her demand for more time – not just for our families, but also for other social relations, leisure, and possibilities[66] – exemplifies one response

[63] M Fidelis, *Women, Communism, and Industrialization in Postwar Poland* (New York, Cambridge University Press, 2010).

[64] Weeks, *The Problem with Work* (n 5) 123–26.

[65] D Alessandrini, 'A Social Provisioning Employer of Last Resort: Post-Keynsianism Meets Feminist Economics' (2013) 4 *World Review of Political Economy* 230; Alessandrini, *Value Making* (n 51).

[66] Weeks, *The Problem with Work* (n 5) 123–26.

to that critique while also acknowledging that, besides work (or care), there are other ways to experience pleasure and fulfilment and contribute to social well-being. And similar calls have been made by feminist labour lawyers. Fudge has recently provoked us to consider a minimum basic income along with a 30-hour workweek as basis for a reconceived labour law and democratic equality.[67] I also conclude my own book on working time with an endorsement of calls for possibly even more drastic working-time reductions, which I see as necessary for more egalitarian and sustainable social relations, but also for more ecologically sustainable economies.[68]

C. Routh

To be clear, in my view, taking social cognisance of domestic (including care) work and devising legal entitlements with reference to the worker-society relationship is not the same as socialist (or other similar) projects wherein the state takes control of workers' lives 'through the provision of state services like child-care centres or collective kitchens', to which, indeed, some feminists object on the basis they curtail domestic workers' autonomy.[69] What is important in a social basis for regulation of domestic work is acknowledgement of the social contribution each worker makes, and development of legal entitlements on the basis of her or his lived experiences, rather than a one-size-fits-all state policy. Instead of *a priori* formulation of legal entitlements, this approach to legal regulation would require extensive participation of domestic workers in the law-making process so that their lived experiences become part of the knowledge-background to legal entitlements. In this conceptual regulatory framework, while some of the legal entitlements such as direct payments, child allowances, parental or elderly-care allowances – none of which as practical policies are unprecedented[70] – could become part of domestic work-related entitlements, there may be a range of others generated in the heterogeneous context of domestic workers' lived experiences globally. It is this socially mediated regulation of work that may be able to better acknowledge domestic workers' non-economic contributions to society.

In this context, the concerns outlined above in relation to the social cognisance of domestic and care work are primarily political problems not conceptual ones, although a conceptual space for democratic politics needs to be simultaneously created. It is rarely a surprise that the state is not neutral (or, for that matter, any social-political idea or entity is not neutral). In either the fictional society of Gilead, or the more empirically observable socialist and post-socialist Poland, the

[67] J Fudge, 'A New Vocabulary and Imaginary for Labour Law: Taking Legal Constitution, Gender, and Social Reproduction Seriously' in D Brodie, N Busby and R Zahn (eds), *The Future Regulation of Work: New Concepts, New Paradigms* (London, Palgrave MacMillan, 2016).

[68] Zbyszewska, *Gendering European Working-time Regimes* (n 8) 233.

[69] Weeks, *The Problem with Work* (n 5) 133.

[70] P England, 'Emerging Theories of Care Work' (2005) 31 *Annual Review of Sociology* 381, 384.

state commands an overwhelming amount of power over the citizenry. The state, or perhaps, the government, has traditionally had its way. However, we will do well to remember that the state is far from a unitary entity. It includes government, opposition parties, individual elected representatives, committees, commissions (often constituted by people of diverse backgrounds), parliament, the judiciary, and so forth. A state's politics is often shaped by continuous deliberation and disagreements by these and other non-state entities (including market actors and institutions). Whether the question is of redistribution of domestic work between men and women, as you suggest, or valorisation of domestic work, it needs to form the basis of democratic politics. A socially focused entitlement framework for domestic work, in principle, has no reason to pre-empt these important debates. In fact, my arguments on social cognisance of domestic work are premised on vibrant democratic societies that value reasoned discussion.

Thus, conceptualisation of a non-productivity value of domestic work does not negate domestic workers' autonomy, but rather requires an appropriate version of democratic politics to convert that autonomy into public policy. I want to make two further points. First, I agree that a coercive state-imposed duty of domestic (including care) work is a possibility, but the 'obligation' in relation to domestic work I mention earlier should be understood as voluntarily assumed reciprocation towards society (ie, once such work is voluntarily undertaken), that is, not a private or coercive duty irrespective of who performs domestic work (women or men). And, second, my point has never been that domestic workers work out of pleasure or love; it is rather that love and emotion cannot be subtracted from domestic work, as you rightly note.

IV. Concluding Remarks

As we have considered here, a key challenge for labour lawyers has been to distance ourselves from, or at least not reproduce, productivity logics and market-based justifications for recognising, valuing, and protecting different forms of work, including those that are necessary for reproduction of life and sociality. We reflected on whether or not feminist scholarship in labour law has successfully overcome this challenge, not necessarily with the view of reaching a conclusion, but rather to illuminate an issue we do not often address as labour lawyers, despite the fact that critical scholarship on work has grappled with the problem of work reification and its colonising power, as well as issues of work refusal and resistance for some time.

This challenge – of, intentionally or not, falling into the trap of productivism – is perhaps inherent in the nature of our field, the normative and political goals of which have evolved around the key figure of a worker-citizen, in its individual and collective form. And yet, even if we continue to elevate and prioritise productive (economic and market-based) contributions as a basis of societal wellbeing and solidarity, praise the satisfaction and fulfilment that work (at least in its best forms) carries for individuals, and the autonomy, freedom, and independence it can offer, we also have to be cognisant of, and address head on, the fact that there are limitations to this approach. While the calls that the 'end of work' is looming may or may not be justified, the reality of full employment – and thus social inclusion and distribution through work as we still narrowly define it – is unlikely to materialise for everyone. At the same time, certain forms of work – such as those of reproducing communities and sociality, caring for people and the planet – are hardly going away, and so it is with them that we, as labour lawyers, must more often engage. These are the tasks and activities that make life itself – with production as only one of its aspects – possible in the first place, whether in capitalist economies, those that are already hybrid,[71] or ones that might yet emerge to operate on entirely different logics.

[71] Feminist geographer JK Gibson-Graham has demonstrated economic hybridity in what are generally considered capitalist contexts, in order to illustrate that capitalism is not a total system that penetrates all areas of life: JK Gibson Graham, 'The Feminist Project of Belonging for the Anthropocene' (2011) 18 *Gender, Place and Culture* 1; JK Gibson-Graham, *A Postcapitalist Politics* (Minneapolis, University of Minnesota Press, 2006).

16

Comment

Theories of Labour Law Assessed from the Perspective of Reflexive Labour Law

RALF ROGOWSKI*

I. Introduction

In order to adequately respond to the so-called 'new world of work', it is essential to develop a sufficient understanding of emergent changes. For this task, theories are required that are capable of understanding the global technological, ideological and political challenges to national labour law and industrial relations and, on this basis, define the role of labour law in managing these changes. I am convinced that an adequate theoretical account of labour law is crucial for the field of labour law to survive.

Twenty years ago, Ton Wilthagen identified in his conclusion to the proceedings of the Royal Netherlands Academy of Arts and Sciences (*Koninklijke Nederlandse Akademie van Wetenschappen*, KNAW) conference in Amsterdam, entitled 'Advancing Theory in Labour Law and Industrial Relations in a Global Context', the need to rethink labour law along a number of lines that seem as pertinent today as they were then. Wilthagen proposed as challenges and routes for advancing labour law theory:

(1) to become multidisciplinary,
(2) to pay close attention to the link between labour law, employment relations, the labour market, industrial relations and the state,
(3) to deconstruct the normative assumptions of neo-liberal economism,

* Professor of Law and Director of the Law and Sociology Programme, University of Warwick, Warwick Law School.

(4) to include a policy dimension, and
(5) last, but not least, to develop a new theoretical frame for labour law based on the notion of reflexivity.[1]

As the present volume demonstrates, we luckily have witnessed lately important developments in theorising labour law that continue the search for an appropriate account and understanding of the role of labour law in modern society. In the following, I shall interrogate the theories and models discussed in the previous chapters and ask if they live up to Wilthagen's suggestions. I do not hide that my comments are guided by the perspective of the theory that I consider the most advanced theory on offer, and this is the theory of reflexive labour law.

II. Multidisciplinarity

Current theories of labour law seem to be as open to borrowing approaches, concepts and insights from other disciplines as was the situation when Wilthagen assembled his group of intellectuals and designed his collection on labour law theory. However, some of the disciplines that were prominent 20 years ago seem to have lost attraction while others have risen in prominence. Industrial relations theory, sociology and political economy are less dominant nowadays, while more hope is put in political and legal theory and in philosophy in general. There seems to be a shift from analytical to normative types of theories in the academic discourse of labour law and industrial relations.[2]

A good example that puts hopes in insights from normative theory is Anja Eleveld's attempt to import concepts from republican theory into labour law. She starts with a convincing criticism of Amartya Sen's capability theory, arguing that Sen's theory is in fact a disguised neoliberal form of promoting human capital. Sen's individualistic approach neglects the social aspects of the employment relationship and favours subjective freedom over collective well-being.

The attraction she sees in republican theory is that it focuses on power relations which underlie labour and employment relations. Republican theory is centrally concerned with aspects of domination, respectively non-domination. It provides justification for labour regulation and employment law as protection of the weaker party in employment relations. Furthermore, republican theory is attractive for Eleveld because it supports and justifies employee participation in company decision-making as democratic control.

[1] T Wilthagen, 'Epilogue: A Research Agenda for the Future' in T Wilthagen (ed), *Advancing Theory in Labour Law and Industrial Relations in a Global Context* (Amsterdam, Koninklijke Nederlandse Akademie van Wetenschapen, 1998).

[2] For labour law see G Davidov, *A Purposive Approach to Labour Law* (Oxford, Oxford University Press, 2016); for industrial relations see W Müller-Jentsch, 'Theoretical Approaches to Industrial Relations' in BE Kaufman (ed), *Theoretical Perspectives on Work and the Employment Relationship* (Ithaca, ILR/Cornell University Press, 2004).

Eleveld's contribution is a refreshingly sober contribution to the heated normative debate in search of an ethical foundation for labour law. She does 'not believe in "foundations" of labour law, nor in foundations of anything else'. However, she believes in the need for justification of domination, and we can ask if there is not a paradox here. The demand for justification is a claim for legitimation. One could have expected an engagement with Jürgen Habermas, whose discourse theory of law is based on similar assumptions but transcends republican theory in crucial respects by putting criticism and the challenge of authority at the centre of a critical theory of democracy. There is scope to apply these ideas to labour law.

Furthermore, even more helpful might have been an engagement with reflexive labour law and, in particular, its notion of reflexivity. If Eleveld would apply 'non-foundationalism' reflexively to her own solution, namely 'non-domination' in line with republican theory, can she really uphold her claim to be against foundationalism? She would find herself in a similar situation like atheists whose claims to be against religion are rejected as just another religion. Republican theory is normative and when applied to labour law it provides 'a normative foundation' for labour law.

III. The Relationship between Labour Law, Employment Relations, the Labour Market, Industrial Relations and the State

As the previous remarks on Republican theory and Habermas' critical theory of democracy already demonstrated, there are a number of similar approaches in political philosophy on offer for normative thinking about labour law (John Rawls is an obvious additional candidate). A common thread in this theoretical tradition is a concern with power, how its use is justified and how it can be opposed.

Andrea Iossa's chapter can be read as a contribution to the more radical wing of this tradition. He develops his ideas for rethinking labour law with explicit reference to the anarchist tradition, which rejects the centrality of the state in modern society. His critique of power analyses implications of the changing relationship of labour law, employment relations, the labour market and the state in the gig economy, which provides for him the basis of an alternative understanding of labour law.

Iossa develops his argument for an 'anarchist labour law' in three steps. He analyses the traditional starting point in justifying labour law – the power imbalance and subordination in the employment relationship – as important for the maintenance and reproduction of the capitalist system. He then argues that labour market deregulation policies resulting from neoliberal economic policies are 'anti-statist' and undermine the traditional employment contract based on unilateral employer authority. In a third step, he argues that new forms of work in the gig economy provide a chance for an anarchist (non-statist) rethinking of the employment relationship.

To my mind, Iossa's line of argumentation is not entirely convincing. It can be questioned if neoliberal economic policies and labour market reforms are anti-statist. Political economy studies of Thatcherism argue the opposite. This United Kingdom (UK) form of neo-liberalism (as well as its successor, New Labour's Third Way) uses the state for pursuing neoliberal economic policy. Neoliberalism is only anti-statist in relation to the welfare state but constitutes in essence an increase in authority and authoritarianism, as Foucauldians and Neomarxist studies have shown.[3] They argue that, overall, neoliberalism leads to an increase in state authority and needs the authoritarian state to suppress opposition to neoliberalism in society.[4]

Insofar as the chances for anti-authoritarian employment relations are concerned, it can be questioned whether the gig economy liberates workers and leaves no role for labour law and the state. It is true that labour law also has the function of 'codification of the authority of the employer' and does not only protect employees. However, the freedom of gig workers is characterised by what Karl Marx called the two sides of bourgeois freedom: to be able to choose freely but also being left alone. Recent legal developments in relation to the employment status of Uber drivers and similar efforts in labour law to protect gig workers only reinforce the important role of legislation and tribunals in providing employment protection and resisting unilateral employer authority.

It is certainly true, as Iossa claims, that the capitalist company is not the only possible economic organisation and that self-organisation of workers should be supported. But here insights from reflexive labour law can help. Self-regulation can be strengthened by proper regulation. A reflexive labour law aims at facilitating self-regulation. If workplaces are 'organised horizontally by and through a collectivity of workers (thus self-organised)', this can be supported by labour law. But for reflexive regulation to be effective it requires reflexivity in self-regulation, as well as an understanding of the positive contribution of reflexive labour law for the self–organisation of workers.

IV. The Normative Assumptions of Labour Law Linked to Neo-Liberal Economism

An example of what Wilthagen called for in terms of debunking or deconstructing normative assumptions of neo-liberal economism is Ania Zbyszewska's and Supriya Routh's conversation on labour law's 'productivity' bias through a feminist lens. They are sceptical about market-based justifications of recognising, valuing, and protecting labour. They accuse labour law of having a productivity bias,

[3] B Jessop, K Bonnett, S Bromley and T Ling, *Thatcherism: A Tale of Two Nations* (Cambridge, Polity, 1988).

[4] B Jessop, *State Theory: Putting the Capitalist State in its Place* (Cambridge, Polity, 1990).

by which they mean that it focuses on productive work rather than work in general. They opt for a broadening of the concept of work that includes unpaid and paid forms of domestic and care work.

This approach is a valuable addition to the law and economics perspective on labour law. Studies assessing labour law from this viewpoint have tended to focus on the link between labour law and labour market policy.[5] Zbyszewska and Routh have little confidence in the capability approach, which is also 'falling into the trap of productivism' because of its inherent neo-liberal orientation towards making human capital more efficient. By focusing on unpaid and paid forms of domestic and care work the authors are able to challenge narrow economistic understandings of labour law and integrate a societal perspective based on feminist thinking.

Zbyszewska's and Routh's contribution is not so much a debate of opposing views but a conversation between friends supporting each other's arguments. However, the conversation would have benefitted from a clearer definition of productivism and what is meant by overcoming the productivity bias. It hints at the end of the contribution at an alternative logic to capitalism where production is only one aspect of the economy and social life. What future work needs to undertake is an assessment of the link of current labour law to neoliberalism and how labour law as an academic project as well as a policy is able to overcome this link. There is room for an assessment of the need for collective action and the role of labour law in this respect. Again, we are entering the territory of reflexive labour law theory and the supportive role of labour law for self-regulation. Reflexive labour law protects and encourages collective action where it is needed and this includes collective action in the field of domestic and care work.

V. The Policy Dimension

An interesting theory that transcends the narrow view of labour law as employment rights is offered by Cristina Inversi. In line with reflexive labour law theory she moves the lens from rights to regulation. With this she becomes able to focus on what Wilthagen calls the policy dimension of labour law.

Her case study is the regulation of working time. She develops a refreshing view on how regulation of working time is linked to self-regulation, by using the perspective of a regulatory space in which negotiations over working time regulations take place. She also has an interest in analysing power dynamics between actors involved in negotiating, producing and applying regulations, and the role of unilateral management decisions. These aspects constitute, for her, an analytical framework for the study of regulatory space.

[5] S Deakin and F Wilkinson, *The Law of the Labour Market: Industrialization, Employment, and Legal Evolution* (Oxford, Oxford University Press, 2005).

The regulation of working time is indeed an interesting case for testing the interplay of regulation and self-regulation. Working time is regulated within multilevel governance in the European Union, and at each level we have different interplays of regulation and self-regulation. These levels include the supranational level,[6] the national level,[7] and many forms of negotiation over working time regulations at local and company level.

My concern, though, is that it is not very clear what the notion of space adds to our understanding of negotiation over regulations. From the perspective of reflexive labour law, it can be suggested that regulatory space identifies conditions for negotiations and the context in which negotiations take place. Nevertheless, the presentation of regulatory space as a framework for research seems rather static and classificatory. There is potential to think further about the link between space and negotiations over regulation and self-regulation and their forms. Future work should explore what concrete policy conclusions can be drawn from using a regulatory space analytical framework.

VI. The New Theoretical Frame for Labour Law Provided by Reflexive Labour Law

The contribution of Alysia Blackham analyses a further important area of labour law, namely anti-discrimination or equality law. She is interested in testing theoretical assumptions against empirical evidence in this area. Equality law is certainly of growing importance in current welfare policies and an interesting testing ground for theoretical considerations. She chooses reflexive labour law as her theoretical frame and assesses it in terms of usefulness and effectiveness. She is critical of the link of reflexive labour law to current systems theory and argues for an alternative critical systems theory as a basis for reflexive law.

Blackham grasps well the hybrid nature of reflexive labour law as both a theory and a new stage in the development of labour law. There is indeed a lively debate in the UK in using reflexive law in the field of equality law and Blackham's comment is itself an indication of the growing interest in the theory and its practical implications.

[6] See A Zbyszewska, *Gendering European Working Time Regimes: The Working Time Directive and the Case of Poland* (Cambridge, Cambridge University Press, 2016); R Rogowski, 'Sustainability and Uncertainty in Governing European Employment Law – The Community Method as Instrument of Governance: The Case of the EU Working Time Directive' in J Barbier, R Rogowski and F Colomb (eds), *The Sustainability of the European Social Model: EU Governance, Social Protection and Employment Policies in Europe* (Cheltenham, Edward Elgar, 2015).

[7] R Rogowski, 'Implementation of the EU Working Time Directive in the United Kingdom' in J Barbier, R Rogowski and F Colomb (eds), *The Sustainability of the European Social Model: EU Governance, Social Protection and Employment Policies in Europe* (Cheltenham, Edward Elgar, 2015).

I agree with Blackham that we need to ask critical questions about the use and the limits of self-regulation. Assessing its effectiveness and subsequent results depends, however, on the questions and the perspectives used. I favour a form of self-regulation that is known as participatory self-regulation[8] which puts emphasis on widening the number of participants and the inclusion of employee representatives in company decision-making and at the place of work. Its effectiveness is assessed differently from asking about the effectiveness of protecting individual rights.

I do not share Blackham's reservations in using Niklas Luhmann's social system theory. His theory provides a powerful tool to analyse the societal context of modern labour law and guides us to ask critical questions. It can be combined, for example, with political economy perspectives, which leads to asking about the switch in welfare policies from social to identity politics. Such questions can highlight the context of equality law and critically assess its current prominence within labour law.

The Luhmannian system theory makes us aware that the academic discourse of labour law is a second-order observation, giving us insights in our theoretical endeavours and above all inviting us to reflect on theory itself. Theory, including labour law theory, is self-description or reflection that always takes place in and is conditioned by social systems.

VII. Concluding Remarks

Let me end with a concluding remark about the contributions in the light of reflexive labour law. All chapters make interesting observations and constitute valuable additions to thinking about the theoretical nature of labour law. They enhance our rethinking of labour law in a rapidly changing economic and societal environment. What is needed, however, is a comprehensive theory which in my view is only offered by reflexive labour law.

Reflexive labour law is both a heuristic theory and a description of the latest stage in the development of modern labour law. It describes trends in modern law that take seriously changing employment patterns, changing corporate structures and changing labour market conditions. It views labour law not only in terms of expressing public goods in the form of rights but provides insights about it as a field of regulation. This field needs new forms of law and it takes seriously the role of soft law. It emphasises the role of law as supportive and facilitative of self-regulation.

[8] R Rogowski, *Reflexive Labour Law in the World Society* (Cheltenham, Edward Elgar, 2013) ch 4 with further references.

What future research needs to undertake, however, is a serious rethinking of labour law as a global field. If we understand labour law as regulation, the importance of global conditions that shape regulation is indispensable. This was the message at Wilthagen's conference in Amsterdam and should also be central in future scholarship. Labour law takes place in the world society and the significance of this fact is increasingly significant for hard law development and even more so for soft law and its use in labour law.

INDEX